Women, Gender and Radical Religion
in Early Modern Europe

Studies in Medieval and Reformation Traditions

Edited by

Andrew Colin Gow
University of Alberta

In cooperation with

Thomas A. Brady, Jr., Berkeley, California
Berndt Hamm, Erlangen
Johannes Heil, Heidelberg
Susan C. Karant-Nunn, Tucson, Arizona
Martin Kaufhold, Augsburg
Jürgen Miethke, Heidelberg
M. E. H. Nicolette Mout, Leiden

Founded by

Heiko A. Oberman†

VOLUME 129

Women, Gender and Radical Religion in Early Modern Europe

Edited by

Sylvia Brown

BRILL

LEIDEN · BOSTON
2007

On the cover: Ferdinand Bol, *Portrait of an Old Woman with a Book* (1651) from the State Hermitage Museum, St Petersburg (inv. no. GE 763), used with permission.

This book is printed on acid-free paper.

A C.I.P. record for this book is available from the Library of Congress

ISSN: 1573-4188
ISBN: 978 90 04 16306 5

Copyright 2007 by Koninklijke Brill NV, Leiden, The Netherlands.
Koninklijke Brill NV incorporates the imprints Brill, Hotei Publishing,
IDC Publishers, Martinus Nijhoff Publishers and VSP.

PRINTED IN THE NETHERLANDS

CONTENTS

ACKNOWLEDGEMENTS

The idea for this essay collection originated with a workshop on "Radical Maternities: Spiritual Motherhood and Female Visionaries in France and England", organized by myself, Cynthia J. Cupples, and Julie Hirst for the 2000 "Attending to Early Modern Women" Conference at the University of Maryland.

Since that workshop, the evolving project of a collection focussed on early modern women and radical religion has benefitted from the good ideas and helpfulness of many people. I wish particularly to acknowledge the late Sylvia Bowerbank, Cynthia Cupples, Andrew Gow, Alison Rowlands, and Kirilka Stavreva. Jennifer Bell, Lindsay Scott, Dorothy Woodman, and the Department of English and Film Studies at the University of Alberta all contributed to the editorial labour required to assemble the collection. Practical help was given by John Considine and Chris Considine (who shared her computer at a critical time). Boris van Gool and Hendrik van Leusen at Brill have been patient and humane publishers, and I thank them warmly.

The cartoon from the Quaker Tapestry is reproduced with the kind permission of the Quaker Tapestry Scheme. The cover image, Ferdinand Bol's "Portrait of an Old Woman with a Book, 1651", is reproduced with the permission of the State Hermitage Museum, St Petersburg.

My most heartfelt acknowledgement comes last, and is reserved for Julie Hirst. Her friendship and support throughout the making of this book made it happen.

ABBREVIATIONS AND CONVENTIONS

The following abbreviations are used.

CSPD   *Calendar of State Papers Domestic*
ODNB   *The Oxford Dictionary of National Biography*
OED   *The Oxford English Dictionary*

In the transcription of early modern texts, the letters i/j and u/v are regularized. If a place of publication is not given, it should be assumed to be London.

CONTRIBUTORS

SARAH APETREI has written a doctoral thesis at Oxford on gender and theology in seventeenth-century women's writing and is now working on mysticism and religious radicalism in the same period. She holds a Past and Present Fellowship at the Institute of Historical Research in London, but lives in Oxford where she is Liddon Fellow in Theology at Keble College, Oxford University.

NAOMI BAKER is Lecturer in Renaissance Literature at the University of Manchester, UK. She has published several articles on seventeenth-century radical religious writing and has recently edited two early conversion narratives, *Scripture Women: Rose Thurgood's "A Lecture of Repentance" and Cicely Johnson's "Fanatical Reveries"* (2005).

SYLVIA BROWN is Associate Professor of English at the University of Alberta. She has edited *Women's Writing in Stuart England: The Mothers' Legacies of Dorothy Leigh, Elizabeth Joscelin and Elizabeth Richardson* and published essays on the textual propagation of evangelical Protestantism—from the first English (and Puritan) dictionary to a translation of *The Pilgrim's Progress* into Inuktitut. She is completing a book on women and the reproduction of godly culture from the Reformation to the aftermath of 1688.

RUTH CONNOLLY completed her PhD on the writings of Katherine, Viscountess Ranelagh and Mary Rich, Countess of Warwick at the National University of Ireland, Cork in 2005. She is currently working at the University of Newcastle as the research associate on an AHRC-funded project to establish a new edition of the poetry of Robert Herrick.

PAMELA ELLIS was awarded an MA in 2003 by the University of Leeds for her dissertation on Mary Ward and models of holiness. She has published articles and lectured on a freelance basis on theology and spirituality, particularly from a feminist perspective.

José Manuel González is Associate Professor of English at the University of Alicante, Spain. He has published extensively on Shakespeare and various aspects of early modern theatre in England and Spain. He is editor of *Spanish Studies in Shakespeare and His Contemporaries* (2006).

Julie Hirst received her doctorate from the University of York. She is interested in women and intersections with history, literature, and religion. She is the author of *Jane Leade: A Biography of a Seventeenth-Century Mystic* (2005).

Stephen A. Kent received his doctorate from McMaster University, Canada, and is Professor of Sociology at the University of Alberta. He has published articles in numerous sociology, history, and religious studies journals, including studies of Indian and Buddhist philosophy, seventeenth-century Quakerism, new religions and related ideologies, and sectarian religions and human rights. His present work concentrates on current alternative belief systems.

Marion Kobelt-Groch teaches in the History Seminar at the University of Hamburg. Her dissertation on women in the German Peasants' War and the Anabaptist movement was published in 1993 as *Aufsässige Töchter Gottes: Frauen im Bauernkrieg und in den Täuferbewegungen*. Her Habilitation on the figure of Judith was published in 2005 as *Judith macht Geschichte: Zur Rezeption einer mythischen Gestalt vom 16. bis 19. Jahrhundert*. Her present research focusses on Protestant funeral sermons for children between the sixteenth and eighteenth centuries.

Bo Karen Lee teaches at Princeton Theological Seminary. She received her BA in Religious Studies from Yale University and is currently completing the PhD program in historical theology at Princeton Seminary. Her research focusses on the history of Christian spirituality, and her dissertation topic is "Sacrifice and Desire: The Rhetoric of Self-Denial in the Mystical Theologies of Madame Jeanne Guyon and Anna Maria van Schurman". She previously taught in the Theology department at Loyola College in Baltimore, Maryland.

Kirilka Stavreva is Associate Professor and Chair of English at Cornell College in Mount Vernon, Iowa, where she teaches and writes about early modern literature, drama, and its performances across historical and cultural divides. Her essays on the drama, popular literature, and gender politics of the Renaissance, as well as on critical pedagogy, have appeared in book collections and journals, such as *The Journal of Medieval and Early Modern Studies*, *Pedagogy*, and *The Journal of Popular Culture*. She is completing a book on the violent speech acts of women in early modern England.

SHEILA WRIGHT teaches eighteenth- and nineteenth-century history in the Centre for Lifelong Learning at the University of York. Her publications include *Friends in York: The Dynamics of Quaker Revival, 1780–1860* as well as papers on Quaker women's journals and spiritual friendships. She is currently working on a study of the status and role of single women in the Society of Friends and on women's social and political activities in York in the late nineteenth century. She was President of the Friends Historical Society for 2006 and is a member of the International Review Panel for the journal *Quaker Studies*.

INTRODUCTION

WOMEN, GENDER, AND RADICAL RELIGION IN EARLY MODERN EUROPE

Sylvia Brown

What is Radical?

Etymologically speaking, radicalism seeks to return to the root, *radix*, to the essentials of a movement or belief.[1] This is the view from the inside. From the outside, radicalism is seen as dangerously innovative and transgressive. Radicals are extremists, heretics, enthusiasts. Whether seen from the inside or the outside, however, radicalism opens possibilities for challenging and reimagining ways of knowing, acting, and believing. Religious radicalism is of urgent concern for the twenty-first century because of the global violence and divisiveness spawned by a range of groups claiming to return to the root, the fundamentals, of their traditions of belief.[2] This alone suggests a timely need to analyse what we have historically labelled as 'radical' in religion and why.

This collection seeks to interrogate and expand the category of 'radical' by examining a narrowly focussed group and period within the tradition of Western Christianity: women whose beliefs, actions, and writings challenged the religious institutions and dominant modes of

---

[1] There is a good discussion of the term by Timothy Morton and Nigel Smith in their introduction to the collection, *Radicalism in British Literary Culture, 1650–1830: From Revolution to Revolution* (Cambridge: Cambridge University Press, 2002), 1–2. See also B. J. Gibbons, *Gender in Mystical and Occult Thought: Behmenism and its Development in England* (Cambridge: Cambridge University Press, 1996), 14.

[2] See Gabriel A. Almond, R. Scott Appleby, and Emmanuel Sivan, *Strong Religion: The Rise of Fundamentalisms around the World* (Chicago: University of Chicago Press, 2003). The authors attribute the global rise of fundamentalisms to a reaction against the secularization of the state and the marginalization of religion—processes begun in the early modern period. Douglas Gwyn considers religious radicalism in the period immediately following the Reformation, particularly among Quakers, as the last attempt at the "sacralization" of the state before the secularization characteristic of modernity set in. See Gwyn, "Apocalypse Now and Then: Reading Early Friends in the Belly of the Beast", in *The Creation of Quaker Theory*, ed. Pink Dandelion (Aldershot: Ashgate, 2004).

confessionalized thinking in early modern Europe. Within this specific historical and cultural context, the essays in the collection individually and together seek to make connections and comparisons—sometimes between groups and figures not usually considered together or not, in themselves, considered radical. Thus, the activism of English Quakers finds resonance with the proselytizing or dissidence of Catholic nuns on the Continent; 'personal revelation' is shown to authorize the writings and resistances of women across confessions; and marginal women and sects are found to have surprising points in common with the 'mainstream', and vice versa.

Although all the essays focus on identifiable historical women, most are also concerned with gender as a dynamic, fluid, and often contradictory discursive system, operating both to challenge and reinscribe orthodoxy. Were radical religious beliefs typically accompanied by radical gender thinking? Or, on the contrary, did radical reconfigurations of religion sometimes depend on a reinscription of social norms? Some of the essays in this collection suggest that radical religion enables something like proto-feminism, while others challenge the connection. Gender is shown, by a number of the essays, to be a key constitutive element for the theologies, identities, and experiences of religious radicals—both women and men. Becoming a martyr or becoming 'nothing' under the divine gaze were ineluctably gendered procedures; women and men, in turn, appropriated the gendered language of martyrdom or self-abnegation for their own individual or communal purposes.

The contributors to this volume come from a range of disciplinary backgrounds, from literary and religious studies to sociology and history, but all of the essays arguably illustrate the pervasive presence and effects of theology in the pre-secular world of early modern Europe, whether as a fully articulated system or as an underlying set of assumptions. When a believer radically reimagines her relationship with the divine—giving God feminine attributes, for instance, or asserting unmediated access to divine wisdom—she necessarily reimagines her relationship with others and with the world. She occupies a potentially new place with respect to culture, authority, and history.[3] Of course, such reimagining and repositioning is risky, and many of the essays chart the complex negotiations

---

[3] See Morny Joy, "God and Gender: Some Reflections on Women's Invocations of the Divine", in *Religion and Gender*, ed. Ursula King (Oxford: Blackwell, 1995), 121–43; also Elizabeth A. Johnson, *She Who Is: The Mystery of God in Feminist Theological Discourse* (New York: Crossroad, 1992).

performed by religiously radical women between the demands of their faith and the deeply ingrained concern for order and fear of innovation that characterized early modern cultures. Many of the essays are therefore stories of survival as well as of resistance.

History

Definitions of radicalism, like definitions of heresy, are historically as well as positionally determined. History changes what counts as orthodox or heretical, radical or not, as the chapter on Mary Ward in this volume suggests. Pamela Ellis begins her essay on Ward by contrasting the praise of a twentieth-century pope for this "incomparable woman", founder of an unenclosed order concerned particularly with the education of girls, with the annihilating condemnation of a seventeenth-century pope who described the "Institutes" she founded as "poisonous growths".

At a formative moment in the study of gender and religion, Rosemary Radford Ruether identified one of the ongoing tasks of feminist theology as the historical "quest" for "alternative traditions" that combat androcentric views of religion and God and affirm women's "participation in prophecy, teaching, and leadership". At about the same time that feminist literary historians were looking for Shakespeare's silenced sisters, Ruether urged historians of religion to make the "marginalized and silenced visible and audible".[4] Sarah Apetrei's essay on the little known, mysterious, but highly prolific exegete "M. Marsin" certainly takes up Ruether's call, but Apetrei goes further by historicizing and thus questioning the categories of 'marginal' and 'radical' as they are applied to Marsin. Apetrei shows that, not only were Marsin's esoteric exegeses of the books of Daniel and Revelation owned by the libraries and clergy of the established Church, Marsin's radical and chiliastic ideas about the preacherly vocation of women and women's education had much in common with the writings and arguments of Mary Astell, a far more 'mainstream' figure both by her apologetics for the

---

[4] Rosemary Radford Ruether, "The Future of Feminist Theology in the Academy", *Journal of the American Academy of Religion* 53, no. 4 (Dec. 1985): 707–9. In the same year was published Moira Ferguson's seminal anthology of 'feminist foremothers' among early modern British writers, *First Feminists: British Women Writers, 1578–1799* (Bloomington: Indiana University Press; Old Westbury, N.Y.: Feminist Press, 1985).

established Church of England as well as by her early inclusion in the canon of early modern women writers.[5]

Apetrei analyses Marsin's radicalism through the optic of her intellectual and writing milieu. Other contributors, like Stephen Kent and Sheila Wright, who both write on Quakers, also consider the extent—as well as the consequences—of their subjects' radicalism by examining their milieux. Kent and Wright, however, focus on family and kinship ties. Kent's essay is based on the analysis of the signatures of women appended to a printed anti-tithe petition presented to the Parliament of 1659: *These several PAPERS…Being above seven thousand of the Names of the HAND-MAIDS AND DAUGHTERS OF THE LORD, And Such as feels the Oppression of Tithes.* By collecting demographic information and corroborating evidence both for signatories' participation in other acts of resistance as well as their clear membership in the Quaker movement (by being fined for attending Meeting, for instance), Kent is able to draw some surprising conclusions from the Cheshire and Lincoln petitions. Contrary to the current scholarly consensus, which assumes that *all* the signatories must be Quakers, Kent's interpretation of his evidence suggests that at least half and probably more of the signatories were not Quakers when they signed (although some became Quakers later, suggesting that the act of signing the petition might have been a possible way into the movement). Kent finds evidence for shared opposition to tithes, however, among women within families, suggesting that "their shared experience of kinship and gender gave them a common basis for opposing tithes, possibly across denominational and sectarian lines".

Taking its evidence from a later stage of Quakerism, Sheila Wright's essay makes vivid some of the domestic costs of becoming a 'Friend'. While Kent's chapter suggests that Quaker activism ran in families and was supported by ties of kinship, Wright uses the spiritual journals of Quaker women ministers to show that it also often caused antagonism within families where Quakerism was not embraced by all. Wright shows that Quaker women ministers found it difficult to reconcile their call to preach and travel with their domestic duties and affections. The narratives which record their struggles to do it all, and sometimes even the physical abuse of relatives enforcing the demands of family duty over

---

[5] Astell, for instance, appears in *First Feminists*, introduced by Ferguson as "the first self-avowed, sustained feminist polemicist in English" (180).

those of the 'inner light', tend, however, to end with family forgiveness and reconcilement. It is possible that the narratives themselves were fashioned to neutralize the irreducible tension between Quaker women's radical preaching and their traditionally ordained domestic identities.

Like Kent's essay, Marion Kobelt-Groch's chapter on the imprisonment (or not) of pregnant Anabaptist women closely examines existing archival records in order to question blanket assessments of this particular group's radical identity and history. Narratives of 'sufferings', ultimately deriving from Christian martyrology, were as important to the Anabaptists on the Continent as they were to the Quakers of Britain. Kobelt-Groch finds that gender, and in particular the condition of pregnancy, was used to add poignancy to stories of Anabaptists 'rotting' away in towers as the price paid for rejecting religious orthodoxy. However, upon looking further into the actual penal treatment of pregnant Anabaptist women, Kobelt-Groch arrives at a much more complicated picture than that presented by Balthasar Hubmaier or by the famous *Martyrs' Mirror*. Clearly, as a class, pregnant Anabaptist women were not denied the traditional privileges afforded their condition, often being allowed to leave prison (if only temporarily) to give birth and even to spend the period of recovery allotted by "the childbed privilege". Although the martyrological narrative of suffering unto death prescribes otherwise, Kobelt-Groch finds cases where women took the opportunity of childbirth respite to recant: like the Quaker women ministers whom Wright discusses, these women may have experienced an irreconcilable conflict between religious and domestic callings but may have found pragmatic solutions that do not lend themselves well to ideologizing narratives, whether of martyrdom or reconcilement.

The End of History: Millenarianism

M. Marsin believed she was one of the "two witnesses" of Revelation 11:3, who were to "prophesy a thousand two hundred and threescore days" at the end of history. Quakers and Anabaptists too were impelled to activism and defiance by a conviction that they were living in the last days.[6] As well as interrogating what counts as 'radical',

---

[6] See Douglas Gwyn, *Apocalypse of the Word: The Life and Message of George Fox* (Richmond, Ind.: Friends United Press, 1986) and *Seekers Found: Atonement in Early Quaker*

a number of the essays in this collection seek to track the theological and epistemological shifts that made it possible for women and men to think and act in ways that were significantly revisionary, stretching and testing what was possible.

Typically for the early modern period, new thinking regenerated old language and stories. "And it shall come to pass in the last days, saith God, I will pour out of my Spirit upon all flesh: and your sons and your daughters shall prophesy…on my handmaidens I will pour out in those days of my Spirit; and they shall prophesy" (Acts 2:17–18). In the Old Testament book of Joel and again in connection with the story of Pentecost in Acts (which repeats the words of Joel 2:28–29), early modern millenarians would have found a way to understand the exceptional behaviour and speech of 'inspired' women. Using the frame of eschatology, such women would have been understood as themselves signifiers of the imminence, even the arrival, of the last days.

Those who were prepared to believe they were living in the last days were also prepared for wonders, for all sorts of exceptional happenings. Thus, millenarianism brought with it exceptional opportunities for women's religious leadership even within a patriarchal culture. Some radicals like Francis Lee thought that women had a special eschatological role. Lee said of Jeanne Guyon, Antoinette Bourignon, and Jane Lead that they were the "triune wonder of the world".[7] M. Marsin analogously used her feminine gender to mark her prophetic status; according to her, the traditional bar on women from interpreting and teaching scripture had actually protected them from the erroneous exegeses propagated by tradition. Now, in the last days, the preaching vocation would no longer belong to men, but to uncorrupted women.

In her essay on the Fifth-Monarchist prophetess Anna Trapnel, Naomi Baker argues that her "millenarian religious and political context was intrinsic to the construction and articulation of her subjectivity".

Experience (Wallingford Pa.: Pendle Hill Publications, 2000). For the Anabaptists, Münster is of course the famous example of the potential of millenarian belief for social upheaval, and became the signal example thereof for early modern people. The Puritans of New England, for example, when first encountering Quaker missionaries, compared them to their "predecessors in Munster" (George Bishop, *New England Judged, Not by Man's, But the Spirit of the Lord* [1661]), 5. See also Mark R. Bell, *Apocalypse How? Baptist Movements during the English Revolution* (Macon, Ga.: Mercer University Press, 2000).

[7] Jane Lead, *The Wars of David* (1700; rpt. 1816). I owe this reference to Julie Hirst. See also B. J. Gibbons, "The Female Embassy", *Gender in Mystical and Occult Thought*, 143–62.

Scholars have largely discussed Trapnel's fastings, trances, and aphasic utterances in terms of gender, but Baker shows that her self-representation, although certainly gendered, is bound up with the more general representational strategies of her sect and used by male Fifth Monarchists like John James as well as women like Trapnel. Both James and Trapnel understood themselves and were understood by the compilers of the texts associated with them as martyrs as well as prophets of the imminent return of 'King Jesus'. For these two radical sectarians, the personal was the apocalyptic.

Linking women's radical speaking and leadership to a millenarian timetable, however, led to inevitable problems. Such a link depended on the understanding that women's interventions were exceptional. So, as the millenarian moment faded, so too did the opportunities for women's exceptional interventions. The Quaker movement has provided the best studied example of this. In the 1650s, Quaker women were testifying in the streets and 'steeple houses' of England and beyond, travelling as far as Newfoundland and the Ottoman Empire in order to bear witness to the 'light'. My own essay in this collection discusses the writings and travels of Mary Fisher as performances which work through the implications of an end-of-days, inner-light theology. Only a couple of decades later, however, Quaker women had been domesticated by designated 'women's meetings'.[8] Revolutionary and millenarian thinking may have remained a part of the internalized spiritual experience of Quakers; nonetheless, as Christine Trevett puts it, a "quieter Quakeress" undoubtedly emerged after 1660.[9]

A second problem with the millenarian support for women's religious agency is that it provides little basis for mainstream change. Thus, radical theologies or social theories that have the potential to transform received ideas about gender are current only in marginal or sectarian movements, and die out with these movements.[10] Still, though radical ideas may emerge at moments of crisis, only to disappear and die, they also tend to be reborn and reinvented. From the feminine personification

---

[8] See Phyllis Mack, Chapter Eight, "The Snake in the Garden: Quaker Politics and the Origin of the Women's Meeting," in *Visionary Women: Ecstatic Prophecy in Seventeenth-Century England* (Berkeley: University of California Press, 1992).

[9] The 'revolution within' in spiritualist religion is discussed by Gwyn in *Seekers Found*. See Christine Trevett, *Women and Quakerism in the 17th Century* (York: Sessions Book Trust, The Ebor Press, 1991) 43–44.

[10] The contribution of nineteenth-century American Quakers to women's suffrage is the clear exception. See Margaret Hope Bacon, *Mothers of Feminism: The Story of Quaker Women in America* (San Francisco: Harper & Row, 1986).

of 'Wisdom' in the Old Testament, the German theosophist Jacob
Boehme, whose writings were transmitted to and translated in England
from the mid-seventeenth century, developed 'Sophia' as an additional
feminine 'person' in the masculine godhead. This radical revision of
trinitarian theology and gender is elaborated even further, as Julie Hirst
shows in her essay, by the leader of the late-seventeenth-century Philadelphian sect, Jane Lead. But it also adumbrates the feminine Divinity
of contemporary feminist theology.[11]

Voices, Bodies, Spaces: Women's Spiritual Authority

Discussions of women's actions, utterances, and interventions in the
early modern period necessarily take up the gendered history of voice,
body, and space. Diane Purkiss has proposed that the authority of
women's prophetic voices in this period depended on an erasure of
the problematic female body. Phyllis Mack has argued, on the contrary,
that spiritual experience was generally gendered feminine, and often
figured as maternal, even for men.[12]

Hirst's essay on Lead shows how central both the experience and the
imagery of maternity was to Lead's spiritual leadership and writing.
But Lead's mysticism transforms the significations attached to gesta-
tion and maternity. As natural processes, these have limits: one can
only be born once 'naturally' and one has only one 'natural' mother.
But spiritually or 'supernaturally', one may be born many times and
have many spiritual mothers. (Lead's involuted visions can compass
her own birth from maternal Wisdom, Sophia, while, at the same
time, Wisdom is conceived and birthed within Lead herself.) Pushing
the gendered language of motherhood this far arguably destabilizes
gender altogether, by cutting loose the 'experience' of maternity from
any sort of essentialist anchor in the body (which is itself destabilized
by its co-extensive habitation of natural and supernatural worlds).

---

[11] See, for instance, Elizabeth A. Johnson's chapters on "Spirit-Sophia", "Jesus-
Sophia", and "Mother-Sophia" in *She Who Is*, 121–87.

[12] Diane Purkiss, "Producing the Voice, Consuming the Body: Women Prophets of
the Seventeenth Century," in *Women, Writing, History, 1640–1740*, ed. Isobel Grundy
and Susan Wiseman (Athens: The University of Georgia Press, 1992). See also Mack,
"Religious metaphor and the female nature" and "Mother and child" in *Visionary
Women*, 18–24, 35–44.

Accordingly, Lead adopts the Behmenist idea of the androgynous Adam as the emblem of prelapsarian perfection. To achieve salvation is to recapture this perfection, which Lead expresses as returning to one's "native country" as well as to a state of "virginity". It is to be not gendered at all, or rather beyond gender.

As Baker suggests in her essay on Trapnel, religious radicals do not do away with the body or gender so much as they refigure and redeploy it "in fluid terms". It is perhaps this willingness to resignify the body—whether at the prompting of divine motions or following the imperatives of the last days—that enables religious radicals to make such surprising, and often powerfully disruptive, interventions. Kirilka Stavreva's essay on the disruptive public speech acts and performances of early Quaker women considers how these women used both their bodies and their acoustic environments to challenge established power in its very own spaces. For Stavreva, it was the very unpredictability of the body, as well as these women's willingness to resignify gender "as needed", that gave them the power to challenge ministers in the pulpit and even King Charles II himself in Whitehall.

These loud Quaker women—who, as Stavreva memorably puts it, understood their prophesying as "releasing the Word into the world through their bodies"—might seem to have little in common with the esteemed and learned Anna Maria van Schurman, who was granted the unique privilege of attending lectures at the University of Utrecht—albeit screened from the view of the other students. Bo Karen Lee's essay on van Schurman charts her transformation late in life from the darling of the *res publica litterarum* to the demonized follower of the sect founded by Jean de Labadie. Lee examines the theology of radical self-denial that van Schurman outlined in her late two-volume spiritual work, *Eukleria*. This theology develops itself through a series of paradoxes, so that wholeness, joy, and even pleasure are achieved only by a radical repudiation of the self that allows the "infinite ocean of divinity" to fill the self entirely. Once bent wholly on scholarly achievement, van Schurman's late spiritual conversion and theological writings ultimately challenge the idea of spiritual progress. Radical repudiation of the self means one never becomes an expert at the spiritual life, and so the distinction between the novice and the master dissolves. One might imagine that van Schurman therefore became meek in old age, but, as Lee points out, her rhetoric shifts along with her theology. She ceases to be apologetic or to seek validation from male authorities:

"the style, tone, and content of her writings reveal a new authority and confidence, rather than a truncated or weakened self". Although Lee is more concerned with the theology of the ungendered self than with the gendered body, Purkiss' argument about the erasure of the problematic female body in order to produce the prophetic voice may indeed apply to both the rhetoric and the argument of the *Eukleria*. One might also apply Stavreva's arguments about the possibilities of silence as resistance. Just as the young Quaker woman refused to engage with Charles II until he stopped talking bawdy and started talking theology (as recorded by Pepys), so van Schurman too refused to keep chattering in the republic of letters and was thereby freed from the dubious honour of being a "*miraculum seu naturae monstrum*".[13] Perhaps, as with the Quaker prophet in Whitehall, her renunciation suggests a willingness to resignify herself as needed in order to gain power—power, at least, to effect discursive shifts.

Spiritualism and Difference

What was the potential of religious radicalism to transcend confessional, national, ethnic, or sexual difference in the early modern period? Clearly, some sectarian identities depended on the violent reinscription of difference. The English Fifth Monarchist Mary Cary predicted as a matter of course the destruction of all who resisted the rule of the Saints.[14] The Spanish nun and missionary Luisa de Carvajal, discussed by José González, explored resistant subjectivities in her poetry by taking on the subject position of Christ, for instance, or reimagining the relationship between humans and nature as one not of domination but of fluid interpenetration. González argues for continuities between her 'radical' poetry and her bold mission to re-convert the English. (Interestingly, unlike Mary Ward, de Carvajal never seems to have run into any opposition to her ambitions from the church hierarchy.) Yet González also remarks that de Carvajal "appropriated the spirit of conquest of those who went abroad to acquire new territories for the

---

[13] This was the French Carmelite Louis Jacob's pronouncement on van Schurman in his *Elogium* (1646), quoted in *Choosing the Better Part: Anna Maria van Schurman (1607–1678)*, ed. Mirjam de Baar et al. (Dordrecht: Kluwer Academic Publishers, 1996), 5.

[14] Mary Cary, *The Little Horns Doom and Downfall* (1651).

Spanish crown". Her mystic contemplation did not prevent her from loathing England and hating its weather.

The Quaker Mary Fisher, however, was "moved of the Lord to go and deliver his Word to the Great Turk", travelling across the globe in order to meet a man who was arguably the most hated and feared ruler of the early modern world. (His only rival, at least in Protestant Europe, was the pope.) My essay asks what enabled a thirty-year-old, uneducated servingwoman from the north of England to dare imagine that she could speak on equal terms, and perhaps find something in common, with the most powerful leader of the Islamic world. The answer lies in the early Quaker commitment to belief in the 'universal light', the spark of the divine present in all women and men, in all peoples of the world. This light is not shared out but is the same light in all, which allowed some early Quakers to declare with perfect sincerity that they were Isaiah or that they were Christ.[15] It also allowed for the possibility of intimate communion with the 'Other'. As Fisher put it in a letter alluding to her meeting with the court of the Great Turk, "there is a love begot in me towards them which is endlesse".

In transferring authority from externals like scripture to the inner light, English Quakers followed in the spiritualist tradition of the radical reformation which likewise privileged the inner experience of direct revelation.[16] Yet it is striking that not only the direct heirs of the spiritualist tradition—the Anabaptists, Quakers, and Behmenists discussed in this collection—but also women from Calvinist, Anglican, and Catholic formations are shown to invoke personal revelation or unmediated experience of the divine, with the result that spiritual authority becomes invested in them: not in priestly mediators, guides, or teachers, but in their own selves, bodies, voices, and writings.[17] For the formerly orthodox Calvinist Anna Maria van Schurman, it was experiential religion, "the gaze of divine Mercy" looking at her, that

---

[15] See for instance, Leo Damrosch, *The Sorrows of the Quaker Jesus: James Nayler and the Puritan Crackdown on the Free Spirit* (Cambridge, Mass.: Harvard University Press, 1996).

[16] See George H. Williams, *Radical Reformation*, 3rd ed. (Kirksville, Mo.: Truman State University Press, 2000).

[17] Elsewhere, I have written about the different kinds of feminine authority and authorship enabled by 'Word' and 'Spirit' respectively. See Sylvia Brown, "The Eloquence of the Word and the Spirit: The Place of Puritan Women's Writing in Old and New England", in *Women and Religion in Old and New Worlds*, ed. Susan E. Dinan and Debra Meyers (New York and London: Routledge, 2001), 187–211.

resolved paradoxes. The Catholic Mary Ward founded her Institutes, and nourished her persistence, from a series of "revelations"—although she was careful, as Ellis points out, to characterize them as "intellectual insights" rather than "visions". M. Marsin, too, combined a thoroughly rationalized method for biblical exegesis with personal revelation.

Thoroughly internalized religious experience could provide the resources, it seemed, for the audacious breaking of boundaries. It may also have had the potential to reach across the religious divisions of early modern Europe. Antoinette Bourignon's most dedicated followers were in Scotland. Bo Karen Lee has made the point—in work beyond the scope of her essay in this volume—that Anna Maria van Schurman, a Calvinist, and Jeanne Guyon, a Catholic, were both able to bridge the hardened confessional differences that defined, often with deadly consequences, the Europe in which they lived. Guyon, for instance, was attended by loyal Protestants on her deathbed, while van Schurman's reformed background was reshaped by her encounter with Jean de Labadie, a former Jesuit turned Calvinist, and her later writings were shot through with themes borrowed from Catholic mysticism.[18]

The final essay by Ruth Connolly takes on the question of European ecumenism directly. But Connolly's subject, Katherine Jones, Viscountess Ranelagh, in her participation in and patronage of the energetically reformative Hartlib-Dury circle, had more sober, limited, and rational aspirations than some of the women discussed in this volume. Her concern, and the concern of many of the figures associated with her, was the reconcilement of the *Protestant* factions of Europe against Catholicism.

---

[18] In another instance, Pierre Poiret was a great admirer of Flemish quietist Antoinette Bourignon and edited her complete works; but he also edited the works of the Catholic mystic Jeanne Guyon. As B. J. Gibbons writes, even if Poiret was "celebrated as 'a great Protestant mystic', he was never averse to finding spiritual truth in the Romanist tradition" (*Gender in Mystical and Occult Thought*, 16). For Lee's comparative reading of van Schurman and Guyon, see "Sacrifice and Desire: The Rhetoric of Self-Denial in the Mystical Theologies of Madam Jeanne Guyon and Anna Maria van Schurman" (Ph.D. diss., Princeton Theological Seminary, 2007). I am also indebted to Lee for discussions of these points over email.

A number of essays in the collection also point out diachronic connections, particularly between forms of radical Protestantism and pre-Reformation Catholic spirituality. M. Marsin and Jane Lead, both active in London at the very end of the seventeenth century, both also revive aspects of Mary as an important soteriological figure. Anna Trapnel's fasts and trances recall medieval mystics able to subsist on the host alone.

Although her vision of toleration was a radical one for her time and place—she openly consorted with Quakers and other Nonconformists at a time in England when simply holding a private religious gathering was punishable by fine, prison, or, if persistent, transportation—it looks less radical to us simply because her vision won. As Connolly points out, Ranelagh was not a marginal woman. She had power and influence in a group that itself had political power and influence, and her advocacy of liberty of conscience with checks against antinomianism (and with exceptions remaining for Roman Catholicism) was eventually adopted by the religious-political culture that emerged in Britain after the Glorious Revolution.

In some ways, Ranelagh was the future. Yet Ranelagh's insistence that godly individuals should be guided by the 'inner light' of natural reason and her millenarian interest in the 'deliverance' of the Jews should remind us that what might look superficially modern, rational, and liberal often has its feet planted in wilder soil. As a whole, this collection seeks to elicit comparisons and connections where they might not usually be made, including the indeterminate region between rational, secular modernity and its radical, sacral underside. Taken together and in themselves, the studies in this volume help us to understand the limits, complexity, and contingency of the radical religious beliefs and practices of early modern women. It is also hoped that they will enable what Rosemary Ruether hoped feminist theology would do: not only tell forgotten stories of women and religion, but also recover radical possibilities and understand what made them imaginable.

Bibliography

Almond, Gabriel A., R. Scott Appleby, and Emmanuel Sivan. *Strong Religion: The Rise of Fundamentalisms around the World*. Chicago: University of Chicago Press, 2003.

Bacon, Margaret Hope. *Mothers of Feminism: The Story of Quaker Women in America*. San Francisco: Harper & Row, 1986.

Bell, Mark R. *Apocalypse How? Baptist Movements during the English Revolution*. Macon, Ga.: Mercer University Press, 2000.

Bishop, George. *New England Judged, Not by Man's, But the Spirit of the Lord: And the Summe Sealed up of New-England's Persecution. Being A Brief Relation of the Sufferings of the People called Quakers in those Parts of America, from the Beginning of the Fifth Month 1656...to the later End of the Tenth Moneth, 1660*. London, 1661.

Brown, Sylvia. "The Eloquence of the Word and the Spirit: The Place of Puritan Women's Writing in Old and New England". In *Women and Religion in Old and New Worlds*. Edited by Susan E. Dinan and Debra Meyers. New York and London: Routledge, 2001.

Cary, Mary. *The Little Horns Doom and Downfall*. London, 1651.

Damrosch, Leo. *The Sorrows of the Quaker Jesus: James Nayler and the Puritan Crackdown on the Free Spirit*. Cambridge, Mass.: Harvard University Press, 1996.

De Baar, Mirjam et al., eds. *Choosing the Better Part: Anna Maria van Schurman (1607–1678)*. Dordrecht: Kluwer Academic Publishers, 1996.

Ferguson, Moira, ed. *First Feminists: British Women Writers, 1578–1799*. Bloomington: Indiana University Press; Old Westbury, N.Y.: Feminist Press, 1985.

Gibbons, B. J. *Gender in Mystical and Occult Thought: Behmenism and its Development in England*. Cambridge: Cambridge University Press, 1996.

Gwyn, Douglas. *Apocalypse of the Word: The Life and Message of George Fox*. Richmond, Ind.: Friends United Press, 1986.

——. "Apocalypse Now and Then: Reading Early Friends in the Belly of the Beast". In *The Creation of Quaker Theory*. Edited by Pink Dandelion. Aldershot: Ashgate, 2004.

——. *Seekers Found: Atonement in Early Quaker Experience*. Wallingford Pa.: Pendle Hill Publications, 2000.

Johnson, Elizabeth A. *She Who Is: The Mystery of God in Feminist Theological Discourse*. New York: Crossroad, 1992.

Joy, Morny. "God and Gender: Some Reflections on Women's Invocations of the Divine". In *Religion and Gender*. Edited by Ursula King. Oxford: Blackwell, 1995.

Lee, Bo Karen. "Sacrifice and Desire: The Rhetoric of Self-Denial in the Mystical Theologies of Madam Jeanne Guyon and Anna Maria van Schurman". Ph.D. diss., Princeton Theological Seminary, 2007.

Mack, Phyllis. *Visionary Women: Ecstatic Prophecy in Seventeenth-Century England*. Berkeley: University of California Press, 1992.

Morton, Timothy and Nigel Smith. "Introduction". *Radicalism in British Literary Culture, 1650–1830: From Revolution to Revolution*. Edited by T. Morton and N. Smith. Cambridge: Cambridge University Press, 2002.

Purkiss, Diane. "Producing the Voice, Consuming the Body: Women Prophets of the Seventeenth Century". In *Women, Writing, History 1640–1740*. Edited by Isobel Grundy and Susan Wiseman. Athens: The University of Georgia Press, 1992.

Ruether, Rosemary Radford. "The Future of Feminist Theology in the Academy". *Journal of the American Academy of Religion* 53, no. 4 (Dec. 1985): 703–13.

Trevett, Christine. *Women and Quakerism in the 17th Century*. York: Sessions Book Trust, The Ebor Press, 1991.

Williams, George H. *Radical Reformation*. 3rd ed. Kirksville, Mo.: Truman State University Press, 2000.

PART ONE

QUAKER WOMEN AND RADICAL ACTIVISM
ACROSS THE BOUNDARIES

PROPHETIC CRIES AT WHITEHALL:
THE GENDER DYNAMICS OF EARLY QUAKER WOMEN'S INJURIOUS SPEECH

KIRILKA STAVREVA*

Almost 375 Quaker women prophesied publicly in the second half of the seventeenth century.[1] A good number of these prophets unleashed their spiritual onslaughts against men at the very pinnacle of state power. Curiously, English state leaders often seemed to expose themselves willingly to these attacks. Among the assailants was one Mary Howgill, Quaker minister, who at "about ten a clock at night" on 7 July 1656, issued this prophetic warning to the Lord Protector of England, Oliver Cromwell, in Whitehall Palace:

> But thou, where thou standest, thy reign shall be but for a time, for misery and great condemnation shall be thy portion, and all them who have forgotten the Lord our God; for we have the Lord to be our strength, and thou who acts against him, the time is come that we are justified, and with him that justifies us shalt thou be condemned, and thou shalt know that thou hadst better that thy tongue had been cloven to the roof of thy mouth, ere these things had been acted in thy name (we are kept in perfect peace).

Howgill was not the first Child of Light to assail Cromwell's ear: several of the travelling ministers known as the First Publishers of the Truth had paid visits to Whitehall before her. Yet something about this female minister's speech must have "pierced" the Protector's conscience

---

* I would like to express my gratitude to Cornell College for supporting my research on early Quaker women with three faculty development grants, to the librarians and staff at the Haverford College Quaker Collection in Haverford, Pennsylvania, and the Library of the Society of Friends in London for helpful assistance and conversations, and to Michael Witmore of Carnegie Mellon University for his thoughtful comments on an earlier version of this article, presented at the 2004 meeting of the Renaissance Society of America.
[1] Phyllis Mack, "The Prophet and Her Audience: Gender and Knowledge in the World Turned Upside Down," in *Reviving the English Revolution: Reflections and Elaborations on the Work of Christopher Hill*, ed. Geoff Eley and William Hunt (London: Verso, 1988), 150n.

to allow for "much discourse" with her in spite of the late hour.[2] Before departing, she left a copy of her scathing call for repentance in Cromwell's hands.

There is little in the content and discursive structure of Howgill's letter to account for the heartfelt response on the part of the Lord Protector. It asks for nothing. It is harsh. Like other Quaker petitions, it directly charges Cromwell with condoning the persecution of Friends, but also with much worse: with worldly corruption and with having "crucified the Lamb of God". Furthermore, it draws a clear line between "we [who] know our being and our habitation with the Lord" and "thou" who are "one with all them that are in the evil".[3] As a cry of woe for the spiritual fall of the Protector, signed "by a Lover of thy soul", and using throughout the socially levelling "thou" so typical of Quaker speech, it strikes an intensely (and inappropriately) personal note. And yet the speaking subject in the "Remarkable Letter" positions herself at a remarkable distance from both her addressee and the discursive context. She refers to herself as one "grafted" into God and immersed into an everlasting divine time transcending distinctions among past, present, and future. Why then, in spite of the antagonizing content of the address, its disregard of social decorum, and the discursive distance which the speaker maintains from her addressee, did it procure Howgill a lengthy conversation with the most powerful man in England late into the midsummer evening?

Clearly, Howgill's address derives its style from Old Testament prophecy as evident from the harshness of its tone, the spiritual distance between speaker and addressee, and the alignment of the speaker with the divine. In a deeply religious culture, such prophesying

---

[2] *A Remarkable Letter of Mary Howgill to Oliver Cromwell, called Protector* (London, 1657), 2–4. The first Quakers to declare the divine message to Cromwell were John Camm and Francis Howgill, who visited the Lord Protector in his chamber "for the most part of an hour" in the spring of 1654, but who were dismissed after Cromwell got tired of trying to convince them of the wisdom of "keeping favour with all" religious persuasions. They were followed by William Pearson in July and then again in November of the same year. In the spring of 1655 Pearson "cleared his conscience" to the Protector and tore the linen cap he wore on his head as a sign of how Cromwell's counsels would be rent into pieces. Pearson, along with Gervase Benson and Thomas Aldam, petitioned for the release of imprisoned Friends later that spring. George Fox clearly impressed Cromwell during their first meeting in March 1655, when he brought tears to the Protector's eyes and succeeded in clearing Friends from the rumours about their alleged plots against Cromwell's life. William Braithwaite, *The Beginnings of Quakerism*, 2nd edition (Cambridge: Cambridge University Press, 1961), 435, 156, 436–37, 180.

[3] *Remarkable Letter*, 2.

was bound to deliver a punch to the addressee, putting him—at least momentarily—out of control of the immediate rhetorical context. In other words, the address constituted, in its disorienting interpellation, injurious speech. As Judith Butler explains,

> To be addressed injuriously is not only to be open to an unknown future, but not to know the time and place of injury, and to suffer the disorientation of one's situation as the effect of such speech. Exposed at the moment of such a shattering is precisely the volatility of one's "place" within the community of speakers....[4]

To establish the underlying cause for the efficacy of Quaker women's prophecies, however, we need to look beyond stylistic resemblances with Old Testament rhetorical models and their injurious potential. In all likelihood, the effect of Howgill's address, and, I would argue, of the spoken addresses of other Quaker women to men in high places, had more to do with performative rhetoric; that is, with style *as embodied* in vocal and gestural delivery.[5] Its impact was due neither exclusively to the exhortative content of the message, nor to its distinctive style, but rather, to the discursive performance, by a woman, of a message that appeared to have been authored by a godly community ("we [who] have the Lord to be our strength").[6] An inalienable—and entrancingly dynamic –element of this performance was the gender of the speaker. It is the performative process of gendering the militant style of the early Quakers by women ministers that constitutes the focus of my inquiry. The agile re-fashioning of deeply ingrained gender identities and hierarchies, accomplished with sensitivity to the human participants and architectural conditions of oral performance, entailed the potential to upset other social identities and hierarchies. As Quaker women shifted gender roles, they upset other relations of power as well. Attentively, relentlessly, and often collectively, they enacted a relation of spiritual

---

[4] Judith Butler, *Excitable Speech: A Politics of the Performative* (New York: Routledge, 1997), 4.

[5] The definition of rhetoric as style *and* delivery follows the prioritization of the elocution stage in the aftermath of the influential reforms in the field of rhetoric instigated by French Renaissance philosopher and rhetorician Peter Ramus. Ramus called for a clear differentiation between the arts of logic and rhetoric. The former included the *inventio* of arguments and their arrangement (*dispositio* or *iudicium*), the latter, style (the use of tropes and figures) and delivery (which received little attention by Ramus and his followers). Walter Ong, *Rhetoric, Romance and Technologies: Studies in the Interaction of Expression and Culture* (Ithaca: Cornell University Press, 1971), 83.

[6] *Remarkable Letter*, 2.

domination over their addressees that injured the prestige of state authority in the very site symbolizing state power.

My methodology in studying the performative discursive agency of Quaker women who prophesied publicly at court brings together what Victor Turner has called "processual symbology" with Butler's focus on speech acts as bodily acts. Like Turner, I approach their symbolic actions with an interest in the "events which may generate new cultural materials (symbols, metaphors, orientations, styles, values, even paradigms) as well as fashion novel patternings of social relationships with traditional cultural instruments". Turner understands these events as performance situations that open up avenues both for adding new signifieds to old signifiers by collective fiat and, more importantly for the purposes of this study, for the enrichment of the public signification of symbolic action through the private construction of meaning. Turner maintains that individually construed shifts in public hermeneutic are possible "if the exegete has sufficient power, authority, or prestige to make his views 'stick'".[7] Like Butler, I suggest that such power can *also* be derived through the bodily aspect of the speech of socially marginalized subjects. For, as Butler argues, embodied speech does not generate a dispositional *habitus* that socializes the subject to act in conformity with the social field. Rather, in her view, embodied speech has the potential to unsettle the *habitus* described by Bourdieu as "embodied history, internalized as second nature and so forgotten as history". The speaking body "exceeds its interpellation, and remains uncontained by any of its acts of speech"; in its unpredictability rests the power to re-signify dominant discourses.[8]

The case studies below present such corporally exceeding speech acts carried out in the culturally prominent seat of state power by speakers lacking the social authority to perform and reform symbolic action. It is important to note that the discursive insurrection of female prophetic speech and its associated principle of silence took place within a dynamic, yet identifiable field of social relationships, actions, and meanings. Quaker women ministers were by no means capable

---

[7] Victor Turner, "Symbolic Studies", *Annual Review of Anthropology* 4 (1975): 149, 150, 154. See also Richard Bauman, *"Let Your Words Be Few": Symbolism of Speaking and Silence among Seventeenth-Century Quakers* (Prospect Heights, Illinois: Waveland Press, 1983), 10–12.

[8] Butler, *Excitable Speech*, 157–58, 155; Pierre Bourdieu, *The Logic of Practice*, trans. Richard Nice (Cambridge: Polity Press, 1980), 56.

of fully controlling the signification of the cultural symbol of their prophesying. But they made concerted efforts to perform their symbolic actions to their best advantage, to exert control over the discursive field at hand and, by extension, over the conduct of social life. Often they succeeded. Essential to these efforts was the dynamic gendering of prophetic speech.[9] To reflect on the rhetorical effects of the injurious speech of Quaker women at court, I analyse its stylistic patterns and attempt to reconstruct its vocal and physical delivery from clues in the written documents. Whenever possible, I attend to the soundscape in which this discourse was embedded, or what Bruce Smith describes as the "constant interaction between speech communities and their acoustic environment".[10]

Gender, Writing, and the Sound of the Word

While no government record of the late-night exchange between Howgill and Cromwell survives, we learn about its instigation from Howgill's *Remarkable Letter*, which was published in the following year, with handwritten copies possibly circulating shortly after her visit to Cromwell's palace. It is from published texts like this one that I have extracted clues about the delivery of the early Quaker women's injurious words. It is then necessary to clarify the relationship between letter and sound in them.

Like many petitions and proclamations published by early Friends, Howgill's letter was probably composed as the next best substitute for a direct address in the event that the minister were denied access to the

---

[9] In her influential monograph on seventeenth-century ecstatic prophecy, Mack discusses the experience of testifying by Quaker ministers, male and female alike, as involving a kind of ungendering, a disengagement of "their individual gendered selves from their personae as prophets". I disagree. While female ministers certainly made use of the dynamic gendering of their own speech acts and those of others, including the symbolic use of womanhood to signify inability to preach or disassociation from the divine, the bodily act of speaking reinstalled gender to rhetorical function. As a result, the speaker's gender came into rhetorical relief even as she shifted the normative descriptors of gender, enhancing its performative range. Mack, *Visionary Women: Ecstatic Prophecy in Seventeenth-Century England* (Berkeley: University of California Press, 1992), 175. See also Elaine Hobby, *Virtue of Necessity: English Women's Writing, 1649–1688* (London: Virago Press, 1988), 38, 48.

[10] Bruce R. Smith, *The Acoustic World of Early Modern England: Attending to the O-Factor* (Chicago: University of Chicago Press, 1999), 51.

head of state, or interrupted before delivering her message. Even though it is a written text, it was meant to be urgently sounded, not consumed privately in the silence of the page. Howgill refers to this and several earlier prophetic addresses to Cromwell as a "cry" against which the Lord Protector had hardened his heart.[11] The urgent sound of such prophesying cries must have been inalienable from their content, for early Quakers refer to the aural qualities of their messages even when discussing written texts. Thus in a 1656 address George Fox charges:

> Let all nations hear the word by sound of writing. Spare no place, spare not tongue nor pen, but be obedient to the Lord God and go through the work and be valiant for the Truth upon earth.[12]

Literally animated by what early Friends imagined as a tremulous soul bearing the divine Word, Quaker writing was conceived of as an acoustic phenomenon. Its rhetorical power was attributed to the power of the *voice* to affect the harmonics of the addressee's body and the soul residing within it, unless, of course, listeners had hardened their hearts against the prophets' cries.[13]

For early Quakers, the aural qualities of prophecy preceded the acts of composition and enunciation. Like many Quaker proclamations, the *Remarkable Letter* was a text that voiced the Word of God dwelling inwardly.[14] For Howgill and other "Children of Light", prophesying, or releasing the Word into the world through their bodies, was an act of

---

[11] *Remarkable Letter*, 3–4.

[12] *The Journal of George Fox*, ed. John L. Nickalls, rev. ed. (Cambridge: Cambridge University Press, 1975), 263.

[13] The popular idea of the musical harmony of the human body and soul derives from Boethius' concept of *Musica humana*, the inaudible harmony of human bodies and souls, of the rational and the irrational. *Musica humana* is one of the three categories of music he elaborates in his treatise *De Institutione Musica*, which was highly influential during the early modern era. (The other two are *Musica mundane*, the harmony of the spheres, and *Musica instrumentalis*, vocal and instrumental music.) Joselyn Godwin, ed., *The Harmony of the Spheres: A Sourcebook of the Pythagorean Tradition in Music* (Rochester, VT: Inner Traditions Intl., 1993), 86.

[14] The seventeenth-century Quaker writer Robert Barclay clearly defines the divine Word as dwelling within the believer: "The Word is nigh, in thy Mouth and in thy Heart; that is the Word of Faith, which we preach." See his *Truth triumphant through the spiritual warfare, Christian labours, and writings of that able and faithful servant of Jesus Christ, Robert Barclay, who deceased at his own house at Urie in the kingdom of Scotland, the 3 day of the 8 month 1690* (London, 1692), 128. As Barclay and others have contended, attending to God's voice within was a major doctrinal difference between Quakers and other Christians in the mid-seventeenth century. For the latter, the Word of God was recorded in the Scriptures and further revelations were no longer possible. While Quakers certainly knew their Scriptures and venerated them as an account of God's messages to

spiritual obedience. It started by opening the ear—the organ that the early moderns believed was the gateway to the heart and by extension to the soul—to the divine call. Thus Dorothy White, the most prolific early Quaker woman writer next to Margaret Fell, relates that her 1659 tract, *A Diligent Search amongst Rulers, Priests, Professors, and People*, was only conceived when she actively heeded the sound of the Word:

> Upon the 25th day of the second moneth, [16]59. as I was passing along the street, I heard a cry in me; again on the 26th day of the same Moneth, the same cry was in me; againe on the 27th day, the same cry was in me, and *as I was waiting upon the Lord in silence*, the word of the Lord came unto me.[15]

White's experience suggests that sounding was an intrinsic aspect of early Quaker prophetic tracts, to a degree that can probably only be matched by the dramatic literature of the early modern era. These were texts which started with the aural perception of the Word in the soul of the believer, which were composed as either blueprints for aural delivery or as recording the memory of such delivery, and which sought their fullness in the immediacy of vocal, polythetic performance.

In one respect at least, this ecstatic conception of Quaker prophecy resembles the calls for willful acceptance of the divine word recurring in early seventeenth-century Protestant sermons: in both types of religious discourse the hearer is portrayed as the receptor of the Word of God. As Wes Folkerth points out in his study of the cultural practice of listening in early modern England, Protestant preachers described hearing as a feminized faculty and underscored its agricultural and reproductive associations, typically resorting to the gospel parable of the sower. According to the parable, just as it takes good soil for a seed to grow and yield harvest, it takes honesty, open-mindedness, attentiveness, and perseverance to accept God's Word and cultivate it in the world.[16] The sermons, Folkerth explains, interpret the Word "as seed, the ear [as] either the vaginal gateway through which the seed must

---

earlier believers, they in no way believed that the Word of God could be restricted to a physical written text. See also Bauman, *"Let Your Words Be Few"*, 25–26.

[15] Dorothy White, *A Diligent Search amongst Rulers, Priests, Professors, and People; and a warning to all sorts high and low, that are out of the doctrine of Christ, and fear not God. Put forth by Dorothy White living in Waymouth* (London, 1659), 1, emphasis added.

[16] Matthew 13:3–23, Mark 4:3–29, Luke 8:5–15.

travel on its way to the earth/heart/womb, or...the womb itself".[17]
The underlying assumption in these interpretations is that the minister
is the one performing the masculine task of spiritual impregnation/
planting, while attentive church-goers are cast in a feminine role as
dutifully penetrable and spiritually fertile. Similar images of penetra-
tion and impregnation were used by early Friends as well. Elizabeth
Stirredge, for example, recalls the powerful ministry of two of the First
Publishers of the Truth thus:

> I was in the Nineteenth Year of my Age, when J. Camm and John Aud-
> land came first to Bristol, in the Dread and Power of the great God of
> Heaven and Earth; and I am a living Witness that his powerful Presence
> was with them, and made their Ministry so dreadful, that it *pierced* the
> Hearts of Thousands.[18]

Yet the gendered imagery of speaker and listener in Quaker religious
discourse deviates in interesting ways from that in the Protestant ministers' sermons. As Stirredge continues her recollection of the impact
of Camm's and Audland's speech, she draws on a different scriptural
narrative:

> But before the Meeting was over, the Spirit of the Lord moved in my
> Heart, and in the Light I came to see my woful and deplorable State,
> which made me to cry to God for Mercy; a Day never to be forgotten
> by me.[19]

To the imagery of overpowering and piercing, evocative of the Annun-
ciation story, wherein Mary is said to have conceived her son as God's
message entered her ear, this Quaker adds a reference to the "quickening" of the divine spirit within her heart/womb. The latter reference
recalls the story in Luke's gospel of the first stirring of Elizabeth's baby
when the pregnant Mary greeted her, followed by Elizabeth's prophetic
blessing on Mary and the fruit of her womb:

> God's blessing is on you above all women, and his blessing is on the
> fruit of your womb. Who am I, that the mother of my Lord should visit

---

[17] Wes Folkerth, *The Sound of Shakespeare* (London and New York: Routledge, 2002),
46–47.

[18] Elizabeth Stirredge, *Strength in Weakness Manifest in the Life, Various Trials, and Christian
Testimony of that faithful Servant and Handmaid of the Lord, Elizabeth Stirredge, Who departed
this Life, at her House at Hempstead in Hertfordshire, in the 72nd Year of her Age*, 2nd edition
(London, 1746), 162, emphasis added.

[19] Stirredge, *Strength in Weakness*, 162–63.

me? I tell you, when your greeting sounded in my ears, the baby in my
womb leapt for joy. Happy is she who has faith that the Lord's promise
to her would be fulfilled.[20]

In her "Christian Testimony" Stirredge portrays the spiritually fertile
listener as somewhat akin to the conceiving Mary, but more so to
the sanctifying Elizabeth. By implication, the bearers of the Word in
her narrative are somewhat masculine, like the angel Gabriel bearing
the message of the Holy Spirit, but also feminine, like the pregnant
Mary.

Such dynamic gendering of speaker and listener is persistent in both
female and male Quaker discourse, and the gender emphasis can go
either way. In an address to the Parliamentarian Army, the famous
Quaker minister Richard Hubberthorne refers repeatedly to his and
other Friends' "tender conscience", meaning conscience that is "susceptible to moral and spiritual influence, impressionable, sympathetic, sensitive to pious emotions"—qualities traditionally gendered as feminine.[21]
The same address he signed in unmistakably masculine terms, as "A
member of his Army, who makes War with the sword of his mouth".[22]
Likewise, in commemorating Elizabeth Stirredge's ministry, her neighbour John Thornton says of the woman who portrayed her convincement in terms of the quickening of the divine within her heart/womb:
"She commonly had a sharp and piercing Testimony against such that
the great Enemy had so misled". According to her own account of her
life, Stirredge's prophetic speech (and her silence) could be not only
unsettling and injurious, but downright deadly. On one occasion, after
staring silently for some forty-five minutes upon Justices of the Peace
and assorted officers who had gathered to assess confiscated Quaker
goods, she felt called to deliver a "dreadful Warning" to the men and
prophesied their sudden "destruction". As she reports,

> the Lord was pleased in a very short Time to fulfill that Testimony on
> them. For in a few Weeks, as they were making Merry at a Feast, Two of
> them died on a sudden after Dinner, and the Rest very hardly escaped,
> about the Year, 1674.

---

[20] Luke 1:42–45.
[21] Rosemary Moore, *The Light in Their Consciences: Early Quakers in Britain 1646–1666*
(University Park: The Pennsylvania University Press, 2000), 6.
[22] "A Word, of Wisdom and Counsel to the Officers and Souldiers of the Army in
England, &c." in *A Collection of the Several Books and Writings of that Faithful Servant of God
Richard Hubberthorn* (London, 1663), 239.

Pregnant with the Word, with an ambiguously gendered spirit that was "greatly enlarged by the mighty Power of the Lord", Stirredge was apparently also adept at piercing ears and hearts in a masculine manner, and capable of sounding the destructive power of divine wrath.[23]

Conceptually and pragmatically then, there was supposed to be little difference between the acoustic make-up of male and female Quaker prophetic discourse. Once the Word entered its prophetic bearers' bodies and souls (the latter considered to be seated in the heart), it dynamized their bodies and voices. The result, frequently referred to as a cry, was an 'audible species' presumably bearing the acoustic signature of the Word. The cry, in turn, either 'pierced' those who opened an eager ear to it and re-tuned the harmonics of their souls, or overpowered and eventually destroyed 'hardened' listeners. It was these acoustic qualities, much more than the semantic content of prophetic speech, that Quakers credited with the power to convince or, alternatively, destroy. Thus Alice Curwen rendered her death-bed testimony of God's imminent conquest of the world "with a Heavenly Melody". Though she requested for someone to record her words, there was apparently little that could be recorded in writing, for, as the witness Anne Martindall recalls, Alice "spoke a long time, but I do remember very few of her words".[24] Still, all gathered at her bedside were "broken into Tenderness" by her melodious prophecy.

Yet in spite of the common origins, transmission mechanism, and reported effect of male and female prophecies, those uttered by Quaker women were much more resented and feared. Misgivings about them surface in the writings of male Friends as well. In 1653, some six years after the Quaker leader George Fox first began 'declaring truth' publicly, he wrote to "Friends in the Ministry", urging them to "quench not your prophecy, neither heed them that despise it, but in that stand that brings you through to the end". When Fox addresses women ministers in particular in the same epistle, however, he is markedly cautionary:

---

[23] Stirredge, *Strength in Weakness*, n.p., 47, 114.
[24] *A Relation of the labour, travail and suffering of that faithful servant of the Lord Alice Curwen. Who departed this life the 7th day of the 6th moneth, 1679. and resteth in peace with the Lord* (London, 1680), n.p. [p. 2].

And ye daughters, to whom it is given to prophesy, keep within your own measure, seeing over that which is without.... Neither be lifted up in your openings and prophecies, lest ye depart from that which opened.[25]

There is a palpable concern here about the women prophets' ability to speak the new "plain" language of the Inner Light without adulterating it with the materiality and dynamics "of carnal talk and talkers".[26] The epistle suggests that when these women added their voices to the Word within, they were prone to lift themselves up above their listeners, depart "from that which opened" within, and engage with the immediate social context of their utterance ("that which is without").

Predictably, Fox's contemporaries from other religious persuasions were much more forthright when responding to the insurrectionary speech of early Quaker women. Quaker women prophets were consistently portrayed as analogous to such notorious disruptors of the social order as scolds and witches. Thus the sectarian Lodowick Muggleton noted the rhetorical 'excess' of Elizabeth Hooton's preaching in Nottinghamshire, before calling her "an old she serpent" who "hath shot forth her poisonous arrows at me in blasphemy, curses, and words, thinking herself stronger than her brethren", and pronouncing her "cursed and damned...to eternity." The mayor of Carlisle chose to criminalize Dorothy Waugh's speaking "against all deceit and ungodly practices" at the marketplace in the town, and had her hauled away and paraded through the streets fitted with a scold's bridle of "a stone weight". New England Puritans routinely made witchcraft accusations against female Quaker ministers who challenged their theocracy.[27] While male Quaker ministers were also imprisoned, publicly whipped, and called witches, the severity of the reaction and punishments levelled against women

---

[25] "No More but My Love": Letters of George Fox 1624–91, ed. Cecil W. Sharman (London: Quaker Home Service, 1980), ep. 35, 17. Curiously, the Minute Book for the Women's Monthly Meetings in Oxfordshire records an excerpt from a different letter from George Fox, dated the 2 of the 11th mo. 1673. It reads, with no reservations whatsoever, "Women are to prophesie, and prophecy is not to be quenched" (BMM I/ix/1, Oxfordshire Public Records Office).

[26] Journal of George Fox, 12; Richard Farnsworth, The Spirit of God Speaking in the Temple of God (London, 1663), 14.

[27] On Hooton, see A Volume of Spiritual Epistles written by John Reeve and Lodowicke Muggleton, (London, 1755; reprint 1820), 227. On Waugh, see The Lambs Defence against Lyes (London, 1656), 29–30. Regarding the persecution of Quaker women in New England, Mack estimates that between 1656 and 1664 New England theocrats levelled half of all witchcraft accusations against Quaker women. See her Visionary Women, 259.

suggests that female prophesying posed unique challenges to cultural norms and social relationships.

Such cultural anxiety was not simply a function of the profoundly unsettling cultural symbol of the outspoken and disorderly woman in a world which, in the mid-seventeenth century, was being turned upside down in a fashion that had little to do with the temporary playful rejection of social order during carnival, nor with the upheavals, reversals, and parodies of social norms dramatized on the stage. Male figures of authority, from leaders of Civil War radical religious groups to civic magistrates, responded to a set of recurrent rhetorical qualities of female prophetic speech. Indeed, as injurious speech, women's prophecies resembled the rhetorical eruptions of early modern scolds and witches. But unlike the exclusively improvisational witch-speak and scolding, the prophecies of women Friends were more likely to incorporate familiar and influential Biblical motifs within their rhetorical contour. With male Publishers of the Truth, prophesying women shared a haunting style, which Jackson Cope describes in a groundbreaking article as marked by "incantatory" rhythms, repetitive word clusters, and persistent slippages between literalness and metaphor.[28] Both men and women attended to the experience of the Word of God opening within to harmonize their bodies and voices with the divine message. But, as perhaps Fox was too well aware, Quaker women prophets did not restrict themselves to adding voice to *Vox*. As the case studies below illustrate, they made full use of the acoustic and visual impact of the ecstatic speaker's female body, whose difference from the costuming, gesture, and sound of high society they strategically underscored, and whose gender they re-signified as needed. They entered domains of political and ecclesiastical power in which low-born women had never set foot before, tuned in to the architectural and acoustic environment, and devised performative ways to deliver the heaviest rhetorical punch in the given setting.

---

[28] Jackson I. Cope, "Seventeenth-Century Quaker Style," *PMLA* 71 (1956): 726–38.

"So did this oppression ring over all the Court"

In numerous petitions to Parliament and King, Quaker women issued stern warnings of divine wrath to men in power.[29] Testifying in person at Whitehall, however, was a more demanding speech act, and also one with larger repercussions. It was not an act that many women Friends were eager to engage in. Even a prophet with a reputation for "sharp and piercing Testimony", such as Elizabeth Stirredge, when called to prophesy at court, resisted for a long time the divine 'opening' within:

> knowing my self to be of such a weak Capacity, I did not think that the Lord would make choice of such a contemptible Instrument as I, to leave my Habitation, and tender Children, that were young and tender, to go to King Charles, which was an Hundred Miles from my Habitation, and with such a plain Testimony as the Lord did require of me; which made me go bowed down many months under the Exercise of it, and often times strove against it; but I could get no Rest, but in giving up to obey the Lord in all Things that he required of me....

In spite of these misgivings, however, Stirredge not only delivered her written testimony into the King's hands, but also gave her voice to the pent up prophetic warning in front of Charles II, reporting "these Words in my Mouth, *Hear Oh! King, and fear the Lord God of Heaven and Earth*". Charles was deeply moved; the account goes on to note "that Paleness came in his Face, and with a mournful Voice he said, *I thank you, Good Woman*". As for the manner of delivering the prophecy, Stirredge notes that as she spoke, "the Dread of the Most High God...made me tremble, and great Agony was over my Spirit".[30] This trembling voice is perhaps signalled by the unusual exclamation point driving a breathless pause within her opening invocation, "Hear Oh! King". The terse internal rhyme of "hear and fear" echoed throughout the written

---

[29] Such warnings include a nationwide petition against tithes, *These Several Papers* (London, 1659) presented to the Rump Parliament with a preface by Mary Forster and signed by 7,000 Quaker women; a petition *For the King and both Houses of Parliament* (London, 1670) against the persecution of Friends by Anne Whitehead, Rebecca Travers, Mary Elson, Susanna Yokely, Priscilla Eccleston, Prudence Wapshott and thirty other women; and an epistle, also addressed *To the King and both Houses of Parliament* (London, 1671), from the Nottinghamshire Quakers Anne Ingall and 97 other women and Thomas Ingall and 118 other men.

[30] Stirredge, *Strength in Witness*, 37, 39–40.

testimony as well, but the effect of Stirredge's short speech was more likely due to the arresting sound of a prophetic message coming from a female body worn out by travel, trembling, and "bowed down" under the weight of her formidable performative task.

The semantic and rhythmic patterns of Quaker female prophecies come across more clearly in the 1662 *Letter to Charles, King of England* by Anne Gilman of Reading. Her verbal attack upon the monarch's ear is mounted in the incantatory mode that was a staple of Quaker speech. Gilman's epistle opens by doubling the signature Quaker violation of the politeness formula, which prescribed the use of 'you' with superiors so as to avoid the impression of 'clownishness' or 'contempt': "What have we done (O King) that such usage we should receive from thy hands, and by thy orders". The very next sentence increases the force of the verbal attack through precise rhythmic and semantic parallelism: "I say, What have we done that we should be haled, many of us, out of our Meetings". Similarly to Howgill's address to Cromwell, Gilman concludes with a declaration that thoroughly changes the rhetorical function of the letter: "And so whether thou wilt hear or forbear, I have cleared my self in the sight of my God concerning thee".[31] Before, she strove to impact the tremulous soul of her royal addressee, sounding her righteous indignation in mounting waves of aural symmetry. The coda, however, transforms the letter into an act of communion between writer and God, an act in which the King is relegated to a marginal role at best.

Of course verbal and rhythmic formulae by no means guaranteed the effect of Quaker women's prophecy upon their socially elevated audiences. Thus Samuel Pepys recorded for 11 January 1664 how the King humourously parried a young Quaker woman's verbal charge upon his conscience:

> This morning I stood by the King, arguing with a pretty Quaker woman that delivered to him a desire of hers in writing. The King showed her Sir J Minnes, as a man fittest for her quaking religion, saying that his beard was the stiffest thing about him. And again merrily said, looking upon the length of her paper, that if all she desired was of that length, she might lose her desires. She modestly saying nothing till he begun seriously to

---

[31] Anne Gilman, *Letter to Charles, King of England* (London, 1662), 6, quoted in Rosemary Foxton, *"Hear the Word of the Lord": A Critical and Bibliographical Study of Quaker Women's Writing, 1650–1700* (Melbourne: The Bibliographical Society of Australia and New Zealand, 1997), 23.

discourse with her, arguing the truth of his spirit against hers. She replying still with these words, "O King!" and thou'd him all along.[32]

The King's lewd reference to Sir John Minnes's lack of stiffness and the length of what the petitioner allegedly desired were clearly aimed to demonstrate his own complacent control over the discursive field and to summon the support of a male community whose suggestive snickering would signal an allegiance to the monarch. Pepys, by all indications an eager member of this discursive community, thus points to one way in which the socially explosive charge of Quaker injurious words could be diffused.

Courtly laughter, however, does not have the last word in the diarist's record. It is undercut by the young woman's silence. This silence successfully resists the King's parodic gendering of the young woman as sexually voracious and blocks his demonstrative power over the court. Hardly at a loss for words, the young woman chooses to curtail what Quakers thought of as the carnal activity of outward speech while physically standing her ground until the King "begun seriously to discourse with her, arguing the truth of his spirit against hers".

For the petitioner, this silence may well have been the effect of attentive listening to what the seventeenth-century Quaker Charles Marshall describes as "the small still voice, moving in man Godwards", one of the fundamental ways through which Friends attained a desired spiritual condition.[33] She would thus have been withdrawing mentally from an outward discursive context dominated by male voices and laughter to achieve a unity with the very object of Quaker faith—God's speech. In the meantime, the modest yet resolute stillness of her body would have re-signified femininity not as driven, in the terms preferred by courtly discourse, by sexual desire, but rather as inwardly contemplative as befitting the wise virgin Sophia. And while there is no reason to suspect that Pepys or others among those gathered at court would have been able to recognize the spiritual significance of Quaker silence, they readily acknowledged that the young woman's performative act

---

[32] *The Diary of Samuel Pepys*, ed. Robert Latham and William Matthews, vol. 5 (Berkeley: University of California Press, 1971), 12. Foxton, *"Hear the Word of the Lord"*, 22, suggests that the "pretty Quaker" was likely Margaret Fell's sixteen-year-old daughter Mary, whose discursive challenge to the King would have been occasioned by George Fox's imprisonment four days earlier, on 7 January 1664.

[33] Charles Marshall, *The Journal of Charles Marshall* (London, 1884), 89. See also Bauman, *"Let Your Words Be Few"*, 21–24.

eventually levelled a discursive field that had been dominated by the
King's party. It was her stillness and silence that led the King to engage
in a conversation on spiritual issues with her, a conversation in which,
as Pepys records, she repeatedly refused to honour the monarch's social
superiority "and thou'd him all along".

While Pepys's diary entry supplies little material to reconstruct the
acoustics of Quaker women's prophecies within the soundscape of
Whitehall palace, Elizabeth Hooton's letter about her "cries" at court,
generically addressed to "Friends", provides numerous clues about the
acoustics and the performative impact of her experience. The letter,
dated "the 17th of the 8th Month [October] 1662", maps the complex
soundscape at Whitehall, Hooton's evolving strategies in acquiring
control over it, and the rapt response of her audience.

When Hooton entered the palace for the first time in October 1662,
probably climbing up from the Thames embankment the Whitehall
stairs that would take her past the chapel, she found herself among a
multitude of watermen, citizens, foreign visitors, palace guards, courtiers, and priests.[34] "Ane old woman above three score yeares old", she
had recently returned from a mission to Barbados and New England,
which had involved imprisonment, whipping, starvation during a
"neire two dayes journey in the willdernes...without any victualls, but
a fewe biskets y^t we brought with us which we soaked in the water",
and an enforced passage back to England that she described as rough
and dangerous.[35] Her body must have been thin and sinewy, her face
bearing the marks of malnourishment and long-term exposure to the

---

[34] On the location of the Whitehall landing used by the public, see *The Diary of
Samuel Pepys*, vol. 10, 484. Simon Thurley also identifies the Whitehall stairs from the
Thames landing as a public slipway in a caption to Wenceslaus Hollar's 1647 engrav-
ing *Whitehall from the Thames*. See his *Whitehall Palace: An Architectural History of the Royal
Apartments, 1240–1698* (London and New Haven: Yale University Press, 1999), 101.
Whitehall's sprawling ground plan made it widely accessible from both the river and
St. James's park, but a public encounter with the King would have been more likely
during his fast-paced strolls through the palace grounds, rather than when he was
hunting in the park. For formal architectural plans, see Thurley, *The Whitehall Palace
Plan of 1670* (London: London Topographical Society, 1998), for Charles's exercising
habits, see John Heneage Jesse, *Memoirs of the Court of England during the Reign of the
Stuarts, Including the Protectorate*, vol. 2 (London: George Bell, 1889), 469–70.

[35] Hooton's age in 1661 and the events in New England are described in a letter in
the Portfolio MSS 3/27 in the Library of the Society of Friends, London, transcribed
in Emily Manners, *Elizabeth Hooton: First Quaker Woman Preacher (1600–1672)* (London:
Headley Brothers, 1914), 30–33; the conditions of the passage to England are referred
to in Portfolio MSS 3/34, quoted in Manners, 36.

elements, as well as the labour of the hundred-mile journey to London from her home.[36] Even if she kept silent as she approached through the long gallery the open court at the heart of the palace, her ascetic looks must have drawn curious attention. Hooton was a Northerner, and her severe style of rural simplicity would have contrasted starkly not only with the colourful velvets and taffetas of the courtiers, but also with the refined fabrics imported from Italy and the Low Countries worn by status-conscious Londoners visiting the court.

In the inner court, a place which Bruce Smith claims was designed for declamation, Hooton would have been met by the loud hum of hundreds of people conversing, a veritable Babel of dialects and languages: courtiers exchanging the gossip of the day, loquacious Londoners boasting the importance of their petitions to the King, servants running about their daily business, pages or soldiers clearing a passage for a personage of importance, foreign visitors exchanging impressions of English sights and customs, watermen hawking their services. In his study of the acoustic world of early modern England, Smith draws attention to the sound of people talking as the most prominent feature of the soundscape of pre-industrial London. Whitehall's inner court was enclosed by sound reflecting walls, its ground covered with sand or gravel—material less sound-absorbing than the mud covering the streets of London. Human speech in this environment, punctuated now and again by the keynote sounds of splashing fountains and birds, would have come across as louder than the constant chatter on the city streets.[37]

The King's entry into the court, perhaps announced by the sight and barking of his beloved small spaniels that accompanied him everywhere, would have quieted the noisy rumble of conversations and asserted his

---

[36] In a later letter to Charles II (undated) in Portfolio MSS 3/50, Hooton points out that "It has cost me abundance of Labour besides charges in roming up to thee this 6 or 7 times an hundred mile a Time" (the distance to London from her home in Leicestershire). Her visits to the court may have well been in obedience to a divine call, as she asserts in the 17 October 1662 letter, but she was also determined to get recompensed for losses incurred by the confiscation of a team of horses belonging to her from her son for refusing to swear an oath. This is evident from her letter "To the King and the Lord Chamberlaine" in Portfolio MSS 3/7.

[37] Smith recalls that in the sixteenth and early seventeenth centuries Whitehall's inner court was known as the 'Sermon Court' or the 'Preaching Court'. The space for outdoor preaching and declamation, it was complete with a pulpit and a sounding board above it. See his *Acoustic World*, 89 for the acoustics of the inner court and ibid., 58 for the prominence of human conversation on the streets of pre-industrial London.

control over the acoustic environment.[38] This is probably when Hooton's voice rose in the stillness. She describes it as "Ring[ing] over all the Court", in analogy to the clear sound of church bells above the city clamour of London. "I waite for Justice of thee o King", she thundered before going on to list her personal grievance against magistrates, sheriffs, and bailiffs who had confiscated her horses and "goods contrary to the law". Judging from Hooton's letter, from this point on, her cries dominated the soundscape of the Court. She relates,

> soe did I open the grievances of our freinds, all over the Nation, the Cry of the Innocent is great, for they have made Lawes to persecute Conscience, and I followed the King wheresoever he went with this Cry, the Cry of the innocent regard, I followed him twice to the Tenace Court, and spoke to him when he went up into his Coach, after he had beene at his sport....

Coming in strong repetitive sound waves, Hooton's distinct Northern voice would have bounced off the reflective walls, drawing the attention of courtiers and visitors not only in the inner court, but of those by the surrounding windows as well. Her voice was the living embodiment of the social metaphor of the crying innocents, and there was no public space in Whitehall—the royal tennis court included—where her social and religious message could be ignored. Nor did she lower her voice or body in the traditional humbling pose of a suitor in front of the sovereign: "I did not Kneele, but I went along by the King and spoke as I went".[39]

Reception of Hooton's acoustic and spiritual challenge to the monarch was mixed. She reports that a royal guard laughed at her, that "the people murmured" in disapproval of her refusal to pay homage by kneeling in front of the King, that there were those who suggested that her performative bravura "was of the devill". On the other hand, one of the King's coachmen and several unidentified visitors to Whitehall were sufficiently taken by her performance to read aloud her letters to the King, adding their voices to hers. Others reproved the guard who laughed and silenced "the gainesayers" protesting against Hooton's usurpation of authority. There were even those, she reports, who wished that they had her spirit and who on two occasions she calls her "disciples". Elizabeth Hooton's audience was clearly split on how

---

[38] Jesse, *Memoirs of the Court of England*, vol. 2, 472.
[39] Portfolio MSS 3/34, transcribed in Manners, *Elizabeth Hooton*, 36.

they interpreted her discursive performance. But in the aftermath of her assured navigation of the soundscape of Whitehall Palace, it was no longer possible to regard the royal addressee of her petition as the unambiguous summit of discursive or spiritual power.

This was not the last of Hooton's prophesyings on this visit to London. As she records excitedly,

> it Came upon me to gett a Coat of sackecloath, and it was plaine to me how I should have it, soe we made that Coat, and the next morning I were moved to goe amongst them againe in Whitehall in sackecloath and ashes, and the people was much stricken, both great men and women was strucken into silence, the witnesse of god was raised in many, and a fine time I had amongst them....[40]

This time, Hooton's performance seems to have been modelled after the two witnesses of unspecified gender in Revelation 11 who were "to prophesy, dressed in sackcloth, for those twelve hundred and sixty days". Injuring the prophets, as any seventeenth-century reader knew, was supposed to provoke them into causing drought, turning water into blood, or afflicting the earth with disease; killing them, once their appointed time had run out, was to bring a violent earthquake and the death of thousands in the city.[41] If, on the first day of her visit to Whitehall, Hooton gained command over the soundscape of the palace by emulating the trumpeting Angel of Revelation, on her second visit she resolutely gendered the characters in the Biblical narrative of the earth's last days as she staged it through her weary, penitent female body, bent with age and hardship.

For all their derision of theatrical 'idolatry', Quaker women prophesying at Whitehall proved adept at utilizing performative strategies when they struck their elite audiences with amazement. Attentive to the architectural and acoustic setting, they showcased 'costumes' and appearances markedly different from those of the fashionable crowd at court and delivered their messages in unforgettable tones and cadences. They heeded closely the divergent responses of the assembled audience and often succeeded in uniting it in a silent contemplation upon the confluences of the present with Biblical history and the part that the prophet and her addressee played in both. As for the signification of the female gender, at least for the duration of their powerful performative

---

[40] Portfolio MSS 3/34, transcribed in Manners, *Elizabeth Hooton*, 37.
[41] Revelation 11:3–13.

acts, it functioned not only as the vehicle for what Phyllis Mack has perceptively described as powerful, polymorphous, and morally ambiguous spirituality, but also for qualities she ascribes to the political sphere: self-consciousness, self-control, practicality, and toughness.[42] No small feat to accomplish at Whitehall.

Bibliography

Manuscript Sources

Minute Book for the Women's Monthly Meetings, BMM I/ix/1. Oxfordshire Record Office, Cowley, Oxford.
Portfolio Manuscripts. Vol. 3. Library of the Society of Friends, London.

Printed Sources

Barclay, Robert. *Truth triumphant through the spiritual warfare, Christian labours, and writings of that able and faithful servant of Jesus Christ, Robert Barclay, who deceased at his own house at Urie in the kingdom of Scotland, the 3 day of the 8 month 1690.* London, 1692.
Bauman, Richard. *"Let Your Words Be Few": Symbolism of Speaking and Silence among Seventeenth-Century Quakers.* Prospect Heights, Illinois: Waveland Press, 1983.
Bourdieu, Pierre. *The Logic of Practice.* Translated by Richard Nice. Cambridge: Polity Press, 1980.
Braithwaite, William. *The Beginnings of Quakerism.* 2nd ed. Cambridge: Cambridge University Press, 1961.
Butler, Judith. *Excitable Speech: A Politics of the Performative.* New York: Routledge, 1997.
Cope, Jackson I. "Seventeenth-Century Quaker Style". *PMLA* 71 (1956): 725–54.
Farnsworth, Richard. *The Spirit of God Speaking in the Temple of God.* London, 1663.
Folkerth, Wes. *The Sound of Shakespeare.* London and New York: Routledge, 2002.
Forster, Mary et al. *These Several Papers.* London, 1659.
Fox, George. *The Journal of George Fox.* Edited by John L. Nickalls. Rev. ed. Cambridge: Cambridge University Press, 1975.
———. *"No More but My Love": Letters of George Fox 1624–91.* Edited by Cecil W. Sharman. London: Quaker Home Service, 1980.
Foxton, Rosemary. *"Hear the Word of the Lord": A Critical and Bibliographical Study of Quaker Women's Writing, 1650–1700.* Melbourne: The Bibliographical Society of Australia and New Zealand, 1997.
Godwin, Joselyn, ed. *The Harmony of the Spheres: A Sourcebook of the Pythagorean Tradition in Music.* Rochester, VT: Inner Traditions Intl., 1993.
Hobby, Elaine. *Virtue of Necessity: English Women's Writing, 1649–1688.* London: Virago Press, 1988.
Howgill, Mary. *A Remarkable Letter of Mary Howgill to Oliver Cromwell, called Protector.* London, 1657.
Hubberthorne, Richard. *A Collection of the Several Books and Writings of that Faithful Servant of God Richard Hubberthorn.* London, 1663.
Ingall, Anne et al. *To the King and both Houses of Parliament.* London, 1671.

---

[42] Mack, "The Prophet and Her Audience", 146.

Jesse, John Heneage. *Memoirs of the Court of England during the Reign of the Stuarts, Including the Protectorate*. Vol. 2. London: George Bell, 1889.

The Lambs Defence against Lyes. London, 1656.

Mack, Phyllis. "The Prophet and Her Audience: Gender and Knowledge in the World Turned Upside Down". In *Reviving the English Revolution: Reflections and Elaborations on the Work of Christopher Hill*. Edited by Geoff Eley and William Hunt. London: Verso, 1988.

———. *Visionary Women: Ecstatic Prophecy in Seventeenth-Century England*. Berkeley: University of California Press, 1992.

Manners, Emily. *Elizabeth Hooton: First Quaker Woman Preacher (1600–1672)*. London: Headley Brothers, 1914.

Marshall, Charles. *The Journal of Charles Marshall*. London, 1884.

Moore, Rosemary. *The Light in Their Consciences: Early Quakers in Britain 1646–1666*. University Park, Pa.: The Pennsylvania University Press, 2000.

Ong, Walter. *Rhetoric, Romance and Technologies: Studies in the Interaction of Expression and Culture*. Ithaca: Cornell University Press, 1971.

The Oxford Study Bible: Revised English Bible with the Apocrypha. Edited by M. Jack Suggs, Katharine Doob Sakenfeld, James R. Mueller. New York: Oxford University Press, 1992.

Pepys, Samuel. *The Diary of Samuel Pepys*. Edited by Robert Latham and William Matthews. 10 vols. Berkeley: University of California Press, 1970–83.

Reeve, John and Lodowick Muggleton. *A Volume of Spiritual Epistles written by John Reeve and Lodowicke Muggleton*. 1755. Reprint, London, 1820.

A Relation of the labour, travail and suffering of that faithful servant of the Lord Alice Curwen. Who departed this life the 7th day of the 6th moneth, 1679. and resteth in peace with the Lord. London, 1680.

Smith, Bruce R. *The Acoustic World of Early Modern England: Attending to the O-Factor*. Chicago: University of Chicago Press, 1999.

Stirredge, Elizabeth. *Strength in Weakness Manifest in the Life, Various Trials, and Christian Testimony of that faithful Servant and Handmaid of the Lord, Elizabeth Stirredge, Who departed this Life, at her House at Hempstead in Hertfordshire, in the 72nd Year of her Age*. 2nd ed. London, 1746.

Thurley, Simon. *Whitehall Palace: An Architectural History of the Royal Apartments, 1240–1698*. London and New Haven: Yale University Press, 1999.

———. *The Whitehall Palace Plan of 1670*. London: London Topographical Society, 1998.

Turner, Victor. "Symbolic Studies". *Annual Review of Anthropology* 4 (1975): 145–61.

White, Dorothy. *A Diligent Search amongst Rulers, Priests, Professors, and People; and a warning to all sorts high and low, that are out of the doctrine of Christ, and fear not God. Put forth by Dorothy White living in Waymouth*. London, 1659.

Whitehead, Anne et al. *For the King and both Houses of Parliament*. London, 1670.

Cartoon used to plan the panel, "The Publishers of the Truth", for the Quaker Tapestry.
Copyright Quaker Tapestry Scheme.

THE RADICAL TRAVELS OF MARY FISHER: WALKING AND WRITING IN THE UNIVERSAL LIGHT

Sylvia Brown

The Quaker Tapestry was begun in 1981 as a means of depicting the 350 years of the history of the Society of Friends. Along with panels dedicated to such generally known Quakers as George Fox and William Penn, the Tapestry commemorates the seventeenth-century traveller Mary Fisher as "one of the many women 'publishers of the truth'".[1] Both the words and the images on this panel constitute a narrative that not only purports to represent Fisher's travels but also suggests *how* they should be read. The Tapestry, however, is only a recent example of a long line of narrative re-fashionings. From the beginning, Fisher's story was told and retold, by herself and by fellow Quakers, by contemporaries and near-contemporaries, in order to challenge the idea of difference in its most global sense. In her first extant piece of writing, a letter to an "unjust judge" written from York gaol, Fisher invoked God "w[hi]ch respecteth no man's person", urging the judge to do justice by doing likewise.[2] Fisher and other early Friends, often to their cost, behaved as if this sort of levelling justice were already a reality in the world, as if the eschatological appearance of the divine Judge who does not unjustly distinguish between persons was happening now, present in an almost performative sense in their words and actions.

---

[1] The Quaker tapestry has 77 panels made by 4,000 men, women, and children. It is on display from April to November each year at the Exhibition Centre in Kendal, Cumbria UK. For more information, see the Exhibition Centre's website www. quaker-tapestry.co.uk. See also *Quaker Faith & Practice*, 3rd ed. [The Yearly Meeting of the Religious Society of Friends (Quakers) in Britain, 2005], 28:13. The cartoon is also reproduced here, along with a delineation of the Society's present position on 'missionary' work: "We long to reach out to those who may find a spiritual home in the Society; we do not claim that ours is the only true way, yet we have a perception of truth that is relevant to all if, as we believe, the light to which we witness is a universal light". How far this non-proselytizing model of witnessing was implicit in the first period of Quakerism is one of the questions of this chapter.

[2] "From Mary Fisher presiner at Yarke", undated, A. R. Barclay MSS., vol. 324, f. 173, Library of the Religious Society of Friends, London. Quoted by Althea Stewart, "Public Justice and Personal Liberty: Variety and Linguistic Skill in the Letters of Mary Fisher", *Quaker Studies* 3 (1998): 143.

This chapter will examine Mary Fisher's travels and extant writings as radical attempts to overcome difference in the light of this eschatological imminence. Of particular concern will be the linkages between sexual, social, ethnic, and religious difference. I hope to show that the radical performative and narrative attempts of early Quakers to dissolve these differences were, although courageous, ultimately uneven in their success. Insisting on the dissolution of difference in one part of the journey or the story often meant not its disappearance but its displacement, on difference being even more deeply etched elsewhere.

The Pattern of Mary Fisher's Journeys

The Quaker Tapestry panel dedicated to Fisher reproduces narrative elements and emphases that have been present from the seventeenth century. Fisher's travels began in England, but the stories of her early journeys among people who might have been assumed to be her own kind, including the English colonists of Barbados and Massachusetts, consist almost entirely of accounts of cruel persecution and endurance. These stories of sufferings, however, point up by contrast the exemplary and glamorous meeting for which Fisher is most famous. Around 1658, Fisher, an unmarried servingwoman from the north of England, travelled across much of what is now Greece and into Turkey in order to meet Sultan Mehmed IV, ruler of the Ottoman Empire, where he lay encamped with his army at Adrianople. Contemporary accounts tell us not only that she made it but emphasize the courtesy with which she was received—a fact that might have been especially surprising to an early modern reader steeped in stereotypes of the cruel and lascivious Turk and acquainted also, perhaps, with claims that the Great Turk was Antichrist himself.[3] Thus, where difference might have been expected, we are offered instead the story of a meeting such as might characterize the millennial fulfillment: one where differences of class, nation, gender, and religion apparently melt away.

Fisher's work as a leveller of difference began almost as soon as she was 'convinced' around the age of thirty, at which time she was a ser-

---

[3] See Christopher Hill, *Antichrist in Seventeenth-Century England* (London: Oxford University Press, 1971), 181–82. English Protestant millenarians typically predicted the destruction of Rome as one of the significant events of the last days; some predicted the destruction of 'the Turk' as well (26, 110).

vant in the household of Richard and Elizabeth Tomlinson in Selby, Yorkshire. Servant, master, and mistress all became Quakers. We are not told what Richard did when he received the Light, but the conversions of Mary and Elizabeth were marked by violent transgression of the gendered boundary between the household and public places. Elizabeth Tomlinson is said to have immediately run into the street, "carried almost off her feet" in her zeal to prophesy.[4] Soon after her convincement, Mary Fisher caused a disturbance in her parish church which led to her imprisonment in York Castle in 1652. She had shouted down the minister of Selby in his pulpit: "Come downe, come downe, thou painted beast, come downe. Thou art but an hireling, and deludest the people with thy lyes".[5] In prison she met two other Quaker women, Jane Holmes and Elizabeth Hooton. The latter was George Fox's first convert, the first of the Quaker women preachers, who would herself set off on a missionary voyage across the Atlantic in 1661.[6] The Quaker Tapestry shows Elizabeth Hooton writing, in the bottom left corner, with Mary Fisher standing over her. This is the first, chronologically, of the surprising places in which Fisher witnessed to the Light. Like the Sultan's court, prison might have seemed to most an unpromising field. Yet, as with the Recusant Margaret Clitherow, who while held in the same gaol 75 years earlier took the opportunity to learn how to read, Fisher used prison to make connections with other Quakers, to sign a tract against false teachers with five others, and to write what seems to have been a reasonably effective letter of admonition to the unjust judge.[7] Accordingly, the Quaker Tapestry depiction of York gaol

---

[4] Phyllis Mack, *Visionary Women: Ecstatic Prophecy in Seventeenth-Century England* (Berkeley: University of California Press, 1992), 168. For Mack's vivid account of Fisher's life and travels, see 168–70.

[5] James Raine, ed., *Depositions from the Castle of York Relating to Offences Committed in the Northern Counties in the Seventeenth Century*, Surtees Society 40 (1861), 54. Fisher pleaded guilty and was fined a sum, 200*l*, which must have been impossible for her to pay. Non-payment of the fine may have been the nominal reason for her imprisonment.

[6] Mack, *Visionary Women*, 168. For Elizabeth Hooton and her travels, see Mack 127–30.

[7] *False Prophets and False Teachers Described* is an invective against ministers who preach for hire and who persecute "the Saints of the most high God". (It also condemns these ministers for lack of hospitality, which has resonance for later narratives about Fisher, as will be discussed below.) *False Prophets* was signed (in the following order) by Thomas Aldam, Elizabeth Hooton, William Pears, Benjamin Nicholson, Jane Holmes, and Mary Fisher, "Prisoners of the Lord at York Castle, 1652" (8). A corporate, rather than an individualistic, model of authorship is often more appropriate for Quaker tracts: Stewart argues for the formative influence of Elizabeth Hooton on Mary Fisher's various writings in "Public Justice and Personal Liberty" (142–48), and it is possible

looks like a schoolroom; whatever its other deprivations, it seems to have been a productive place for discussion and writing.

A year later (moving across the bottom panel of the cartoon), in December 1653, Fisher and another woman Friend, Elizabeth Williams, headed south to witness in Cambridge. There, some scholars of Sidney Sussex College asked them (no doubt in mockery), "*how many Gods there were?*" The women answered, "*but one God*; and told them, *they had many that they made Gods of* ", at which the scholars laughed and scoffed. Fisher and Williams then told them they "*were Antichrists*, and that *their Colledg was a Cage of unclean Birds, and the Synagogue of Satan*". Arrested for preaching, and brought before the mayor of Cambridge, William Pickering, they were sentenced to be stripped and whipped at the market cross. The first recorder of this persecution, an "Eminent Hand" who may have been a sympathetic magistrate in Cambridge, noted that they "never whinched . . . and all the while they were in their punishment, they sang and rejoiced".[8]

The "Eminent Hand" also noted that "no man knows" by what law these women were punished, "for they neither did beg or steal".[9] In 1653, travelling Quakers were a relatively new problem for civic authorities, particularly in the South of England. Mary Fisher and Elizabeth Williams were the first to be punished by invoking the prohibitions and penalties of an Elizabethan Act against vagrancy, designed "for punishment of rogues, vagabonds, and sturdy beggars".[10] The writer of the 1654 tract evidently thought that this was a misapplication of the Act, but Pickering's response, soon to be imitated by other magistrates in

---

that they composed the letter to the unjust judge, sent as "From Mary Fisher presiner at Yarke", together. At the end of the manuscript draft or copy of this letter, a note in the same hand indicates that two out of the three men Fisher was pleading for were reprieved. See Stewart, 143–44.

[8] *The First New Persecution; Or a True Narrative of the Cruel Usage of two Christians, By the Present Mayor of Cambridge. As it was Certified from thence by an Eminent Hand* (London, 1654), 3–4, 6. "*A Postscript*" [7] gives "notice to all men, That none of the *Justices* of the Town had any hand in this barbarous and unlawfull act, saving Mr. *William Pickering* Mayor". See also Joseph Besse, *A Collection of the Sufferings of the People Called Quakers*, vol. 1 (1754), 84–85. Besse evidently depended on the earlier tract, but identifies the two women by name, whereas *The First New Persecution* merely describes them as "two Northern Women, the one of them about 50. the other about 30. years old" (3).

[9] *First New Persecution*, 5.

[10] St. 39 Eliz. cap. 4. See William C. Braithwaite, *The Beginnings of Quakerism*, 2nd ed., rev. by Henry J. Cadbury (Cambridge: Cambridge University Press, 1955), 445. Fisher and Williams seem to have been awake to the possibility that they might be charged as beggars, for in their interrogation they were at pains to point out that they "*paid for what they called for*". *First New Persecution*, 4.

other towns, shows that he defined the Quaker women's essential crime as illegitimate travel: transgression beyond the patriarchal bounds of their own parishes and families. He wanted to know where they came from, their names, and their husbands' names. Their reply to the last question—"*they had no husband but Jesus Christ, and he sent them*"—seems to have been the incendiary spark:

> Upon this the Mayor was in a great rage, and thrust them to the dore of his house, and said they were whores, and made a Warrant to the Constable to *whip them at the Market-Crosse untill the blood came.*[11]

Pickering's rage may have been fuelled by his own sense that these women were not simply vagrants, not simply homeless and husbandless whores; the fact that he "thrust them to the dore of his house" might suggest that he desired, by violence, to make them simply so. In fact, Fisher and Williams did more than merely step over the usual social and gender boundaries. Their travel—particularly as it was narrativized and moralized for Quaker readership, for the consumption and propagation of new Quaker preachers and travellers—stretched, refashioned, and problematized the 'normal' boundaries that defined home and away. Seemingly unhoused and unsupervised, Fisher and Williams in truth travel under the directive of the universal Husband, Christ, to whose authority even a male magistrate like Pickering ought to be subject. Furthermore, coming to a university town, where they might reasonably expect a civil hearing for 'the Truth', Fisher and Williams meet instead with "barbarous Usage".[12] Such paradoxes—finding barbarity in the supposed regions of Christian civility, and vice versa—become a sustained pattern in the narratives of Mary Fisher's later travels as well.

Fisher made her vagrant way across England, rebuking priests in public places of worship and drawing punishment on herself for doing so.

---

[11] *First New Persecution*, 4. In *Masterless Men: The Vagrancy Problem in England 1560–1640* (London: Methuen, 1985), A. L. Beier lists the three main sorts of vagrant women as "those looking for husbands who had deserted them, prostitutes, and unmarried pregnant girls" (52). Any unaccompanied travelling woman was likely to be sexualized as a whore, as is apparent from Thomas Harmon's classification of female vagabonds in his immensely popular *A Caveat For Commen Cursetors Vulgarely called Vagabones* (1567, with another edition in 1573). Vagrants of either sex were seen as "a menace to the social order because they broke with the acceptable norms of family life" (Beier, *Masterless Men*, 51).

[12] The phrase is Joseph Besse's, a slight but telling embroidery on his source. *Collection of the Sufferings*, vol. 1, 85.

In 1654, she was imprisoned for twelve weeks for "testifying to the Truth, in the place of publick Worship" at Pontefract, Yorkshire. (The year before she had spent six months in gaol for the same offense in the same place.) In 1655, she was imprisoned in Buckinghamshire with other Quakers "for giving Christian Exhortations to the Priests and People".[13]

Fisher continued her travels across the Atlantic, heading to Barbados at the end of 1655 and arriving in New England in July 1656 with another female companion, Ann Austin.[14] Fisher and Austin are usually credited as the first Quakers to land in America,[15] and the final two tableaux along the bottom of the Quaker Tapestry panel record the ill-treatment they met with there. At first, the governors of Massachusetts refused the women permission to land in Boston. They seized about a hundred books from their luggage (which were later burnt by the public executioner) and then transported Fisher and Austin to prison. There, their bodies were thoroughly and, as early accounts emphasize, immodestly searched for witchmarks, and they were forbidden to communicate with anyone "to prevent the Spreading of their corrupt Opinions". After five weeks in gaol, the two women were forcibly transported back to Barbados.[16] To underline the cruelty of the Puritan governors and the fortitude of the Quaker women, the tapestry emphasizes 'old' Ann Austin's decrepitude; analogously, early accounts stress that Austin was already the mother of five children when she travelled to Boston.[17] The tapestry also imports the story of Mary Dyer, who was executed in Boston in 1660 after repeatedly defying an order of banishment on pain of death.[18] Mary Dyer's fate

---

[13] Besse, *Collection of the Sufferings*, vol. 2, 90; vol. 1, 75.

[14] Braithwaite, *Beginnings of Quakerism*, 402. Sometime in 1656, Fisher is also reported to have made her way to Newfoundland with Hester Biddle—perhaps en route to Barbados? See Catie Gill and Elaine Hobby, "Hester Biddle", *ODNB*.

[15] Mack, *Visionary Women*, 131. Mack also notes that Elizabeth Harris arrived simultaneously in Maryland.

[16] Besse, *Collection of the Sufferings*, vol. 2, 177–78.

[17] Humphrey Norton, *New-England's Ensigne* (1659), 7. George Bishop, *New England Judged, Not by Man's, But the Spirit of the Lord...* (1661), 12.

[18] Before her conversion to Quakerism, Dyer was associated with the infamous New England Antinomian, Anne Hutchinson, and publically "accompanied her" on the occasion of Hutchinson's excommunication. See David D. Hall, ed., *The Antinomian Controversy, 1636–1638: A Documentary History* (Middletown, Connecticut: Wesleyan University Press, 1968), 281; also Johan Winsser, "Mary Dyer and the 'Monster' story", *Quaker History* 79 (1990): 20.

makes clear what was at stake in these repeated defiances of civil and religious authority: nothing less than martyrdom.[19]

The forced return to Barbados gave Fisher the chance to preach to a more receptive audience—for a short time at least. Writing to Margaret Fell from the island in November 1656, the Quaker missionary Henry Fell noted that Fisher "hath been very serviceable here".[20] By April 1657, she was back in London, whence she dated a letter to those in Barbados who had benefitted from her preaching:

> Dear hearts go on in the power and might of our God, that you may conquer the whole earth, and rule over the inhabitants thereof, go on, look not back, press forwards.[21]

The vision of Friends 'conquering' and 'ruling' the whole earth has more to do with Fisher's sense of eschatological imminence—the power and might of God are at the point of being universally revealed—than with any early blueprint for the British Empire. As early Quakers tended to do in their writings, Fisher was pushing the language of worldly things—in this case, the language of *imperium*—to an extreme in order to figure a spiritual truth. It was perhaps this sense of the unstoppable momentum of the Light spreading throughout the world that propelled Fisher and five companions to set out almost immediately on travels more ambitious than any she had yet undertaken.

In July 1657, Fisher, along with John Perrot, John Luffe, John Buckley, Mary Prince, and Beatrice Beckley, set out for Leghorn (Livorno), a usual staging port for travel to the Levant. Their initial idea seems to have been to convert the Jews and Turks of Jerusalem, but at some point they took on the more ambitious plans of travelling to Rome, to convert the Pope, and to Adrianople, to convert the Great Turk. After distributing books, meeting with local Jews, and fending off the Inquisition in Leghorn, the group travelled on to the island of Zante,

---

[19] Besse likened the persecutions suffered by Mary Fisher and her Cambridge companion Elizabeth Williams to "the Proto-Martyr *Stephen*". *Collection of the Sufferings*, vol. 1, 85.

[20] Quoted by Mack, *Visionary Women*, 169. It is possible that Fisher may have made other preaching stops along the way. Besse reported that in 1658 Humphrey Highwood of Nevis, then nominally an English colony and northwest of Barbados in the Lesser Antilles archipelago, was imprisoned for giving a "friendly Reception" to Mary Fisher and two Quaker men. *Collection of the Sufferings*, vol. 2, 352. See also note 14.

[21] Portfolio MSS, vol. 33, f. 112. Library of the Religious Society of Friends, London. Quoted by Mack, *Visionary Women*, 169.

then under the rule of Venice. There they split up. Perrot and Buckley travelled overland, up the Peleponnese, while Luffe, Prince, Beckley, and Fisher sailed via Crete to Smyrna (Izmir), where all met again late in 1657.[22] In Smyrna, the group clearly made known their intention to convert the Great Turk but were hindered by the English consul there and sent packing back to Venice.[23] Landing at Zante because of bad weather, the group again split up. This time, Mary Fisher and Beatrice Beckley set off for the encampment of Mehmed IV at Adrianople, while Buckley sailed to Constantinople and Perrot and Luffe returned to Venice.[24] John Perrot, writing to Edward Burrough after his arrival in Venice, reported that

> the Lord caused his winde to put us into Zant Iland where I left Mary Fisher and B. B. [i.e., Beatrice Beckley] to passe into Moreah againe into Turky which is in sight of that Iland to goe towards Andaniople [sic] where we hear the Turkes Emperour lyes with his armie being as is supposed six dayes Journey from the place where they may land as the Lord Makes way for their passage, blessed be the Lord I left them both in a meet state to proceed.[25]

Very probably, Fisher and her companions believed that the unexpected landing at Zante was a sign that they should not abandon their plan to seek an audience with the Great Turk. The English consul at Smyrna may have refused any official sanction or help, but Fisher and Beckley evidently believed that the world-conquering power and might of God was with them, allowing them not only to circumvent representatives of the English state but to dare to seek an audience with the ruler of what was arguably the most powerful and feared imperium of the early modern world.

What made possible a meeting between a thirtyish servingwoman from the North of England, unmarried and probably minimally edu-

---

[22] Stefano Villani, *Tremolanti e Papisti: Missioni Quacchere nell'Italia del Seicento* (Rome: Edizioni de Storia e Letteratura, 1996), 33–45.

[23] The English consul at Marseilles, John Aldworth, wrote to Secretary John Thurloe in April 1658: "From Smirna I have advice of the 27. February, that thear was theare arrived six Quakers, 3 men and 3 women, who pretended to goe to convert the grand signior; but the consill at Smirna hindered them; so they are gone to Venice, pretending to convert the Jewes". *A Collection of the State Papers of John Thurloe*, vol. 7 (1742), 32.

[24] Villani, *Tremolanti e Papisti*, 45. Mary Prince apparently remained in Smyrna for a short while.

[25] Caton MSS, vol. 320/1, f. 161. Library of the Religious Society of Friends, London.

cated, and the Great Turk—a ruler whom Fisher's companion John
Perrot addressed as "above all Princes and Kings…the greatest in
all parts of the Earth"?[26] And in what spirit did Mary Fisher (and
Beatrice Beckley) approach this meeting? Was it merely a millenarian
gesture, an almost impossibly audacious attempt at proselytizing the one
notorious tyrant whose conversion would signify that God had indeed
'conquered' all the world? Or was it an attempt, startlingly before its
time, at something like a broad ecumenism, at finding common ground
between one of the radical sects of Christianity and Islam?

Chasing the Universal Light: Mary Fisher's Writings

The theological principle that made it possible for Quakers to imagine
the radical dissolution of difference—whether that meant converting the
Great Turk or speaking with him as an equal—was that of the universality of divine light in every person. What made them particularly
disruptive was their willingness to *enact* this principle. Their distinctive
language, gestures, and actions were themselves witnesses to the universal Light, whose presence in every man and woman demanded the
dismantling of all divisive barriers. Thus, Quakers famously refused the
class-inflected customs of addressing social superiors with the formal
'you' and of removing hats as a gesture of subservience. They kept
their hats on and addressed everyone as 'thou'.[27] Ethnic, and even more
radically, religious differences within and beyond Christendom were also
subject to the dissolving power of the Light. In the mid 1650s, George
Fox famously advised Quaker ministers,

> …be patterns, be examples in all countries, places, islands, nations, wher-
> ever you come; that your carriage and life may preach among all sorts
> of people, and to them. Then you will come to walk cheerfully over the
> world, answering to that of God in every one; whereby in them ye may
> be a blessing, and make the witness of God in them to bless you.[28]

As this exhortation suggests, cheerful walking over the world was
expected of ministers like Mary Fisher in this first stage of Quakerism.

---

[26] John Perrot, *A Visitation of Love and Gentle Greeting of the Turk* (1658), 3.
[27] See Adrian Davies, "Holy Language" and "Fashioning the Body" in *The Quakers in English Society, 1655–1725* (Oxford: Clarendon, 2000), 51–57.
[28] John L. Nickalls, ed., *The Journal of George Fox*, rev. ed. (London: Religious Society of Friends, 1975), 263.

Moreover, travelling ministers were not conceived as delivering truth
to the unenlightened regions of the world, but rather as going out and
meeting truth where it might be found—which is in *all* parts of the
earth—recognizing and responding to "that of God in everyone". In
these formative and heady first years of Quaker witnessing, Fox set up
a paradigm of reciprocity for early Quaker missionaries which allowed
for the possession of truth by others, and perhaps even for their possession of 'other' truth. At the very least, it prepared travelling Quakers
for the experience of recognizing commonality and minimizing divisive
difference.

Only a single letter by Mary Fisher mentions her meeting with
Mehmed IV—this will be discussed below—but other extant short writings by her work through the implications of accepting the universality
and sole authority of the divine light. For instance, a short manuscript
piece, titled "The light the true teacher & the condemnation of false
teachers" and given the date 1656 begins:

> I am the light of the world, & lighteth every man that cometh into the
> world, saith Christ learne of me I am the way to the father noe man
> cometh unto the father but by me who lighteth every man that cometh
> into the world that all men through him might beleive....[29]

A later hand than the first copyist has emended this passage to make
it less repetitious, but the repetition in fact emphasizes the universality of the divine light, and thus of salvation.[30] Fisher is combining a
number of scriptural passages here, of which the principal, John 14:6,
"no man cometh unto the Father, but by me", potentially works against
the universality of salvation, seeming particularly to cut off those who
do not accept that Jesus was the Son of God, viz. Jews and Muslims.
Yet early Quakers made active overtures to Jews and Muslims, on the
explicit basis that they already had the Light in them.[31] Fisher frames the

---

[29] Portfolio MSS, vol. 33, f. 38. Like *False Prophets and False Teachers*, this short manuscript piece goes on to condemn "the ministry of the world...who preaches for gifts
& rewards".

[30] The later hand has also added, above the title, the attribution to "Mary Fisher"
and added the date of 1656. It is possible that this piece was retrospectively ascribed
to Mary Fisher, as appropriate to one who had visited the Great Turk.

[31] Samuel Fisher wrote that redemption is truly tendered to all "of every Nation,
Tongue, Kindred, and People" even though all but a few "put it away from themselves,
by not turning to the teachings of that Light, Word, and Grace of God that is nigh in
their hearts...else all, even *Gentiles*, as well as *Jews, Heathens*, and *Indians* as well as *Eng-*

potentially excluding passage by repetitions that emphasize the presence of the Light in every person, without exception: "every man…every man…all men". Since this Light is, moreover, emphatically internal, *within* every person, Fisher counsels mistrust of any of the external, conventional sources of teaching or grace:

> …this is the light which comes from christ, who saith learne of me, this teacher you will find as you ly in your beds, & as you goe up & downe, & when they say loe here is christ, or loe there is christ, you need not goe forth,…the ministry of the world say the letter is the light, & the scriptures is the word, & the steeplehous is the church, & sprinkleling of infants is the baptisme, which is contrary to the scriptures, which saith the church is in God[.][32]

Coincident with the beginning of her travels, Fisher was formulating—and likely delivering her formulation as a 'short paper' to a Quaker meeting—the practice of going "up & downe" to seek the Light in unexpected places. The logic of her paper suggests that any 'church' that claims a monopoly on light or truth or faith shows, by that very claim on exclusivity, that its light does not come from Christ. Fisher's specific targets are the Bible taken as the sole authoritative Word of God, the physical church or 'steeplehouse' as a place set aside, and baptism as the rite of entry into the Church—all of which draw jurisdictional and exclusionary boundaries. By radically internalizing access to the Light, so that it is 'within' all men irrespective of externals, Fisher and the early Quakers provided theological justification for rejecting *all* jurisdictional and exclusionary boundaries—extending even to boundaries between Christian and Islamic worlds.

Nonetheless, as the theology of universal light potentially let in Jews and Turks who also possessed it, so it shut out unforgivingly those who rejected it. Fisher, in common with other early Quakers, seems harshest

---

lish-men and *Christians* (so called) and among each of these, all, as well as any of them, have some measure of that Grace nigh them, which in the least measure is sufficient to heal and help them". *The Testimony of Truth Exalted by the Collected Labours of … Samuel Fisher* (n.p. [London?], 1679), 656. Part of this passage is quoted by Kathleen Thomas in "An Evaluation of the Doctrine of the Inward Light as a Basis for Mission—as exemplified by Quaker approaches to Jews and Muslims in the seventeenth century", *Quaker Studies* 1 (1996): 54–72. Thomas discusses George Fox and Margaret Fell Fox in their approaches to Jews and Muslims, arguing that George Fox became increasingly willing to recognize the light that Muslims already possessed, even modelling his later epistles to them on the style of the Qur'an.

[32] Porfolio MSS, vol. 33, f. 38.

when writing to fellow Christians, particularly other English sectaries, who although seemingly closer in identity have therefore erred more unforgivingly in rejecting the Light so nearly available to them. Fisher's undated letter "To them that are called Anabaptists in Barbados" condemns another sectarian group that found refuge on the island for being 'out of the light'. After using this formula once, Fisher then varies the trope of exclusion to that of being 'shut out of the scriptures':

> ...you who are conformable to the world, you are shut out of the scriptures, & you who respect persons for their gay cloathing, you are shut out of the scriptures, & you who give flattering titles unto men, you are shut out of the scriptures...it is the same with you now who are building upon the scriptures letter, which is none of yours, but belongeth to them on whom the ends of the world is come....[33]

While the repetition in "The light the true teacher" hammered home the universality of the light given to all, the identical rhetorical strategy here does the opposite. Every iteration of 'you are shut out' seems to score more deeply the lines of difference and exclusion. The Anabaptists, who fetishize 'the scriptures letter' as the authoritative Word of God, thereby paradoxically shut themselves out of 'the scriptures', by which Fisher means something more figuratively expansive as well as inward—something more like 'the light'. As we will see again later, the radical undermining of difference by a theology of universal Light did not entirely do away with difference among the early Quakers: difference returned, with a vengeance and often with bitterness.

Mary Fisher's letter to the Anabaptists of Barbados also makes mention of the other doctrinal point that motivated her radical travels: the present realization of 'the ends of the world'. In another of her writings, "concerning putting of[f] the hat", she declared, "christ is now appearing, which is the light of the world, & noe covering can stand before him which is made by the falne [i.e. fallen] wisdome".[34] Chiliastic fervour was a galvanizing force for many mid-seventeenth-century sects in England, as has been well documented.[35] Millenarian thought

---

[33] Portfolio MSS, vol. 33, f. 40.

[34] "A paper given forth by M F concerning putting of[f] the hat", Portfolio MSS, vol. 33, f. 35.

[35] See, for instance, B. S. Capp, "Extreme Millenarianism", in *Puritans, the Millennium, and the Future of Israel: Puritan Eschatology 1600 to 1660*, ed. Peter Toon (Cambridge and London: James Clarke & Co, 1970), 66–90, and idem, *The Fifth Monarchy Men: A Study in Seventeenth-Century English Millenarianism* (London: Faber 1972); Keith Thomas,

of this period generally recognized the conversion of the Jews as a signal event for the imminent second coming of Christ. The Quakers, however, were the one group that made practical attempts to convert both Jews and Muslims—generally unsuccessful.[36]

In one way, however, success was not the point. A distinctive feature of Quaker apocalypticism of the 1650s was the readiness of Friends to live as if 'the ends of the world' had already come, to perform the signs of apocalypse. It was during this period that Friends like Solomon Eccles became well known for walking naked with a pan of burning coals and brimstone on the head, exhorting all around to repent.[37] Yet such performances were merely the overflowing of something that was, like the Light, essentially inward. For the Quakers of this period, the Second Coming was an historical event that was happening within each convinced believer. George Fox recounted meeting, while in Plymouth prison in 1656, Baptists and Fifth Monarchy Men who were prophesying that Christ would come and begin his reign of a thousand years that very year.

> And they looked upon this reign to be outward, whenas he was come inwardly in the hearts of his people to reign and rule ther .... So they failed in their prophecy and expectation, and had not the possession of him.[38]

Fisher's letter to the Anabaptists of Barbados accuses them of the same fixation on outward things, so that they too neither possess Christ

---

Religion and the Decline of Magic: Studies in Popular Beliefs in Sixteenth- and Seventeenth-Century England (Harmondsworth: Penguin, 1973), 166–71. See also William Lamont, *Godly Rule: Politics and Religion, 1603–1660* (1969; rpt. Aldershot: Gregg Revivals, 1991), 31–32, for a reminder that millenarian thinking was not restricted to radical sects.

[36] Christopher Hill, "'Till the Conversion of the Jews'", in *Millenarianism and Messianism in English Literature and Thought 1650–1800*, ed. R. H. Popkin (Leiden: E. J. Brill, 1988). For Quaker attempts to convert Muslims, see Nabil Matar, *Islam in Britain 1558–1685* (Cambridge: Cambridge University Press, 1998), 132–36.

[37] Eccles processed in this manner through three Bartholomew Fairs between 1660 and 1663, as he recounted in a broadside composed in Newgate prison in the latter year: "*The Lord God is coming with all his Saints about him, to execute judgement upon all...I am your Sign from the dreadful Lord God; who hath sent me three several times, to leave you inexcusable*" [*Signes are from the Lord to a People or Nation, To Forewarn Them of some Eminent Judgment Near at Hand* (1663)]. See also Richard Bauman, "Going Naked as a Sign: The Prophetic Mission and the Performance of Metaphors", in *Let Your Words Be Few: Symbolism of Speaking and Silence Among Seventeenth-Century Quakers* (Cambridge: Cambridge University Press, 1983), 84–94.

[38] Nickalls, ed., *Journal of George Fox*, 261.

nor (according to her variant metaphor) 'the scriptures' because such possession is possible only for those "on whom the ends of the world is come". It is clear from this formulation that, far from being a universal experience, the end of the world is already happening only for and within some;[39] like walking in the Light, it is an inward state not shared by everyone, although theoretically available to everyone. At the beginning of Fisher's paper concerning the hat, she attempts to articulate this difficult concept in terms of perceiving beyond normal human temporality:

> They who are of God, that doth discerne, the ground, the rise, the being of that which is out of times, comprehending time, who this can fathom, the depth, the length of it, & receiveth it hath eternall life in himselfe....[40]

Thus, the primary difference between those who are in and those who are out is discernment—the ability to fathom, and thus participate, in God's eternal being.

Mary Fisher's one account of her meeting with Mehmed IV carefully characterizes the meeting not as an attempt at conversion—which is how scholars have loosely described it—but rather as an encounter where both commonalities and differences, what is shared and what is not, are acknowledged. If Fisher's visit to Mehmed IV was simply an attempt at conversion, it was a failure. If it was, on the other hand, an encounter where both difference and commonality were accepted, then it was radical in a more enduringly useful sense. In other words, although we may rightly read the meeting as a challenge to early modern hierarchies of civilized European and barbaric other, or of gender and class, approaching it through Fisher's own writing might alert us to further revisionary possibilities. In particular, can one read the meeting as an irenical exchange between Christianity and Islam?

Fisher's sole letter about the encounter is the best ground to test the hypothesis that she saw it less as the missionary's deliverance of truth to

---

[39] Douglas Gwyn argues that George Fox's message, "Christ is come to teach and lead his people himself", led to a "present-centred apocalypse from within", generating the pentecostal and charismatic activity of the first phase of Quakerism. See "Apocalypse Now and Then: Reading Early Friends in the Belly of the Beast", in *The Creation of Quaker Theory*, ed. Pink Dandelion (Aldershot: Ashgate, 2004), 143. See also T. L. Underwood, "Early Quaker Eschatology", in *Puritans, the Millennium, and the Future of Israel*, ed. P. Toon, 91–103.
[40] Portfolio MSS, vol. 33, f. 34.

the unenlightened and more as the act of "answering to that of God in every one". Here is the letter in full:[41]

> Tho[mas] Killam Tho[mas] Aldam and John Killam with your dear wives.
>
> My dear Love salutes you all in one, you have been often in my remembrance since I departed from you, and being now returned into England and many tryalls such as I was never tryed with before, yet have I borne my testimony for the Lord before ye King unto whom I was sent, and he was very noble unto me, and so were all that were about him, he and all that were about him received the words of truth without contradiction, they do dread the name of God many of them and eyes his Messengers, there is a royall seed amongst them, which in time God will raise, they [are] more near truth then many Nations, there is a love begot in [me] towards them which is endlesse, but this is my hope concerning them that he who hath caused me to love them more then many others will also raise his seed in them unto which my love is, Neverthelesse though they be called Turkes the seed in them is near unto God, and their kindnesse hath in some measure been shewne towards his servants after ye word of ye Lord was declared to them, they would willingly to have me to stay in the country, and when they could not prevaile with me they proffered me a man and a horse to go five dayes Journey, that was to Constaninople where but I refused and came safe from them the English are more bad most of them, yet there hath a good word gone thorow them, & some have received it but they are few, so I rest with my dear love to you all.
> Your dear sister Mary Fisher
> From London the 13. day of the 1 month (.58.)[42]

In this letter, Fisher is careful to mark the limits of agreement between herself and the Turkish court. Her delineation is grounded in a sober honesty that recognizes the extent to which the Turks remain different as well as a chiliastic expectation that they will grow yet nearer the truth and thus into greater likeness. "The King", she writes, and "all that were about him received the words of truth without contradiction", and they "eye" (that is, give countenance to) God's messengers. Fisher suggests that she was listened to; she does not claim that she persuaded,

---

[41] Words in square brackets are difficult to read because of wear to the page. Quoted by permission of the Library of the Religious Society of Friends, London.

[42] Caton MSS, vol. 320/1, f. 164. Modern dating for this letter would be 13 March 1659: Quakers called that month "First Month" since the new year under the Julian Calendar (used at this time in England) was generally counted from 25 March. Fisher had met with the Great Turk the summer before; according to Stefano Villani's *ODNB* article on Mary Fisher, she was in Leghorn in December 1658 and returned to England thereafter.

let alone converted, anyone. Yet she found some common ground and, even more clearly, proximity. Many of the Turks "dread the name of God" and "they [are] more near truth then many Nations...the seed in them is near unto God". Fisher explicitly recognized that she and her Islamic hosts worshipped the same God. Her metaphors of proximity, moreover, suggest that the spiritual geography of the world is much different than its physical geography: that peoples who might seem alien and far away are in fact 'nearer' than those who seem more like.[43] Fisher's metaphor of the 'seed' may be understood as a variant on the universal Light: it is a distinctively cabalistic metaphor for the fragmented and scattered spark of the divine which will be gathered up again in the last days, used by Jacob Boehme and also by Fisher's companion, John Perrot.[44] But Fisher further specified that "there is a royall seed amongst them, which in time God will raise". 'Royall seed' was used by Quaker writers in this period for the Quakers themselves.[45] Thus Fisher clearly expected that Friends, a new chosen people, would arise within the Ottoman Empire. Not all would convert—'amongst' suggests a scattering of seed rather than a universal sowing—but the very presence of seed and the promise of growth in this particular part of the world carries world-changing promise beyond the conversion merely of the English. John Perrot, in the tract he published from prison in Rome in 1658, when he could not deliver his word to the ruler of the Ottoman Empire in person, seemed to promise this possibility. "If Gods Seed in thee comes to live", he wrote to the Great Turk, "thy Seed may replenish every Island and Continent of this Earth".[46]

---

[43] Fisher's idea that Muslims were "more near truth then many Nations" was not idiosyncratic, nor merely restricted to Quakers. Islam's strict rules against representational images made Muslims more sympathetic for iconoclastic Protestants. See Matar, *Islam in Britain*, 123–25 for Elizabethan attempts to forge strategic ties with the Turks on the basis of a shared abhorrence of the 'scandal' of images in Catholic Europe.

[44] See, for instance Jacob Boehme's metaphorical use of 'seed' throughout *Aurora, that is, the Day-Spring, or Dawning of the Day in the Orient, or Morning-Rednesse in the Rising of the Sun, that is, the Root or Mother of Philosophie, Astrologie, & Theologie*, trans. John Sparrow (1656). For Perrot's use of the term, see note 46 below. On Boehme, Cabala, and the vexed relationship between Behmenism and Quakerism, see B. J. Gibbons, *Gender in Mystical and Occult Thought: Behmenism and its Development in England* (Cambridge: Cambridge University Press, 1996), especially chapter 6, "Behmenism and the Interregnum Spiritualists".

[45] As in William Caton's *The Moderate Enquirer Resolved...Concerning the Contemned People Called Quakers Who are the Royal Seed of God* (London, 1658); cf. also John Perrot's *To the Suffering Seed of Royalty, Wheresoever Tribulated upon the Face of the Whole Earth* (1661).

[46] Perrot, *A Visitation of Love, and Gentle Greeting of the Turk*, 17. While imprisoned in Rome, Perrot also wrote an epic poetic work which he published as *A Sea of the Seed's*

Fisher's letter, however, also demarcates the limits of universality. Although by travelling to meet the Great Turk she had acted out the implications of "the light of the world" that "lighteth every man", she recognized that difference remains. Fisher's toleration of difference, however, is played out against a background of millennial unfolding. The difference of the Turks is tolerated because God has yet to raise his seed in them. The English, however, seem to have had their chance and rejected it: "the English are more bad most of them" since most have rejected the "good word" that has been sown amongst them. Fisher may have had in mind the hostility of the English whom she met in the Ottoman empire: the unhelpfulness of the consul at Smyrna and the English Ambassador at Constantinople in particular contrasting with the courtesy and helpfulness of the Turks. While the latter offered an escort for her from Adrianople to Constantinople, the English Ambassador at Constantinople, Sir Thomas Bendish, evidently told Fisher and her companion Beatrice Beckley to get out of town for being "scandalous to our nation and religion".[47] Thus, although Fisher's meeting with the Great Turk seems full of heroic potential for overturning the rigidly inscribed system of differences of the early modern period, we find in the narration of that meeting a displacement rather than an overturning of difference. The theology of the light in every man makes theoretically possible the inclusion of literally every human being—Turks also—in the schema of salvation. Yet the very reports which seem to document progress towards this comprehensively universal salvation seem always to be framed by accounts and excoriation of those who despite being apparently 'nearer' the light have rejected it and therefore, paradoxically, have shown it to be *not* universal. It is to early narratives of Mary Fisher's travels and their

---

Sufferings, Through which Runs a River of Rich Rejoycing in 1661. See Nigel Smith, "Exporting Enthusiasm: John Perrot and the Quaker Epic", in *Literature and the English Civil War*, ed. T. Healey and J. Sawday (Cambridge: Cambridge University Press, 1990), 248–64.

[47] Bendish wrote to Oliver Cromwell on 24 July 1658 of Quakers arriving from Zante by way of Morea. John Buckley had made his own way to Constantinople, where Mary Fisher and Beatrice Beckley arrived by foot after their audience with the Great Turk at Adrianople. Bendish wrote to Cromwell (diplomatically, perhaps, given the Lord Protector's sympathy towards Quakers) that he first tolerated these Quakers in Constantinople "so long as theer comportment was offencelesse". But when they became "insufferable...by reason of their disturbances of our divine exercises, and severall notorious contempts of mee and my authority, I friendly warned them to returne, which the two women did quietly, but John Buckly refusing, I was constrained to shipe him hence". *A Collection of the State Papers of John Thurloe*, vol. 7 (1742), 287.

persistent founding of universalism on difference—sometimes violent difference—that I now turn.

Narrative Embroideries and Silences: Overcoming and Reinscribing Difference

In 1661, George Bishop gave the first full report of Mary Fisher's encounter with Mehmed IV, including purported exchanges between them:

> ...Then *he* bad *her speak the Word of the Lord to them, and not to fear, for they had good hearts and could hear it* —and *strictly* charged *her* to speak the *Word* she had *to say from the Lord, neither more or less, for they were willing to hear it, be it what it would.*[48]

By this account, Fisher finds, at the end of her long journey, not an infidel ripe for conversion, but one who already speaks in the Light—Mehmed IV talks like a Quaker! He recognizes that the Word of the Lord in the messenger is identical with what lives in the hearts of the recipients of the message. In this sense, they are not so much messenger and recipients as fellow witnesses. Fisher's exchange with the scholars of Sidney Sussex College, in which she and her companion were mockingly asked *"how many Gods there were?"* and gave the answer back *"but one God"*, stands in ironic shadow when viewed in the light of this later encounter. Bishop's narrative throughout is built on the assumption that his reader will recognize that Fisher and the Court of Mehmed IV, however else they differ, share a reverence for the 'Truth', the 'Word', and the 'one God'.

Yet, as Mary Fisher's letter from London carefully delimits the extent of what is shared, so too does Bishop's narrative suggest—and then tactfully remains silent about—where agreement ends.

> *They* were *also* desirous of *more* words than *she* had *freedom* to speak, and asked *her, What she thought of their Prophet Mahomet? She* Replied, That *she* knew *him* not, but the *Christ,* the *true* Prophet, the *Son of God,* Who was *the Light of the World,* and *enlightneth every man that cometh into the World,* Him she knew:—And *further* concerning *Mahomet,* she said, *That they might judge of him to be true or false, according as the Words and Prophesies he spake were either true or false,* Saying, *If the Word that the Prophet speaketh come to pass, then shall ye know that the Lord hath sent that Prophet, but if it come not to pass, then shall ye know that the Lord never sent him.*—To which *they* confessed and said, *It was Truth.*[49]

---

[48] Bishop, *New England Judged,* 20.
[49] Bishop, *New England Judged,* 20.

As Bishop presents it, both parties veered near to the kindling point of difference between them: their differing emphases on Mohammed and Jesus as the defining figures for their faiths, and their incompatible understandings of each. Interestingly, Fisher is reported to use the universalist language of her paper on "The light the true teacher": Christ is *the Light of the World*, and *enlightneth every man that cometh into the World*". Yet she uses it here to make an exclusivist argument, that Christ (and not Mohammed) is "the *true* Prophet" and, moreover, "the *Son of God*". Her Turkish hosts would have agreed with neither of these assertions. They do not, however, voice their disagreement, perhaps restrained by their own cultural values of hospitality to strangers.

Thus, what is not said here is as important as what is said; the common ground is staked out by *silence*, itself so important to Quaker practice. As reported by Bishop, the exchange sounds like negotiation, in which Fisher and her Islamic interlocutors find common referents and a common language. They agree on the means and the terms by which agreement may be found, even if they stop short of fully articulated agreement. So, when asked what she thought of Mohammed, Fisher's answer is, "*That they might judge of him to be true or false, according as the Words and Prophesies he spake were either true or false*". To which they "confessed"—ambivalently suggesting acknowledgement or concession but also, more strongly, the declaration of an article of faith—and said, "*It was Truth*".[50]

Even if we can find here the ingredients of an irenical meeting remarkable for the seventeenth century, still, the seeming dissolution of difference in Bishop's account of the meeting—between a Muslim and a Christian, between a Turkish man and an English maiden, between the ruler of the most powerful empire in the world and a servingwoman—depends on the reinscription of difference elsewhere. In his 1661 tract, titled *New England Judged*, Bishop embeds his account of Fisher's travels in the Ottoman Empire within a larger critique of the Christian, English governors of Massachusetts.

---

[50] These criteria for judging a true prophet may have been formulated collectively by Fisher and her companions precisely for their encounters with Muslims. They also appear in John Perrot's *A Visitation of Love and Gentle Greeting of the Turk*: "Will not that which trieth all peoples and Nations, try all Elders and Prophets also in all Nations…doth not this give testimony of a true Prophet, when the Word of the Prophet cometh to pass according to his Prophecie, that the Prophet shall be known to the people that the Lord hath truly sent him?" (19). Perrot's tract notably avoids direct mention of Christ.

Bishop directs how Fisher's later meeting with the Great Turk is to be read by first inviting critical judgment of her reception among those who should have been her like. When Mary Fisher and Anne Austin landed in Boston in 1655, after coming (as Bishop puts it in a scathing apostrophe to the rulers of Massachusetts) "*some* Thousands of Miles in *Love* to Visit *You*", they were received not with gratitude but were rather stripped and searched for witch-marks. "And with such Barbarousness", Bishop writes (and his choice of word is significant), "that One of them, a Married Woman and a Mother of Five Children [that is, Anne Austin], suffered not the like in the bearing of any of them into the World".[51] The "barbarousness" of the Puritan governors of Massachusetts is exemplified by their sexualized violence towards women's bodies. But Bishop then extends the critique to include what the Puritans failed to do as well as what they did. Their great failure was the failure of hospitality. They failed to welcome and listen to those who had travelled so far just to speak with them. Bishop continues: "Is *this your* Entertaining of *Strangers, your* Civility, *your* Manhood to *those* who travel'd so many *Thousands* of *Miles* to *Visit You* in the *Movings* of the *Lord*?"[52] In these passages, 'civility' and its opposite 'barbarousness' are gendered and sexualized. Civility is associated with a disciplined manhood, which respects and does not seek to uncover the modesty and maternity of female bodies and which shows appropriate love in the exercise of a just hospitality. The civil man's barbaric opposite violates and exposes his victim.

When George Bishop emphasizes that Mary Fisher undertook her astounding journey to Adrianople alone and unprotected, we are clearly meant to recall and compare the sexually abusive treatment Fisher and Austin received at Boston two years earlier. Yet the spectre of rape haunts the passages where Fisher goes to meet the Turk as well. Bishop begins his account of Fisher's travels in the Ottoman Empire by describing her as "a Maiden Friend" who, "*moved* of the *Lord* to *go* and deliver his *Word* to the *Great Turk*", travelled five or six hundred miles "very Peaceably without any abuse or injury". When she met with fearful citizens at Adrianople, who did not dare accompany her further for fear of the "Displeasure" of the Great Turk, she "passed

---

[51] Bishop, *New England Judged*, 5, 12.
[52] Bishop, *New England Judged*, 12–13.

alone" through the encampment of his army.[53] It is interesting to note that neither Bishop nor the Quaker Tapestry acknowledge that Mary Fisher was in fact not alone during her journey to Adrianople. Both John Perrot and Thomas Bendish make clear that she was accompanied, as was the custom among travelling Quakers, by another woman, Beatrice Beckley, about whom nothing much else is known.[54] Bishop shapes his narrative to emphasize Fisher's sexual vulnerability, although it is invoked primarily to demonstrate its powerlessness against one "moved by the Lord".[55] Nonetheless, it is an irony that a story that is in one way about the transcendence of gender—Fisher is under the protection of no father or husband and disregards the female imperative of keeping to her house in a big way—in another way depends on reminding the reader about the violability of the female body.

Unlike the Puritan elders of Massachusetts, Mehmed IV shows himself a model of manly civility in Bishop's as in Fisher's own account. He and his entire entourage treat Fisher with impeccable courtesy, and he shows concern for the dangerousness of her travelling.[56] Perhaps recalling the abuse suffered by Fisher in Cambridge and by Quaker women ministers generally when they were faulted for travelling "with no husband but Jesus Christ", Bishop may have intended to point up the contrast. Still, the way that Bishop's narrative sets up the encounter with Mehmed IV activates not simply comparisons with barbarous treatment by supposedly 'civil' authorities; I suggest it also activates latent cultural anxieties about the violations of body and belief that English travellers had come to expect from the Turk.[57]

---

[53] Bishop, *New England Judged*, 19.

[54] See Perrot's letter to Edward Burrough, referenced in note 25.

[55] Dropped travel companions (to make Mary Fisher seem more vulnerable and more heroic) may also feature in the transmission of Fisher's own account of the meeting with Mehmed IV. Her letter in the Caton MSS is a copy of a lost original. But does it record the trace of an omitted reference to John Buckley, who was awaiting Beatrice Beckley and Mary Fisher in Constantinople? Note the cancellation, reproduced from the manuscript: "they proffered me a man and a horse to go five dayes Journey, that was to Constaninople ~~where~~ but I refused and came safe from them" (Caton MSS, vol. 320/1, f. 164).

[56] "*He told her, It was dangerous Travelling, especially for such a one as she, and wondred that she had passed so safe so far as she had*; Saying, *It was in respect to her, and kindness that he profered it* [i.e. a "Guard" to bring her to Constantinople], *and that he would not for any thing she should come to the least hurt in his Dominions:* (A *Worthy* Expression of so great a Prince)" (*New England Judged*, 20).

[57] See "'Turning Turke': Conversion to Islam in English Writings", in Matar, *Islam in Britain*, 21–49.

Gerard Croese, writing his *General History of the Quakers* nearly forty years after Bishop, expressed some scepticism about Fisher travelling all that way by herself. It is an "Example of the strange and ardent Resolution of [Quaker] Women...almost too great, and therefore the less Credible", for which there is no other testimony or witness "besides the Woman herself".[58] Although writing after George Bishop, Croese seems not to have used his account, since he professes never to have been able to learn what Fisher said to Mehmed IV. Croese, however, not only also stresses that she travelled all alone, with no Beatrice Beckley in sight, "regarding neither the circumstances of Nature, nor the weakness of her Sex", but he goes further and omits the rest of Fisher's travelling companions as well. Thus, the difficulties with the English consul at Smyrna become a confrontation between a recalcitrant official and one resolute young woman. Moreover, Croese, who claims personal experience of Ottoman rule in his time as a Dutch minister in Smyrna, makes explicit all of the latent cultural fear and aversion towards the 'Great Turk' that seems so pointedly missing from either Fisher's letter or Bishop's narrative:

> ...a Monster of a Man, a Deformed sight both in Body and Mind, as if one strove with the other how to offend, of a black Complexion, with a flat broad Nose and Mouth, stupid, logger-headed, cruel, fierce, as to his Aspect, and besides other marks upon his Body, had a Scar beneath his Eye-lid...a Testimony of his Boisterous and Cruel Disposition....[59]

Croese only makes crudely explicit what lurks beneath Bishop's, and perhaps even Fisher's own, account of heroic witnessing. The Universal Light, with all its levelling potential, shines all the brighter against a latent field of violent, racialized, sexualized difference.[60]

---

[58] Gerard Croese, *The General History of the Quakers Containing the Lives, Tenents, Sufferings, Tryals, Speeches and Letters of the most Eminent Quakers, Both Men and Women* (1696), Book II, 274. Originally published in Latin as Gerardi Croesi *Historia Quakeriana...Libri III* (Amsterdam, 1695).

[59] Croese, *General History of the Quakers*, Book II, 275–76. For Croese's statement that he was in his younger days "Minister of the Gospel of *Jesus Christ* our Lord" in Smyrna, see 270. Croese—not a Quaker himself, though supposedly sympathetic to the Society of Friends—got much of his material from Willem Sewel who it seems was so disappointed with Croese's misinterpretations that they helped impel him to write his own history of the Quakers. See David J. Hall, "Willem Sewel", *ODNB*.

[60] See also Portfolio MSS, vol. 30.31, a nineteenth-century versified version of Fisher's story for Quaker children where the threat of rape and violence is made explicit: Fisher appears before the Great Turk as "one who would / Your royal harem grace", and "A moment o'er the Christian's head / The flashing weapons hung" (ff. 7, 17).

Conclusion

In her essay on Quaker women's travel narratives, Susan Wiseman suggests that early Quakers like Elizabeth Hooton, Mary Dyer, and Mary Fisher sought out experiences of violent differentiation in order to articulate their own beliefs by refusal and defiance—by difference itself. They returned again and again to places from which they had been expelled, "re-enacting and repeating a cycle of witness, imprisonment, whipping, banishment, return", particularly among the Puritan governors of the New World. These enactments locked Quakers and Puritans into violent polemical exchanges, of which George Bishop's *New England Judged* gives us a specimen, in which each side took fierce pains to differentiate themselves from the other.[61]

Nonetheless, it is against this backdrop that Quakers sought out commonality, the light that "lighteth every man that cometh into the world". As well as acknowledging the irrepressible return of difference, it is worth remembering that the theology of Universal Light enabled spectacular defiances of the normal early modern rules for gender, class, ethnicity, and religious identity—so spectacular that, as Gerard Croese observed, they are sometimes scarcely credible. Although set off by the foil of difference, these defiances were grounded on sameness, on the absolute identity of the divine spark wherever it was released and acknowledged. Thus prophets were true prophets wherever and whenever they spoke 'Truth': whether in the Bible or in Massachusetts, within Islam or at a Quaker meeting.

In 1697, in South Carolina whither she had emigrated with her second husband, Mary Cross (née Fisher) looked after a shipwrecked English Quaker named Robert Barrow who wrote home to his wife of his "landlady and nurse...one whose name you have heard of, a Yorkshire woman, born within two miles of York; her maiden name was Mary Fisher, she that spake to the great Turk".[62] To the end of her life, Mary

---

[61] Susan Wiseman, "Read Within: Gender, Cultural Difference and Quaker Women's Travel Narratives" in *Voicing Women: Gender and Sexuality in Early Modern Writing*, ed. Kate Chedgzoy, Melanie Hansen, and Suzanne Trill (Keele, Staffordshire: Keele University Press, 1996), 161.

[62] Villani, "Mary Fisher", *ODNB*. See also Jonathan Dickinson, *God's Protecting Providence...in the remarkable deliverance of Robert Barrow* (Philadelphia; rpt. London, 1700), 88.

After meeting with the Great Turk, Mary Fisher's career of witnessing and defiance did not end. In 1662, she married William Bayly, a shipmaster and Quaker preacher

Fisher remained famous around the world—around the Quaker world
at least—for one particular remarkable travel encounter. In the various
historical accounts and representations of this meeting, commonality
and difference are held in a tension that is precarious, but which also
has the potential to be productive. For this reason, even beyond the
instrinsic interest of her story, Fisher remains a provoking example
of the "strange and ardent resolution of women" for the present.

Bibliography

Manuscripts

Caton MSS. Library of the Religious Society of Friends, London.
Portfolio MSS. Library of the Religious Society of Friends, London.

Published Works

Aldam, Thomas, Mary Fisher, Jane Holmes, Elizabeth Hooton, Benjamin Nicholson,
    and William Pears. *False Prophets and False Teachers Described*. N.p., 1652.
Bauman, Richard. *Let Your Words Be Few: Symbolism of Speaking and Silence Among Seven-
    teenth-Century Quakers*. Cambridge: Cambridge University, Press, 1983.
Beier, A. L. *Masterless Men: The Vagrancy Problem in England 1560–1640*. London:
    Methuen, 1985.
Besse, Joseph. *A Collection of the Sufferings of the People Called Quakers*. 2 vols. London, 1754.
Bishop, George. *New England Judged, Not by Man's, But the Spirit of the Lord: And the Summe
    Sealed up of New-England's Persecution. Being A Brief Relation of the Sufferings of the People
    called Quakers in those Parts of America, from the Beginning of the Fifth Month 1656...to the
    later End of the Tenth Moneth, 1660*. London, 1661.
Boehme, Jacob. *Aurora, that is, the Day-Spring, or Dawning of the Day in the Orient, or Morn-
    ing-Rednesse in the Rising of the Sun, that is, the Root or Mother of Philosophie, Astrologie, &
    Theologie*. Translated by John Sparrow. London, 1656.
Braithwaite, William C. *The Beginnings of Quakerism*. 2nd ed. Rev. by Henry J. Cadbury.
    Cambridge: Cambridge University Press, 1955.
Capp, B. S. "Extreme Millenarianism". In *Puritans, the Millennium, and the Future of Israel:
    Puritan Eschatology 1600 to 1660*. Edited by Peter Toon. Cambridge and London:
    James Clarke & Co., 1970.

---

from Poole in Dorset, whom she had been visiting in Newgate prison. While pregnant,
she defended her husband from an officer of the law, and was struck and thrown
violently to the ground—twice—for her efforts (Besse, *Collection of the Sufferings*, vol. 1,
388). She and William evidently worked as a team and were attacked as such in *The
Letter Sent by Robert Rych to William Bayly and Mary Fisher, Called his Wife* (1669). William
Bayly died in 1675, and in 1682 Mary emigrated to America with her second Quaker
husband, John Cross, a "cordwainer" or shoemaker. She died in Charlestown, South
Carolina in 1698. Her granddaughter, Sophia Hume, became a well-known Quaker
writer in America. See also Christine Trevett, *Women and Quakerism in the 17th Century*
(York: Sessions Book Trust, The Ebor Press, 1991), 65.

——. *The Fifth Monarchy Men: A Study in Seventeenth-Century English Millenarianism*. London: Faber, 1972.

Croese, Gerard. *The General History of the Quakers Containing the Lives, Tenents, Sufferings, Tryals, Speeches and Letters of the most Eminent Quakers, Both Men and Women*. London, 1696.

Davies, Adrian. *The Quakers in English Society, 1655–1725*. Oxford: Clarendon, 2000.

Dickinson, Jonathan. *God's Protecting Providence, Man's Surest Help and Defence, in Times of the Greatest Difficulty, and Most Eminent Danger Evidenced in the Remarkable Deliverance of Robert Barrow*. Philadelphia; rpt. London, 1700.

Eccles, Solomon. *Signes are from the Lord to a People or Nation, To Forewarn Them of some Eminent Judgment Near at Hand*. London, 1663.

The First New Persecution; Or a True Narrative of the Cruel Usage of two Christians, by the present Mayor of Cambridge. As it was certified from thence by an Eminent Hand. London, 1654.

Fisher, Samuel. *The Testimony of Truth Exalted, By the Collected Labours of that Worthy Man, Good Scribe, and Faithful Minister of Jesus Christ, Samuel Fisher*. N.p. [London?], 1679.

Gibbons, B. J. *Gender in Mystical and Occult Thought: Behmenism and its Development in England*. Cambridge: Cambridge University Press, 1996.

Gwyn, Douglas. "Apocalypse Now and Then: Reading Early Friends in the Belly of the Beast". In *The Creation of Quaker Theory*. Edited by Pink Dandelion. Aldershot: Ashgate, 2004.

Hall, David D., ed. *The Antinomian Controversy, 1636–1638: A Documentary History*. Middletown, Connecticut: Wesleyan University Press, 1968.

Hill, Christopher. *Antichrist in Seventeenth-Century England*. London: Oxford University Press, 1971.

——. "'Till the Conversion of the Jews'". *Millenarianism and Messianism in English Literature and Thought 1650–1800*. Edited by Richard H. Popkin. Clark Library Lectures 1981–1982. Leiden: E. J. Brill, 1988.

Lamont, William. *Godly Rule: Politics and Religion, 1603–1660*. 1969. Reprint Aldershot: Gregg Revivals, 1991.

Mack, Phyllis. *Visionary Women: Ecstatic Prophecy in Seventeenth-Century England*. Berkeley: University of California Press, 1992.

Matar, Nabil. *Islam in Britain 1558–1685*. Cambridge: Cambridge University Press, 1998.

Nickalls, John L. ed. *The Journal of George Fox*. Rev. ed. London: Religious Society of Friends, 1975.

Norton, Humphrey. *New-England's Ensigne: It being the Account of Cruelty, the Professors Pride, and the Articles of their Faith; Signified in Characters Written in Blood, wickedly begun, barbarously continued, and inhumanly finished…by the…Priests and Rulers in New-England*. London, 1659.

Perrot, John. *A Visitation of Love and Gentle Greeting of the Turk and Tender Tryal of his Thoughts for God, and Proof of the Hearts of his Court, and the Spirits of People Round about Him, in his own Dominion, and the Inhabitants of the Earth that are Borderers upon his Skirts, in their Declared Religious Ways*. London, 1658.

Quaker Faith & Practice. 3rd ed. The Yearly Meeting of the Religious Society of Friends (Quakers) in Britain, 2005.

Raine, James, ed. *Depositions from the Castle of York Relating to Offences Committed in the Northern Counties in the Seventeenth Century*. Publications of the Surtees Society. Vol. 40. Durham: Published for the Society by F. Andrews, 1861.

Rich, Robert. *The Letter Sent by Robert Rych to William Bayly and Mary Fisher, Called his Wife*. London, 1669.

Smith, Nigel. "Exporting Enthusiasm: John Perrot and the Quaker Epic". In *Literature and the English Civil War*. Edited by Thomas Healey and Jonathan Sawday. Cambridge: Cambridge University Press, 1990.

Stewart, Althea. "Public Justice and Personal Liberty: Variety and Linguistic Skill in the Letters of Mary Fisher". *Quaker Studies* 3 (1998): 133–59.

Thomas, Keith. *Religion and the Decline of Magic: Studies in Popular Beliefs in Sixteenth- and Seventeenth-Century England*. Harmondsworth: Penguin, 1973.

Thurloe, John. *A Collection of the State papers of John Thurloe, Esq; Secretary, First, to the Council of State, and Afterwards to the Two Protectors, Oliver and Richard Cromwell. In Seven Volumes*. London, 1742.

Trevett, Christine. *Women and Quakerism in the 17th Century*. York: Sessions Book Trust, The Ebor Press, 1991.

Underwood, T. L. "Early Quaker Eschatology". In *Puritans, the Millennium, and the Future of Israel: Puritan Eschatology 1600 to 1660*. Edited by Peter Toon. Cambridge and London: James Clarke & Co., 1970.

Villani, Stefano. *Tremolanti e Papisti: Missioni Quacchere nell'Italia del Seicento*. Rome: Edizioni de Storia e Letteratura, 1996.

Wiseman, Susan. "Read Within: Gender, Cultural Difference and Quaker Women's Travel Narratives". In *Voicing Women: Gender and Sexuality in Early Modern Writing*. Edited by Kate Chedgzoy, Melanie Hansen, and Suzanne Trill. Keele, Staffordshire: Keele University Press, 1996.

Watts, Michael. *The Dissenters: From the Reformation to the French Revolution*. Oxford: Clarendon Press, 1978.

Winsser, Johan. "Mary Dyer and the 'Monster' story". *Quaker History* 79 (1990): 20–34.

SEVEN THOUSAND "HAND-MAIDS AND DAUGHTERS OF THE LORD": LINCOLNSHIRE AND CHESHIRE QUAKER WOMEN'S ANTI-TITHE PROTESTS IN LATE INTERREGNUM AND RESTORATION ENGLAND[1]

Stephen A. Kent

Hopes ran high among religious sectarians in 1659 that Parliament was about to abolish the widely-hated tithe system. With the sectarian sympathizer Henry Vane granting radicals an official ear inside the assembly, Quakers and others pinned their tithe abolition aspirations on his efforts.[2] Obligatory tithe payment was among the most bitterly contested issues of the day, with persons legally required to provide a tenth of their "annual produce of land or labour taken as a tax for the support of the Church and clergy".[3] On religious grounds, dissenters abhorred having to support a religious institution with whose teachings and practices they disagreed, not the least because they believed that the New Covenant announced by Jesus eliminated many practices (including mandatory tithes) described in the Old Testament (Matt. 23:23; Heb. 7:1–28). Moreover, to tithe opponents, their collection felt like a property rights violation,[4] and their payment caused severe financial hardship to many persons who lived on the margins of poverty and famine. They were disincentives to people who might otherwise attempt

---

[1] My appreciation goes to Malcolm Thomas and Joanna Clark for their assistance with materials at the Library of the Religious Society of Friends, London, and to Susan J. Hutton, Ken Hutton, Kelly Laycock, Jessie Meikle, Julie Neilson, Linda Distad, and Susan Raine for their careful assistance with data tabulation, presentation, editing, and proofreading. I also gratefully acknowledge the assistance of the Isaac Walton Killam Fellowship at the University of Alberta, which provided me with the travel money necessary for the British research.

[2] See J. H. Adamson and H. F. Folland, *Sir Henry Vane: His Life and Times, 1613–1662* (Boston: Gambit, 1973), 389; William C. Braithwaite, *The Beginnings of Quakerism*, 2nd ed. (Cambridge: Cambridge University Press, 1961), 457–58; Barry Reay, "The Quakers, 1659, and the Restoration of the Monarchy", *History* 63 (1978): 196–203; Violet A. Rowe, *Sir Henry Vane the Younger: A Study in Political and Administrative History* (London: Athlone Press, 1970), 223–24.

[3] Laura Brace, *The Idea of Property in Seventeenth-Century England* (Manchester: Manchester University Press, 1998), 15, see 17.

[4] Brace, *The Idea of Property*, 28, 37.

to improve their lives,[5] and the fact that some lay persons demanded tithes because they owned land with historical tithe-rights attached to them (called impropriations) was especially galling.[6] Attempting, therefore, to present a front of opposition to tithes in 1659 when it appeared that some parliamentary support existed for their position, Quakers organized two anti-tithe petitions, and the names of the signatories to one of those has survived.

On 14 June—almost two weeks before the first of the two Quaker petitions—Parliament received a petition from tithe opponents in the western counties, and Vane himself championed its conclusions about tithe abolition.[7] The resulting parliamentary discussion was inconclusive, with members agreeing to devise a tithes-substitute of some kind. Then, on 27 June, Friends (i.e., Quakers) resuscitated the debate when they turned over to Parliament a second anti-tithe petition, signed by more than 15,000 persons from around the country.[8] To their angry disappointment, however, Parliament decided to continue the tithe system in default of a suitable substitute for ministry support, and it underlined its decision by issuing a proclamation that "tithes should be paid properly now that it had decided for them".[9] Regrettably, the signatories' names on the first Quaker petition are not extant. On 20 July, however, the second collection of anti-tithe petitions that Quakers intended for Parliament was sent to the legislative body, although it is

---

[5] Barry Reay, "Quaker Opposition to Tithes, 1652–1660", *Past and Present* 86 (February 1980): 106.

[6] Christopher Hill, *Economic Problems of the Church: From Archbishop Whitgift to the Long Parliament* (Oxford: Clarendon Press, 1956), 155–167; see H. Larry Ingle, *First Among Friends: George Fox and the Creation of Quakerism* (Oxford: Oxford University Press, 1994), 57.

[7] *The Humble Petition of Many Well-affected Persons of Somerset, Wilts, and Some Part of Devon, Dorset and Hampshire, to the Parliament of the Commonwealth of England, Against Tithes. Together with the Parliaments Answer Thereunto, and Resolves Thereupon* (London: Livewel Chapman, 1659) [Wing/H3479]; Ronald Hutton, *The Restoration: A Political and Religious History of England and Wales 1658–1667* (Oxford: Clarendon Press, 1985), 49.

[8] *The Copie of A Paper Presented to the Parliament: And Read the 27th of the fourth Moneth, 1659. Subscribed by more than fifteen thousand hands. Thus Directed: To the Parliament of England, from many thousand of the free-born people of this Common-Wealth* (London, Giles Calvert, 1659), Thomason/147:E.988[24].

[9] Ronald Hutton, The Restoration: A Political and Religious History of England and Wales, 1658–1667 (Oxford: Clarendon Press, 1985), 49; see also George Thomason, *Catalogue of the Pamphlets, Books, Newspapers, and Manuscripts Relating to the Civil War, the Commonwealth, and Restoration, Collected by George Thomason, 1640–1661*, vol. 2 1908, Reprint. (Nendeln, Liechtenstein: Kraus Reprint, 1961), 244 (669. f. 21 [56]).

not clear if any Quakers actually presented it to members themselves.[10] The collection contained the signatures of 7,746 women.[11] These petitions, complete with printed signatory names, were bound in a book that has survived, but the frequent mention of this book in discussions both of Quaker women and of the late Interregnum in general has not yet led to an extensive analysis of the signatories themselves.

This chapter makes a preliminary attempt to locate the petitions in the context of the lives of many of the women who signed it. Working with primary and secondary sources at the Library of the Religious Society of Friends, London, along with public records and printed sources in Chester and Lincoln, I have identified events in the biographies of many signatories that allow me to place their involvement with the anti-tithe petitions in a diachronic perspective.[12] Specifically, I used marriage, birth, and death records, sufferings accounts, and miscellaneous Quaker records to make tentative determinations about how many of the signatories and their relatives from these two shires were Quakers either when they signed or at a subsequent period in their lives. I paid special attention to instances, either before or after the petition-collection was sent to Parliament, in which the signatories or their immediate relatives were involved in other anti-tithe protests. By taking this biographical, diachronic approach to the lives of the signatories, I am able to provide a preliminary estimate of how many of the signatories were *not* Quakers and may have supported tithe abolition from within other religious backgrounds. Certainly the historical records from the mid-to-late 1650s are uneven, and many of the names that have survived present ambiguous evidence about the persons whom they represent. Undoubtedly, future scholars will both expand and correct this work. Nevertheless, it stands as an initial attempt to enter into the lives of women who chose to petition their government on a burning issue of the day.

---

[10] Hutton, *Restoration*, 47, indicates that the petition "was produced but not presented in July," so it is not clear if Parliament as a body ever saw it.

[11] *These Several PAPERS Was* [sic] *sent to the PARLIAMENT the twentieth day of the fifth Moneth* [sic], *1659. Being above seven thousand of the Names of the HAND-MAIDS AND DAUGHTERS OF THE LORD, And Such as feels the Oppression of Tithes...* (London: Mary Westwood, 1659).

[12] I chose to examine the signatories from these shires only because of the quality of the extant Quaker records that exist at Library of the Religious Society of Friends, London, and the respective public records offices. I plan to publish a similar analysis of Somerset.

*The "Hand-Maids and Daughters of the Lord" Book and the
Petitions That It Contains*

The book itself consists of a two-page (unnumbered) preface by Mary
Forster (1619?–86), followed by seventy-two pages of petitions and
typeset signatures from various parts of England and one petition
from Wales. A friend of George Fox, Forster was a Quaker who lived
in London and wrote several pamphlets and testimonies.[13] Petitioners
are identifiable from twenty-nine geographical locations (almost all of
which are shires), although four petitions fail to identify the parts of
the country from which they came. The appearance of the petitions
does not follow any particular order, nor does the presentation of the
signatories' names. While some names appear more than once, it may
not be the case that, as Stevie Davies concludes, "a few signed twice",[14]
but just as likely that the repetitions indicate relatives (including mothers
and daughters) whose families circulated a small number of names.[15]

The introductions or prefaces to the various petitions themselves
vary in content from very brief statements to rather long anti-tithe
treatises, and no authors are given for any of the texts. (We cannot
be certain, therefore, that women wrote any of them, but the fact
that several introductions to petitions refer to the signatories as "we"
makes it highly likely that women composed at least some of them.)[16]
Since the petitions printed for Mary Westwood do not tell us how the
names were collected, we can only speculate that Quakers gathered
them at the same time that they collected the (presumably all male)

---

[13] "Dictionary of Quaker Biography", Library of the Religious Society of Friends,
London; see also Phyllis Mack, *Visionary Women: Ecstatic Prophecy in Seventeenth Century
England* (Berkeley: University of California Press, 1992), 181.

[14] Stevie Davies, *Unbridled Spirits: Women of the English Revolution: 1640–1660* (London:
The Women's Press, 1998), 92.

[15] Working with the birth records from this period, for example, one is struck by
how frequently a child has the same name as the parent of the same sex. Moreover, a
number of women among the shires' petitions have names qualified as "senior", "elder",
or "junior". See, for example, "Ellen Burgess, elder" followed by "Ellen Burgess" in
the Cheshire petition. See *These Several PAPERS*, 25. "Eliz. Smith, junior" appears in
the Lincolnshire petition. See *These Several PAPERS*, 32.

[16] Perhaps the clearest example appears in the introduction to the petition from
London and Southwark, which begins, "To you which should do justice, we who are
of the female kind, whose names are underwritten, do bear Testimony against Priests
and Tithes…" *These Several PAPERS*, 53.

signatories for the 27 June petition.[17] Most historians probably share the assumptions expressed by Davies, that "[t]he ranks of names are arranged by area, just as they were gathered in by nationwide local [Quaker] Meetings",[18] and some evidence from the book itself supports this view. The petitions from Lancashire and Nottingham identify the signatories as Friends,[19] but no other prefaces mention Quakerism. It may well have been that, in some shires, Quakers, who indisputably were key figures in the petitions' production, went outside their own group in order to boost the number of names and show the extent of opposition that diverse women felt toward tithe payment. (This issue will reappear in the conclusion of this study.) We do not even know whether the women were able to sign their names, a skill sometimes taken to be a minimal indicator of writing ability.[20] We do know, however, that Quakerism's central figure, George Fox, probably initiated the idea for a petition of this kind in 1657, realizing that tithes burdened women as well as men.[21] Consequently, the names-collection effort may have extended over a considerable length of time.

---

[17] See Braithwaite, *Beginnings of Quakerism*, 458.

[18] Davies, *Unbridled Spirits*, 92.

[19] *These Several PAPERS*, 8, 31.

[20] Margaret Spufford, "First Steps in Literacy: The Reading and Writing Experiences of the Humblest Seventeenth Century Spiritual Autobiographers", *History* 4, no. 3 (October 1979): 427, 435. I have my doubts, however, whether all of the signatories were actually able to sign their names. Margaret Fell's daughter, Sarah, for example, appears in the Lancashire petition, even though she was only six years old at the time. See Isabel Ross, *Margaret Fell: Mother of Quakerism* (New York: Longmans, Green and Co., 1949), 43 and *These Several PAPERS*, 8. People in that era were most likely to begin writing at age seven, if they were fortunate enough in their education to get that far. See Spufford, "First Steps", 410. In the Lincolnshire petition, Elizabeth Robinson's name appears (*These Several PAPERS*, 32), but in a January 1654/5 deed involving land use in which seven people were involved, she was the only person simply to leave her mark (which were her initials, 'ER') and not her signature (Index of Names, BRA 1765/1/8/2, Lincoln Records Office, Lincoln).

[21] The editor of Fox's "Cambridge Journal", Norman Penney, included a footnote about the 1659 petition. Referring to a manuscript in the Religious Society of Friends Library, he concluded, "[t]his paper against tithes was apparently suggested by Fox. He writes, under the date 1657, "For all women friends to sett their hands against tythes they may freely as they are moved...for the women in the truth feeles the weight as well as the men.... And soe if all the women friends in England, send up their hands against Tythes, I shall send them by women to the parliament, for many have sent up their names and some have not, but have been stopped...G: ff:". George Fox, *The Journal of George Fox*, ed. Norman Penney, 2 vols. 1911, Reprint. (New York: Octagon Press, 1973), 1:468 n. for p. 385.

Scholars seem divided as to whether all of the signatories were Quakers—as Isabel Ross and Barry Reay claim[22]—or Quakers and other sectarian women. Maureen Bell, for example, identified two Baptists who signed from London.[23] Certainly, women's economic plight, especially when caused by widowhood, could have contributed to many non-Quakers signing the local petitions.[24] Twenty signatories, for example, from the sixty-two recorded from Cambridgeshire and the Isle of Ely, were widows, and signers from other areas occasionally designated themselves in that manner.[25] Likewise, the Cheshire petition specifically mentioned the plight of widows.[26] Perhaps worth noting is that the lead names in the first petition reproduced in the 1659 book are those of the prominent Quaker leader and widow, Margaret Fell, along with seven daughters, listed from oldest to youngest.[27] Most religious organizations that co-existed with Quakerism did not share early Friends' penchant for record-keeping, so it will be impossible to discover much, if anything, about most non-Quaker women, if any of their names (beyond the ones Bell identified) now stare at us from across three centuries. I will be able to draw cautious conclusions, however, about the number of non-Quaker and Quaker signatories from Cheshire and Lincoln after analysing the names from those shires, but these conclusions must not be generalized to the signatories from other parts of the country.

---

[22] Ross indicates that the petition bore "the signatures of 7,000 women Friends". Ross, *Margaret Fell*, 42. Reay says that the petition was "signed by seven thousand Quaker women from all over the nation". Reay, "Quaker Opposition", 110.

[23] Maureen Bell named Elizabeth Poole and Sarah Attaway as Baptists. "Mary Westwood Quaker Publisher", *Publishing History* 23 (1988): 25.

[24] On the plight of widows in the seventeenth century, see Alice Clark, *Working Life of Women in the Seventeenth Century* (London: Routledge & Kegan Paul, 1982), 86–87, 137; and Miranda Chaytor and Jane Lewis's introduction therein (xxx–xxxi). Also, Bonnie S. Anderson and Judith P. Zinsser, *A History of Their Own: Women in Europe from Prehistory to the Present*, 2 vols. (New York: Harper & Row, 1988), 1:140–45. Michael Roberts concluded that "[b]etween a fifth and a half of all women may have been left in this position [of widowhood] in different early modern communities". See his "'Words They are Women, and Deeds They are Men': Images of Work and Gender in Early Modern England", in *Women and Work in Pre-Industrial England*, ed. Lindsey Charles and Lorna Duffin (London: Croom Helm, 1985), 127–28.

[25] *These Several PAPERS*, 37, 49.

[26] *These Several PAPERS*, 20.

[27] Bonnelyn Young Kunze, *Margaret Fell and the Rise of Quakerism* (Stanford: Stanford University Press, 1994), x–xi, 134.

The Lincolnshire Petition

Quakers first entered Lincolnshire in 1654 when George Fox and several others challenged ministers in their "steeplehouses" and spoke to congregants in independent "separate" meetings.[28] Within a short time, Quakers had established meetings in Gainsborough, Glentworth, Sturton, and Lincoln.[29] In 1654 also, William Dewsbury travelled through Lincoln, and at different times in 1656 Quakers James Naylor and Richard Farnsworth visited that city in attempts to mediate unspecified issues within the Quaker community.[30] Lincoln donated £12 for "service abroad" to help offset Friends' missionary expenses between March 1657 and March 1658.[31]

Table 1: Analysis of Lincolnshire's 1659 "Handmaids"

# of Women in Quaker Records						# of Women Not in Quaker Records			
Pre-signing			Post-Signing						
possible	probable	certain	possible	probable	certain	possible	probable	certain	
(a)*	(b)	(c)	(d)	(e)	(f)	(g)	(h)	(i)	
4	0	10	23	36	21	0	5	81	
n = 14 (= 8%)			n = 80 (= 44%)			n = 86			180
n = 94 (= 52%)						(= 48%)			= 100%

* See Appendix A for the names in each lettered category.

Despite the fact that Fox won over the sheriff of Lincoln during his 1654 trip,[32] persecution of Quakers began that same year. In Ninth Month (November), a crowd descended on John Whitehead after he apparently challenged the minister in Lincoln Cathedral, and soldiers who intervened probably saved his life.[33] Also that month, Elizabeth Hooton challenged the minister at Beckingham, which landed her in Lincoln Castle prison for five months.[34]

---

[28] *Journal of George Fox*, vol. 1, 149.
[29] Braithwaite, *Beginnings of Quakerism*, Map 1.
[30] Braithwaite, *Beginnings of Quakerism*, 174, 244, 565; see also 127.
[31] Braithwaite, *Beginnings of Quakerism*, 324.
[32] *Journal of George Fox*, vol. 1, 150.
[33] *Journal of George Fox*, vol. 1, 152.
[34] Joseph Besse, *A Collection of the Sufferings of the People Called Quakers* (London: Luke Hinde, 1753), vol. 1, 346; *Journal of George Fox*, vol. 1, 152.

Beckingham was also the location where, in 1655, John Pidd suffered ten weeks' imprisonment for tithe payment refusal.[35] Again in 1658, he spent six months in prison, presumably for the same offence.[36] A woman named Anne Pid (spelled with one 'd') was a petition signatory from the shire, and Quaker death records from Lincolnshire indicate that an "Ann Pidd", married to John and residing in Barmbee [*sic*: Barnby?], Nottinghamshire, died in 1675.[37]

If, in fact, this Ann(e) Pidd was the wife of tithe resister John, then she was one of nine Quaker signatories whose husbands were tithe resisters either before or after their wives signed. Elizabeth Pid's husband, Richard "and Joseph Stokes were detained several Weeks in Lincoln Castle for Tithes, till discharged by Order of a Committee of Parliament".[38] Over a decade later, Richard (listed as being from Beckingham), had goods worth £17 3s. 6d. taken from his household for holding Quaker meetings at the Pid(d) house.[39] In the same year that Ann Frotheringham's name appeared on the anti-tithe petition, both her husband Vincent and their son were imprisoned for their tithe resistance,[40] along with Robert Whitman, whose wife, Susanna, also

---

[35] Besse, *Collection of the Sufferings*, vol. 1, 346. See also entry for "John Pidd", Clerk of Monthly Meeting, Society of Friends in Lincolnshire, Harold W. Brace Collection, 2 Brace 3/20 2,000, Lincolnshire Records Office.

[36] Besse, *Collection of the Sufferings*, vol. 1, 347.

[37] *These Several PAPERS*, 32. Marriage records indicate that Ann Handley of Long Lednam, Lincolnshire, married John Pidd of Beckingham in 1657. They were members of Broughton and Gainsboro Monthly Meeting. See Digested Copy of the Registers of Births of the Quarterly Meeting of Lincolnshire [1632–1837], Library of the Religious Society of Friends, London. On the death of Ann Pidd of Barmbee [*sic*?], Nottinghamshire, see Digested Copy of the Registers of Burials of the Quarterly Meeting of Lincolnshire [1656–1837], Book 807:338, Library of the Religious Society of Friends.

[38] Besse, *Collection of the Sufferings*, vol. 1, 347.

[39] Besse, *Collection of the Sufferings*, vol. 1, 351. I cannot determine whether the families of Anne Pid(d) and Elizabeth Pidd were related, but evidence exists that the husbands, John and Richard, suffered together for their tithe opposition: "Richard Pidd, John Pidd, & Arnold Trueblood of Beckingham were upon the three & twentieth Day of the ninth Month 1658 brought to Lincoln Goale [*sic*] for Tithes at the suit of George Farthing where they Remained many weeks[.] Arnold Trueblood died in the Goale[. T]he other was Released by Committee of Parliament". See entry for "Richard Pidd, John Pidd, & Arnold Trueblood", 2 Brace 3/20 2,000.

[40] Ann was the "wife/widow of Vincent of [South Hykeham/] Welbourn [yeoman]" who had seven children and whose husband died in 1682. See entry for "Frotheringham, Ann", Index of Quaker Names, Harold W. Brace Cards, Lincolnshire Records Office.

affixed her name to the petition.[41] Subsequently, in 1668, Vincent again went to prison for his tithe opposition.[42] Signatory Martha Teff risked serious injury for her beliefs as Quaker persecution accounts report:

> *William Teff*, of Middle Rason, for going into the Steeplehouse there, and witnessing against the Priest's Deceit in the yeare 1655 was Knockt downe by John Wetherhog of the same Towne, and then ha[u]led out. The said William Teff for Reproving some people for their swearing and prophaneness in Markett Rason in the yeare 1655 [*sic*: 1658?], the Rude Multitude fell upon him & his wife [Martha] Stoning and beating them and driving them out of towne.[43]

Subsequently, William went to prison in 1660 for his tithe resistance.[44] Another Quaker woman who signed the 1659 petition from Lincolnshire was Mary Trueblood, whose husband Arnold had died in Lincoln gaol after having been imprisoned along with Richard and John Pidd in late 1658.[45]

---

[41] Besse, *Collection of the Sufferings*, vol. 1, 347. Robert and Susana (with one 'n') Whitman had a son, Robert, in 1654 and another son, John, in 1660. See Births to 1690, Digested Copy of Supplement Registers of Marriages, Births and Burials of the Quarterly Meeting of Lincolnshire [1618 {*sic*} to 1672], Book 826:55, Library of the Religious Society of Friends.

[42] Besse, *Collection of the Sufferings*, vol. 1, 349.

[43] "Sufferings" entry under "William Teff", 2 Brace 3/20 2,000. The problem over dating the incident in Markett Rason (or Market-Raison) stems from the fact that Besse described what seems to be the same incident, and dates it to 1658 (Besse, *Collection of the Sufferings*, vol. 1, 347). Quaker birth records indicate that William and Martha Teff had two sons: John (b. 1650) and Nathan (b. 1660). See "Supplemental Births", Digested Copy of Supplement Registers of Marriages, Births and Burials of the Quarterly Meeting of Lincolnshire. Daughter Jane died in 1670 (see "Death, Lincolnshire" ibid.).

[44] Besse, *Collection of the Sufferings*, vol. 1, 347.

[45] Entry for "Richard Pidd, John Pidd & Arnold Trueblood", 2 Brace 3/20, 2,000. In 1660, Mary remarried with William Burdett of Beckingham ("Marriages to 1700", Digested Copy of Supplement Registers of Marriages, Births, and Burials of the Quarterly Meeting of Lincolnshire, Book 807:129). In 1670, Burdett suffered a fine of £2 12s. 4d. for having Quaker meetings at his house (Besse, *Collection of the Sufferings*, vol. 1, 351). Mary had at least three children with Arnold: Elizabeth, John (b. 1654), and William (b. 1658). See "Index of Quaker Names", Harold W. Brace Cards.

Table 2: Persecuted Female Quakers and their Relatives—Lincolnshire's 1659 Signatories

	Refusing to Pay Tithes		Disrupting Sermons and Challenging Ministers		Refusing to Pay Church Maintenance		Refusing to Swear Oaths		Hosting Quaker Meetings		Public Disruptions		Contempt of Authority		Unspecified	
	Pre-signing	Post-Signing	Pre-Signing	Post-Signing	Pre-Signing	Post-Signing	Pre-Signing	Post-Signing	Pre-Signing	Post-Signing	Pre-Signing	Post-Signing	Pre-Signing	Post-Signing	Pre-Signing	Post-Signing
RELATIVES	*Pid, Anne (I) 1655; (I) 1658; *Pid, Elizabeth (I) 1658; *Trueblood, Mary (I) 1658; *Frothering-ham, Ann (I)1659 ▲ hands; - Whitman, Susanna (I) 1659 ▲	*Teff, Martha (I) 1660; *Davie, Elizabeth ■ (I) 1661; *Tate, Alice (D) 1662 h and s; - Garland, Mary (I) 1667; *Frothering-ham, Ann (I) 1668	*Teff, Martha (B) 1655		- Thorton, Anne (D) 1657			*Davie, Elizabeth ■ (I) 1662; *Tate, Alice (I, F) 1662		*Pid, Elizabeth (D) 1670	*Teff, Martha (B) 1658?			- Harrison, Jane (I) 1660 h and s		
SELVES								- Wilson, Ellen (I) 1662		- Parker, Mary (D) 1670; - Tate, Alice (D) 1670						- Smith, Margaret (I) 1662; - Northern, Ann (E) 1663 ■

KEY

* = multiple persecutions
■ = spelling discrepancy
▲ = cannot date event within 1659
• = reason for imprisonment unspecified

(B) = Beaten
(D) = Distraint
(E) = Excommunicated from Established Church
(F) = Fines
(I) = Imprisoned

fh = future husband
h = husband
s = son

N.B. because of multiple persecutions, the total number of incidents = 23, involving 12 relatives (10 husbands and 2 sons) and 6 female signatories

Four women whose names appear on the Lincolnshire anti-tithe petition—Mary Parker, Margaret Smith, Alice Tate, and Ellen Wilson—suffered for their Quaker faith in subsequent years. In 1670, both Mary Parker and Alice Tate suffered distraints for holding Quaker meetings in their houses.[46] Earlier, Alice's husband, Charles, refused to take an oath in 1662, for which he suffered a month's imprisonment and a 30s. fine.[47] That year must have been a difficult one for the Tate family, since Quaker records report: "Taken from Charles Tate A Poore man for Priest Healy for tithes to the value of 12s., one cow worth 40s".[48] In addition, at another (but undated) time, "Priest Healy" took another 17s. 64d. worth of hemp for a 5s. tithe owed to him.[49] In 1662, Margaret Smith and Ellen Wilson were among a number of Quakers who were committed to prison for refusing to swear;[50] they had signed the anti-tithe petition roughly three years earlier. Elizabeth Davie's husband, "Samuell Davey had taken from him two Calves worth £1. 13s. 4d. for the Steeplehouse Assessment by Edward Austin & Robert [?], the demand was 6s. 7d. in the yeare 1661".[51] The following year his travails continued: he first suffered imprisonment for unspecified reasons but then returned to gaol for twenty-two weeks for refusing to swear the Oath of Allegiance.[52] Mary Garland's husband, William, went to gaol in 1667/68 for his tithe refusal.[53] Jane Harrison's husband, Robert, had to appear before a judge in May 1660 for not paying toward the repairs of the local church. In typical Quaker fashion, he refused to remove his hat in court and was thrown in gaol for Contempt of Authority.[54]

---

[46] Besse, *Collection of the Sufferings*, vol. 1, 351.

[47] Besse, *Collection of the Sufferings*, vol. 1, 348. Quaker records indicate that Charles Tate of Newbigg was buried in 1666. Alice Tate of Haxey, the widow of Charles, remarried with John Barrow of Haxey in 1671 and was buried in 1672. See "Tate, Alice" of Haxey, Index of Quaker Names, Harold W. Brace Cards.

[48] 2 Brace 3/20, 2,022.

[49] 2 Brace 3/20, 2,028.

[50] Besse, *Collection of the Sufferings*, vol. 1, 348.

[51] Entry for "Samuell Davey", 2 Brace 3/20, 2,000.

[52] Besse, *Collection of the Sufferings*, vol. 1, 348. Samuel and Elizabeth Davie became the parents of a daughter, Marie, in 1656. See Digested Copy of the Registers of Marriages of the Quarterly Meeting of Lincolnshire [1657–1836], Book 826:55, Library of the Religious Society of Friends, London. I am assuming that Samuel Davie, Samuell Davey, and Samuel Davey were the same man.

[53] Besse, *Collection of the Sufferings*, vol. 1, 349.

[54] Besse, *Collection of the Sufferings*, vol. 1, 347. Jane Smith and Robert Harrison married in 1657 and had a child named Jane in 1661. See Digested Copy of the Registers of

The number of signatories that we can identify (with varying degrees of certainty) as having involvement in Lincolnshire Quakerism is around 52%. These numbers can never be taken as precise representations, given the uneven nature of the records. That caution acknowledged, it is still worth considering the interpretation that a substantial portion of the women who signed the anti-tithe petition in this shire were not Friends. The likely impact of tithes on others in the communities in which Friends lived makes it probable that people outside of Quakerism shared some of the resentments that Quakers felt and were willing to go at least as far as signing the anti-tithe petition.

The Cheshire Petition

The first Quaker convert in Cheshire had been a member of an Independent congregation whose preacher had sent him to a northern shire in order to enquire about the Quakers in July 1653.[55] Later that year, Quakers John Lawson and Richard Hubberthorne travelled to various Cheshire locations (including Chester, Malpas, Morley, and Wrexham), recruiting extensively among existing Independent communities. These Quaker missionaries, and a few of their converts, quickly drew the ire of Presbyterian ministers, their congregations, and local officials. By November 1653, Hubberthorne sat in Chester's Northgate Prison,[56] and other Friends suffered at the hands of angry mobs and furious preachers. Among these early Quaker sufferers was Richard Hitchcock, who in 1653 "utter[ed] a Christian Exhortation to the People" at the end of public worship, which led to the mayor sending him to gaol. The gaoler put "him in Irons in a dark Place called *Dead Man's Room*, where condemned Persons were usually put; there was he kept above thirteen Weeks from his Wife and many Children".[57] Extant Quaker

---

Marriages of the Quarterly Meeting of Lincolnshire, Book 807:127 and Digested Copy of the Registers of Births of the Quarterly Meeting of Lincolnshire, Book 823:2.

[55] Hugh Barbour, *The Quakers in Puritan England* (New Haven: Yale University Press, 1964), 49; Braithwaite, *Beginnings of Quakerism*, 123; Norman Penney, ed., *The First Publishers of Truth* (London: Headley Brothers, 1907), 16–19.

[56] Braithwaite, *Beginnings of Quakerism*, 125.

[57] Besse, *Collection of the Sufferings*, vol. 1, 99. A manuscript on file in the Mayors' Files 1 of the Chester Corporation (probably from 1656) indicates that Hitchcock was gaoled for fifteen weeks. See S. B., "Quakers in Chester 1653–1656", *The Cheshire Sheaf* 5 (January–December 1970): 12.

records do not provide us with the name of Richard Hitchcock's wife, but an "Ursala Hitchcock" was among the Cheshire signatories.[58]

Table 3: Analysis of Cheshire's 1659 "Handmaids"

# of Women in Quaker Records						# of Women Not in Quaker Records			
Pre-Signing			Post-Signing						
possible	probable	certain	possible	probable	certain	possible	probable	certain	
(a)*	(b)	(c)	(d)	(e)	(f)	(g)	(h)	(i)	
4	20	28	10	52	41	14	9	271	
n = 52 (= 12%)			n = 103 (= 23%)			n = 294			449
n = 155 (= 35%)						(= 65%)			= 100%

* See Appendix B for the names in each lettered category.

An examination of Quaker records does indicate, however, that seven or more of the women who signed the petition had been involved with protesting against tithes and the ministers who received them in the years before 1659. For challenging a preacher after a sermon, Mary Endon suffered four days' imprisonment in 1654.[59] In 1656, Margret Wood was imprisoned for four weeks for "sundry causes" involved with her testifying "against the Vices and Corruptions of those Times".[60] Two years later, signatory Mary Milner was imprisoned seven weeks for tithe refusal, and the goods that she lost in payment were worth three

---

[58] *These Several PAPERS*, 25.

[59] Besse, *Collection of the Sufferings*, vol. 1, 100; Anthony Hutchins, *Caines Bloudy Race Known by Their Fruits. Or, a True Declaration of the Innocent Sufferings of the Servants of the Living God* (London: Thomas Simmons, 1657), reprinted in F. Sanders, "The Quakers in Chester Under the Protectorate", *Chester Archaeological Society Journal* ns, XIV (1908): 42; see also Mack, *Visionary Women*, 421.

[60] Besse, *Collection of the Sufferings*, vol. 1, 100. Another account gives a somewhat clearer picture of what happened: "Sarah Adgit and Margret Wood, coming to this City [Chester], were moved to go to a Steeple-house; Sarah spake a few Words when the Priest had done; Margret Spake not in the Steeple-house at all; they were both taken before William Wright, and by him committed to prison, and kept above four Weeks, though (as aforesaid) one of them spoke not at all in the Steeple-house". See Hutchins, *Caines Bloudy Race*, 43. Apparently Wood was imprisoned because of the actions of her friend. For a general discussion of Quaker women challenging clergymen and others, see Phyllis Mack, "Gender and Spirituality in Early English Quakerism, 1650–1665", in *Witnesses for Change: Quaker Women over Three Centuries*, ed. Elisabeth Potts Brown and Susan Mosher Stuard (New Brunswick: Rutgers University Press, 1989), 38, 43–45. On Margaret Wood, see Mack, *Visionary Women*, 417.

times the value of the initial tithe demand.[61] Three years before Mary died in 1673, her husband, Richard, was "fined 20£ for a Meeting at his House, [and] had Goods taken from him worth 37£".[62] Some time between 1653 and 1656, Sisly (or Cisly) Cleaton of Runkorn Parish "had taken from her one Warming-Pan worth 6s. for tythe-flax, and she had none, being sued at Law, and cast [i.e. decided] by a false Oath for the use of Coll. [Colonel] Brook". She signed the 1659 petition,[63] as did Margret Royl, who may have been the "Widow Royle" who had a cow, a load of beans, and a bed hilling (i.e. a quilt or covering) taken for refusal to pay tithes in the early-to-mid 1650s.[64] During the mid 1650s, Anne Janney (whom I presume to be the "Ann Janney Senior" who signed the petition) lost a cow and a heifer worth considerably more than the 13s. that she owed in tithe payments.[65] Also during this period, Ellin Boulton (presumably the same "Elin Boulton" who signed the petition) had four pewter dishes, a pewter bowl, a pot, and a candlestick confiscated after not paying for the repair of the "steeplehouse" at Runkorn.[66] In the mid 1650s, Deborah Maddock ran afoul of the mayor after she delivered a letter to him from the imprisoned Edward Morgan. The mayor was offended at how "unreverently" she behaved toward him—even telling him that "there is no respect of persons with God"—so he got a constable to throw her in the hole in prison called "Little Ease" for four hours.[67] A parish register from Nantwich indicates

---

[61] Besse, *Collection of the Sufferings*, vol. 1, 102; *These Several PAPERS*, 24.

[62] Besse, *Collection of the Sufferings*, vol. 1, 104. Quaker burial records indicate that Mary Milner of Helsebey [*sic*: Helsby], wife of Richard, and a member of the Cheshire Monthly Meeting, died in 1673 and was buried in Whitley.

[63] Hutchins, *Caines Bloudy Race*, 78; *These Several PAPERS*, 22.

[64] Hutchins, *Caines Bloudy Race*, 78. When Margaret Royle died in 1668, Quaker records indicated that she was a widow. See Digested Copy of the Registers of Burials of the Quarterly Meeting of Cheshire and Staffordshire [1655–1837], Book 218:15, Library of the Religious Society of Friends, London.

[65] *These Several PAPERS*, 24; Hutchins, *Caines Bloudy Race*, 80.

[66] *These Several PAPERS*, 22; Hutchins, *Caines Bloudy Race*, 81.

[67] Quoted in Hutchins, *Caines Bloudy Race*, 49. Besse described Little Ease as a place "devised for Torture, of which we find the following Description: 'It was an Hole hewed out in a Rock, the Breadth and Cross from Side to Side was seventeen Inches, from the Back to the Inside of the great Door at the Top, seven Inches, at the Shoulders eight Inches, at the Breast nine Inches and a Half; from the Top to the Bottom one Yard and a Half, with a Device to lessen the Height, as they are minded to torment the Person put in, by Draw-boards, which shoot over the two Sides to a Yard Height, or thereabout.' In this Place they tormented many of those who were induced with Christian Courage to reprove the Vices either of Ministers, Magistrates, or People." *Collection of the Sufferings*, vol. 1, 100.

that a "Margret Knevit" married John Faulkner in 1648, and in the mid 1650s "John Falkener" had goods taken from him for not paying tithes. It seems likely that the Margret Falkner who signed the petition was his wife.[68] Finally, we also know that Oliver Cromwell's second son, Henry, had imprisoned signatory Elizabeth Morgan (d. 1666)[69] and Richard Hickock (both from Chester) early in 1656 as they ministered to English troops in Dublin, Ireland, probably because he feared the group's influence on soldiers and thought that Quakers were "not very consistent with civil government".[70]

At least five women suffered for their Quaker beliefs several years after signing the petition. Dorothy Deane was imprisoned in 1663 for her tithe opposition, and Anne Janney had goods distressed to the value of £28 18s. for an unpaid tithe of £7 4s. 10d.[71] In August 1670, Ann Marsland of Hanford was fined a substantial amount—£20—for holding numerous meetings at her house.[72] Margret Coppock, whose name appears twice on the petition,[73] suffered two fines in 1670 and one in 1671. Quaker persecution records do not indicate what the first fine in 1670 was for, but the second one that year and the fine in 1671 were for attending meetings. Mary Stretch (who may have been the signatory Mary Strach) had the misfortune of being thrown in prison in 1665 simply for attempting to visit her fellow Quakers who were already in gaol.[74]

One of the people whom Stretch was attempting to visit was Edward Alcock, who was sent to prison for two months (along with seventeen other attenders) for holding a Quaker meeting in his family's house.[75] From serving time in winter without receiving necessary food, one person died. Soon after Alcock's release, he was gaoled for another

---

[68] Nantwich Parish Register, vol. 1, Cheshire Records Office; Hutchins, *Caines Bloudy Race*, 83; *These Several PAPERS*, 25.

[69] Digested Copy of the Registers of Burials of the Quarterly Meeting of Cheshire and Staffordshire, Book 218:7, 13; see also Mack, *Visionary Women*, 416 and Davies, *Unbridled Spirits*, 239–40. Elizabeth Morgan and her husband resided in Chester.

[70] Quoted in Braithwaite, *Beginnings of Quakerism*, 215; see also 216, 388 n. 10.

[71] Besse, *Collection of the Sufferings*, vol. 1, 104. I am assuming that the "Dorothy Deane" mentioned in Besse is the same "Dorothy Deen" who signed the petition (*These Several PAPERS*, 23).

[72] Davies, *Unbridled Spirits*, 240–41.

[73] *These Several PAPERS*, 22, 25.

[74] *These Several PAPERS*, 23; Besse, *Collection of the Sufferings*, vol. 1, 104.

[75] Besse, *Collection of the Sufferings*, vol. 1, 104.

four months, this time for attending a meeting.[76] His difficulties with authorities, however, dated back to 1653, when he and five other men suffered distress of £11 10s. for travelling two miles to a Quaker meeting.[77] The following year, Edward married Ellen Halle before a justice of the peace, and in 1657 Ellen Alcock gave birth to a daughter whom they named Marie. Living in Moberly, she signed Cheshire's anti-tithe petition, and before the end of 1659 she gave birth to another daughter, Martha.[78]

The five other men whose goods were distrained along with Alcock's in 1653 were John Worthington, Thomas Jannery, Thomas Potts, Richard Burgess, and Robert Milner. Most (if not all) of these men were related to women who would sign the anti-tithe petitions six or so years later. In this incident from 1653, John Worthington lost a young horse, and in subsequent confrontations over the next few years lost a brass pan, two pewter dishes, and one pair of iron-bound cart wheels because he failed to meet his tithe obligations.[79] At some point John was married to Mary Worthington, since a few months after Mary signed the petition she gave birth to a daughter named Hannah, while she and her husband lived at Pownal. In 1669 another daughter, Martha, died.[80] The names of both Mary and Martha Worthington appeared as signatories on the list, as did six others with the same last name. Five signatories share the surname Janney, although Thomas Janney appears to have been married to a woman named Margery whose name does not appear. Two of his daughters, however, were Martha and Elizabeth, and both of those names appear as signatories.[81] Thomas Janney had numerous run-ins with officials throughout the mid 1650s for his tithe resistance, losing at various times a mare, two cows, a pewter dish, and four stools.[82]

---

[76] Besse, *Collection of the Sufferings*, vol. 1, 104.

[77] Besse, *Collection of the Sufferings*, vol. 1, 100.

[78] Entry for "Alcock, Ellen", MF 63/1, Digested Copy of the Registers of Births of the Quarterly Meeting of Cheshire and Staffordshire, Book 232:151, 152 and Book 217:3, 5; *These Several PAPERS*, 24.

[79] Hutchins, *Caines Bloudy Race*, 79, 82.

[80] Digested Copy of the Registers of Births of the Quarterly Meeting of Cheshire and Staffordshire, Book 217:5 and Book 232:151; Digested Copy of the Registers of Burials of the Quarterly Meeting of Cheshire and Staffordshire, Book 235:11 and Book 218:17.

[81] Digested Copy of the Registers of Burials of the Quarterly Meeting of Cheshire and Staffordshire, Book 235:8.

[82] Hutchins, *Caines Bloudy Race*, 79, 82.

Two signatories named "Mary Pot" appear in the 1659 petition, and we cannot know if one woman signed twice or two signatories shared the same name. In any case, a "Thomas Pott" shows up in Quaker records, and in October 1655, a justice of the peace married Mary Heald and Thomas Pott, the two having publicized their marriage intention over several market days.[83] At various times throughout the mid 1650s, Mary and Thomas lost two heifers, a brass pot, and a coat for refusing to pay tithes that they owed.[84] Mary and Thomas Pott buried a daughter, Marie, in 1665, and in that same year Thomas was among the eighteen persons imprisoned for attending a Quaker meeting at Edward Alcock's house and subsequently imprisoned with Alcock for another four months.[85] He lost goods in 1671 for refusing tithes,[86] and by 1684 the condition of his family's finances was dire. He received a £20 fine for holding a meeting in his house:

> but he being very poor, the Officers, who broke open his doors, and rifled his House, could find no more Goods than amounted to 3£. 0s. 6d. Which they took, and the poor Man and his Family were obliged to seek Lodging at their Neighbours Houses.[87]

We know nothing more about the family's fate.

Three other women who shared Mary Pott's maiden name, Heald, signed the anti-tithe petition, typically with variant spellings—although it is impossible to determine if they were related through either blood or marriage. According to Quaker records, signatory "Elizabeth Heeld" gave birth to a son, James, in 1658, and died in Moberly (i.e., Mobberley), Cheshire, in 1664.[88] She and her husband, Thomas, lost a heifer in the mid 1650s for his failure to provide tithe-corn to the local minister, Robert Barlow.[89] Margaret Heald of Mobberley also appears in Quaker

---

[83] Entry under "Pott, Mary", October 1655, MF 63/1.

[84] Hutchins, *Caines Bloudy Race*, 79, 82.

[85] Digested Copy of the Registers of Burials of the Quarterly Meeting of Cheshire and Staffordshire, Book 235:7 and Book 218:11; Besse, *Collection of the Sufferings*, vol. 1, 104.

[86] Besse, *Collection of the Sufferings*, 105.

[87] Besse, *Collection of the Sufferings*, 105.

[88] Digested Copy of the Registers of Births of the Quarterly Meeting of Cheshire and Staffordshire, Book 232:151 and Book 217:3; Digested Copy of the Registers of Burials of the Quarterly Meeting of Cheshire and Staffordshire, Book 235:6 and Book 218:9.

[89] Hutchins, *Caines Bloudy Race*, 80.

burial records for 1667,[90] and a "Margret Heeld" had affixed her name
to the 1659 petition.[91] Anne Lambe (also a family name that appears
twice among the signatories, without the 'e') married Robert Heald
on 22 August 1654,[92] and a person named "Anne Heeld" appears in
the 1659 petition. The surname, but not the given name, of Richard
Burgess also appears in existing Quaker records, and four women with
the same last name, three of whom spelled it with only one 's', are in
the anti-tithe petition.[93] Jeffrey Burgess, along with the familiar Cheshire
Quakers—Thomas Janney, Thomas Pott, and Edward Alcock—went
to jail for four months in 1665 for attending a Quaker meeting, and
Jeffrey had apparently buried his Quaker wife, Ellen, three years earlier.[94] Again, it is impossible to determine whether any family connection existed between Richard Burgess and these signatories or their
families. Robert Milner and his signatory wife, Ann, had a daughter,
Rachell, a few months before Ann signed the 1659 petition. Perhaps
this child helped allay the grief they certainly felt for having buried
a son, Samuel, the year before.[95] As an educated guess, therefore, the
six men (Worthington, Janney, Potts, Burgess, Milner, and Alcock) who
suffered distraint of goods in 1653 were Quakers who had relatives by
blood or marriage who also opposed tithes, even if these relatives were
not necessarily Friends themselves.

---

[90] Digested Copy of the Registers of Burials of the Quarterly Meeting of Cheshire
and Staffordshire, Book 218:13.

[91] *These Several PAPERS*, 24.

[92] Entry for "Heald, Anne", MF 63/1.

[93] The signatories were "Ellen Burges, Margery Burges, Margret Burges, and Ellen
Burgess, elder". A "Margaret" Burgess appears in Quaker records as having married
"William" and given birth to a child named "Joseph" in 1657 (Digested Copy of the
Registers of Births of the Quarterly Meeting of Cheshire and Staffordshire, Book
232:152). In 1664, William Burgess, along with John Worrall and Thomas Janney,
went to prison for refusing to pay tithes (Besse, *Collection of the Sufferings*, vol. 1, 104). In
Cheshire Records Office, the Nantwich Parish Register, vol. 1, has a "Richard Burges"
marrying Margaret Podmore, but the year is uncertain (probably 1653). Perhaps worth
mentioning is that an informer against the Quakers in 1666 was named John Burges
(Besse, *Collection of the Sufferings*, vol. 1, 104).

[94] Digested Copy of the Registers of Burials of the Quarterly Meeting of Cheshire
and Staffordshire, Book 218:7 and Book 235:3. She was buried in Mobberley.

[95] *These Several Papers*, 24; Digested Copy of the Registers of Births of the Quarterly
Meeting of Cheshire and Staffordshire, Book 232:151 and Book 217:5; Digested Copy
of the Registers of Burials of the Quarterly Meeting of Cheshire and Staffordshire,
Book 235:1 and Book 218:3. The child's name was recorded as "Milnor, Samuel", and
he was listed as the "son of Robert and Ann" from "Pownall See, Cheshire".

Table 4: Persecuted Female Quakers and their Relatives—Cheshire 1659 Signatories

Refusing to Pay Tithes

Pre-signing — RELATIVES:
- Boulton, Sarah (D) mid 1650s h
- *Brown, Elin • (D) mid 1650s h
- *Burtonwood Mary (D) mid 1650s h
- Falkner •, Margret (D) mid 1650s h
- Heeld •, Elizabeth (D) mid 1650s h
- *Janney, Martha & Elizabeth (D) mid 1650s (D,F) mid 1650s
- *Pot •, Mary (D) mid 1650s h
- Sarret, Eliz.
- Strettel •, Mary (D) mid 1650s h

Pre-signing — SELVES:
- Cleaton, Cisly • (D) mid 1650s
- *Janney, Ann • Senior (D) mid 1650s
- Milner, Mary (I,D) 1658

Post-signing — RELATIVES:
- Falkner• Margret (I) 1666 h

Post-signing — SELVES:
- Deen •, Dorothy (I) 1663
- *Janney, Ann • Senior (D) 1663
- *Sarrat, Elizabeth• (D) 1683

Disrupting Sermons and Challenging Ministers

Pre-signing — RELATIVES:
- *Morgan Eliz. (I) mid 1650s h (i)

Pre-signing — SELVES:
- Endon, Mary (I) 1654
- Wood, Margret (I) 1656

Refusing to Pay Church Maintenance

Pre-signing — RELATIVES:
- *Janney, Martha & Elizabeth (D,F) mid 1650s
- Brown Elin • (D) 1658 h

Pre-signing — SELVES:
- Boulton Elin • (D) mid 1650s

Refusing to Swear Oaths

Pre-signing — RELATIVES:
- *Morgan Eliz. (I) 1656 h

Hosting Quaker Meetings

Post-signing — RELATIVES:
- *Alcock, Ellen (I) 1665 h
- Milner, Mary (F, D) 1670 h
- *Pot•, Mary (D) 1684 h

Post-signing — SELVES:
- Marsland, Anne • (F) 1670

Attending Quaker Meetings

Pre-signing — RELATIVES:
- *Alcock, Ellen (F) 1653 h
- *Janney, Martha & Elizabeth (D) 1653 h / 1653 f
- Milner, Ann (D) 1653 h
- *Morgan, Eliz. (I) 1653 h
- Worthington, Martha (D) 1653 f
- Worthington, Mary (D) 1653 h

Post-signing — RELATIVES:
- *Alcock, Ellen (I) 1665 h
- *Pot•, Mary (I) 1665 h
- (I) 1665 h
- Falkner• Margret (I) 1666 h
- *Harrison, Ann (I)1668 h
- *Morgan Eliz. (D) 1670 h

Post-signing — SELVES:
- *Coppocock•, Margret (F) 1670
- (F) 1670
- (F) 1671

Holding Quaker Membership

Pre-signing — RELATIVES:
- *Morgan Eliz. (I) mid 1650s h

Pre-signing — SELVES:
- *Morgan Eliz. (I) 1656
- Maddock, Deborah (I) mid 1650s

Post-signing — SELVES:
- *Sarrat Elizabeth (I) *1684

Refusing to give Hat Honour

Pre-signing — RELATIVES:
- *Morgan Eliz. (I) 1657 h

Visiting Imprisoned Quakers

Post-signing — SELVES:
- Strachan• Mary (I) 1665

KEY * = multiple persecutions   • = spelling discrepancy

(D) = Distraint   (F) = Fines   (I) = Imprisoned   (i) = imprisoned for actions of another

d = daughter   f = father   fh = future husband   h = husband

[1] = Quaker records do not indicate the reason for this fine
[2] = The precise reason for her imprisonment in Ireland is unclear
[3] = Was not reverent to a mayor
[4] = Absence from the national worship

N.B. Because of multiple persecutions, the total number of incidents = 48, involving 17 relatives (3 fathers and 14 future husbands and husbands) and 10 signatories

A few other signatories were married to men who had histories of tithe-opposition dating back into the 1650s. James Brown, husband to Elin (Ellin), was one of several persons in 1658 who had 50s. taken from him for refusal to pay a 2s. fee in relation to the operation of the local church.[96] Previously, on two occasions between 1653 and 1656, James had lost goods, including one yoke of oxen, for tithe refusal.[97] Edward Morgan, husband of signatory Elizabeth (whom Henry Cromwell had imprisoned), suffered because of his faith numerous times in the 1650s. In 1653, he went to gaol for nine weeks for attending a Quaker meeting.[98] Some time later, a Quaker named Edmond Ogden challenged a minister after a sermon, and apparently as a 'guilt-by-association' punishment, the angry mayor brought Morgan out of his own house and imprisoned him (as well as Ogden himself) for Ogden's impertinence.[99] Again, at some unspecified time between 1653 and 1656, this same mayor, Richard Bird (or Burd), threw Morgan into prison for apparently no other reason than that the official saw the Quaker walking down the street.[100] In 1656, Morgan complained "to the Mayor against a Servant who had robbed him, but refusing to Swear, the Mayor discharged the Thief, and sent Edward himself to Prison, where he was detained eleven Weeks, and then privately released".[101] The next year, 1657, he had another unfortunate encounter with the mayor when he complained to the official about "a drunken Fellow, who had grossly abused him, [and] was sent to *Little Ease* for not pulling off his Hat when he made that Complaint, and the drunkard went unpunished".[102] The gross abuse involved Joh. [John?] Fletcher, "a notorious common drunkard known to be all the City over... [who] came and called Edw. Morgan Cuckold, and his Wife a Whore in the presence of many people, and railed so on Edw. that he could not in

---

[96] Besse, *Collection of the Sufferings*, vol. 1, 102. In 1648, James and Ellin Browne had a son named James, then a daughter, Elin, in 1653 (Digested Copy of the Registers of Births of the Quarterly Meeting of Cheshire and Staffordshire, Book 217:1).

[97] Hutchins, *Caines Bloudy Race*, 78.

[98] Hutchins, *Caines Bloudy Race*, 39; Besse, *Collection of the Sufferings*, vol. 1, 99.

[99] Hutchins, *Caines Bloudy Race*, 41–42.

[100] Hutchins, *Caines Bloudy Race*, 42.

[101] Besse, *Collection of the Sufferings*, vol. 1, 100; see also Hutchins, *Caines Bloudy Race*, 45–49.

[102] Besse, *Collection of the Sufferings*, vol. 1, 101. The account in Hutchins differs slightly from Besse's account, having Morgan thrown into Little Ease for refusing to swear when he made his complaint (*Caines Bloudy Race*, 60–61, 74).

quiet follow his imployment...."[103] Morgan appears again in 1670 as a person who suffered greatly under the Conventicle Act when officers distressed goods "five or six Times the Value of the fines".[104]

Signatory Mary Burtonwood and her husband Henry were members of Cheshire Monthly Meeting, and Henry had a long history of tithe resistance that Mary seems to have supported. During the period 1653 to 1656, Henry lost three cows to the local parish minister, which were worth roughly three times what he owed in tithes. Previously he had lost another cow to the same minister for tithe-payment refusal.[105] Mary may already have been married to Henry during this period and hence felt the loss of these goods directly, because Quaker records list them as having buried a daughter, Mary, in 1657, and as parents to Samuel (b. 1655) and another Mary (b. 1658). They resided in Ashton, a village seven miles northeast of Chester.[106] Similarly, William Sarret had goods taken worth £5 10s. for failure to provide tithe-corn worth £1 6s. 8d., and spent seven weeks in prison for his resistance.[107] The exact date of this incident is uncertain, but around the same period (1655) he and his wife Eliz[abeth] became parents to a son named John.[108] Elizabeth was a signatory to the petition, and a few months after signing it she once again gave birth to a son whom they named John.[109] (Probably the earlier son died, but no records indicate this.) Elizabeth suffered distraint in 1683 for tithe refusal, and in the next

---

[103] Hutchins, *Caines Bloudy Race*, 60–61.

[104] Besse, *Collection of the Sufferings*, vol. 1, 105. "[T]he Conventicle Act of 1664 struck at the rank and file of nonconformity. Any one over 16 years of age apprehended at a meeting held under pretext of religious worship but not conducted according to the liturgy of the Church of England became subject to the penalties of the Act, provided that more than five persons other than members of the household were present. In the first instance the punishment was to be three months' imprisonment or a fine of not more than five pounds; for a second offence the penalties were doubled; on the third occasion, after a trial by jury, the accused was to be sentenced to transportation for seven years to one of the American colonies, Virginia and New England excepted" (Gerald Cragg, *Puritanism in the Period of the Great Persecution, 1660–1688* [Cambridge: Cambridge University Press, 1957], 11–12).

[105] Hutchins, *Caines Bloudy Race*, 77; *These Several PAPERS*, 22.

[106] Digested Copy of the Registers of Burials of the Quarterly Meeting of Cheshire and Staffordshire, Book 218:3; Digested Copy of the Registers of Births of the Quarterly Meeting of Cheshire and Staffordshire, Book 217:1, 3.

[107] Hutchins, *Caines Bloudy Race*, 78.

[108] Digested Copy of the Registers of Births of the Quarterly Meeting of Cheshire and Staffordshire, Book 217:1.

[109] *These Several PAPERS*, 22; Digested Copy of the Registers of Births of the Quarterly Meeting of Cheshire and Staffordshire, Book 217:5.

year she suffered substantial goods-confiscation (worth £17 8s.) for her absence from the national worship.[110]

An interesting commentary appeared in a Quaker account of the goods-confiscation suffered by Hugh Strettle during the mid-1650s. (Unfortunately, the text gave no dates for the incidents, but subsequent scholarship determined that all of them occurred between 1653 and 1656.)[111] According to the account,

> Hugh Strettle for tythe-Corn of the value of 11s. 6d. Had taken from him by two Justice Writs, two Sacks of Oats worth 1£ 8s. and the Constable of the Town being troubled at it, asked the priest how he took so much, seeing he professed not to take trebble [triple] damage of any: The Priest answered, That it cost him so much in Justices Dinners, and their men, for Warrants, and for a Judgment....[112]

Presumably Strettle could have used those sacks of oats, since in 1655 his wife Mary gave birth to a son, James, and then in 1657 to another son, Amos. Mary (spelling her surname as "Strettel") included her name on the 1659 petition.[113]

Finally, and in addition to several husbands already discussed, John Falkner (husband of probable signatory Margret) was imprisoned six months for attending a Quaker meeting in 1666 at Thomas Janney's house.[114] James Harrison, who was married to signatory Ann, lost goods valued at £28 18s. over his refusal to pay tithes in 1663, and three years later spent five months in gaol for attending a Quaker meeting.[115]

The Cheshire petition carried by far the most signatures of the two that I examined here, and what is striking about it, and was also true of the Lincolnshire petition, was the number of women in the same families who signed it. This petition contained thirty-two clusters of two or more consecutively listed people with the same surnames (seven

---

[110] Besse, *Collection of the Sufferings*, vol. 1, 110, 111. As an aside, Elizabeth appears to have had a long life, with her death not being recorded until 1712 (Digested Copy of the Registers of Burials of the Quarterly Meeting of Cheshire and Staffordshire, Book 218:109).

[111] S.B., "Quakers in Chester", 10.

[112] Hutchins, *Caines Bloudy Race*, 80.

[113] Digested Copy of the Registers of Births of the Quarterly Meeting of Cheshire and Staffordshire, Book 217:3, Book 232:152, Book 222:151, and Book 217:1; *These Several PAPERS*, 24.

[114] *These Several PAPERS*, 25; Besse, *Collection of the Sufferings*, vol. 1, 104. Cheshire Records Office, Nantwich Parish Register 1 has John Faulkner marrying a widow named Margret Knevit on 7 April 1648.

[115] Besse, *Collection of the Sufferings*, vol. 1, 104.

consecutive names in the case of the 'Worthington' signatories) which suggests that relatives—mothers and daughters, sisters, or other relatives sharing the same name—expressed together their opposition to tithes.[116] By no means should we assume that all (or in some cases, any) of the women within each cluster of surnames were necessarily Quakers, since women within families could have shared opposition to tithes but not been involved in the Quaker faith. These clusters of names, however, suggest that tithe opposition was strong among the women of many families, and that their shared experience of kinship and gender gave them a common basis for opposing tithes, possibly across denominational and sectarian lines.

Conclusion

Despite inevitable imprecision, these findings allow us to make a few observations about both the signatories and their possible meaning for Quaker history. First, the large percentage of apparent non-Quakers who signed the 1659 petition strongly suggests that many Baptists, extreme Independents, and members of various sects like the Fifth Monarchists affixed their names in these two shires.[117] Based upon available evidence, only about 50% of the signatories to the petition in Lincoln appear in Quaker records, as do only about 35% of the names in the Cheshire petition (see Tables 1 and 3, and Appendices A and B). Isabel Ross's belief, shared by Barry Reay and Stevie Davies, that the "7,000 Handmaids" petition contains strictly Quaker names therefore seems unlikely, however true it may be for some shires. More appropriate seems to be Maureen Bell's conclusion about it, which is that

> [t]here is at least a suggestion here that the petition might provide evidence of a common cause between different sects in the summer of 1659 and of the way in which a shared political objective, for sectarian women at least, might cut across the boundaries separating sects which were in other respects hostile to each other.[118]

Tithe-opposition cut across several theological boundaries, and some women may have realized the heightened vulnerability that destitute

---

[116] Lincolnshire had seven clusters of two or more consecutive surnames.
[117] See Michael R. Watts, *The Dissenters* (Oxford: Clarendon Press, 1978), 151.
[118] Bell, "Mary Westwood", 25.

widows faced when having to meet tithe obligations. Moreover, tithe-payment burdened everyone whose families had to pay them, so it is likely that a number of relatives and friends supported the Quakers' anti-tithe efforts while continuing to pay them themselves. As historian Barry Reay pointed out, "[w]hen a [Q]uaker labourer was imprisoned in 1658 for small tithes the townspeople of Leverton in Lincolnshire paid the amount due and he was let free". Likewise, Reay said Wiltshire and Somerset records suggest that sometimes neighbours harvested the crops of Quakers who were imprisoned because of their opposition to tithes.[119] Clearly, therefore, non-Quakers in various communities either shared Quakers' hostilities to tithe-payment, or felt driven by friendship or family ties to support them in their efforts. Social radicals like the Quakers "saw tithes as the issue which could unite the concerns of the rural population with the religious programme of the separatists".[120]

Second, researchers must wonder about how many women were partners with their spouses in tithe-resistance but whose contributions were buried by patriarchal assumptions among the recorders of early Quaker history (see Tables 2 and 4). In the best of moments, records from the first decades of Quakerism are uneven in their quality and quantity (although far better than other Interregnum and Restoration groups), and many women's stories have likely been lost. Most tithe-sufferings records, for example, describe the punishment that occurred to the man of the household when he refused tithe payment, yet the distraints and property confiscations that subsequently befell him certainly impacted his wife along with other family members. One wonders about the extent to which women's suffering in domestic settings remains lost to the historian's gaze. Reading, however, the extant accounts of the Quaker women who suffered and occasionally died opposing tithes, it becomes clear that their numerous acts of resistance were simultaneously socio-political, religious, and deeply personal.

Third, analyses of persons' names in relation to the geographical locations in which they lived might reveal significant patterns about the collection of the signatures. Women who were supportive of the anti-tithe campaign may not have signed the petitions simply because the name-collectors did not get to particular sections of the shires or collect at particular Quaker, Independent, or Baptist meetings. While

---

[119] Reay, "Quaker Opposition", 113.
[120] Brace, *The Idea of Property*, 49.

collecting signatures at religious services would have been the most efficient way to gather names, we simply do not know who did the collecting and how they did it. Moreover, it seems impossible for us ever to know anything about most of the signatories, and their names in the petition may be the only historical evidence that these women ever lived, struggled, and died.

Appendices

Appendix A: the Relationships Between Lincolnshire's 1659 Signatories and Quakerism

(Names [totalling 180] taken from *These Several PAPERS*, 32–33)

a: Surnames and Names (4) that Possibly Appear in Pre-Signing Quaker Records:
Makaril, Katharine; Makaril, Katheren; Marshall, Hollen; Thorton, Anne

b: Names (0) that Probably Appear in Pre-Signing Quaker Records:

c: Names (10) that Certainly Appear in Pre-Signing Quaker Records and 1659 Records Without a Specified Month:
Ashley, Margaret; Davie, Elizabeth; Fotherby, Sarah; Frotheringham, A.; Garland, Mary; Harrison, Jane; Harvey, Anne; Thorton, Anne; Whitman, Susanna; Wright, Martha

d: Surnames and Names (23) that Possibly Appear in Post-Signing Quaker Records:
Bainton, Eliz.; Berrier, Anne; Berrier, Mary; Boot, Eliz.; Brown, Anna; Carie, Didolis; Crosby, Anne; Cussons, Susanna; Fisher, Anne; Foster, Anne; Mathews, Elizabeth; Morris, Anne; Pheasant, Anne; Pheasant, Anne; Pheasant, Mary; Phillips, Jane; Rosse, Anne; Rose, Mary; Trueblood, Mary; Waterfal, Anne; Waterfool, Eliz.; Waterfal, Elizabeth; Williamson, Eliz.

e: Names (36) that Probably Appear in Post-Signing Quaker Records:
Barnard, Eliz.; Beck, Anne; Billidge, Susanna; Clark, Eliz.; Fisher, Prudens; Foster, Mary; Gathorn, Eliz.; Gibson, Mary; Greswel, Mary; Harpham, Eliz.; Harrison, Eliz.; Hempsted, Mary; Higham, Eliz.;

Hobson, Anne; Holland, Susanna; Makepeace, Anne; Manby, Anne; Maple, Mary; Northern, Anne; Northern, Eliz.; Northern, Sence; Parker, Anne; Parker, Eliz.; Robinson, Eliz.; Scot, Mary; Sharp, Alice; Smith, Eliz.; Robinson, Eliz.; Scot, Mary; Sharp, Alice; Smith, Eliz.; Smith, Eliz., junior; Smith, Ellen; Smith, Mary; Sowter, Mary; Spain, Anne; Turner, Mary; West, Eliz.; White, Bridget; Winsor, Alice

f: Names (21) That Certainly Appear in Post-Signing Quaker Records:
Armstrong, Dorothy; Chapman, Cassandra; Hempsted, Jane; Hooton, Ursala; Hudson, Mary; Hutchinson, Eliz.; Jackson, Eliz.; Leverton, Anne; Marshal, Eliz.; Mell, Dorcas; Northern, Mary; Oliver, Mary; Parker, Mary; Pid, Anne; Pid, Eliz.; Pid, Kath.; Recket, Anne; Smith, Margaret; Tate, Alice; Teff, Martha; Wilson, Ellen

g: Surnames and Names (0) That Possibly Do Not Appear in Quaker Records:

h: Surnames and Names (5) that Probably Do Not Appear in Quaker Records:
Brumby, Ellen; Classon, Sarah; Mason, Eliz.; Mosse, Sarah; Wilson, Mary

i: Surnames and Names (81) that Do Not Appear in Quaker Records:
Bagaley, Anne; Beck, Alice; Beck, Rachel; Bellamy, Anne; Blackney, Mary; Brinckler, Alice; Burroughs, Ursala; Chandler, Mary; Chanler, Mary; Cook, Anne; Crosby, Mary; Cussons, Mary; Darlinton, Margret; Day, Rebecka; Dounham, Margret; Drury, Isabel; Fletcher, Eliz.; Foster, Dorothy; Foster, Ellen; Freestone, Anne; Garton, Anne; Gaskin, Eliz.; Gaunt, Anne; Gaunt, Ellen; Gibson, Ellenor; Gilliot, Ellin; Haigham, Elizabeth; Haldenby, Anne; Harris, Anne; Hart, Ester; Hempsted, Anne; Hird, Anne; Hobson, Eliz.; Hobson, Frances; Jarnil, Eliz.; Johnson, Anne; Kirk, Eliz.; Kirk, Sarah; Lee, Eliz.; Lightfoot, Jane; Lumkin, Mary; Marston, Margret; Milner, Anne; Norton, Thomasin; Otter, Sarah; Packins, Mary; Pannel, Ruth; Parrot, Susanna; Pickaver, Dorothy; Pickaver, Katherine; Preston, Jane; Rawbuck, Dorothy; Robinson, Grace; Rogers, Eliz.; Sanders, Jane; Scot, Grace; Seagrave, Frances; Seaton, Hannah; Sharp, Anne; Sherman, Anne; Shoreman, Anne; Smith, Susan; Stelworth, Anne; Stoker, Anne; Streaton, Alice; Swayer, Katheren; Thistleton, Mary; Thomlinson, Anne; Thompson, Sarah; Thorton, Rebecca; Torksey, Susanna; Trevis, Mary; Turington, Bridget; Westwood, Jone; White, Mary; Whiteworth, Anna; Wilkinson, Elizabeth; Wilkinson, Jane; Winch, Anne; Woolsey, Eliz.; Wray, Eliz.

*Appendix B: The Relationships Between Cheshire's 1659
Signatories and Quakerism*

(Names [totalling 449] taken from *These Several PAPERS*, 21–25)

*a: Surnames and Names (4) that Possibly Appear in Pre-Signing Quaker
Records:*
Baddeley, Eliz.; Baddeley, Margret; Hitchcock, Ursala; Janyou, Anne

b: Names (20) that Probably Appear in Pre-Signing Quaker Records:
Andrews, Kathern; Ashbrook, Eliz.; Clare, Mary; Edge, Jone; Falkner,
Margret; Hall, Eliz.; Hall, Eliz.; Heeld, Anne; Heeld, Elizabeth;
Heeld, Margret; Higenson, Margret; Monk, Margret; Moor, Eliz.;
Pot, Mary; Pot, Mary: Royl, Margret; Steward, Elin; Strach, Mary;
Sudlow, Elizabeth; Wyrral, Eliza

*c: Names (28) that Certainly Appear in Pre-Signing Quaker Records and 1659
Records Without a Specified Month:*
Alcock, Ellen; Boulton, Sarah; Bradbury, Eliz; Bradford, Mary; Brad-
ford, Mary; Brock, Mary; Brown, Elin; Burtonwood, Mary; Bushel,
Deborah; Cleaton, Cisly; Endon, Mary; Harrison, Ann; Hobson,
Elizabeth; Hough, Sebel; Janney, Ann Senior; Maddock, Deborah;
Milner, Ann; Milner, Mary; Morgan, Eliz.; Parker, Margret; Pritchard,
Mary; Sarrat, Eliz.; Shield, Constant; Smith, Alice; Smith, Eliz.;
Stretch, Ellin; Strettel, Mary; Wood, Margret

*d: Surnames and Names (10) that Possibly Appear in Post-Signing Quaker
Records:*
Baker, Margret; Baker, Margret; Barker, Elliner; Bradshaw, Sarah;
Crosby, Kathern; Eaton, Kathern; Jackson, Mary; Lamb, Elizabeth;
Painter, Juliana; Parcival, Widdow

e: Names (52) that Probably Appear in Post-Signing Quaker Records:
Amery, Anne; Barker, Margret; Barker, Margret; Baxter, Elin;
Boare, Ann; Briggs, Eliz.; Brown, Sarah; Burges, Elizabeth; Burges,
Elizabeth; Burges, Ellen; Burges, Margery; Burges, Margret; Burgess,
Ellen elder; Cawly, Mary; Chorley, Eliz.; Crosby, Eliz.; Crosby, Eliz.;
Croxton, Eliz.; Davenport, Alice; Hall, Mary; Hall, Mary; Hill,
Kathern; Hucksly, Jane; Janney, Martha; Janney, Mary; Janney, Mary;
Jones, Elin; Lamb, Ann; Lewis, Eliz.; Loanes, Mary; Lownds, Jane;

Maddock, Anne; Miller, Mary; Milner, Eliz.; More, Jane; Moreton, Anne; Mosse, Alice; Oakes, Margery; Owen, Sarah; Pickring, Eliz.; Pickring, Elizabeth; Pickring, Mary; Rowland, Margret; Shaw, Ellin; Shaw, Mary; Shepherd, Kathern; Smith, Mary; Smith, Mary; Stoniard, Eliz.; Swan, Eliz.; Touchet, Margret; Wardley, Anne

f: Names (41) That Certainly Appear in Post-Signing Quaker Records:
Armit, Fran.; Ashton, Elizabeth; Barker, Ellinor; Bower, Anne; Buckly, Alice; Bushel, Eliz.; Bushel, Eliz.; Cash, Mary; Challiner, Alice; Coppock, Margret; Coppock, Margret; Davenport, Mary; Deen, Dorothy; Hall, Hester; Hand, Dorothy; Hare, Dorothy; Hatton, Eliz.; Holm, Joan; Key, Mary; Lownds, Margery; Marbury, Hannah; Marsland, Anne; Pass, Eliz.; Pickring, Margret; Pickring, Margret; Rylance, Kathern; Sarrat, Anne; Sharples, Margery; Sharples, Mary; Sheild, Ann; Steel, Dorothy; Taylor, Alice; Taylor, Mary; Walley; Alice; Worthington, Frances; Worthington, Martha; Worthington, Mary; Worthington, Mary; Worthington, Mary; Worthington, Sarah; Yarwood, Margret

g: Surnames and Names (14) That Possibly Do Not Appear in Quaker Records:
Buckly, Amy; Burges, Alice; Dicks, Anne; Eaton, Margery; Eaton, Margret; Furnifall, Katheren; Gandy, Elizabeth; Hatton, Ellinor; Hatton, Katherin; Hatton, Priscilla; Hignet, Alice; Pearson, Cisly; Peirson, Elizabeth; Simpson, Ann

h: Surnames and Names (9) that Probably Do Not Appear in Quaker Records:
Crosby, Elin; Croxton, Mary; Griffeth, Eliz.; Greffeth, Mary; Hill, Jone; Hill, Mary; Hill, Sarah; Janney, Elizabeth; Ridgway, Alice

i: Surnames and Names (271) that Do Not Appear in Quaker Records:
Adlington, Eliz.; Alexander, Dorothy; Allen, Dorothy; Anderton, Elin; Anderton, Eliza.; Anderton, Kathern; Anderton, Mary; Andrews, Eliz.; Andrews, Jane; Antrobus, Elin; Armstrong, Joan; Arnefield, Hester; Arstenstal, Ellen; Astel, Eliz.; Baker, Anne; Baker, Hannah; Barrow, Margret; Bealy, Ellen; Bealy, Margret; Beard, Sibel; Beck, Kathern; Becket, Ann; Beely, Mary; Beeston, Eliz.; Berrington, Mercy; Berry, Ann; Bertles, Elin; Bettily, Anne; Blemily, Anne; Booth, Dorothy; Bostock, Mary; Boulton, Elin; Bowdon, Elizabeth; Bowler, Ann; Bradshaw, Eliz.; Bradshaw, Mary; Bramal, Ann; Bramal, Elizabeth; Bretton, Marget; Brierwood, Kathern; Brierwood,

Mary; Bristoe, Eliz.; Broadhouse, Margret; Browant, Mary; Brown, Anne; Brown, Grace; Brownant, Eliz.; Brownant, Mary; Brumbly, Hester; Burdiken, Jane; Bushel, Mary; Buttely, Eliza.; Candwel, Margret; Carrington, Ellin; Cartwright, Margret; Cash, Anne; Chanler, Jane; Chorley, Margret; Colley, Jane; Cook, Ellin; Cordal, Margret; Cotgrean, Ellinor; Court, Sarah; Cowley, Eliz.; Crabb, Priscilla; Crosby, Hannah; Davenport, Elin; Dawson, Ellin; Dawson, Mary; Deakin, Jane; Dewsberry, Ellinor; Dewsberry, Margret; Ducker, Eliz.; Dunbabin, Jane; Dunbabir, Margret; Ellet, Grace; Falkner, Eliz.; Evans, Eliz.; Felor, Elizabeth; Felor, Sibel; Fisher, Mary; Forrest, Elnor; Foxley, Katheren; Frinson, Anne; Fryer, Eliz.; Garnet, Margret; Gatlist, Margret; Gerrard, Mary; Ghorst, Sarah; Gilbert, Mary; Glover, Elizabeth; Glover, Ellin; Goulden, Elizabeth; Grange, Ellin; Gravener, Jane; Graves, Mary; Green, Eliz.; Green, Mary; Hale, Eliz.; Hall, Ann; Hall, Elin; Hall, Elin; Hall, Ellin; Hampton, Jone; Hamsley, Mary; Hamson, Margret; Hare, Jane; Hare, Mary; Harrup, Margret; Hasel, Eliz.; Hasfort, Mary; Hasul, Margret; Haywort, Amy; Heath, Margery; Hilbert, Elizabeth; Hibert, Mary; Hide, Ellin; Hitchin, Margery; Hitchinson, Kathern; Hollenshed, Ellen; Holm, Ann; Holm, Ellin; Holm, Rebecca; Holm, Margret; Hoyd, Elizabeth; Husall, Eliz.; Hutton, Eliz.; Jackson, Jane; Jamon, Mary; Johnson, Alice; Johnson, Anne; Jones, Alice; Kalshaw, Kathern; Kelshal, Eliz.; Kerkcum, Katheren; Kilshaw, Eliz.; Lagh, Isabel; Ledsome, Anne; Leech, Elizabeth; Leigh, Ann; Leigh, Mary; Liversticke, Susanna; Lloyd, Dorothy; Lloyd, Jane; Lloyd, Margret; Loranson, Ann; Lounds, Anne; Lownds, Alice; Maddock, Sarah; Maddocks, Susanna; Madley, Kathern; Mallory, Mary; Mear, Dorothy; Mear, Eliz.; Meer, Margret; Mercer, Sarah; Midlehurst, Margret; Miller, Jane; Miller, Margret; Millington, Anne; Millington, Katheren; Millington, Mary; Millor, Alice; Mills, Kathern; Milner, Margret; Moberly, Elin; Moberly, Eliz.; Moreton, Eliz.; Moreton, Margret; Morral, Elizabeth; Morrice, Eliz.; Morrice, Mary; Mountford, Mary; Naylor, Dorothy; Newby, Elizabeth; Nicklas, Jane; Nicholas, Alice; Nicholas, Jane; Nicson, Elin; Norman, Margret; Oussoncroft, Anne; Owen, Martha; Owen, Margery; Pasley, Alice; Perrin, Eliz.; Perrin, Lettice; Picker, Ellin; Picker, Margaret; Pickring, Alice; Pike, Anne; Pike, Eliz.; Pike, Mary; Plant, Isabel; Pownal, Margret; Pownal, Mary; Preston, Elin; Pricket, Ermine; Probbin, Fran.; Read, Anne; Ridgway, Margret; Robinson, Elizabeth; Rowbottom, Ann; Rowlison, Elinor; Royle, Frances; Ryther, Kathren; Sanders, Alice; Sanderson,

Mary; Sanky, Margret; Sargeant, Darcas; Sarrat, Eliz; Sergeant, Hannah; Shak-shaff, Alice; Sharples, Anne; Shaw, Hester; Shaw, Jane; Shaw, Rebecca; Sheart, Kathren; Sheply, Elizabeth; Sibert, Anne; Sikes, Sibel; Simcock, Widdow; Skelton, Fran.; Stockley, Katheren; Stringer, Eliz.; Suddern, Mary; Sutton, Ann; Swan, Mary; Taylor, Tomasine; Thorncroft, Isabel; Thorncroft, Sarah; Tomasin, Mary; Tomlisson, Dorothy; Tomlisson, Fran.; Tomlisson, Jane; Tomlisson, Jane; Tomlisson, Margret; Tomlisson, Mary; Tomson, Anne; Tumkin, Dorothy; Underwood, Elinor; Underwood, Margaret; Vandrey, Mary; Walker, Fran.; Walker, Kathern; Warrington, Margret; Warrington, Mary; Warton, Mary; Watmore, Hannah; Weaver, Eliz.; Wharmbee, Lydia; Whitakers, Elin; Whitcars, Cisly; Widart, Eliz.; Widdens, Alice; Williams, Margaret; Williams, Mary; Williamson, Elin; Williamson, Martha; Wooly, Margaret; Wood, Eliz.; Wood, Elizabeth; Wood, Jone; Wooker, Anne; Worthington, Anna; Worthington, Elizab.; Woyd, Ann; Yardly, Dorothy; Yardly, Eliz.; Yardly, Fran.; Yate, Eliz.; Yayler, Eliz.

Bibliography

Manuscript Sources

Cheshire Sources
MF [Microfilm] 63/1 [Wilmslow]. St Bartholomews' Early Registers 1558–1667. Cheshire Records Office.
"Dictionary of Quaker Biography". Unpublished Files, Library of the Religious Society of Friends, London.
Digested Copy of the Registers of Births of the Quarterly Meeting of Cheshire and Staffordshire [1647/8–1837]. Library of the Religious Society of Friends, London.
Digested Copy of the Registers of Burials of the Quarterly Meeting of Cheshire and Staffordshire [1655–1837]. Library of the Religious Society of Friends, London.
Nantwich Parish Register, vols. 1–5. Transcribed. Library of the Religious Society of Friends, London.

Lincolnshire Sources
Harold W. Brace Cards. Index of Quaker Names. Lincolnshire Records Office.
Index of Names. Lincolnshire Records Office.
2 Brace 3. Clerk of Monthly Meeting, Society of Friends in Lincolnshire. Harold W. Brace Collection. #66 6600–6699. (Spalding Monthly). Lincolnshire Records Office.
Digested Copy of the Registers of Births of the Quarterly Meeting of Lincolnshire [1632–1837]. Library of the Religious Society of Friends, London.
Digested Copy of the Registers of Burials of the Quarterly Meeting of Lincolnshire [1656–1837]. Library of the Religious Society of Friends, London.
Digested Copy of the Registers of Marriages of the Quarterly Meeting of Lincolnshire [1657–1836]. Library of the Religious Society of Friends, London.

Digested Copy of Supplement Registers of Marriages, Births, and Burials of the Quarterly Meeting of Lincolnshire [1618 (sic) to 1672]. Library of the Religious Society of Friends, London.

Printed Sources

Adamson, J. H. and H. F. Folland. *Sir Henry Vane: His Life and Times (1613–1662)*. Boston: Gambit, 1973.

Anderson, Bonnie S. and Judith P. Zinsser. *A History of Their Own: Women in Europe from Prehistory to the Present*. 2 vols. New York: Harper & Row, 1988.

B., S. "Quakers in Chester 1653–1656". *The Cheshire Sheaf* 5 (January–December 1970): 9–28.

Barbour, Hugh. *The Quakers in Puritan England*. New Haven: Yale University Press, 1964.

Bell, Maureen. "Mary Westwood Quaker Publisher". *Publishing History* 23 (1988): 5–66.

Besse, Joseph. *A Collection of the Sufferings of the People Called Quakers*. 2 vols. London: Luke Hinde, 1753.

Brace, Laura. *The Idea of Property in Seventeenth-Century England: Tithes and the Individual*. Manchester: Manchester University Press, 1998.

Braithwaite, William C. *The Beginnings of Quakerism*. 2nd ed., revised by Henry J. Cadbury. Cambridge: Cambridge University Press, 1961.

Clark, Alice. *Working Life of Women in the Seventeenth Century*. Introduction by Miranda Chaytor and Jane Lewis. London: Routledge & Kegan Paul, 1982.

The Copie of A Paper Presented to the Parliament: And Read the 27th of the fourth Moneth, 1659. Subscribed by more than fifteen thousand hands. Thus Directed: To the Parliament of England, from many thousand of the free-born people of this Common-Wealth. London, Giles Calvert, 1659, Thomason/147:E.988[24].

Cragg, Gerald. *Puritanism in the Period of the Great Persecution 1660–1688*. Cambridge: Cambridge University Press, 1957.

Davies, Stevie. *Unbridled Spirits: Women of the English Revolution: 1640–1660*. London: The Women's Press, 1998.

Fox, George. *The Journal of George Fox*. Edited by Norman Penney. 2 vols. 1911. Reprint, New York: Octagon Press, 1973.

Hill, Christopher. *Economic Problems of the Church: From Archbishop Whitgift to the Long Parliament*. Oxford: Clarendon Press, 1956.

The Humble Petition of Many Well-affected Persons of Somerset, Wilts, and Some Part of Devon, Dorset and Hampshire, to the Parliament of the Commonwealth of England, Against Tithes. Together with the Parliaments Answer Thereunto, and Resolves Thereupon. London: Livewel Chapman, 1659.

Hutchins, Anthony. *Caines Bloudy Race Known by Their Fruits. Or, a True Declaration of the Innocent Sufferings of the Servants of the Living God*. London: Thomas Simmons, 1657. Reprinted in F. Sanders, "The Quakers in Chester Under the Protectorate". *Chester Archaeological Society Journal* n.s. XIV (1908): 29–84.

Hutton, Ronald. *The Restoration: A Political and Religious History of England and Wales, 1658–1667*. Oxford: Clarendon Press, 1985.

Ingle, H. Larry. *First Among Friends: George Fox and the Creation of Quakerism*. Oxford: Oxford University Press, 1994.

Kunze, Bonnelyn Young. *Margaret Fell and the Rise of Quakerism*. Stanford: Stanford University Press, 1994.

Mack, Phyllis. "Gender and Spirituality in Early English Quakerism, 1650–1665". In *Witnesses for Change: Quaker Women over Three Centuries*, edited by Elisabeth Potts Brown and Susan Mosher Stuard. New Brunswick: Rutgers University Press, 1989.

——. *Visionary Women: Ecstatic Prophecy in Seventeenth Century England*. Berkeley: University of California Press, 1992.

Penney, Norman, ed. *The First Publishers of Truth*. London: Headley Brothers, 1907.

Reay, Barry. "Quaker Opposition to Tithes, 1652–1660". *Past and Present* 86 (February 1980): 98–120.

——. "The Quakers, 1659, and the Restoration of the Monarchy". *History* 63 (1978): 193–213.

Roberts, Michael. "'Words They are Women, and Deeds They are Men': Images of Work and Gender in Early Modern England". In *Women and Work in Pre-Industrial England*, edited by Lindsey Charles and Lorna Duffin. London: Croom Helm, 1985.

Ross, Isabel. *Margaret Fell: Mother of Quakerism*. New York: Longmans, Green and Co., 1949.

Rowe, Violet A. *Sir Henry Vane the Younger: A Study in Political and Administrative History*. London: Athlone Press, 1970.

Spufford, Margaret. "First Steps in Literacy: The Reading and Writing Experiences of the Humblest Seventeenth Century Spiritual Autobiographers". *History* 4, no. 3 (October 1979): 407–35.

These several PAPERS Was [sic] sent to the PARLIAMENT the twentieth day of the fifth Moneth, 1659. Being above seven thousand of the Names of the HAND-MAIDS AND DAUGHTERS OF THE LORD, And Such as feels the Oppression of Tithes. London: Mary Westwood, 1659.

Thomason, George. *Catalogue of the Pamphlets, Books, Newspapers, and Manuscripts Relating to the Civil War, the Commonwealth, and Restoration, Collected by George Thomason, 1640–1661*. 1908. Reprint, Nendeln, Liechtenstein: Kraus Reprint, 1961.

Watts, Michael R. *The Dissenters*. Oxford: Clarendon Press, 1978.

"TRULY DEAR HEARTS":[1] FAMILY AND SPIRITUALITY IN QUAKER WOMEN'S WRITINGS 1680–1750

Sheila Wright

Quaker women and their spiritual writings in this period have been awarded a great deal of attention by historians, but their familial relationships have received less attention.[2] In this chapter I want to explore how Quaker women represent themselves and their spirituality in relation to their family in their writing. Using the private correspondence, diaries, and published journals of a group of Quaker women, the majority of whom were ministers, I will suggest that for Quaker women their relationships with their family were directly connected to and inter-linked with their spirituality.[3] Their spirituality influenced and guided the way they represented their inter-familial relationships, and as Rebecca Larson suggested "brought about redefinitions of familial roles".[4] Friends' concept of family was rooted in the 1656 Epistle from the Elders of Balby. Clauses in this document dealt with all aspects of the Society of Friends, but, specifically, clauses seven to nine dealt with marriage and family relationships.[5] Out of this document developed a highly institutionalised idealism for the conduct of the personal lives

---

[1] "The Journal of Susanna Morris, 1682–1755", in *Wilt Thou Go on My Errand?: Journals of Three 18th Century Quaker Women Ministers*, ed. Margaret Hope Bacon (Wallingford, Pa.: Pendle Hill Publications, 1994), 76. Morris used this term of endearment repeatedly in her letters to her children.

[2] See Phyllis Mack, *Visionary Women: Ecstatic Prophecy in Seventeenth Century England* (Berkeley: University of California Press, 1992); Christine Trevett, *Women and Quakerism in the 17th Century* (York: Sessions Book Trust, The Ebor Press, 1991); Rosemary Moore, *The Light in their Consciences: Early Quakers in Britain 1646–1666* (University Park, Pa.: The Pennsylvania University Press, 2000); Elaine Hobby, *Virtue of Necessity: English Women's Writing 1649–88* (London: Virago, 1988). For a later period, see Camilla Leach, "Quaker Women and Education from the Late Eighteenth to the Mid-Nineteenth Century" (Ph.D. diss., King Alfred's College, Winchester, 2003).

[3] Many of the original texts have been lost and I have had to use some much edited and consequently, homogenised versions; in particular, the thirteen volumes of Quaker journals edited by William and Thomas Evans in the nineteenth century.

[4] Rebecca Larson, *Daughters of Light: Quaker Women Preaching and Prophesying in the Colonies and Abroad, 1700–1775* (New York: Knopf, 1999), 134.

[5] Epistle from the Elders at Balby, 1656, Papers of Marsden Monthly Meeting, FRM 1/39, Lancashire Record Office.

of members, giving the Society its distinctive paradigms of family and creating a more specific and extended concept of family than was generally the case in secular society in the late-seventeenth and early-eighteenth century. As a consequence, the Meeting formed an extended family subject to regulation along familial lines, creating in Friends a sense of belonging to a larger, wider group than their immediate kinship network. For women ministers especially, the 'extended' Quaker family influenced the way in which they viewed both their own families as well as the 'family' of the Meeting.[6] One of the most frequent manifestations of this concept was the archetypal 'Mother in Israel' who, as Phyllis Mack has suggested, "made the transition between ecstasy and sanctified daily life at least a partial reality".[7] Margaret Fell was deemed by Quakers to be the original 'Mother in Israel', but successive, experienced Quaker women ministers were to a greater or lesser extent endowed with a 'mother' role within the Meeting and particularly in the nurturing of inexperienced women ministers.[8] This emphasis on the 'mother' as a quasi-universal protector of the family of the Meeting, and indeed the whole Society, gave added meaning to the maternal role. It raised the position of women both within the Quaker home and within Quaker society by emphasising their responsibility for not only achieving a high level of spirituality for their own family and their adherence to the tenets of Quakerism but also the spirituality and behaviour of members of the Meeting.

The journals used for this chapter were either published or written between 1680 and 1750 and are not limited to any specific group of Quaker women, but the majority, if not all, Quaker journals were written by, or contain the writings of, deceased ministers.[9] Although

---

[6] Leach, "Quaker Women and Education", 69–74.

[7] For a discussion of the significance of the Mother in Israel concept, see Mack, *Visionary Women*, 215–35, 287–93; Larson, *Daughters of Light*, 164.

[8] Young Quaker women ministers referred to experienced ministers as 'Mothers in Israel'. Joan Vokins was "a nursing mother over the young convinced". See Elspeth Graham et al., eds., *Her Own Life: Autobiographical Writings by Seventeenth-Century English-women* (London: Routledge, 1989), 211. Sarah Stephenson described Catherine Phillips, Rachel Wilson, and "diverse others...as nursing mothers to me", and Esther Tuke "[k]indly took me under her wing and was indeed a tender Mother in Truth". *Memoirs of the Life and Travels in the Service of the Gospel of Sarah Stephenson* (London, 1807) 16, 20. Men were less frequently referred to as 'fathers' of the church.

[9] The Society of Friends has no formal ministry. Male and female could minister if called to do so by divine inspiration. To be 'recognised' as a minister, a Friend stood up and ministered in Meeting, and if the ministry was deemed suitable by Friends, he/she would then be approved a minister by the Meeting of Ministers and Elders.

the act of writing or confessing to a journal was considered to encourage and enhance progress in the search for a stronger personal faith, the journals were also written in the expectation that Friends would read them as an example of a godly life lived. In addition, to some extent the raison d'être for publication was to show the Society in a good light and to encourage an 'ideal' of spirituality, and even though many manuscript journals exist, these have generally been edited by someone, at some time. Most Friends' published journals went through a series of rigorous editorial processes; firstly, by the original editor and secondly, by the London Morning Meeting committee for publications. As a consequence of this editorial process, the journals we inherit may well represent a serious misrepresentation of the author's intention. In addition, many were written retrospectively, altering the 'voice' of the text to comply with the aspirations or beliefs of the autobiographical persona and the perceived requirements of her audience.[10] Despite all these disadvantages, Quaker women's published journals retain their validity as a source of evidence.

Linda Peterson has suggested that in the seventeenth century "the spiritual autobiography unlike the domestic memoir, does not particularly

---

All ministers could in theory travel, so long as the desire to travel was divinely inspired and was approved by their Meeting. Travelling ministers were issued with a certificate of introduction and recommendation to the Meetings they were visiting.

[10] George Fox established a 'style' for Quaker journals to which women seeking a 'voice' were likely to conform. This was reinforced by The Morning Meeting editorial committee which was originally established in 1673 to edit and publish George Fox's works, in particular his journal. It consisted of ministers who were in London at the time the committee met. In theory, the committee vetted all manuscripts published under the auspices of the Society. The minutes of the Meeting show that many manuscripts were either refused or severely altered by the committee. For example, the minutes for "30.7.1764" read: "Having deliberately considered a paragraph in Elizabeth Bathurst's book...it is agreed that Luke Hinde reprint the four last pages, leaving out that paragraph". Morning Meeting Minute Book, Vol. 6, 1765–1783, p. 41, Library of the Religious Society of Friends, London. See also David J. Hall, "'The Fiery Trial of their Infallible Examination': Self Control in the Regulation of Quaker Publishing in England from the 1670s to the Mid-Nineteenth-Century", in *Censorship and the Control of Print in England and France 1600–1910*, ed. Robin Myers and M. Harris (Winchester: St Paul's Bibliographies, 1992), 76–82; Thomas O'Malley, "Defying the Powers and Tempering the Spirit: A Review of Quaker Control over their Publications 1672–1689", *Journal of Ecclesiastical History* 33, no. 1 (1982): 72–88; Christine Trevett, "'Not Fit to be Printed': The Welsh, The Women and the Second Day's Morning Meeting", *Journal of the Friends Historical Society* 59, no. 2 (2004): 115–44. For the problems of using women's autobiography, see Sidonie Smith, *A Poetics of Women's Autobiography: Marginality and the Fictions of Self-Representation* (Bloomington: Indiana University Press, 1987), 45–49.

concern itself with marriage, the home, or the family".[11] But while the
majority of Quaker journals in this period can be read as conversion
narratives which generally focus on the women's spiritual life, their
struggles with hostile external authorities, and their progress to enlightenment, I would suggest that in the period from the Restoration into the
early eighteenth century many did include domestic details and advice
as to how to deal with the conflicting commitments of family and home
and the need to serve God.[12] In contrast to a Catholic nun, a Quaker
woman gifted in the ministry did not withdraw from 'the world' and
could maintain a high level of spiritual practice while also performing
her role as daughter, wife, and mother. The balancing act required to
fulfil both her spiritual role and her domestic role frequently created
agonizing tensions, not least of which was how to deal with the dual
demands of serving God and the family.

Family Conflict and Conversion to Quakerism

Conflicts created by conversion to Quakerism frequently resulted in
the emergence of writings that can be considered to be confessional
tools, the act of writing of the distress caused by familial conflict having a cathartic effect upon the writer. Confessing to a journal allowed
women to express the feelings of guilt and anguish brought about by
conflict arising from the need for absolute obedience to God and the
confrontation with family which so often resulted. While this guilt
could be associated with confrontation with family members, it was
also connected to conflict with the customs of secular society in the

---

[11] Linda H. Peterson, *Traditions of Victorian Women's Autobiography: The Poetics and Politics
of Life Writing* (Charlottesville and London: University Press of Virginia, 1999), 10.

[12] Peterson, *Traditions*, 5–16. For Quaker women's spiritual autobiography, see Kate
Peters, "Patterns of Quaker Authorship 1652–1656", *Prose Studies* 17, no. 3 (1994):
6–24; Mary A. Schofield, "'Women's Speaking Justified': The Feminine Quaker Voice
1662–1797", *Tulsa Studies in Women's Literature* 6, no. 1 (1987): 61–77; Felicity A. Nuss-
baum, *The Autobiographical Subject: Gender and Ideology in Eighteenth-Century England* (Baltimore
and London: Johns Hopkins University Press, 1989), 154–77; Cristine M. Levenduski,
Peculiar Power: A Quaker Woman Preacher in Eighteenth-Century America (Washington and
London: Smithsonian Institution Press, 1996), 100–108; Carol Edkins, "Quest for
Community: Spiritual Autobiographies of Eighteenth-Century Quaker and Puritan
Women in America", in *Women's Autobiography: Essays in Criticism*, ed. Estelle Jeleneck
(Bloomington: Indiana University Press, 1980), 39–52.

late-seventeenth and early-eighteenth century.[13] Seventeenth-century
domestic patriarchalism was justified by reference to selected scriptural
passages and established and enshrined within English law. This social
and legal structure defined relationships between the young and their
parents and husbands and wives and upheld expectations of behaviour
to which Friends subscribed, including the expectation that children
"obey their parents in the Lord".[14] Texts advising men and women on
acceptable familial relationships abounded in the seventeenth century,
many extolling the virtues of the obedient, dutiful wife. These included
Richard Braithwaite's *The Good Wife, Or a Rare One Amongst Women* and
others in which a man was cautioned to ensure that his wife be no
"gadder abroad".[15] But Milton in his epic poem *Paradise Lost* sought a
more equitable arrangement emphasising companionship over procreation and partnership rather than subservience.[16]

Despite their best efforts, men in the seventeenth century could not
provide a unified 'voice' with regard to the position of women; in reality, because women in this period did not form a homogenous group,
they could negotiate a route through these restrictions. Quaker women
constantly challenged many elements of existing social mores, and their
lifestyle was often in sharp contrast to the imagery of the ideal 'Good
Wife'. These women had different priorities, as Joan Vokins made clear
when she asserted, "I could not take comfort in husband or children,
house or land, or any visibles, for want of the marriage union with the
lamb of God".[17] And although, in theory, the bodies of Quaker women
were subjected to the authority of husbands or fathers, they frequently
found that the demands of their spiritual role called for disobedience to
male authority and even intransigence in the face of intense pressure

---

[13] See Sara Mendelson and Patricia Crawford, *Women in Early Modern England 1550–1720* (Oxford: Clarendon, 1998), 126–48; Lawrence Stone, *The Family, Sex and Marriage in England, 1500–1800* (Harmondsworth: Penguin, 1979), 127–44, 217–25; Alan Macfarlane, *Marriage and Love in England: Modes of Reproduction 1300–1840* (Oxford: Basil Blackwell, 1987), 119–208.

[14] Advice no. 9, Epistle from the Elders at Balby.

[15] Margaret J. M. Ezell, *The Patriarch's Wife: Literary Evidence and the History of the Family* (Chapel Hill and London: University of North Carolina Press, 1987), 36–61.

[16] Barbara K. Lewalski, "Milton on Women—Yet Once More", *Milton Studies* 6 (1974): 3–20.

[17] Quoted in Graham et al., *Her Own Life*, 215.

to change their beliefs.[18] Taking their cue from writers such as the Leveller Katherine Chidley, who had sharply remarked, "I know of no true Divinity that teacheth men to be Lords over the Conscience", a Quaker woman could, if forbidden by a husband from performing a godly duty, "after proper prayer and reflection, follow God's will" and be obedient only to her True Husband, Christ.[19]

This spiritual prioritising of obedience had a potentially divisive effect, restricting familial authority to earthly matters. As a result, the diametrically opposed demands of the secular and spiritual created tensions between expectations of a woman's temporal behaviour and the spiritual demands of the Inner Light. In an attempt to limit the resulting antagonism, Friends took the Biblical injunction against excessive love of family or friends seriously: "people must learn to hate them in comparison to God, even while God's love in our hearts enlarges our own love not only to relatives but to all humanity"—advice which appears to have had some resonance for Quaker women.[20] Jane Hoskens, Margaret Lucas, Alice Hayes, and Elizabeth Ashbridge all placed the fulfilment of their calling to the Inner Light before their obedience to their family or husbands.

In 1714, aged 21, Jane Hoskens, in direct opposition to her parents, left England and went to Philadelphia as an indentured servant to escape their disapproval of her conversion to Quakerism. She claimed that it was her duty, saying she thought "it might be for my good to go, for that by being among strangers, I might with more freedom serve God".[21]

---

[18] Robbie Smith, "Female 'Intransigence' in the Early Quaker Movement from the 1650s to About 1700, with Particular Reference to the Northwest of England". M.A. diss., University of Lancaster, 1990.

[19] Katherine Chidley, *The Justification of the Independent Churches of Christ* (London, 1641). Although Chidley's writing preceded the emergence of Quakerism in the 1650s, the writing of Leveller women such as Chidley was influential in the formation of Friends' attitudes and ideas relating to the position of women. For the formation of Quakerism, see William C. Braithwaite, *The Beginnings of Quakerism*, 2nd ed., rev. by Henry J. Cadbury (Cambridge: Cambridge University Press 1961); for Levellers and Quakerism, see Adrian Davies, *The Quakers in English Society 1655–1725* (Oxford: Clarendon Press, 2000), 64–75; see also Hilary Hinds, *God's Englishwomen: Seventeenth-Century Radical Sectarian Writing and Feminist Criticism* (Manchester and New York: Manchester University Press, 1996), 49.

[20] Katherine A. Damiano, "On Earth as it is in Heaven": Eighteenth-Century Quakerism as Realized Eschatology" (Ph.D. diss., The Union of Experimenting Colleges and Universities, 1988), 180.

[21] *The Life of that Faithful Servant of Christ Jane Hoskens*, in *The Friends House Library: Comprising Journals, Doctrinal Treatises and other writings of members of the Religious Society of Friends*, ed. William Evans and Thomas Evans (Philadelphia, 1837), 460–61.

She represented her parents as a repressive influence who held back her spiritual progress and duty, suggesting that through the act of leaving and the severing of parental emotional bonds—inevitably resulting in loneliness—she would be free to pursue her call from God and enabled to forge a more powerful, emotional relationship with Him.

For some young Quaker women, disobedience in the pursuance of their Quaker faith resulted in physical abuse from their families. Margaret Lucas, for instance, in *An Account of the Convincement and Call to the Ministry of Margaret Lucas*, related the cruelty she endured from both her uncle and her aunt. Her introduction to Friends came through her business dealings with the Quaker Samuel Taylor.[22] When she first began attending the Friends Meeting and refused to go to church, her uncle drove her from home and, in an attempt to persuade her to abandon Quakerism, blackmailed her both emotionally and financially. In the first instance, he told her if she would "promise, that I would never be a Quaker, he would give me a deed of gift, that at his and my aunt's decease, I should have all they were worth".[23] He then suggested that if she would become a Presbyterian, he would "take the shop and bear the loss he might sustain in selling it off; for he thought the removing me out of the way of shame and disgrace, as he called it, might be a means of altering my resolution". Both offers she declined, telling them she "could not do it". Margaret's continued attendance at Meeting and her obstinate defiance of her uncle resulted in a series of physical and psychological attacks from her aunt, who whipped her and parodied the dress of Quaker Ministers by wearing "a black hood and a green apron". But Margaret remained defiant, altering her speech and adopting the 'thee and thou' form, which caused a further angry confrontation with her aunt who seized the fire shovel and struck her. In 1721, her uncle parted her from her sister for fear that her Quakerism was infectious, and in the same year threatened to use her inheritance to pay off her father's debts. By this date, the financial consequences of her family's anger were serious: her aunt had frightened away the pupils from the school she had opened around 1719 and told anyone who came into

---

[22] *An Account of the Convincement and Call to the Ministry of Margaret Lucas, late of Leek, in Staffordshire* (London, 1797). Margaret Lucas was born Margaret Brindley in London in 1701. Her father kept a china shop on the corner of Fetter Lane in London which, when he died intestate in 1708, appears to have been managed by her uncle. Margaret took over the running of the shop in 1718, and Samuel Taylor acted as her business advisor.

[23] *An Account of the Convincement...of Margaret Lucas*, 49.

Margaret's shop that Margaret was "the new made Quaker" in an attempt to reduce her trade. Holding Margaret's left arm, which was next to her,

> when I used the plain language, she pinched me very bad; and so often renewed her pinches, that it was very hard for me to bear them.... When she was gone, I tried to unbutton my sleeve, but my arm being so prodigiously swelled, I could not....my hand and arm swelled to such a degree, that,...I could scarcely shut my fingers.... My fingers were swelled, stiff, and useless, for I could neither close nor stir them.[24]

In her writing, she represents herself as strong and determined in the face of considerable opposition to her convincement to Quakerism, but she absolves herself from accusations of intransigence by asserting that her defiance was in response to the leadings of the Spirit. This detailed account of her sufferings had two purposes: it was written to encourage and uplift her readers to a deeper, more steadfast faith and to exemplify the trials through which, as a Quaker minister, it was necessary to travel in pursuit of the Inner Light, while also serving as an articulation and reinforcement of her own beliefs. In 1725, Margaret married the Quaker Samuel Lucas, "a worthy and well respected [man]". Her family's reconciliation with her Quakerism was never absolute, but they eventually behaved "lovingly and affectionately to my kind husband; and, afterwards were very tender of our children, my aunt exceedingly so".[25]

Marriage

By the 1670s, spiritual equality between Quaker men and women had become enshrined within Quaker doctrine, and these ideals overflowed into the organisation of the Society, giving Quaker women unprecedented levels of responsibility. Women who were granted a share in the governance of their church expected a share in the regulation of their family and consequently a greater degree of equality within the marriage relationship. These concepts of equality were enhanced by the omission of the promise to 'obey' in the marriage service, releasing

---

[24] *An Account of the Convincement...of Margaret Lucas*, 51–52, 63–109; quote taken from 73–4, 76.
[25] *An Account of the Convincement...of Margaret Lucas*, 120.

women from the restraints of subservience and placing them on a more equal footing.[26] As Jacques Tual has perceptively commented, Quaker couples established "a very novel relationship with their mates", resulting in Friends' belief that marriage was a bond of equals based on love, reaching levels of spiritual union which "regained a paradisaical state of innocence and spirituality".[27] For Friends, these precepts were exemplified in the union of George Fox and Margaret Fell, and in Fox's declaration upon marriage to Fell that she was his equal both in temporal and spiritual matters.[28]

In contrast to secular advice books of the mid-eighteenth century which emphasise submission of the wife to her husband, those in the seventeenth century frequently characterised wives as being "an equall with him in the yoake".[29] Friends' origins in the Puritan tradition ensured that they too upheld these concepts of marriage; John Bell asserted that his wife, Deborah, was a "true and faithful yoke-fellow".[30] But although this might mean that Friends had a heightened sense of awareness of equality within marriage and that Quaker women were more equal than most, these women were not truly equal to men.

Decisions relating to marriage were frequently portrayed as an inner struggle which entailed finding a balance between earthly needs and pleasures and the fulfilment of a spiritual calling. In many instances, Quaker women either rejected marriage or delayed marriage until they were considerably older and often past child-bearing age.[31] Delay or celibacy were linked to a concern that earthly love could become more important than the love of God; consequently, this would be the cause

---

[26] Equality is fundamental to the Quaker marriage service which has no gender distinctions in the promises and no exchange of rings. See Davies, *The Quakers in English Society*, 91–100. Equality was also present in Meeting for Worship where married and unmarried women sat together unlike in the Anglican church.

[27] Jacques Tual, "Sexual Equality and Conjugal Harmony: The Way to Celestial Bliss", *Journal of the Friends Historical Society* 55 (1988): 164, 165.

[28] Fox was 45 and Fell was 55 when they married. Fox denied that there were any carnal or sensuous purposes for the marriage, rejecting the idea of marriage as being for procreation. There was some resentment amongst Friends, who questioned the justification for this marriage. See Trevett, *Women and Quakerism*, 90.

[29] Sir Thomas Overbury, *His Wife with Additions of New Characters*, quoted in Ezell, *The Patriarch's Wife*, 38.

[30] *Life of Deborah Bell*, in *The Friends House Library*, 5.

[31] Larson, *Daughters of the Light*, 135–36. Larson found Quaker women ministers were on average ten years older upon marriage than the general Quaker population. See also Richard T. Vann and David Eversley, *Friends in Life and Death: The British and Irish Quakers in the Demographic Transition, 1650–1900* (Cambridge: Cambridge University Press, 1992), 80–128.

of both personal and marital conflict. For women ministers who did marry, marriage was a serious prospect involving much heart-searching to ensure that a marriage partner was not only equal in earthly matters but also equal in spiritual growth. To achieve this balance, Quaker women diligently sought God's guidance and approval in their choice of a marriage partner. Ann Young's choice of husband was by "divine appointment", and she acknowledged that "some good hand I think was evidently witnessed in joyning us together". Deborah Bell conceded that her marriage to John Bell in 1710 was undertaken "with a great awfulness and reverence".[32] Divine guidance was also required when choosing a place to live and when moving house, as John Bell discovered when he suggested to Deborah soon after their marriage that they move to London. She felt the indications were not right, but some years later she "saw the way clearly, and had a certain evidence that the Lord would be with us, and own us in that undertaking. This removed all doubts, and I freely consented".[33]

Although generally married Friends lived in comparative harmony, for some their adherence to the strictures of Quakerism could cause conjugal friction. Alice Hayes was born in 1657, and before she was twenty years old she left home to go into service where she met her husband, Daniel Smith. Over the following six years, she struggled to find a true faith, finally joining the Friends. As a consequence of her convincement, her relationship with her husband deteriorated, and he became "very unkind and his love turned into hatred and contempt". When dressing for Meeting, he would "take away my clothes". She hints of other cruelties which she thought "not proper here to mention".[34] He also threatened her with abandonment: "if you do not leave off going to the Quakers, I will sell all that I have, and pay every one their own and go and leave you". Her response was to remain steadfast and defiant, claiming that her determination came from God, telling him, "if it be so, I cannot help it...I could not go against that interest I had in God".[35] Like Margaret Lucas, she represented her defiance as obedience to God, emphasising that it was the leading of the Inner

---

[32] Diary of Ann Young (1701–1790), MFR 2791/3, British Library. *Life of Deborah Bell*, 11.
[33] *Life of Deborah Bell*, 17.
[34] *A Short Account of Alice Hayes (a Minister)* in *The Friends House Library*, vol. 2, 68–72.
[35] *A Short Account of Alice Hayes*, 73.

Light which dictated her actions. Since the Inner Light, she argued, bestowed sanctity on the individual, as a recipient of its leadings she was able to deny personal responsibility for her wifely disobedience, undermining the authority of her husband. In time, Alice Hayes and her family were reconciled, and her narrative turns from the pain of suffering to the joy of reconciliation, as she transformed her tormentor into a model of tolerance. He became resigned to her Quakerism: "My dear husband's love returned and he continued to his life's end a loving and tender husband, and an indulgent father to our children".[36]

Elizabeth Ashbridge's story echoes that of Alice Hayes and provides a rare life story which details all the vicissitudes experienced by a woman in search of both spiritual and temporal fulfilment. As Cristine Levenduski has noted, "the multivocality of her text makes it much more than a preacher's conversion narrative".[37] Like Jane Hoskens, Ashbridge also left England to escape the displeasure of her father, having eloped with an unsuitable young man. She too signed up as an indentured servant and, after many trials, found a new life in America.[38] Underlying the narrative of her struggle to find both temporal and spiritual contentment, as Levenduski suggests, is a deep psychological need to replace the bond between herself and her father, and this breaks through the story of both her search for a church that satisfies her spiritually and a human relationship that fulfills her temporal needs. Her quest for a spiritual 'home' takes her through a variety of churches until, finally, she encounters the Quaker meeting within which she finds the familial bonds that she has been seeking.[39] But while her conversion to Quakerism brought her spiritual comfort, it created conflict between herself and her husband, damaging the already unhappy relationship with the only 'family' she had and emphasising the importance of the familial sanctuary she found in the Friends Meeting.

Ashbridge describes the beginning of her struggles with her husband as a "Tryal of my Faith"—immediately elevating her sufferings to a

---

[36] *A Short Account of Alice Hayes*, 75.

[37] Levenduski, *Peculiar Power*, 4.

[38] Daniel B. Shea, ed., "Some Account of the Fore Part of the Life of Elizabeth Ashbridge", in *Journeys in New Worlds: Early American Women's Narratives*, ed. William L. Andrews (Madison, Wis.: University of Wisconsin Press, 1990), 119–177. It is thought that Ashbridge wrote the text in the late 1740s, but no original version of this journal appears to exist. The extent copies include a manuscript copy and other copies based on the first edition of 1774.

[39] Levenduski, *Peculiar Power*, 74, 82–84.

higher realm—and then proceeds to establish her husband as a man
increasingly angered by her adherence to Quaker customs and doctrine.
He put her through numerous trials to test her commitment to Quakerism, including threatening her with a pen knife and telling her not to
go to Meeting or he will "cripple you, for you shall not be a Quaker".[40]
But his actions and threats only served to strengthen her convincement,
enabling her to confront her husband, establish her priorities, and defy
his authority. In her *Life*, Elizabeth recalls asking:

> "My Dear, art thou willing to let me go to a Meeting?" at which he
> flew into a rage, saying "No you shan't". I then Drew up my resolution
> and told him as a Dutyfull Wife ought, So I was ready to obey all his
> Lawfull Commands, but where they imposed upon my Conscience, I
> no longer Durst: For I had already done it too Long and wronged my
> Self by it, & tho' he was near & I loved him as a Wife ought yet *God
> was nearer than all the World to me* & had made me sensible this was the
> way I ought to go, the which I Assured him was no Small Cross to my
> own will, yet had Given up My heart, & hoped that he that Called for
> it would Enable me the residue of my Life to keep it steadyly devoted
> to him, whatever I suffered for it, adding I hoped not to make him any
> the worse Wife for it. But all I could Say was in vain; he was Inflexible
> and Would not Consent.[41]

Ashbridge mixes obedience as a "dutyfull wife" with obedience to
God, representing herself as a wife who, although wishing to be obedient and dutiful, had to be disobedient to serve God, regardless of
the consequences. Finally, she depicted her husband as the loser in
this struggle, not herself, for she had God to sustain her. While she is
determined in her adherence to her beliefs, in the same paragraph she
turns her disobedience into a plea of loyalty to her marital relationship,
suggesting that it is through spiritual fulfilment and obedience to God
that she can ultimately become a good wife. Ashbridge ends her narrative by recalling her husband's act of grudging reconciliation as he
tells her, "If it be of God I can't over throw it, & if it be of yourself
it will soon fall".[42]

It is in these narratives that we can most easily identify the conflicting
loyalties to which Quaker women ministers were subject. Ashbridge and
Hayes represent the destruction wrought on their marital relationships

---

[40] Shea, ed., "Some Account of the Life of Elizabeth Ashbridge", 161–66.
[41] Shea, ed., "Some Account of the Life of Elizabeth Ashbridge", 165–66. Emphasis
added.
[42] Shea, ed., "Some Account of the Life of Elizabeth Ashbridge", 167.

by their insistence on becoming Friends as a necessary sacrifice and trial through which followers of the Inner Light had to pass to achieve true enlightenment. But while they may have emphasised their struggle to live by their convictions in their writings, these women ultimately gained strength and closure on their tribulations when they were able to end their narratives with an emphasis on forgiveness and family reconciliation. The ability to heal the pain caused by their disobedience and the consequent realignment of family relationships reflect a fundamental aspect of Friends' belief in the essential goodness of mankind. The imperative to write of the ultimate forgiveness of the perpetrator of suffering, provoked by intransigent behaviour and transgressions against prevailing social conventions, was an act of purification for the writer and a lesson in forgiveness for her readers.

These narratives of conflict are not widespread. In most Quaker women's writings, familial relationships are presented as harmonious and loving, and there is no lack of love expressed for husbands or children. Ruth Follows, ministering in America, wrote to her husband of her "unfeigned love to thee and my dear and tender children...and although it is so ordered that we are separated one from another outwardly, yet I am near to you in spirit". Mary Weston finished her letter "with a heart full of the sincerest and best of love I am capable of expressing to thy dear self and our well belov'd daughter who with ye is dearer to me than life itself".[43] When husbands or wives died, loss was expressed in words of palpable pain, and even God's consoling presence could not lessen the distress. In 1663, Ann Camm's husband, John died: "How hard it was, and how great a loss to me, to part with so dear and tender a husband, is far beyond what I can express". And when Deborah Bell died, her husband wrote, "She was a loving and affectionate wife, and the gift of God to me, and as such I always prized her".[44]

---

[43] Samuel Stansfield, ed., *Memoirs of Ruth Follows: For Sixty Years a Minister in the Society of Friends with Extracts from her Letters* (Liverpool: C. Bentham, 1829), 117. Letter dated 3.6.1751, Diary and Letters of Mary Weston (1711–1766), Quaker Women's Diaries, MFR 2791/5, British Library. This is one of a series of loose leaf letters pasted into the back of the journal. The date here, and in all subsequent references to dates, conforms to Quaker usage, where '6' refers to 'Sixth Month'. England adopted January (rather than March) as the first month of the new year, along with the Gregorian calendar, in 1752.

[44] *A Short Account of the Life of Ann Camm* in *The Friends House Library*, vol. 4, 476; *Life of Deborah Bell*, 5.

Family and Travelling in the Ministry

Quaker women who travelled in the ministry did so in response to a calling from the Spirit or Inner Light, and husbands and family were not expected to challenge or prevent a woman from travelling. Consequently, it was essential for a Quaker woman minister to have a spiritually compatible and understanding mate, someone to whom they could leave the care of home and children when they were away. Most journals in this period suggest an acceptance of the need for wives to travel, but as Susanna Morris counselled, it was necessary to have the call to undertake a ministerial journey and to wait for "the consent of husband and good Friends".[45] Once permission was granted, the decision as to where and when to travel was divinely ordered, and women ministers had to await the 'leadings of the Spirit' as to destination or return home. As Ann Mercy Bell of York, away ministering in 1745, admitted to her "Suffering Husband", it "would be more desirable than ever to me to find myself clear and be at Liberty to return to thee my dear husband and my dear children, whom I oft remember with near affection", but she explained that she did not consider herself free to leave London to return to York until God indicated that her ministerial duty was done.[46] And Ruth Follows, ministering in America in 1748, cautioned her husband and children that her absence was God's work, and that they all should be "wholly resigned to his will", advising them that since it was in obedience to "the Lord that I am where I am, I sincerely desire that I may continue in obedience to his pure and holy will, although it be a very great trial and at times comes near almost to my life".[47]

While husbands and children were not allowed to interfere with spiritual duty, leaving children caused considerable anxiety, as Ruth Follows admitted when departing on her first ministerial journey in 1748: "I left all to His divine protection, my dear husband and sweet babes, my eldest about six and youngest about three years old...but as I stood resigned to the will of God, he gave me strength in weakness".[48] Often

---

[45] "The Journal of Susanna Morris" in *Wilt Thou Go on My Errand*, 44.

[46] Ann Mercy Bell to Nathaniel Bell, 26.6.1745, Ann Mercy Bell's Journal and Correspondence, 1745–1786, microfilm reel 173, York Monthly Meeting, York Friends Archives.

[47] Letter dated 21.3.1748 in Stansfield, ed., *Memoirs of Ruth Follows*, 117.

[48] Stansfield, ed., *Memoirs of Ruth Follows*, 18.

separated from family by great geographic and cultural distance, and with infrequent and unreliable mail, Quaker women inevitably suffered from loneliness. Mary Weston wrote to her husband from Philadelphia in 1750 that he "may be assured [we] are not exempt from the passing of lonely weeks" and complained, "I have not yet gott the long letter thou writes of".[49] Despite the practical difficulties involved in leaving husbands, home, and most often children for long periods when away travelling, Quaker women ministers had to follow their calling. Domestic and familial duties could not interfere with their spiritual work.

Conclusion

A Quaker woman minister's life was fused to her spiritual calling, which was the primary motivation for her actions and for her reactions to her own personal life. Unlike other sects, Quakerism required a level of integrated spirituality that permeated all aspects of a Friend's life. Being a member of the elite within the Society of Friends did not simply involve attending Meeting on First Day but demanded an exceptionally high level of spiritual dedication. This placed a heavy responsibility on Quaker women ministers to ensure that they led exemplary lives, not only as representatives of their sect but especially as symbols of good faith and practice within the family. Consistently, their writing represents their spirituality and their 'calling' to be of greater importance than the demands of family and suggests that conflict with the family was a test to be suffered by true Friends in pursuance of enlightenment. This is not to suggest that the family was unimportant to these women or that conflict was to be welcomed, but it has to be considered that the needs of family were frequently secondary to their spiritual role. Because the Society of Friends elevated the concept of the family to a place at the very heart of its organisation and its existence, it endowed Quaker women with especially heavy responsibilities as spiritual leaders, as carers of the membership, and as educators of the next generation. This, when combined with their duties as custodians of the harmony and purity of their own homes bestowed upon women not only an elevated position within the Society but also accorded them levels of

---

[49] Letter dated 3.10.1750, Diary and Letters of Mary Weston. The 'we' is an interpolation; the pronoun is missing in the original manuscript.

equality and influence within the domestic sphere which were not generally present for women outside the Society of Friends.

Bibliography

Manuscript Sources

Bell, Ann. Journal and Correspondence, 1745–1786. York Monthly Meeting. York Friends Archives.
"Epistle from the Elders at Balby, 1656". FRM 1/39, Papers of Marsden Monthly Meeting. Lancashire Record Office.
Morning Meeting Minute Book. Library of the Religious Society of Friends, London.
Weston, Mary (1711–1766). Diary and letters. MFR2791/1, Quaker Women's Diaries. British Library Microfilm Series.
Young, Ann (1701–1790). Diary. MFR2791/3, Quaker Women's Diaries. British Library Microfilm Series.

Printed Sources

An Account of the Convincement and Call to the Ministry of Margaret Lucas, late of Leek, in Staffordshire. London, 1797.
Bacon, Margaret Hope, ed. *Wilt Thou Go on My Errand?: Journals of Three 18th Century Quaker Women Ministers*. Wallingford, Pa.: Pendle Hill Publications, 1994.
Braithwaite, William C. *The Beginnings of Quakerism*. 2nd ed., revised by Henry J. Cadbury. Cambridge: Cambridge University Press, 1961.
Chidley, Katherine. *The Justification of the Independent Churches of Christ*. London, 1641.
Damiano, Katherine A. "On Earth as it is in Heaven": Eighteenth Century Quakerism as Realized Eschatology. Ph.D. diss., The Union of Experimenting Colleges and Universities, 1988.
Davies, Adrian. *The Quakers in English Society 1655–1725*. Oxford: Clarendon Press, 2000.
Edkins, Carol. "Quest for Community: Spiritual Autobiographies of Eighteenth-Century Quaker and Puritan Women in America". In *Women's Autobiography: Essays in Criticism*, edited by Estelle Jeleneck. Bloomington: Indiana University Press, 1980.
Evans, William and Thomas Evans, eds. *The Friends House Library: Comprising Journals, Doctrinal Treatises and other Writings of Members of the Religious Society of Friends*. 14 vols. Philadelphia, 1837–1850.
Ezell, Margaret J. M. *The Patriarch's Wife: Literary Evidence and the History of the Family*. Chapel Hill and London: University of North Carolina Press, 1987.
Graham, Elspeth et al., eds. *Her Own Life: Autobiographical Writings by Seventeenth-Century Englishwomen*. London: Routledge, 1989.
Hall, David J. "'The Fiery Trial of their Infallible Examination': Self Control in the Regulation of Quaker Publishing in England from the 1670s to the Mid Nineteenth Century". In *Censorship and the Control of Print in England and France 1600–1910*, edited by Robin Myers and M. Harris. Winchester: St Paul's Bibliographies, 1992.
Hinds, Hilary. *God's Englishwomen: Seventeenth-Century Radical Sectarian Writing and Feminist Criticism*. Manchester and New York: Manchester University Press, 1996.
Hobby, Elaine. *Virtue of Necessity: English Women's Writing 1649–88*. London: Virago, 1988.
Larson, Rebecca. *Daughters of Light: Quaker Women Preaching and Prophesying in the Colonies and Abroad, 1700–1775*. New York: Knopf, 1999.

Leach, Camilla. "Quaker Women and Education from the Late Eighteenth to the Mid-Nineteenth Century". Ph.D. diss., King Alfred's College, Winchester, 2003.

Levenduski, Cristine M. *Peculiar Power: A Quaker Woman Preacher in Eighteenth-Century America*. Washington and London: Smithsonian Institution Press, 1996.

Lewalski, Barbara K. "Milton on Women—Yet Once More". *Milton Studies* 6 (1974): 3–20.

Macfarlane, Alan. *Marriage and Love in England: Modes of Reproduction 1300–1840*. Oxford: Basil Blackwell, 1987.

Mack, Phyllis. *Visionary Women: Ecstatic Prophecy in Seventeenth Century England*. Berkeley: University of California Press, 1992.

Memoirs of the Life and Travels in the Service of the Gospel of Sarah Stephenson. London, 1807.

Mendelson, Sara and Patricia Crawford. *Women in Early Modern England 1550–1720*. Oxford: Clarendon Press, 1998.

Moore, Rosemary. *The Light in Their Consciences: Early Quakers in Britain 1646–1666*. University Park, Pa.: The Pennsylvania University Press, 2000.

Nussbaum, Felicity A. *The Autobiographical Subject: Gender and Ideology in Eighteenth-Century England*. Baltimore and London: Johns Hopkins University Press, 1989.

O'Malley, Thomas. "Defying the Powers and Tempering the Spirit: A Review of Quaker Control over their Publications 1672–1689". *Journal of Ecclesiastical History* 33, no. 1 (1982):): 72–88.

Peters, Kate. "Patterns of Quaker Authorship 1652–1656". *Prose Studies* 17, no. 3 (1994): 6–24.

Peterson, Linda H. *Traditions of Victorian Women's Autobiography: The Poetics and Politics of Life Writing*. Charlottesville and London: University Press of Virginia, 1999.

Schofield, Mary Anne. "'Women's Speaking Justified': The Feminine Quaker Voice 1662–1797". *Tulsa Studies in Women's Literature* 6, no. 1 (1987): 61–77.

Shea, Daniel B., ed. "Some Account of the Fore Part of the Life of Elizabeth Ashbridge". In *Journeys in New Worlds: Early American Women's Narratives*, edited by William L. Andrews. Madison, Wis.: University of Wisconsin Press, 1990.

Smith, Sidonie. *A Poetics of Women's Autobiography: Marginality and the Fictions of Self-Representation*. Bloomington: Indiana University Press, 1987.

Smith, Robbie. "Female 'Intransigence' in the Early Quaker Movement from the 1650s to About 1700, with Particular Reference to the Northwest of England". M.A. diss., University of Lancaster, 1990.

Stansfield, Samuel, ed. *Memoirs of Ruth Follows: For Sixty Years a Minister in the Society of Friends with Extracts from her Letters*. Liverpool: C. Bentham, 1829.

Stone, Lawrence. *The Family, Sex and Marriage in England, 1500–1800*. Harmondsworth: Penguin, 1979.

Trevett, Christine. *Women and Quakerism in the 17th Century*. York: Sessions Book Trust, The Ebor Press, 1991.

———. "'Not Fit to be Printed': The Welsh, The Women and the Second Day's Morning Meeting". *Journal of the Friends Historical Society* 59, no. 2 (2004): 115–44.

Tual, J. "Sexual Equality and Conjugal Harmony: The Way to Celestial Bliss". *Journal of the Friends Historical Society* 55 (1988): 162–73.

Vann, Richard T. and David Eversley. *Friends in Life and Death: The British and Irish Quakers in the Demographic Transition, 1650–1900*. Cambridge: Cambridge University Press, 1992.

PART TWO

PROPHETESSES: RADICAL REVISIONS OF KNOWLEDGE, GENDER, BODY, SELF

.

"BREAK DOWN THE WALLS OF FLESH":
ANNA TRAPNEL, JOHN JAMES, AND FIFTH MONARCHIST
SELF-REPRESENTATION

Naomi Baker

During one of her trances, as her body is overwhelmed by "the Spirit" like "a mighty gale", Anna Trapnel is asked to describe her physical symptoms.[1] She initially obliges, speaking for a while of her "distemper", but then abruptly seems to change the subject: "I told them, to speak of my body, was but lost time; but if they would hear of Divine things…it was my delight to tell of the unfoldings of God".[2] Through dismissing physical categories in order to focus on spiritual matters, Trapnel apparently exhibits the "[disavowal] of the subject body" observed by Diane Purkiss in the writings of female prophets of the seventeenth century, where the prophets seek to "locate themselves more and more firmly in spiritual rather than physical spheres".[3]

For one ostensibly uninterested in her body, however, Anna Trapnel spends a surprising amount of time describing it. Her apparent lack of concern with the physical in the above passage follows a lengthy and precise anatomisation of her bodily sufferings:

> [I] could not rise out of my bed all that fortnight, but as five lifted me out one night; and I was so extream earthy, even as lead, that they had much ado to lift me into bed again, and I slept not, but talked night and day, the pourings forth of the spirit was such, when I did slumber, and that was but little, but then I felt my pain and weakness very much;…sometimes my bones hath been shaken in my flesh, my joints unloosed, and sometimes great pains, as if my bones had been pulled asunder: such torture hath seized upon me, and sick fits, that the parties which watched by me hath bowed me double, to keep breath in me,

---

[1] Anna Trapnel, *A Legacy for Saints* (1654), 29.

[2] Trapnel, *Legacy*, 29–30.

[3] Diane Purkiss, "Producing the Voice, Consuming the Body: Women Prophets of the Seventeenth Century", *Women, Writing, History: 1640–1740*, ed. Isobel Grundy and Susan Wiseman (Athens: The University of Georgia Press, 1992), 150, 151.

when I have been cold, and my breath cold within me, and to sence a
breathing out my last breath...much ado I had to speak.[4]

The leaden weight of Trapnel's body is on one level set against the
lively "pourings forth of the spirit", yet far from being occluded or dissolved, the heavy, painful materiality of the body remains the central
focus of Trapnel's self-representation in this passage.

Trapnel's body, whether tortured or restored, is in fact displayed
prominently throughout her writings.[5] Maintaining a precise material
context for her experiences, Trapnel tells us, for example,

> how I was that night after Mr Greenhil was gone; about the ninth hour,
> that night an extream pain seized on me, and my throat was very sore,
> and a swelling in my mouth, which even stopt my breath, and Satan
> violently seized on me, tempting me strongly, that my breath that night
> might be stopt, and I might have a quincy in my throat[.][6]

The supernatural order works alongside, rather than obliterates, the
physical realm: Satan and "a quincy" are presented as entirely compatible entities.[7] Elsewhere in her writings, Trapnel imagines falling
"from the top to the bottom of the stairs" and breaking her limbs,
again focusing attention on the material image of her broken, suffering
body.[8] Her experiences are repeatedly evoked in startlingly sensuous
terms: "the Sent of dead sculls turned out of the grave was still in my
nostrils", she claims in one episode, "and my body like unto a clod
of earth, and pain working up to my heart".[9] The physical figures
the supernatural, but the metaphorical terms through which Trapnel
represents her spiritual struggles, such as when she depicts herself

---

[4] Trapnel, *Legacy*, 29.

[5] Recent critical attention to Trapnel's display of her body includes Susanna B.
Mintz, "The Specular Self of Anna Trapnel's *Report and Plea*", *Pacific Coast Philology* 35
(2000): 1–16; Hilary Hinds, who discusses Trapnel's "blissfully corporeal vision of the
state of grace", in "Soul-Ravishing and Sin-Subduing: Anna Trapnel and the Gendered
Politics of Free Grace", *Renaissance and Reformation* 25, no. 4 (2001): 117–137, 131; and
Maria Magro, "Spiritual Autobiography and Radical Sectarian Women's Discourse:
Anna Trapnel and the Bad Girls of the English Revolution", *Journal of Medieval and
Early Modern Studies* 34, no. 2 (2004): 405–437. Magro notes that Trapnel "makes a
spectacle of her body" and describes her raptures as "visually compelling" (414, 420).
Diane Purkiss discusses Trapnel's representations of her sufferings in "Producing the
Voice" (139–58).

[6] Trapnel, *Legacy*, 31.

[7] 'Quinsy' is an inflammation of the throat (*OED*).

[8] Anna Trapnel, *Anna Trapnel's Report and Plea* (1654), 6.

[9] Trapnel, *Legacy*, 40.

"wallowing in blood and pained with wounds", continue to place her tortured body centre stage.[10]

Trapnel claims that she would rather "be out of the body then in it", echoing the apostle Paul as she states: "I was desirous to be out of the body, I longed to be dissolved".[11] Her desire for dissolution nevertheless emerges in the context of a graphically described illness: "I lay in the strength of the fever, burning very much within, but without like a clod, and my stomack being shut up...I did so burn in my throat and stomack".[12] As Elaine Scarry observes, "the person in great pain experiences his own body as the agent of his agony", generating an acute sense of alienation from the body whose pain simultaneously announces its inescapability.[13] Trapnel's fantasies of freedom from the body are swiftly followed by the recognition that such release is impossible, leading her to ask "how I should live in the body[?]"[14] The divine plan for her life, it seems, must be played out in physical terms: "live in the body...to the glory of God", she is instructed.[15]

Testifying to the "glory" inscribed in Trapnel's tortured body involves displaying this body to a wide audience, transgressing the rules of decorum sanctioning the display of the suffering female form.[16] The editor of *A Legacy for Saints* confirms the significance of Trapnel's body as witness: her "sore sickness" enables God's power to be "demonstrated upon her in a visible way: whereby God would seem as by a visible sign to manifest that the Invisible God dwells in her".[17] Her body has already been a "visible sign" to those in her immediate vicinity, such as when her "outward man [was] altered on a sudden, to the view of

---

[10] Trapnel, *Legacy*, 13.

[11] Trapnel, *Legacy*, 28, 27. See Philippians 1:23–25 and 2 Corinthians 5:1. Thanks to Crawford Gribben for these and other biblical references. Esther Gilman Richey discusses Trapnel's reliance on Pauline models in *The Politics of Revelation in the English Renaissance* (Columbia: University of Missouri Press, 1988), 196–218.

[12] Trapnel, *Legacy*, 27.

[13] Elaine Scarry, *The Body in Pain: The Making and Unmaking of the World* (Oxford: Oxford University Press, 1985), 47.

[14] See Phillipians 1:23–25, where Paul also concedes that he must "remain in the flesh".

[15] Trapnel, *Legacy*, 28.

[16] Mintz notes Trapnel's "blatant exposure of her body to shameful visibility" ("Specular Self", 5). Frances E. Dolan discusses the "indecorum" of displaying the suffering female body in "'Gentlemen, I Have One Thing More to Say': Women on Scaffolds in England, 1563–1680", *Modern Philology* 92, no. 2 (Nov 1994): 157–78, 162.

[17] Trapnel, *Legacy*, 21.

those that have been in the house".[18] The publication of her story, her
editor implies, is motivated by a desire to allow others to share in this
visual witness.

Readings of Trapnel's self-representations, including those that have
discussed the significance of her enfeebled body, have tended to privilege
gender as the primary framework through which to make sense of these
often mystifying writings. On the one hand, Trapnel's catatonia has been
identified as an expression of the inevitable 'pathology' of a woman
projecting her voice in this era.[19] On the other, Trapnel has been identified as a "politically astute stuntwoman" whose "trances" operate as a
tactical cover for her subversive activity.[20] Both approaches tend to posit
a clearly gendered self behind Trapnel's prophetic voice. Sue Wiseman
counters this trend, observing that Trapnel's texts are "not attributable
to a single subject or voice", as her prophetic discourse "[presents] us
with no unified and gendered subject-position". Wiseman makes an
exception for the autobiographical element of Trapnel's writing, however, which she claims is "written from a gendered subject-position".[21]
Any attempt to separate the prophetic from the autobiographical in
Trapnel's work nevertheless occludes the extent to which Trapnel's millenarian religious and political context was intrinsic to the construction
and articulation of her subjectivity.

Trapnel's male Fifth Monarchist counterparts remain a notable
absence in most discussions of her work. Placing Trapnel within an
exclusively female prophetic and authorial tradition—one critic writes
of "Trapnel and her sisters"[22]—divorced from the work of her fellow
sectarians, potentially obscures the Fifth Monarchist framework of her
texts, leading to specific sectarian strategies of self-representation being
identified in more simply gendered terms. In this chapter, I examine

---

[18] Trapnel, *Legacy*, 12.
[19] Readings of Trapnel in relation to gender and illness include Purkiss, "Producing
the Voice", 151; Phyllis Mack, *Visionary Women: Ecstatic Prophecy in Seventeenth-Century
England* (Berkeley: University of California Press, 1992), 108–112; Hilary Hinds, *God's
Englishwomen: Seventeenth-Century Radical Sectarian Writing and Feminist Criticism* (Manchester
and New York: Manchester University Press, 1996), 100–102.
[20] Stevie Davies, *Unbridled Spirits: Women of the English Revolution 1640–1660* (London:
The Women's Press, 1998), 162.
[21] Sue Wiseman, "Unsilent Instruments and the Devil's Cushions: Authority in Seventeenth-Century Women's Prophetic Discourse", in *New Feminist Discourses*, ed. Isobel
Armstrong (London and New York: Routledge, 1992), 187, 189.
[22] See Magro, where "Trapnel and her sisters" are seen to contribute "to the shaping
of emergent female authorial consciousness" ("Spiritual Autobiography", 430).

Trapnel's writings alongside representations of the Fifth Monarchist John James, executed for treason following his alleged involvement in an uprising in 1661, whose experiences are related in the anonymous tract *A Narrative of the Apprehending, Commitment, Arraignment, Condemnation and Execution of John James* (1662). Paralleling Trapnel's self-constructions, James is depicted in the tract relating his story as passive, weak, self-alienated and self-abnegating. Through emphasising James's helplessness, the author locates him within a tradition of martyrological representation where victimisation and physical weakness operate as the grounds for spiritual triumph.[23] Trapnel's emphasis on her sufferings is likewise generated within a martyrological framework, suggesting the significance of motifs of martyrdom for Fifth Monarchist self-representation more generally.

Fifth Monarchists were by no means unique in harnessing the power of suffering to their cause: the tradition of "suffering for the Truth's sake", as Knott states, was "at the heart of Protestant Christianity", and such discourses were heavily deployed by other sectarian groups, notably the Quakers.[24] Despite being widely appropriated across a broad theological spectrum, however, the representation of martyrdom is centrally concerned with the establishment and policing of boundaries between religious and social groups.[25] Accounts of martyrdom, which conform to clearly defined conventions, are not primarily individualistic narratives, but are aimed instead at particular audiences, working to consolidate specific communities of faith. The body of the martyr performs and is displayed for a wider audience in order to witness to specific versions of the truth.[26] As Nigel Smith notes, "the meaning of the body became a matter of inter-sectarian dispute" in this era.[27] Representations of the body, including the martyred body, operate within sectarian writings as a key means by which sects sought to differentiate themselves from

---

[23] See John R. Knott, *Discourses of Martyrdom in English Literature, 1563–1694* (Cambridge: Cambridge University Press, 1993), 32.

[24] Knott, *Discourses of Martyrdom*, 1. For a discussion of Quaker martyrdom see Knott, 216–55.

[25] As Brad S. Gregory observes, "'us' and 'them' could scarcely have been clearer" than in martyrs' trials and public deaths. See his *Salvation at Stake: Christian Martyrdom in Early Modern Europe* (Cambridge, Mass.: Harvard University Press, 1999), 142.

[26] The root meaning of 'martyr' is 'witness'. See Knott, *Discourses of Martydom* 12. See also Elizabeth A. Castelli, *Martyrdom and Memory: Early Christian Culture Making* (New York: Columbia University Press, 2004), 120–21.

[27] Nigel Smith, *Perfection Proclaimed: Language and Literature in English Radical Religion 1640–1660* (Oxford: Clarendon Press, 1989), 15.

other ostensibly similar groupings. Trapnel's suffering, 'martyred' body
is thus a site where the truth of Fifth Monarchism is defined, displayed,
and vindicated. The "unfoldings of God" are not suppressed, then, by
talk "of the body" in her writings, but are spectacularly witnessed in
the rhetorical display of her suffering.

Christian martyrological traditions were rooted in accounts of the sufferings of Old Testament prophets, and the New Testament consolidated
the connection of martyrdom with "vision and inspiration by the Holy
Spirit".[28] The prophetic associations of martyrdom coincided with its
apocalyptic implications. As Castelli observes, the New Testament made
"persecution an organizing feature of the triumphant story it told",
while "the gruesome portraits of righteous suffering and vindication in
the book of Revelation wrote the story of Christian suffering...with a
driving apocalyptic beat".[29] Revelation suggests that Antichrist will be
defeated once sufficient numbers of martyrs take their place beneath
the altar, implying that each act of martyrdom works to hasten the end
times.[30] The prophetic and apocalyptic overtones of martyrdom reso-
nated strongly with Fifth Monarchists. The sect, comprised of women
and men labelled by their contemporaries as "the worst of men, the
Scum and very froth of baseness", crystallised at the beginning of the
1650s.[31] Proclaiming the imminent millennial reign of Christ on earth,
they adopted an unusually detailed, practical, and social vision of the
coming revolution, which would instigate the rule of the saints over
the masses.[32] Fifth Monarchists set themselves apart from other sectarian groups by emphasising their own potentially violent agency in the
inauguration of this era, indicating why they were a particularly "potent
and dangerous synthesis" of the radical revolutionary impulses grip-
ping some sections of English society in the mid-seventeenth century.[33]
Their millennial fervour was relatively short-lived: severe repression

---

[28] Knott, *Discourses of Martyrdom*, 21.

[29] Castelli, *Martyrdom and Memory*, 36.

[30] Revelation 6:9–11. See Gregory, *Salvation at Stake*, 142.

[31] Anon., *London's Glory, or, the Riot and Ruine of the Fifth Monarchy Men* (1661). Cited
in B. S. Capp, *The Fifth Monarchy Men: A Study in Seventeenth-Century English Millenarianism*
(London: Faber and Faber, 1972), 82.

[32] See Capp, *Fifth Monarchy Men*, 175.

[33] Capp, *Fifth Monarchy Men*, 15–16, 20. See also Capp 1–14 and Crawford Gribben, *The Puritan Millennium: Literature and Theology 1550–1682* (Dublin: Four Courts
Press, 2000), 154.

after the Restoration meant that the group had largely disbanded by the end of the 1660s.

Given their revolutionary aspirations, the Fifth Monarchist tendency to portray themselves in helpless and impotent terms in their life writings can come as something of a surprise. Instead of asserting the political and spiritual agency of the saints, Fifth Monarchist life writings frequently emphasise their passivity. Quakers often describe a process of guarding the word of God within themselves until the time is ripe for its proclamation, but Trapnel's will plays no role in her apprehension or delivery of divine truth. Instead, her body, selfhood, and consciousness are wholly overridden by the force of God's word which speaks through her. The editor of *A Legacy for Saints* similarly presents the work of God as the violent overthrow of the self: "God begins to break down the Walls of flesh in a Creature, in such a rending way, upon those ruines he raiseth up a foundation of Heaven and of Glory to be admired".[34]

The editor's formulation of personal destruction as the means of achieving wider social and spiritual glory draws attention to the apocalyptic martyrological perspective underlying the seemingly paradoxical self-representations of the Fifth Monarchists. Rather than the feeble physical self being an end in itself, personal annihilation within Fifth Monarchist frameworks operates as a microcosm of the coming social apocalypse. All fleshly constructs must be destroyed in order that a new social order can be established, a process undergone prophetically by the Fifth Monarchist messenger. Representations of the annihilation of the self therefore characteristically develop into generalised statements predicting social destruction, indicating the extent to which the personal is indivisible from the public and collective in this discourse:[35]

> Oh what is the Carcasse, the Vessel? They are nothing, but when these are gone, then where am I but there where I am made perfect in thy selfe; thou wilt bring thine into the Grave before thou raisest them up to live; til thou comest and puttest a sentence of death upon all things here below, they wil not look upon that which is glorious.[36]

---

[34] Trapnel, *Legacy*, 27.

[35] Megan Matchinske notes that apocalyptic texts equate "the personal with the universal, the individual with the national". "Holy Hatred: Formations of the Gendered Subject in English Apocalyptic Writing, 1625–1651", *English Literary History* 60, no. 2 (Summer 1993): 349–77, 354.

[36] Anna Trapnel, *The Cry of a Stone* (1654), 44–45.

The personal, then, is apocalyptic in these writings. Trapnel insists on the millennial significance of her sufferings, which she sees as inaugurating the wider "pulling downe" that will usher in the "fifth monarchy":[37]

> The Lord is building his Temple...The Souldiers slight thy handmaid, but she matters not, they shall and must consider in time; they say these are Convulsion-fits, and Sickness, and diseases that make thy handmaid to be in weakness; But oh they know not the pouring forth of thy spirit, for that makes the body to crumble, and weakens nature; In these extraordinary workings thou intendest to shew what is coming forth hereafter; something is a coming forth, there is so Lord; and oh how does thy handmaid bless thee![38]

The pain of her 'crumbling' body is inextricable from her expectation of an imminent end to social injustice: "this weakness on thy body is that the power of thy God may be made manifest".[39]

The framework of martyrdom means that the "powerlessness", or the "dislocation from subject as active agent", that Matchinske reads as a problem for women to negotiate in their articulation of millennial "holy hatred" is in fact inextricable from the apocalyptic authority of both female and male Fifth Monarchists.[40] Martyrological models uniquely reconcile the passive, tortured body with the projection of a prophetic voice. Scarry argues in general for the irreconcilability of the suffering body with the power inherent in the possession of a voice, but notes that the figure of Christ, the ideal martyr, shatters the separation of body and voice, becoming a model for the reconciliation of pain and power.[41] The 'voice' in Trapnel's texts does not operate at the level of 'personal' expression, however, any more than the theatrical display of her body can be understood in simply narcissistic terms.[42] "I go not about to vindicate myself, but Truth", she declares.[43]

Trapnel's emphasis on her physical weakness is thus generated within the specific sectarian frameworks shaping her self-representations, rather

---

[37] Trapnel, *Cry*, 36.
[38] Trapnel, *Cry*, 29.
[39] Trapnel, *Legacy*, 26.
[40] Matchinske, "Holy Hatred", 359, 360.
[41] Scarry, *Body in Pain*, 27–59, 213–14.
[42] Mintz comments that Trapnel is "obviously fascinated by herself", arguing that "she repeatedly directs our attention *not* toward God but toward Anna Trapnel" ("Specular Self", 8).
[43] Trapnel, *Report and Plea*, sig. A2.

than solely in relation to her gender. Sectarian models of the self are not divorced from gendered categories, but gender is frequently deployed in fluid terms in sectarian writings, in relation to wider political, theological, and social discourses. Magro argues that "antirationalist" sectarian discourse was "feminized", suggesting that radical Puritan groups were "coded as feminine".[44] Millennial prophetic discourse has also been identified as a "predominantly 'masculine' genre", however, and Fifth Monarchists presented themselves as possessing masculine privileges of social and political authority.[45] Discourses of martyrdom, like those of radical religion, rendered gender a "remarkably malleable dimension of contingent earthly identity".[46] "The martyr's death", notes Castelli, "is a masculine death", as confirmed by Latimer's famous challenge to his fellow martyr Ridley to "plaie the manne".[47] 'Masculine' valour was nevertheless set against 'feminine' physical weakness in order to establish the heroism of the martyr: Ridley described his fellow martyr, a "man of God", as "like unto a great bellied woman" in order to emphasise his physical incapacity.[48] Stories of female martyrdom carried particular power because of the alignment of 'feminine' physical frailty with the necessary vulnerability of the martyr.[49] Indicating the gendered ambivalences of martyrological representations, Foxe cites the example of Julitta, an early female martyr who demanded that women

> [c]ease to accuse the fragilitie of feminine nature. What? Are not we created of the same matter, that men are? Yea, after Gods image and similitude are we made, as lively as they. Not fleshe onely God used in the creation of the woman, in signe and token of her infirmitie and weakenes, but bone of bones is she, in token that she must be strong in the true and livyng God.[50]

Through insisting that martyred women exhibit masculine "bones", representing strength, Julitta not only rejects traditional narratives of

---

[44] Magro, "Spiritual Autobiography", 406, 405, 408.

[45] Matchinske, "Holy Hatred", 370.

[46] Castelli, *Martyrdom and Memory*, 61.

[47] John Foxe, *The Second Volume of the Ecclesiasticall History, Contaynng the Actes and Monumentes of Martyrs* (1576), 1662. Latimer's phrase echoes the story of the early Christian Polycarp's martyrdom, when a voice from heaven encourages him to "play the man" (Castelli, *Martyrdom and Memory*, 62).

[48] Foxe, *Second Volume*, 1678.

[49] Knott describes accounts of Anne Askew's martyrdom in these terms. *Discourses of Martyrdom*, 57.

[50] John Foxe, *The First Volume of the Ecclesiasticall History conteyning the Actes and Monuments of the Martyrs of Jesus Christ* (1576), 96.

feminine helplessness but also represents masculinity in emphatically physical terms: female 'flesh' fuses with male 'bones', rather than with male 'spirit', in this passage. Martyrdom not only redefines femininity, then, but also foregrounds the fleshly nature of men. Whether made of 'flesh' or 'bones', however, the martyr is ultimately aligned with a disempowered corporeal role more typically cast as feminine than masculine.[51]

The terms within which John James's identity is constructed illustrate both the 'feminized' discourse of martyrdom informing Fifth Monarchist representations and the extent to which the language of weakness, intersecting as it does with categories of social status, was deployed within the sect in order to figure the alternative terms of Fifth Monarchist spiritual and social ascendancy. *A Narrative* relates the experiences of the low-born James, whose Fifth Monarchist allegiances culminated in his execution in 1661. The narrative is penned by a sympathetic observer, but includes lengthy transcriptions of James's own words, thus allowing access, albeit mediated, to the self-representations of a man facing desperate social, economic, and religious circumstances in this period. John James began his working life as a small-coal man, but was unable to continue that "calling" because of physical "weaknesse". He turned instead to ribbon-weaving, which entailed a life of extreme poverty. He "had much adoe for this many years to get Bread for his Family", and describes how "many a night he has not been able to take his rest, for the sore and painful labour he had taken the day before with his weak body, to get food for his poor Family".[52] Along with others of the largely illiterate underclass of mid-seventeenth-century England, he became involved in the Fifth Monarchy movement, believing that "he did own the *Fifth Kingdom* which must come".[53]

As he was preaching to a congregation in Whitechapel, London, in October 1661, James was arrested for treason. A neighbour claimed to have overheard him stating that "Out of the mouths of Babes and Sucklings hast thou ordained strength because of thine Enemies".[54] The authorities believed that such biblical references were being used

---

[51] For a discussion of the disempowerment of embodiment, see Scarry's account of torture, *Body in Pain*, 27–59. Purkiss notes the feminisation of "bodily weakness" in "Producing the Voice", 144.

[52] *A Narrative of the Apprehending, Commitment, Arraignment, Condemnation and Execution of John James* (1662), 25, 27.

[53] *A Narrative*, 9.

[54] *A Narrative*, 7.

to stir an uprising, associating James with a Fifth Monarchist rising of that year. James denied involvement in any plot, but the threat to social order entailed in his descriptions of both the king and the nobles of England as "blood-thirsty and tyrannical men" was sufficient to justify his execution.[55] His destitute family was ordered to pay extortionate fees for his execution, while the hangman menacingly threatened that "if he would not give him Five pounds, he would torture him exceedingly". Unable to pay, James cast himself on his executioner's mercy, and was ultimately perceived as fortunate for dying from hanging before his bowels were removed and burnt. He was decapitated, and his body was dismembered.[56]

John James is constructed in passive, enfeebled terms in the narrative, fulfilling the necessary requirements of the ideal Christian martyr.[57] Depictions of his weakness play on his low social status, yet James adopts the terminology employed to denigrate the poor as the language of his self-justification, stating, like countless women alongside him, that God "chooseth the weak and foolish things of the world to confound the mighty". He resists social impotence through invoking the commonplace biblical theme that "the way of the Lord was and is many times, to use the poorest of his People to do his work".[58] James's self-denigrating language reaches a climax at the moment of his execution, when he is allowed to offer a final, public prayer. He praises God that "such a poor worm as is before thee can call thee Father, that such a poor worm before thee can come and take hold of thee". He refers to himself as a "poor worm" nineteen times in the prayer, elsewhere describing himself as "a *poor low deformed worm*, yea a *flea*".[59] James's terminology nevertheless echoes that of Psalm 22, a text frequently interpreted in Messianic terms, so that his apparently self-abnegating language aligns him with Christ.[60] His 'weakness' is thus redefined as the terms of his ultimate triumph.

James employs ambivalent images of himself as God's instrument, representing himself and his fellow sectarians as weapons in the hands of Christ: "Jesus Christ must come by his Kingdom, and that is, He

---

[55] *A Narrative*, 15.
[56] *A Narrative*, 26, 46.
[57] Castelli, *Martyrdom and Memory*, 55.
[58] *A Narrative*, 8–9.
[59] *A Narrative*, 35–36, 43–46.
[60] See Psalm 22:6.

shall use his People in his hand as his *Battle-ax and Weapon of War* for
the bringing in the kingdoms of this World into subjection to Him".[61]
James's collective objectification of the Fifth Monarchists as a "Battle-
ax" on the one hand evacuates the saints of personal agency, displac-
ing their actions onto Christ. This manoeuvre echoes the tortuous
negotiations of female authors of this era with representations of their
agency.[62] On the other hand, though, as is the case in the writing of
many women, this strategy provides the ultimate legitimation for the
saints' actions, here taking the form of a clear justification for Fifth
Monarchists to act as God's instruments in the violent overthrow of
the authorities.

Elsewhere in his account, James again presents himself as alienated
from his body, which is objectified in inanimate terms:

> this poor weak body has been often near the gates of death in my own
> thoughts, and others, and now that the Lord should make choice of so
> poor a Carcass to put it off at such a rate, Oh…blessed be God! let
> him take it.[63]

James thus echoes Trapnel's objectification of and dissociation from
her body, demonstrated for instance as she responds to a persecutor's
demands for her body with the statement: "take it, if it will do you any
good".[64] Refigured in alienated terms as 'the sacrifice', James's suffering
body enables the ultimate elevation of his identity:

> he had look'd upon all their Instruments of death, and was filled with
> Joy and Peace unutterable, but when he had any thoughts of living he
> had nothing but trouble and distraction; for alas (said he) what will my
> Life signifie but little; but my Blood will cry aloud, it will speak louder
> than all my life.[65]

The fact that James's blood will "cry aloud" identifies him with the
martyrs of Revelation, as the apparent passivity of his death is reinterpreted as a powerful act, working to usher in the reign of Christ on
earth. His death will also become articulate through its narrativisation,
providing a platform for the display and vindication of Fifth Monarchist

---

[61] *A Narrative*, 34.
[62] For analysis of female authors' negotiations with agency, see Hinds, *God's Englishwomen*, 96–97.
[63] *A Narrative*, 28.
[64] Trapnel, *Report and Plea*, 27.
[65] *A Narrative*, 28.

truth through its depiction of his godly suffering. Apocalyptic and Christological models of martyrdom therefore enable the apparently helpless defeat of Fifth Monarchist saints such as James to be refigured in wholly alternative terms in the writings of the sect.

The theatrical display of Trapnel's sufferings in her texts similarly works to construct her identity in martyrological terms. *A Legacy for Saints*, as its title suggests, is presented as a final testimony, to be read when its author has "gone hence, and shall be no more seen".[66] The tract was published during her lifetime, yet the voice of the author derives authority from its apparent positioning beyond the grave. Trapnel's status as 'martyr' is further secured in *A Report and Plea*, an account of her trial and imprisonment, where she structures her experiences around persecution, echoing other Protestant narratives in which the examination was the pivotal arena for the martyr's testing and triumph.[67] Trapnel's writings are infused with the language of martyrdom. She refers to her "fiery tryals" and parallels her illness with Christ's period of entombment, aligning herself with the ultimate act of martyrdom as she proclaims that she, too, is about to be resurrected.[68]

Foxe's *Acts and Monuments* emphasised the patient endurance of the martyrs, highlighting their calm willingness to comply with their fates as evidence of the godliness of their cause.[69] These victims are often seen to rejoice at the opportunity to sacrifice their lives for the truth. The night before his execution, for instance, Ridley serenely stated "to morrow I must be married" and "shewed hym self to be as mery as ever he was at any tyme before", while Julitta "[embraced] the sentence as a thing most sweete and delectable".[70] John James, as we have seen, similarly speaks of his "joy and peace" as he examines the "instruments of death". "*Here comes my Bride-men*", he announces, as his executioners arrive, "imbracing them with much joy".[71] Trapnel's euphoria in the midst of her suffering, as she is fuelled by "liquors and flagons from heaven" and the "pure hony that is reviving", is generated within the same tradition. Her allusions to her "excellent sweet" raptures redefine her agony as an occasion for festive celebration, demonstrating her

---

[66] Trapnel, *Legacy for Saints*, 12.
[67] Knott, *Discourses of Martyrdom*, 49–50.
[68] Trapnel, *Legacy*, 23, 27–28.
[69] Knott, *Discourses of Martyrdom*, 5, 8.
[70] Foxe, *Second Volume*, 1661; Foxe, *First Volume*, 96.
[71] *A Narrative*, 38.

ability to experience pleasure in the midst of pain and thus working to identify her as an ideal martyr.[72]

Trapnel's torments, including her lengthy periods of fasting, might appear to be self-inflicted rather than the result of persecution. While self-induced sufferings were potentially readable as signs of holiness before the Reformation, such experiences were dubious markers of godliness within a post-Reformation context.[73] In their anxiety to emphasise saints' readiness to suffer for their faith, however, accounts of martyrdom often insist so heavily on the self-sacrificial nature of the act that the agency of the executioner is occluded.[74] It is James, not his persecutors, for instance, who ensures that his body is tied: "But, said he, *Must not the sacrifice be bound?* One answered, *Yea, it must be bound with Cords*: he rejoicing, said, so he had heard".[75] Imitating Christ, James is presented as actively surrendering his own existence. His final speech and prayer are said to have brought his body "very low", suggesting that he has consciously reached the point of death before any action is taken by his executioners. The event is framed as the culmination of an act already performed by James on himself, as he appears to eradicate his own feeble body.

Trapnel, however, is anxious to deny that she is the author of her own misery, rejecting any suggestion of 'self-end' as she portrays herself as the helpless victim of supernatural forces. "I was tortured in my body", she states, "as if [Satan] had the full possession thereof".[76] Her body is the object of divine as well as Satanic assaults. The semi-violent encounters demonstrate her helplessness in the face of an intrusive deity:

> When I have closed my eyes, thinking to sleep, they have on a sudden been forced open.... Another time when I laid my self to sleep, something as it were pulled me by the shoulder, with this voice, it is better for thee to wake, I will shew thee thy Saviour in the Mount;...At another season

---

[72] Trapnel, *Cry*, 23, 37.

[73] See Stephen Greenblatt, "Mutilation and Meaning", in *The Body in Parts: Fantasies of Corporeality in Early Modern Europe*, ed. David Hillman and Carla Mazzio (New York and London: Routledge, 1997), 230.

[74] See Castelli, *Martyrdom and Memory*, 53.

[75] *A Narrative*, 38. The early Christian martyr Pionius similarly placed the cords around his own neck and those of his companions. See Castelli, *Martyrdom and Memory*, 99.

[76] Trapnel, *Cry*, 5, 8.

> when I have shut my eyes, immediately they have been unclosed, and my
> Saviour presenting his speech to me that he said to his Disciples[.][77]

Trapnel's depiction of God's physical impact upon her, forcing open her
eyes and pulling her by the shoulder, is generated by her perception of
the position of God in relation to mankind. Through describing God's
violation of her body, Trapnel constructs a clear spatial distinction
between herself and the divine. Whatever her rapturous apprehensions
as she lies on her bed, or her sense of 'the spirit' speaking through
her, God is ultimately exterior to the self in her writings. "How I had
erred", she laments, "in that I had held forth before I sickned, that
God dwelt essentially in his saints":

> so the Lord said to me, should I thy God dwell in thee, as I am in my
> essentiall glory, thou couldst not breathe in the body, but immediatly
> thou woudst dye in the body, it could not bear such a weight of glory:
> therefore I shine on thee on beams and streams of glory, which produces
> those effects spoken of in Scripture[.][78]

Trapnel's insistence that God dwells outside, rather than within, the
self, so that her body bears the marks of his external influence, is
crucial to her self-differentiation from other sectarians such as the
Quakers.[79] Contemporaries often confused Fifth Monarchists with
Quakers, suggesting the significant degree of overlap between the two
radical religious groups. Quaker doctrines of the Light within nevertheless implicitly merged self and divine, a radical position abhorred by
Trapnel: "[S]ome poor creatures call themselves Christ", she laments,
"because of this oneness with Christ, they will have no distinguishing,
thou wilt make them to know that there is a difference between Head
and Members".[80] Trapnel's representation of God as physically external to the self is a means of asserting his essential 'difference' from
mankind. In *The Cry of a Stone*, Trapnel differentiates Fifth Monarchists
from other sects in these terms, opposing those who are "for a crucified
Christ" to those for "a Christ within". Trapnel elevates the former as
the only true form of accepting Christ, stating that "if they have not

---

[77] Trapnel, *Legacy*, 36–37.
[78] Trapnel, *Legacy*, 36.
[79] Hinds notes that Trapnel's texts "make quite clear how important the distinctions
and differences between sects are" ("Soul-Ravishing and Sin-Subduing", 123).
[80] Trapnel, *Cry*, 66.

a footing in a crucified Christ, in God manifest in the flesh, then let not thine embrace them".[81]

Trapnel's construction of God as emphatically other to the self leads to His voice being projected in material terms in her text. God's Word is figured in *A Legacy for Saints* as a physical presence outside of the self:

> it followed me where ever I went; sometimes as I have been going along the streets, I have looked behind me, thinking I had heard some locall voice, a voice without me, but sure it was because I was unacquainted with the voice of the Spirit speaking in, or to the soul; I oft-times turned back when I have been going along the streets, to see who it was that spake, taking that for visible which was invisible[.][82]

As with Quaker constructions of the Light and the 'self', absolute distinctions of 'interior' and 'exterior' cannot be maintained in this discourse of God and the self. Trapnel frames her perception of God's voice speaking in the street as youthful folly, implying that God was, after all, speaking individually to her soul. Yet this voice is nevertheless located as speaking 'to', rather than 'in' the self, as the text maintains a crucial distinction between her own interiority and the voice of God. It is this consciousness of God's separate existence from the self which induces the initially mistaken identification of God's Spirit as a "locall voice" that follows her down the street.

Trapnel's use of her suffering to witness to the external impact of God upon her body, alongside the apocalyptic terms through which her passivity operates as the grounds for her revolutionary agency, indicates the manner in which her writings deploy physical descriptions in order to construct and police the boundaries of sectarian belief. While their self-representations drew on widespread motifs of martyrdom, the specific terms in which Fifth Monarchists constructed themselves as suffering saints worked to embody and vindicate their particular brand of apocalyptic thinking. In view of the radical agenda that it supports, it is perhaps unsurprising that Trapnel's depiction of herself as martyr, as we shall see, boldly rejects some key tenets of Protestant discourses of martyrdom in this era.

Martyrdom occupied an ambivalent place within Reformed thought, maintaining as it did a focus on the body of the saint which did not

---

[81] Trapnel, *Cry*, 57–58.
[82] Trapnel, *Legacy*, 7–8.

accord easily with Protestant rejection of "somatic holiness".[83] Protestant dubiousness concerning the visibility of the martyred body, or spiritual investment in this entity, did not prevent Foxe from "[lingering] over abuses of the body" in his accounts, capitalising on the theatrical power of death-scenes to enhance the heroism of the Marian victims.[84] Foxe nevertheless minimises the presence of the miraculous or the supernatural in his *Acts and Monuments*, elements intrinsic to pre-Reformation depictions of the suffering of the saints. Pre-Reformation accounts of Christian martyrdom depicted victims as participating in the Passion of Christ, an interpretation of martyrdom usually rejected in Protestant accounts, where victims were more likely to imitate apostolic models of persecution.[85] Downplaying the intervention of the divine, Foxe emphasised the "heroic faith of the individual", as the martyr remained emphatically human throughout his or her ordeal.[86]

James's martyrdom is described with a poignant simplicity that largely accords with Protestant narratives of martyrdom. Messianic parallels, as we have seen, however, reverberate throughout his text. The moment of his death, for instance, explicitly parallels Christ's Passion: he "said aloud (lifting up his hands) *Father, into thy hands I commit my spirit*".[87] Trapnel also overtly draws on pre-Reformation models of martyrdom. Her experiences are made to parallel those of the early Christians as she refers to the threat of "wild beasts", deploying biblical terminology which simultaneously evokes the fate of the early Christians: "Thou hast a people in this nation, who have thy name upon them, therefore thou wilt not let out the boars, and the wild beasts against them".[88] As this passage suggests, Trapnel differentiates herself from orthodox Protestant martyrs through emphasising her miraculous preservation, echoing accounts of early Christians such as Thecla, who were rescued from persecution through divine intervention.[89] In her accounts of her lengthy fasts, Trapnel draws attention not to her physical frailty but

---

[83] See Greenblatt, "Mutilation and Meaning", 230.
[84] Knott, *Discourses of Martyrdom*, 10.
[85] Knott, *Discourses of Martyrdom*, 45.
[86] Knott, *Discourses of Martyrdom*, 46.
[87] *A Narrative*, 46.
[88] Trapnel, *Cry*, 24. See Psalm 80:13.
[89] Models of supernatural preservation preventing martyrdom can be traced back to biblical accounts including those of Daniel and the three Hebrew men, preserved from fire and from wild animals. For a discussion of Thecla, see Castelli, *Martyrdom and Memory*, 134–71.

to the supernatural strength by which she is sustained: "that a poor creature should subsist without sustenance, what a gazing is there at this poor thing, while you forget the glory that is in it".[90] Her illnesses, similarly, allow her to stage her body as the site of miraculous healing: God is "putting forth his Power, both for the removing of the distemper from soul and body".[91] Two of her texts, notably, conclude with images of her "health and strength", as Trapnel emphasizes the supernaturally maintained well-being of her body after its temporary incapacities.[92] As well as drawing on corporeal images to figure the experience of grace,[93] Trapnel's miraculously sustained body displays a corporeal manifestation of supernatural presence and power at odds with orthodox Protestantism.

Pre-Reformation narratives of martyrdom, as Knott states, "often give the impression that Christ is actually present", so that the bodies of the saints, and subsequently their shrines, are tangibly marked by holiness. The presence of the supernatural sets the martyr apart as uniquely purified in such accounts.[94] Trapnel's dramatic display of her body participates in this tradition. Her ability to survive beyond all natural capacity sets her apart from others. "Which of all our ministers", she asks, "can hold out thus many hours without a cordial?"[95] Although anxiously denying any "self-end" in her "singular" status, Trapnel does not ultimately deny this singularity.[96] As we have seen, however, Trapnel's textual identity is a vehicle for the transmission and consolidation of a collective identity. The fact that her calling, as with the early martyrs, is undoubtedly one which distinguishes her "from more ordinary and fallible human beings"[97] ultimately points to the elite

---

[90] Trapnel, *Cry*, 38. Trapnel's miraculously sustained self-starving body clearly evokes the experiences of medieval fasting female saints. See Carolyn Walker Bynum, *Holy Feast and Holy Fast: The Religious Significance of Food to Medieval Women* (Berkeley and Los Angeles: University of California Press, 1987). Nancy A. Gutierrez conversely argues that early modern female food refusal "is a practice distinct from...medieval patterns", but she excludes Trapnel's writings (which she merges with Quaker texts) from her analysis. See her *"Shall She Famish Then?" Female Food Refusal in Early Modern England* (Aldershot: Ashgate, 2003), 6, 21.

[91] Trapnel, *Legacy*, 23.

[92] Trapnel, *Cry*, 76 and Anna Trapnel, *Strange and Wonderful Newes from White-hall* (1654), 8.

[93] See Hinds, "Soul-Ravishing and Sin-Subduing", 117–37.

[94] Knott, *Discourses of Martyrdom*, 45.

[95] Trapnel, *Report and Plea*, 18.

[96] Trapnel, *Cry*, 5.

[97] Knott, *Discourses of Martyrdom*, 45.

prophetic status of the saints within Fifth Monarchist thinking, rather than to mere narcissism. While Foxe denied the 'odour of sanctity' surrounding earlier accounts of martyrdom, Trapnel's sensual evocation of her encounters with the divine, where her body is visibly marked by the supernatural as she imbibes "the sweet odour of the savour of the spirit", emphatically re-creates it in the name of her version of radical religious truth.[98]

Purkiss has noted the "uncanny return of what had been forgotten or repressed by orthodox Protestant culture", namely the "believer's body as the site of [supernatural] power", in relation to the fasting of female prophets.[99] The differences between the perhaps more orthodox narrative depicting James's martyrdom and the terms in which Trapnel's prophetic body is displayed may endorse Purkiss's gendered reading of this "uncanny return", where "women are characteristically the bearers of this kind of knowledge".[100] Trapnel's 'mystical' spirituality, a spirituality drawing her back to pre-Reformation models, cannot be divorced, however, from her radical Puritanism. As Nigel Smith states:

> Radical religious writers, especially learned ones, were using medieval and sixteenth-century Catholic, reformed and radical, mystical and spiritual writings in order to extend the boundaries of their own spiritual experiences, both psychologically and politically. That Catholic works were used should come as less of a surprise when it is realized that the emphasis upon direct divine inspiration put them in the same position as Catholic spiritual writers.[101]

Presenting herself within the context of pre-Reformation martyrdom, Anna Trapnel makes her prophetic body the site where Fifth Monarchist truth, a truth centred on "direct divine inspiration" and the paradoxical agency of martyrdom, is demarcated, published, and vindicated. The presentation of her suffering within this context aligns the overthrow of the self with an imminent social and spiritual revolution. Within such a context, to speak of her tortured body is not "lost time" but is at the heart of her Fifth Monarchist mission.

---

[98] Knott, *Discourses of Martyrdom*, 46; Trapnel, *Legacy*, 27.
[99] Purkiss, "Producing the Voice", 145.
[100] Purkiss, "Producing the Voice", 225n22.
[101] Smith, *Perfection Proclaimed*, 17.

Bibliography

Anonymous. *A Narrative of the Apprehending, Commitment, Arraignment, Condemnation and Execution of John James*. London, 1662.

——. *London's Glory, or, the Riot and Ruine of the Fifth Monarchy Men*. [London,] 1661.

Bynum, Carolyn Walker. *Holy Feast and Holy Fast: The Religious Significance of Food to Medieval Women*. Berkeley and Los Angeles: University of California Press, 1987.

Capp, B. S. *The Fifth Monarchy Men: A Study in Seventeenth-Century English Millenarianism*. London: Faber and Faber, 1972.

Castelli, Elizabeth A. *Martyrdom and Memory: Early Christian Culture Making*. New York: Columbia University Press, 2004.

Davies, Stevie. *Unbridled Spirits: Women of the English Revolution 1640–1660*. London: The Women's Press, 1998.

Dolan, Frances E. "'Gentlemen, I Have One Thing More to Say': Women on Scaffolds in England, 1563–1680". *Modern Philology* 92, no. 2 (November 1994): 157–78.

Foxe, John. *The First Volume of the Ecclesiasticall History conteyning the Actes and Monuments of the Martyrs of Jesus Christ*. London, 1576.

——. *The Second Volume of the Ecclesiasticall History, Contayning the Actes and Monumentes of Martyrs*. London, 1576.

Greenblatt, Stephen. "Mutilation and Meaning". In *The Body in Parts: Fantasies of Corporeality in Early Modern Europe*. Edited by David Hillman and Carla Mazzio. New York and London: Routledge, 1997.

Gregory, Brad S. *Salvation at Stake: Christian Martyrdom in Early Modern Europe*. Cambridge, Mass.: Harvard University Press, 1999.

Gribben, Crawford. *The Puritan Millennium: Literature and Theology 1550–1682*. Dublin: Four Courts Press, 2000.

Gutierrez, Nancy A. *"Shall She Famish Then?" Female Food Refusal in Early Modern England*. Aldershot: Ashgate, 2003.

Hinds, Hilary. *God's Englishwomen: Seventeenth-Century Radical Sectarian Writing and Feminist Criticism*. Manchester and New York: Manchester University Press, 1996.

——. "Soul-Ravishing and Sin-Subduing: Anna Trapnel and the Gendered Politics of Free Grace". *Renaissance and Reformation* 25, no. 4 (2001): 117–37.

Knott, John R. *Discourses of Martyrdom in English Literature, 1563–1694*. Cambridge: Cambridge University Press, 1993.

Mack, Phyllis. *Visionary Women: Ecstatic Prophecy in Seventeenth-Century England*. Berkeley: University of California Press, 1992.

Magro, Maria. "Spiritual Autobiography and Radical Sectarian Women's Discourse: Anna Trapnel and the Bad Girls of the English Revolution". *Journal of Medieval and Early Modern Studies* 34, no. 2 (2004): 405–437.

Matchinske, Megan. "Holy Hatred: Formations of the Gendered Subject in English Apocalyptic Writing, 1625–1651". *English Literary History* 60, no. 2 (Summer 1993): 349–377.

Mintz, Susanna B. "The Specular Self of Anna Trapnel's *Report and Plea*". *Pacific Coast Philology* 35 (2000): 1–16.

Purkiss, Diane. "Producing the Voice, Consuming the Body: Women Prophets of the Seventeenth Century". In *Women, Writing, History 1640–1740*. Edited by Isobel Grundy and Susan Wiseman. Athens: The University of Georgia Press, 1992.

Richey, Esther Gilman. *The Politics of Revelation in the English Renaissance*. Columbia: University of Missouri Press, 1988.

Scarry, Elaine. *The Body in Pain: The Making and Unmaking of the World*. Oxford: Oxford University Press, 1985.

Smith, Nigel. *Perfection Proclaimed: Language and Literature in English Radical Religion 1640–1660*. Oxford: Clarendon Press, 1989.

Trapnel, Anna. *Anna Trapnel's Report and Plea*. London, 1654.
——. *A Legacy for Saints*. London, 1654.
——. *Strange and Wonderful Newes from White-hall*. London, 1654.
——. *The Cry of a Stone*. London, 1654.
Wiseman, Susan. "Unsilent Instruments and the Devil's Cushions: Authority in Seventeenth-Century Women's Prophetic Discourse". In *New Feminist Discourses*. Edited by Isobel Armstrong. London and New York: Routledge, 1992.

A "REMARKABLE FEMALE OF WOMANKIND": GENDER, SCRIPTURE, AND KNOWLEDGE IN THE WRITINGS OF M. MARSIN

Sarah Apetrei

Between 1694 and 1701, a woman of some means produced at least fifteen (self-funded) theological tracts, many of which appeared in two or more editions, and some of which exceeded one hundred pages in length.[1] Few other seventeenth-century women writers published more than ten times in their lifetime.[2] Even the celebrated Mary Astell was less prolific. The reflections of this theologian, located in the contemporary discourses of both millenarian mysticism and advocacy for women, are illustrative of the dynamic religious and literary context of the 1690s. Yet "M. Marsin" (whose full name is unknown) remains one of the least discussed female figures of the period. Fortunately, she has been rescued from oblivion in recent years by William E. Burns, Tim Hitchcock, and Christopher Hill,[3] who have provided much of the groundwork for further research and have demonstrated the significance and exceptionality of her work.

Marsin's literary career did not begin in 1683, as the Wing Short Title Catalogue indicates. The unfortunate confusion of the anonymous satire *The Women's Advocate, or, Fifteen Real Comforts of Matrimony*, published in that year, with her 1697 *Womans Advocate* has carried over to various catalogues. Burns has drawn attention to the absurdity of the attribution, and the most cursory comparison of the bawdy humour of the 1683 *Women's Advocate* and Marsin's earnest prose confirms his point. In fact, Marsin began to write in 1694, following a series of earthquakes

---

[1] See bibliography.
[2] Famous exceptions include Aphra Behn, Margaret Cavendish, Eleanor Davies, Margaret Fell, Elinor James, Jane Lead, Dorothy White, and Hannah Woolley.
[3] Christopher Hill, *The English Bible and the Seventeenth-Century Revolution* (London: Penguin, 1993), 156, 407–9; William E. Burns, "'By Him the Women will be delivered from that Bondage, which some has found intolerable': M. Marsin, English Millenarian Feminist", in *Eighteenth Century Women: Studies in their Lives, Work and Culture*, ed. Linda V. Troost, vol. I (New York: AMS Press, 2001), 19–38; Tim Hitchcock, "Marsin, M. (*fl.* 1696–1701)" in *ODNB*.

and volcanic explosions which had shaken the territories of South Italy in the previous year, and the island of Jamaica in June 1692. It was perhaps in the year 1693, following the dissemination of this news, that she made her decision to travel to London. Her starting point is impossible to know, as the only indication she gives of her origin is the vaguest radius from the capital. In 1697 she describes how "I did dare do no other then leave and venture the little concern I had, and come about a Hundred Miles to acquaint the Nation, what God is a going to do".[4]

The reports from Jamaica and Italy—particularly those relating to volcanic activity, which seemed to her to portend the opening of hell[5]—convinced M. Marsin of the imminent second coming of Christ. She came to believe that this would be precipitated by the opening of the "sealed book" of Revelation 5, which implied a full and definitive exposition of Scripture (her own). There were a number of points which required clarification to reach this perfect synthesis, including the obscure "figurative speeches" which dealt with the status of the Jews in salvation history, the Holy Spirit, predestination, and other eschatological paradigms. Her views on some of these questions evolved over time, as autograph corrections on her publications indicate.[6] As Marsin's millennial expectations heightened, so did her understanding of her role as herald of the truth. She defended in radical terms her claim to a unique and almost prophetic dispensation as a woman and argued from Scripture the possibility of such a vocation for others of her sex. While her prose is often impenetrable and turgid, at intervals Marsin fires the imagination with her humanity, her audacity, her eccentricity, and her advocacy for her sex.

Yet her profile is still strikingly absent from the usual canons of early modern women writers: notably the Brown University Women Writers Project, but also the massive anthological literature of recent years.[7]

---

[4] *All the Chief Points Contained in the Christian Religion* (1697), 16.

[5] Marsin understood the eruptions of Vesuvius to be physical manifestations of hellfire, a notion perhaps derived from Henry More, who expected that the earth would be consumed by a conflagration at the end of time, precipitated by volcanic and subterranean fires. See *An Explanation of the Grand Mystery of Godliness* (Cambridge, 1660), 238–40.

[6] See for example the Bodleian copy of *This Treatise Proving Three Worlds* (1696), 8° Y 35 Th., in which Marsin modified her doctrine of election in a brief note below the Advertisement.

[7] Some recent examples include James Fitzmaurice et al., eds., *Major Women Writers of Seventeenth-Century England* (Michigan: University of Michigan Press, 1997); Randall

There are a number of reasons for this enduring obscurity. In the first place, Marsin falls between all kinds of stools. Her works do not obviously belong to the genres of poetry, prophecy, devotional writing, or polemic; a little like Astell, she was principally a theologian and exegete. As a religious figure, however, she is even more difficult to classify. A radical, but an adherent of no particular Dissenting group, she has been described rather fittingly as "the first and only Marsinite".[8] Her theological system is certainly nothing if not idiosyncratic. Moreover, any research on Marsin eventually meets a blind alley when it comes to reconstructing any sort of biographical information. There is no internal allusion which might lead us to a family or a literary circle. No references to her works, derisory or complimentary, have been found in contemporary literature, and it is generally accepted that her works did not circulate widely. Her very name has been thought to be pseudonymous, which leaves the biographer with few available leads.

However, it is my conviction that certain misleading assumptions about Marsin have contributed to her obscurity. First, I do not think that "Marsin" is obviously a pseudonym. While I acknowledge the possibility of a reference to the "Marprelate" alias,[9] I consider it more plausible that "Marsin" was authentic, particularly given the numerous variations on the name which appear in different editions (Mersen, Mercin, and Marcin). There were Marsins in the East Riding of Yorkshire and in Wirksworth in Derbyshire in the early to mid-eighteenth century, and the will of a "Marie Martyn, or Marsin" was drawn up in 1646 in the parish of St Clement Danes, Middlesex.[10] While it would be difficult to demonstrate a genealogical link, it is certain that Marsin or Mersen

---

Martin, ed., *Women Writers in Renaissance England* (London: Longman, 1997); Paul Salzman, *Early Modern Women Writers: An Anthology 1560–1700* (Oxford: Oxford University Press, 2000); Betty S. Travitsky and Anne Lake Prescott, eds., *Female and Male Voices in Early Modern England: An Anthology of Renaissance Writing* (New York: Columbia University Press, 2000).

[8] Hitchcock, "Marsin".

[9] See Burns, "'By Him the Women will be delivered'", 20.

[10] The East Riding Marsins seem to have an inauspicious history: an Ann Marsin was charged for assault in March 1762 (see Grimston Family of Grimston Garth and Kilnwick archives at East Riding of Yorkshire Archives and Records Service, Catalogue Ref. DDGR/34/88) and a Mary Marsin was cited in a bastardy case in 1780 (East Riding Quarter Session Records, QSF/288/C/15). See also Parish Registers for Wirksworth and Middleton-by-Wirksworth, Derbyshire (1608–1899) in which the baptisms of the children of a Ferdinand Marsin or Marsen are recorded in 1703 and 1706; and the Prerogative Court of Canterbury Will Registers, Fines Quire Numbers: 1–62 (1647), Cat: PROB 11/199.

was indeed an authentic family name in seventeenth-century England. The name was, however, French or Flemish, which raises the possibility of immigrant origins.[11]

Second, it seems possible that M. Marsin was read more widely and with greater approval than has commonly been recognized. It would be problematic simply to accept her boast in *Two Remarkable Females of Womankind* (1701) that "some well-read Gentlemen acknowledge, since they have read my Books, and that of the Deity; that I write agreeable to the most Ancient Authors of the Primitive times".[12] Indeed, the criticisms which she acknowledges of her use of the apocryphal text 1 Esdras, and of her tendency to "heap Scriptures one upon Back of another", have more of a ring of truth to them.[13] It is equally hard to demonstrate whether or not her *All the Chief Points Contained in the Christian Religion* (1697) ever arrived at the palaces of "the Lord Bishops" to whom it was respectfully addressed.[14] On some extant texts there are individually handwritten amendments which seem to be painstakingly transcribed onto each of these particular editions, indicating a limited circulation. Yet an investigation into the provenance of a number of her publications, which have found their way into such unlikely collections as that of the St George's Chapter Library at Windsor Castle, yields some intriguing evidence about the enduring audience for her writings.

A copy of *The Womans Advocate* (1697) survives at Trinity College, Cambridge, and was donated by the Whig clergyman and writer Francis Wrangham (1769–1842), Archdeacon of the East Riding, at his death. Wrangham's interest in Judaism and eschatology, reflected in his prize-winning poem of 1794, "The Restoration of the Jews", may have stimulated an interest in the philo-semite Marsin. Similarly, *A Full and Clear Account the Scripture gives of the Deity* (1700) found its way into Canterbury Cathedral Library via the collection of a nineteenth-century high-churchman, Benjamin Harrison, Archdeacon of Maidstone. His interest in the apocalyptic visions of Daniel and St John perhaps explains

---

[11] "Marsin" seems to have been a corruption of the name of the Wallonian town Marchin, southwest of Liège, as in the title of "Comte de Marchin", often called "Marsin".

[12] *Two Remarkable Females of Womankind* (1701), 15.

[13] *The Womans Advocate* (1697), 5; *Two Sorts of Latter Days* (1699), 44.

[14] *All the Chief Points Contained in the Christian Religion* (1697), 16.

his attention to Marsin's own exposition of these texts.[15] Another clergyman, William Torkington of Huntingdonshire, owned a copy of *All the Chief Points Contained in the Christian Religion*.[16] A bound volume of Marsin's tracts became part of the Baptist minister and academic Joseph Angus' personal library and was bequeathed to Regent's Park College in Oxford in the late nineteenth century.[17] Three volumes of Marsin's tracts were also preserved in the Duke of Manchester's Collection of Theological Literature at Tandaragee Castle.[18] Perhaps most interestingly, a collection of seven of Marsin's works was presented as a prize "to mary Lyneall December the 8 1710"—a mark of respectability.[19]

In her own day, Marsin made conscious efforts to target the poor and common reader. Her advertisement in *This Treatise Proving Three Worlds* (1696) expressed the hope "that the price being small, it might the easier be attained by all".[20] She invariably published in octavo and used Cheapside booksellers. Despite this, and her often unorthodox views, her works seem to have been preserved largely in the hands of senior clergymen. Naturally this is precisely the kind of collector who might afford a considerable library of eschatological works, and Marsin probably had other, less well-established readers. However, an "establishment" interest in Marsin is nonetheless curious. It raises questions about her personal marginality, but also about the marginality of the kinds of views which she represented and about the boundaries of theological acceptability and intellectual respectability. I want to ask some further questions about Marsin's interests and influences, to argue for her distinctiveness as a theologian and to assess how she might enrich approaches to both women's writing and radical religion in this period.

---

[15] See Benjamin Harrison, *Prophetic Outlines of the Christian Church and the Antichristian Power as Traced in the Visions of Daniel and St. John* (London: Francis & John Rivington, 1849).

[16] This was bequeathed to the parish of Broughton in 1737 and was eventually integrated into the Cambridge University Library.

[17] Shelfmark Angus 2.f.14 (1).

[18] These volumes were purchased by Harvard University in 1942, and are listed as EC65.M3594.700f, EC65.M3594.697f, and EC65.M3594.697f.

[19] Copy held at Henry E. Huntington Library (Rare Books), shelfmark 249553–249560. My thanks to Stephen Tabor at the Huntington Library; Joanna Ball at Trinity College, Cambridge; Keith O'Sullivan at Canterbury Cathedral Library; Sue Mills at Regent's Park College, Oxford; Emily Walhout at the Houghton Reading Room, Harvard University; and Nicholas Smith at Cambridge University Library for their helpful advice.

[20] *This Treatise Proving Three Worlds* (1696), 302.

Marsin: Her Task and her Gender

The convention among many seventeenth-century women writers of conceding the frailty of their sex and their unworthiness as authors is well-known. This gendered apology has been interpreted by an earlier generation of feminist commentators as a symptom of the tendency of women writers to 'kiss the rod', or to collude in their own subjection. Quite recently, efforts have been made to treat such modesty tropes with greater subtlety and to recognise the ways in which they function ambiguously and even ironically.[21] There is not only, however, a rhetorical subtext to such modesty topoi. Disentangling the 'weaker vessel' metaphor also, rather unexpectedly, bears out a powerful theological *vindication* for women's writing. The ambiguous quality of 'weakness' need not necessarily be understood as an inherent moral disability but can be associated with the very 'meekness' and worldly insignificance which often characterized great spiritual leaders in the Christian tradition.

It is easy to identify a biblical precedent for the special election of the disempowered. In the early history of Israel, a series of improbable protagonists led the nation through its most significant episodes: Gideon, Jeremiah, David, and even Moses each represented marginal origins. Youth, social inferiority, and, indeed, criminality did not disqualify these men from remarkable vocations. Neither were women excluded from participating in the sacred narrative, judging from the instrumentality of female protagonists such as Deborah, Miriam, Esther, and Ruth in the divine plan. Crucially, the Christian Gospel radically affirmed that the kingdom of heaven belonged to the poor and humble, and that divine glory was most appropriately displayed in "jars of clay" (2 Corinthians 4:7). The rich and powerful, said Christ, could as easily penetrate the kingdom of God as a camel the eye of a needle. Anyone who read the Sermon on the Mount might conclude that authentic spirituality was the exclusive province of the lowly.

Such a message could authorize the claims of disenfranchised men and women to a greater facility for spiritual advancement. Defenders of the controversial mystic Antonia Bourignon, whose lack of 'humane

---

[21] For example, Patricia Pender's unpublished paper on "Arresting Silence: Reading Modesty Rhetorically", presented July 2005 at *Still Kissing the Rod?: Early Modern Women's Writing in 2005* Conference, St Hilda's College, Oxford.

learning' was considered contemptible, rebuked her critics, pointing out that "the Learned had no regard" for Christ himself.[22] Indeed, certain radical and literalist religious movements were populated by unexceptional men and women who came to understand that priesthood and privilege of an unworldly kind belonged especially to them. The question of individual agency in the case of such claims is a difficult one: how did a religious writer, preacher, or prophet, convinced of the divine origins of their message, understand their own relationship to the words they used? Quaker theologians often justified the ministry of women by emphasising that it was Christ himself speaking through them, who "in the Male and the Female is one".[23] This rather circular reasoning makes a virtue of weakness, but in doing so subordinates the human voice to that of God. However, in the case of M. Marsin at least, both her humanity and specifically her gender played important roles in her sense of vocation and her understanding of the message she heralded.

Marsin's authorial sensibilities are not devoid of conventional humility. She understands her human weakness in precisely the terms I have described above: as the perfect showcase for God's revelation. She describes how "God has made choice of so weak an Instrument" (herself), so that "his power might the more eminently appear therein".[24] This sentiment is repeated elsewhere: in *The Figurative Speeches* (1697), she rejoices that God has "opened his Word, whereby Knowledge may be increased; and this he hath done by weak means, that his glory might the more eminently appear".[25] In *The Womans Advocate*, she hopes that "thro my weakness his Power might be exalted".[26] It is clear that Marsin sees her disempowered state as an actual advantage and even as a precondition for her particular ministry.

There is no apology for Marsin's gender; it is her very womanhood which permits her to criticize the misguided Church and its male authorities, who have corrupted their entire sex by their deviation from scriptural truth. As she colourfully puts it, "it is the He-Goats that have eaten the good Pastures, and trodden down the residue, and fouled the

---

[22] George Garden, *An Apology for M. Antonia Bourignon* (1699), 1.
[23] Margaret Fell, *Womens Speaking Justified, Proved and Allowed of by the Scriptures* (1667), 12.
[24] "To the Reader" in *The Near Approach of Christ's Kingdom*.
[25] *The Figurative Speeches*, 127.
[26] *The Womans Advocate*, 4.

deep Waters".[27] By withholding Scripture from women throughout centuries of spiritual oppression, the Church has inadvertently vindicated women as the authentic representatives of the Gospel because in their suffering they have participated in the Cross.[28] Therefore, "God often chuses to shew forth his Power…on that side by whom this Offence was not committed"—in other words, through women. She insists that

> our Teachers need not wonder that the knowledge of the lost Truths should come out by a Woman, and that Women should have Light herein. For they have had no hand in overturning the Bible; for that has been done by the Wise and Learned of this World.[29]

Of course, the reference to the "Wise and Learned" is somewhat ironic, and implies the inconsequentiality of knowledge which is humanly acquired. Elsewhere, she specifically states that "God chuseth not the Wise and Learned of this World to discover the Secrets in his Word".[30] In the fine intellectual cobwebs woven by men at the universities and in the pulpits, the plain meaning of Scripture has been tangled and obscured. Only the fresh insights of an uncluttered (female) mind can restore the truth to the world.

Gender is not the only theme of Marsin's subversive gospel. The Old Testament provides her with ample evidence of the calling of all kinds of marginal groups. She seems to feel a special affinity with 'the Poor' and 'the mean and low things of the Earth', who are described as the brethren of Christ and who will be chosen as part of his Elect at the second coming. In her frequent attacks on the doctrine of predestination, she insists that neither the poor, nor children who die in innocence, will be damned. She is able to reflect that "the poor, that here have known nothing but misery" are "thereby made uncapable of shewing mercy": a rather immoderate conclusion, but one which ultimately reflects her humanity. Her emphatic repudiation of the doctrines of original sin and reprobation elsewhere indicate a sympathy (probably unconscious) with the contemporary taste for theodicy, reflected in the works of Leibniz and Malebranche. Whatever her ambivalence about the moral capacity of the poor, Marsin consistently affirms that "It is not their Wisdom, Grandeur, or Greatness that made them acceptable with God". She

---

[27] *Truth Vindicated*, 25.
[28] *The Womans Advocate*, 4.
[29] *Two Remarkable Females*, 21.
[30] *The Womans Advocate*, 4.

quotes 1 Samuel 2:8, the prophecy of a woman, to powerful effect: "*He raised up the Poor out of the dust, and lifteth up the beggar from the dunghil, to set them among Princes, and to make them inherit the Throne of Glory*".[31]

This advocacy for the poor dovetails with Marsin's defence of women's instrumentality. Women, with the economically oppressed, belong to the class of people most commonly characterized by the virtue of humility. The Virgin Mary emerges as the patron or emblem of the marginalized, who was "but of small appearance in this World", but who, as her *Magnificat* celebrates, confounded "the high and lofty in their own imaginations".[32] Marsin is not, however, complacent about the injustices of subjection and does not glorify the state of oppression. She describes with anger how "the Beast ... would not permit any woman so much as to Read the Word: For which, when man acts contrary to God, then God acts contrary to man".[33] (The Beast refers, of course, to the Church of Rome.) The deprivation of religious education for women is described here as an act of rebellion against God. For this reason, Marsin, as a woman, has been given exclusive insight.

Marsin's understanding of the power balance between the genders is framed by the biblical narrative. In *The Womans Advocate*, she explains that "Man was given the Ruling Power" because "Woman was first in the Transgression", appearing to accept conventions about Eve's guilt and its implications for the female sex. However, Marsin places a special emphasis on the role of the Virgin Mary in reversing Eve's legacy. Her gender is given a soteriological significance, where Marsin points out that "the Lord Christ, to restore fallen Mankind, came of a Woman".[34] This hints at the notion of a 'second Eve', recalling the antithesis of Adam and Christ in 1 Corinthians 15. Marsin's parallelism implies that the subjection of women postdated Eve, and that the equality of the sexes reflects the 'perfect state' of Eden and is a feature of Christ's redemption of creation and the promise of heaven. This is most explicit in *Good News to the Good Women* (1700), where she envisions a time in which "the Husband will not be above the Wife, nor the Wife above the Husband; but as they were in the first Creation, before Sin entred into the World". The conception of Christ through Mary "without Man" signifies the restoration of womankind. Marsin explains:

---

[31] *The Figurative Speeches*, 117, 119.
[32] *The Womans Advocate*, 4.
[33] *The Womans Advocate*, 4.
[34] *The Womans Advocate*, 1–2.

But the Lord of Life coming by a Woman, he who is the Reconciler
between God and his Creature, by him the Women will be deliver'd from
that Bondage, which some has found intollerable.[35]

Marsin drives home the significance of Mary's gender and its implications for other women by making an explicit parallel between herself
and the Virgin Mother. Indeed, the very title of *Two Remarkable Females
of Womankind* refers specifically to Mary and to Marsin herself, who
both appear at crucial moments in salvation history to act "as Signs
of the times".[36] Just as God chose Mary to bring forth the first age of
Christ, so he elected Marsin to proclaim his return. Thus Mary provides a powerful vindication for Marsin's missionary activity, and she
is able to argue forcefully that "those that refuse the Truth, because
it comes forth by a Woman, may as well refuse to be saved by Christ,
because he came by a Woman".[37] Unlike the young Mary Astell, for
whom "Mary's priviledge" represented the object of hopeless desire,[38]
M. Marsin herself found validation in the Virgin's calling.

---

[35] *Good News to the Good Women* (1700), 3–4. The representation of Mary as the
'second Eve' was as old as Justin Martyr, and there even existed a patristic tradition
associated with the fifth-century theologian Fulgentius, that the "Virgin Mary...*restored
all womankind, as Christ did all mankind*". See Simon Birckbek, *The Protestants Evidence Taken
Out of Good Records* (1635), 138. A related mystical tradition can be detected in Tauler,
who declared that "In her was restored what had been lost in Paradise", in Mechtild
of Magdeburg's mariology, and in the "Sophia" cult in Behmenist thought. See B. J.
Gibbons, *Gender in Mystical and Occult Thought* (Cambridge: Cambridge University Press,
1996), 62–4. Variations on the theme in contemporary English literature include Milton's references to the saving work of "the seed of the woman" in *Paradise Lost* and a
discussion of the parallel in Peter Heylyn's *Theologia Veterum* (1654), 148. The currency
of the 'second Eve' paradigm in the late seventeenth century is reflected in a contemporary tract entitled *The Female Advocate* (1700), a response to a misogynistic wedding
sermon. The pseudonymous author known as "Eugenia" may have consciously referred
to Marsin's *Womans Advocate* (1697), although a more probable source is Sarah Fyge's
more famous *Female Advocate*, published in 1686. Eugenia describes Mary's restorative
role and her interplay with Eve, commenting that, "since it hath pleased God so far
to repair the honour of our Sex, as to send a Saviour into the World by the means of
a Woman, methinks that should more than recompense for the consequences of the
other...." *The Female Advocate* (1700), 24.
  For more general surveys of the place of Mary in Protestant theology and political
culture, see Helen Hackett, *Virgin Mother, Maiden Queen* (New York: St Martin's Press,
1995); Bridget Heal, "Images of the Virgin Mary and Marian Devotion in Protestant
Nuremberg", in *Religion and Superstition in Reformation Europe*, ed. Helen Parish and William G. Naphy (Manchester: Manchester University Press, 2003); and Beth Kreitzer,
Reforming Mary (New York: Oxford University Press, 2004).
[36] *Two Remarkable Females*, 3.
[37] *Truth Vindicated*, 105.
[38] Mary Astell, "In emulation of Mr Cowley's Poem", in Ruth Perry, *The Celebrated
Mary Astell* (Chicago: University of Chicago Press, 1986), 403.

Women, Scripture, and the Latter Days

The 'remarkable' nature of the two women featured in Marsin's *Two Remarkable Females of Womankind* may indicate that their dispensation is exceptional. However, Marsin is quick to associate the ministry of other women in Scripture with that of Mary, particularly those women to whom Christ appeared after the Resurrection. She makes the connection explicit, describing how, just "as the Lord came by a Woman, so after he arose, he appeared first to the Women".[39] In fact, it is Marsin's conviction that women in general have been entrusted with the task of preaching the Word. Her evidence for this conclusion is naturally biblical. She found references to women preachers throughout the Bible—the first in Psalm 68:11. The King James version reads: "The Lord gave the word: / Great the company of those that published it". Drawing on the scholarship of the separatist Henry Ainsworth (1569–1622), Marsin noted that "in Hebrew it is, great the Company of the *She-Publishers....* But our Translators have not honestly done it, according to the Text".[40] In using this verse to vindicate women's preaching, she had a precedent in Sarah Jones, a prophetic writer of the 1640s. Jones envisioned the employment of "new threshing instruments" in the mission of the Church, specifically the "shee preachers" of Psalm 68:11, who will "hold forth Christ, publish the Gospel, take in and cast out, exercising the power of Christ".[41]

Marsin's appeal to scriptural precedent for women preachers does not stop at the "Prophecie" of the Psalmist. In *Good News to the Good Women*, she trawls through the whole of Scripture, identifying all the good and powerful women who were instrumental in the proclamation of the kingdom and who demonstrated that their sex "should be restored to that perfect state Woman was in before the Fall".[42] Elsewhere, she explains Jeremiah's vision of "*a new thing in the earth*" in which "*a Woman shall compass a Man*" (Jer. 31:22) as a prediction of her own authoritative ministry of exposition,[43] but the preaching vocation is not restricted to herself. She considers the Psalmist's words to be fulfilled

---

[39] *The Near Aproach*, 19.
[40] *Two Remarkable Females*, 16. See Henry Ainsworth, *Annotations upon the Book of Psalmes* (Amsterdam, 1617), Psalm LXVIII: V 12.
[41] Sarah Jones, *To Sions Lovers, Being a Golden Egge to Avoid Infection* (1644), sig. A4r.
[42] *Good News to the Good Women*, 5.
[43] *Two Remarkable Females*, 5–9.

in the Gospels, in which "the Lord made Women the Publishers of the Messiah's first coming". Her examples are Elizabeth, the woman of Samaria, and those who testified to the Resurrection. Even St Paul is called in to support her claim. His reference in Romans 16 to the female "servant" or "deacon" known as Phoebe, who Marsin insists was "an Instructor…but not otherwise a Servant", is set up against his prohibitions on women's speaking. As she puts it,

> As to what the Apostle speaks in contradiction hereunto, he declares he speaks it from himself, in that he *saith*, He *suffers not a Woman to teach*, 1 Tim. 2.12. But his, nor no Man's Words are of force, as to what they speak in contradiction to the Word of God.[44]

Marsin's radical refutation of the authority of Paul in this matter destabilizes her entire exegetical framework, which rests on the premise that all contradictions within Holy Scripture can be resolved by literal or figurative interpretation. She explains her rejection of certain Pauline texts by emphasizing, as modern feminist exegetes do, the context of his proscriptions, "considering how they were spoken", and the "plain Contradictions" in other parts of his corpus.[45] Her willingness to privilege some biblical examples above others is an inevitable consequence of her private enterprise and reflects her inability to conform to theological conventions about women's subjection. Having dismantled the biblical obstacles to women's participation, she attempts to rally members of her sex in her own generation, to preach the second coming:

> And O ye Women! be sound in your Duty; now the word is given according to promise, that at the time of the end, Knowledge should be increased. That you may prepare for, and Publish the coming of the Lord according to the Prophecie [Ps. 68:11].[46]

The reasoning that only women could repair the damage done by the "he-goats" of the Church eventually brings Marsin to its natural application in the re-gendering of the profession of preacher.

The 'feminist' implications of Marsin's exegesis resonate with the insights of other defences of women in the period which argue from Scripture. Christine de Pizan in the early fifteenth century had invoked the figure of Mary Magdalene to defend the value of a woman's testimony, while Moderata Fonte and Lucretia Marinella, both around

---

[44] *Two Remarkable Females*, 16.
[45] *Good News to the Good Women*, 15.
[46] *Two Remarkable Females*, 18.

1600, had reinterpreted the creation story to conclude that women were made from a nobler substance. Heinrich Cornelius Agrippa criticized a literal interpretation of Paul's prohibitions, which only touch the "outside" of his meaning and not "the inner part".[47] The English *Querelle des Femmes* had generally focussed on questions about women's moral nature, requiring new angles on the story of Eve. However, a new vitality and a departure from strictly humanist genres and arguments characterized religious writing about the moral status of women in late-seventeenth-century England.

Margaret Fell's *Women's Speaking Justified* (1666) justly remains the best-known of the Quaker treatises on the subject.[48] Fell deals deftly and systematically with the difficult passages on women, contextualizing Paul's prohibitions and insisting on the authority of divine revelation, regardless of the gender of its agent. Her exposition implies an ultimate subservience to Christ as the source of legitimacy, but also relies upon an inward and unmediated hermeneutic. The meaning illuminated by the Spirit transcends traditional interpretations. Like Marsin, the Quakers saw Scripture as a 'sealed book' which had been opened in the last days of humankind for the increase of divine knowledge. However, Marsin admonishes those who fail to "take the plain Letter of the Word", but prefer to construct interpretations "according to their own Fancy".[49] Such as these, she claims, "have made the Scriptures like a Nose of Wax"; meaning that, in their hands, it becomes malleable and unstable.[50] Her reproach looks a little weak in the light of her dependence on her own personal insight and on figurative meanings which dissolve apparent inconsistencies. It seems clear that she shared with spiritualising interpreters of Scripture an epistemology which released the believer from both conventional readings and methodologies.

Almost as famous as Fell's treatise is Mary Astell's "Preface" to *Some Reflections Upon Marriage*, added to the third edition in 1706. This lively commentary on biblical heroines and passages about women contains some startling and penetrating analysis. This is particularly true of Astell's exposition of Paul's prohibitions, which are understood

---

[47] Heinrich Cornelius Agrippa von Nettesheim, *The Glory of Women*, trans. "H. C. Gent." (1652), 45.

[48] See earlier contributions from Richard Farnworth, *A Woman Forbidden to Speak in the Church* (1655) and George Fox, *The Woman Learning in Silence* (1656).

[49] *Truth Vindicated*, 93.

[50] *The Womans Advocate*, 11.

contextually or allegorically, and their universality disproved in light of other parts of Scripture. The point of Astell's survey is to demonstrate that the equality of women is the purpose of the Creator. She insists that it is "the Custom of the World" which "has put Women...into a State of Subjection" and cleverly refers to the claims of various *male* authors that "in the Original State of things the Woman was the superior" and that "before the Fall there was a greater equality between the two Sexes".[51] It is her intention to make a theological case for the moral equivalence of men and women, which she does to devastating effect. Yet Scripture is secondary to Reason in the debate, since the issue affects humanity in general and is not confined to the circumstances of the biblical writers.[52]

Astell's exercise was not entirely theoretical. It was her conviction, of course, that women's circumstances would be vastly improved by advancing their education. She appealed to Queen Anne to patronise this cause, warning that if she refused, then women could bid

> Adieu...to those Halcyon, or, if you will, *Millennium* Days, in which the Wolf and the Lamb shall feed together, and a Tyrannous Domination, which nature never meant, shall no longer render useless, if not hurtful, the Industry and Understandings of half Mankind![53]

This vision, loaded as it is with references to Isaianic prophecy, seems to have an eschatological tone which would accord well with Astell's insistence upon a prelapsarian equality. She reminds us, entirely unwittingly, of the curious appeal of highly gendered apocalyptic imagery in the 1680s and 90s, as well as the large body of contemporary literature which advocated for women's education.

Religious Knowledge and Women's Writing in the 1690s

While Marsin's attempts at a 'feminist exegesis' were composed at least five years prior to Astell's 1706 "Preface", it is possible that she was familiar with Astell's *A Serious Proposal to the Ladies* (1696). The *Proposal*

---

[51] Mary Astell, "Preface", *Some Reflections Upon Marriage*, 3rd edition (London, 1706), v. Her first source may have been a translation of Agrippa's *Female Pre-eminence* and her second is definitely William Whiston, *A New Theory of the Earth* (London, 1696), 170: "The Female was then very different from what she is now; particularly she was in a state of greater equality with the Male".

[52] Astell, "Preface", vii.

[53] Astell, "Preface", xxiv.

set out the case for an all-female college devoted to the religious instruction of girls and ladies of quality. Astell was not the first to conceive of
such an institution; Margaret Cavendish had wittily imagined a "Female
Academy" in 1662, while Edward Chamberlayne in 1671 and Clement
Barksdale in 1675 had each envisaged a similar "colledge of maids".[54]
Yet the influence of Astell's associated exposition of the principle of
women's moral and intellectual equality set her scheme apart. To a
greater extent than Bathsua Makin's treatise or the English translation
of Anna Maria van Schurman,[55] the *Proposal* proved an inspiration to a
generation of women. The poets Lady Mary Chudleigh and Elizabeth
Thomas, the Anglo-Saxon scholar Elizabeth Elstob, and the popular
writer Lady Mary Wortley Montagu each acknowledged an intellectual
debt to Astell. Marsin too may have been influenced by the *Proposal*, as
in 1701 she articulates her desire for

> a House or School for the Instruction of young Women in Piety and
> Knowledge in the fear of the Lord, and that Women may be instructed
> how to read the Scriptures, so as to understand what they read.[56]

There are obvious parallels here with the religious character of Astell's
academy. This comment appears in *Two Remarkable Females of Womankind*,
following Marsin's biblical vindication of the "She-publishers", and links
into an account of "the increasing of Knowledge at the time of the
end".[57] The eschatological significance of Marsin's "House or School"
for women thus becomes transparent. Religious instruction is a means
of achieving the universal reception of the Gospel: one of the crucial
preconditions of Christ's return.

In this way Marsin suggests a bridge between the humanist movement
for women's education in the 1690s, represented by Astell, Chudleigh,
Montagu, and Damaris Masham, and the more radical mysticism
which characterized other forms of women's writing in the period. The
fin de siècle saw the circulation of works by a number of charismatic
female figureheads. Antonia Bourignon's mystical tracts were published

---

[54] Margaret Cavendish, "The Female Academy" in *Playes Written by the Thrice Noble,
Illustrious and Excellent Princess, the Lady Marchioness of Newcastle* (1662); Edward Chamberlayne, *An Academy or Colledge* (1671); Clement Barksdale, *A Letter Touching a Colledge
of Maids* (1675). See also Bridget Hill, "A Refuge from Men: The Idea of a Protestant
Nunnery", *Past and Present* 117 (November 1987): 107–30.
[55] Anna Maria van Schurman, *The Learned Maid* (1659). Bathsua Makin, *An Essay
to Revive the Antient Education of Gentlewomen* (1673).
[56] *Two Remarkable Females*, 18.
[57] *Two Remarkable Females*, 19.

posthumously in English between 1696 and 1699, and the movement associated with her personality was not insignificant. The veneration she attracted was such that she was accused of setting herself up as a "God-woman" comparable to Christ.[58] The Philadelphian Society, however, is best known for its fostering of spiritual mothers, notably Jane Lead, a key figure in the circle which formed around John Pordage in the 1650s known as the 'Seekers', and the author of mystical meditations heavily influenced by Jacob Boehme. Interestingly, the Philadelphians were impressed enough by Part II of Mary Astell's *A Serious Proposal* to advertise it in their *Theosophical Transactions* in 1697.[59] A crucial feature of this sequel was the development of Astell's epistemology, which envisaged the revelation of "the Eternal Word and Wisdom of GOD" functioning both spiritually and rationally.[60] Her philosophical dependence on the Platonist theology of Henry More and Nicolas Malebranche in this matter may have appealed to the theosophists. Certainly there is a common emphasis in Astell, Lead, Bourignon, and Marsin on the way in which divine knowledge is received.

For Astell, the faculty of Reason is instrumental in the somewhat mystical process of communion with Christ, the Wisdom of God, for Reason itself is a spark of the divine mind. It surpasses Scripture as a tool for interpreting nature and, as 'the candle of the Lord', it enlightens the soul. For Lead and Bourignon, spiritual understanding is a similarly internal experience. There are parallels between Lead's desire to dispose of the body, "this lump of Earth", and Astell's exhortation to put aside "these Mud-walls that enclose our Earthly Tabernacle".[61] Scripture takes second place in a religious epistemology which dissolves fleshly concerns—even the written Word. The function of an educational institution as a place in which knowledge is mediated may seem a little superfluous in this philosophical context, but for Astell, at least, the faculties of the mind and soul required formation to be exercised responsibly. With Marsin, she may well have considered that "neither the Heavenly, nor Earthly Wisdom, or Riches are attainable without Labour".[62]

---

[58] John Cockburn, *Bourignianism Detected* (1698), 19.

[59] See Paula McDowell, "Enlightenment Enthusiasms and the Spectacular Failure of the Philadelphian Society", *Eighteenth-Century Studies* 35, no. 4 (Summer 2002): 520n24.

[60] Astell, *A Serious Proposal Part II* (1697), 156.

[61] Jane Lead, *The Revelation of Revelations* (1683), 10; Astell, *A Serious Proposal Part II*, 160.

[62] *Two Remarkable Females*, 22.

Marsin, by contrast, claims to derive all her knowledge from the literal testimony of Scripture. Like Jane Lead and Antonia Bourignon, she understands her task as the 'unsealing' of the 'Book of Life'; unlike Lead and Bourignon, this implies a definitive and reasoned exposition of Holy Writ, rather than spiritual illumination.[63] The sealed book of Revelation 5 is a continuous theme in Marsin's writings, and it is clear that she considers herself the eschatological instrument of its opening. This process seems to require lengthy surveys of obscure texts, which result in insights such as the analogy of the material "heavens and the earth" to "the powers and people".[64] Curiously, 'Reason' plays a critical role in Marsin's enterprise and seems to occupy a place in her thought comparable to Mary Astell's philosophical system. She is insistent that there is nothing in God's Word which is "contrary to Reason", anticipating Astell's comment on Scripture, "I find nothing there that offends Reason".[65] There is little out of the ordinary here.

More strikingly, both Astell and Marsin borrow the illuminist imagery used by the Cambridge Platonists to account for the activity of Reason. Marsin's assertion that "right Reason and Conscience is the Light which God hath set up in the Soul" is virtually interchangeable with Astell's later affirmation that "Reason is that light which GOD himself has set up in my mind to lead me to Him".[66] For all Marsin's pretensions to a rational exposition, however, she is dependent on a more transcendent and subjective form of revelation for her very vocation and certainly for many of her more figurative interpretations. Her own significance arises from the obscurity of divine truth, concealed even from the penetrations of Reason, and the clarity which she has uniquely received. In the end, she belongs to the company of seventeenth-century mystics and not to the rationalists or rhetoricians. Her theological identity is ultimately Gnostic, and more spiritualist than she would admit.[67]

---

[63] See Lead, *The Revelation of Revelations*, and Garden, *An Apology*, 13. Also Marsin, *The Figurative Speeches*, 165; *Truth Vindicated*, 104; *An Answer to Dr Whitby*, 38; *Two Remarkable Females*, 17–18.

[64] *The Womans Advocate*, 6.

[65] *Two Remarkable Females*, 19; Astell, *The Christian Religion* (1705), 19.

[66] *Truth Vindicated*, 31; Astell, *The Christian Religion*, 7. See for example Peter Sterry on "the Candle of Reason" in *The Spirit Convincing of Sinne* (1645), 10.

[67] See her account of "spiritual baptism" in *The Christian Belief*, 101–103, and of the "Spiritual Signification" of the Eucharist in *An Answer to Dr Whitby*, 46–7.

Yet Marsin's engagement with current philosophical as well as theological language, and her points of intersection even with the unlikely
Astell, reflect the extent to which dominant and radical discourses
could converge. There is, indeed, nothing specifically gendered about
this interplay. However, it is striking that two intellectual cultures
which shared an internalized epistemology—the radical spiritualism
of the Quakers and Philadelphians and the rational mysticism of the
Neoplatonists—also produced some of the most prolific and gender-
conscious female writers of the age. While it is important to avoid the
banal identification of mysticism and femininity, this coincidence seems
to be central to approaches to women's religious writing of the period.
As a case study, Marsin synthesizes some of the central critical themes
of women's literature—authorial agency, gender and Scripture, social
injustice—and also draws our attention to the importance of religious
knowledge as a source of authorization. She also embodies the intellectual paradoxes of Enlightenment, without any consciousness of an
inner tension. Pointing to the iconoclasm of biblical criticism and the
supremacy of Reason with one hand, with the other she holds out her
radical faith in Providence, revelation, and the imminent restitution of
an Eden where women and men would enjoy fullness of wisdom and
equality of stature.

Bibliography

Ainsworth, Henry. *Annotations Upon the Book of Psalmes*. Amsterdam, 1617.
Anonymous. *The Truest and Largest Account of the Late Earthquake in Jamaica, June the 7th,
     1692*. London, 1693.
Astell, Mary. *Astell: Political Writings*. Edited by Patricia Springborg. Cambridge: Cam-
     bridge University Press, 1996.
——. *The Christian Religion, As Profess'd by a Daughter of the Church of England*. London,
     1705.
——. *A Serious Proposal to the Ladies, for the Advancement of their True and Greatest Interest: By
     a Lover of her Sex*. London, 1694.
——. *A Serious Proposal to the Ladies. Wherein a Method is Offer'd for the Improvement of their
     Minds. Part II*. London, 1697.
——. *Some Reflections Upon Marriage, Occasioned by the Duke and Dutchess of Mazarine's Case;
     Which is Also Considered*. 3rd ed. London, 1706.
Barksdale, Clement. *A Letter Touching a Colledge of Maids, or, A Virgin-society written August
     12, 1675*. London, 1675.
Birckbek, Simon. *The Protestants Evidence Taken Out of Good Records*. London, 1635.
Burns, William E. "London's Barber-Elijah: Thomas Moor and Universal Salvation
     in the 1690s". *Harvard Theological Review* 95 (July 2002): 277–290.
——. "'By Him the Women will be delivered from that Bondage, which some has

found intolerable': M. Marsin, English Millenarian Feminist". In *Eighteenth Century Women: Studies in their Lives, Work and Culture*. Edited by Linda V. Troost. Vol. I. New York: AMS Press, 2001.

Cavendish, Margaret. "The Female Academy". In *Playes Written by the Thrice Noble, Illustrious and Excellent Princess, the Lady Marchioness of Newcastle*. London, 1662.

Chamberlayne, Edward. *An Academy or Colledge, Wherein Young Ladies and Gentlewomen may at a Very Moderate Expence be Duly Instructed in the True Protestant Religion, and in All Vertuous Qualities that may Adorn that Sex*. London, 1671.

Chudleigh, Lady Mary Lee. *A Ladies Defence OR The Bride-Womans Counsellor Answered*. 2nd ed. London, 1701.

——. *The Poems and Prose of Mary, Lady Chudleigh*. Edited by Margaret J. M. Ezell. New York: Oxford University Press, 1993.

Cockburn, John. *Bourignianism Detected, or, The Delusions and Errors of Antonia Bourignon, and her Growing Sect which may also Serve for a Discovery of all other Enthusiastical Impostures*. London, 1698.

"Eugenia". *The Female Advocate, or, A Plea for the Just Liberty of the Tender Sex, and Particularly of Married Women Being Reflections on a Late Rude and Disingenuous Discourse*. London, 1700.

Fell, Margaret. *Womens Speaking Justified, Proved and Allowed of by the Scriptures*. London, 1666.

Fox, George. *The Woman Learning in Silence: or, The Mysterie of the Womans Subjection to her Husband*. London, 1656.

Fyge, Sarah. *The Female Advocate, or, An Answer to a Late Satyr Against the Pride, Lust and Inconstancy of Woman*. London, 1686.

Garden, George. *An Apology for M. Antonia Bourignon*. London, 1699.

Gibbons, B. J. *Gender in Mystical and Occult Thought: Behmenism and its Development in England*. Cambridge: Cambridge University Press, 1996.

Grundy, Isobel and Susan Wiseman, eds. *Women, Writing, History: 1640–1740*. Athens: University of Georgia Press, 1992.

Hackett, Helen. *Virgin Mother, Maiden Queen: Elizabeth I and the Cult of the Virgin Mary*. New York: St Martin's Press, 1995.

Harrison, Benjamin. *Prophetic Outlines of the Christian Church and the Antichristian Power as Traced in the Visions of Daniel and St. John*. London: Francis & John Rivington, 1849.

Heal, Bridget. "Images of the Virgin Mary and Marian Devotion in Protestant Nuremberg". In *Religion and Superstition in Reformation Europe*. Edited by Helen Parish and William G. Naphy. Manchester: Manchester University Press, 2003.

Heylyn, Peter. *Theologia Veterum, or, The Summe of Christian Theologie*. London, 1654.

Hill, Bridget. "A Refuge from Men: The Idea of a Protestant Nunnery". *Past and Present* 117 (November 1987): 107–30.

Hill, Christopher. *The English Bible and the Seventeenth-Century Revolution*. London: Penguin, 1993.

Hitchcock, Tim. "M. Marsin". In *Oxford Dictionary of National Biography*. Oxford: Oxford University Press, 2004.

Irwin, Joyce. "Anna Maria van Schurman and Antoinette Bourignon: Contrasting Examples of Seventeenth-Century Pietism". *Church History* 60, no. 3 (September 1991): 301–15.

Jones, Sarah. *To Sions Lovers, Being a Golden Egge to Avoid Infection*. London, 1644.

Kreitzer, Beth. *Reforming Mary: Changing Images of the Virgin Mary in Lutheran Sermons of the Sixteenth Century*. New York: Oxford University Press, 2004.

Kunze, Bonnelyn Young. *Margaret Fell and the Rise of Quakerism*. Basingstoke: Macmillan, 1994.

Lead, Jane. *The Revelation of Revelations. Particularly as an Essay Towards the Unsealing, Opening and Discovering the Seven Seals, the Seven Thunders, and the New-Jerusalem State*. London, 1683.

Mack, Phyllis. *Visionary Women: Ecstatic Prophecy in Seventeenth-Century England*. Berkeley: University of California Press, 1992.

Makin, Bathsua. *An Essay to Revive the Antient Education of Gentlewomen*. London: 1673.

Marsin, M. *All the Chief Points Contained in the Christian Religion, and those Great Truths in the Word which we have not had a Right Apprehension for Almost Thirteen Hundred Years, Never Since the Rise of the Beast*. London, 1697.

———. *An Answer to Dr. Whitby, proving the Jews are not to be Called into the Gospel of the Christian Warfare*. London, 1701.

———. *The Christian Belief Shewing What a Christian Ought to Believe*. London, 1697.

———. *The Figurative Speeches: by which God has Veiled his Secrets Contained in His Word, Until the End of the Time*. London, 1697.

———. *A Full and Clear Account the Scripture Gives of the Deity and All the Mistakes Removed Relating Thereunto*. London, 1700.

———. *Good News to the Good Women, and to the Bad Women Too that will Grow Better the Like to the Men, but Here the Women are Put in the First Place*. London, 1700.

———. *The Near Aproach of Christ's Kingdom, Clearly Proved by Scripture With a Certain Account of the Signs of the Present Times*. London, 1696.

———. *A Practical Treatise, Shewing When a Believer is Justified By Faith Without the Deeds of the Law*. London, 1696. [Appeared in 1697 as *A Clear and Brief Explanation upon the Chief Points in the New Testament*.]

———. *A Rehearsal of the Covenant by Moses Made With the Children of Israel*. London, 1697.

———. *Some of the Chief Heads of the Most Miraculous Wonders, that have of late been in Christendom* (London, 1694). [Reissued in 1697 with *The Womans Advocate*.]

———. *This Treatise Proving Three Worlds, Fondations* [sic] *Mentioned in Scripture*. London, 1696.

———. *Truth Vindicated Against All Heresies. The Seed of the Woman and the Seed of the Serpent Distinguished*. London, 1698 and 1700. [A version also appeared in *Two Sorts of Latter Days* in 1699.]

———. *Two Remarkable Females of Womankind*. London, 1701.

———. *Two Sorts of Latter Days, Proved from Scripture*. London, 1699.

———. *The Womans Advocate. Shewing the Reason According to Scripture or the Scripture Reason why God Hath Brought to Light the True Meaning of His Word by an Unexpected Hand*. London, 1697.

McDowell, Paula. "Enlightenment Enthusiasms and the Spectacular Failure of the Philadelphian Society". *Eighteenth-Century Studies* 35, no. 4 (Summer 2002): 515–33.

More, Henry. *An Explanation of the Grand Mystery of Godliness*. Cambridge, 1660.

Patrides, C. A. *The Cambridge Platonists*. London: Edward Arnold, 1969.

Perry, Ruth. *The Celebrated Mary Astell*. Chicago: University of Chicago Press, 1986.

Ray, John. *Three Physico-Theological Discourses*. 2nd ed. London, 1693.

Rogers, G. A. J., J. M. Vienne, and Y. C. Zarka, eds. *The Cambridge Platonists in Philosophical Context: Politics, Metaphysics, and Religion*. Dordrecht: Kluwer Academic, 1997.

Smith, Catherine. "Jane Lead: The Feminist Mind and Art of a Seventeenth-Century Protestant Mystic". In *Women of Spirit: Female Leadership in the Jewish and Christian Traditions*. Edited by Rosemary Ruether and Eleanor McLaughlin. New York: Simon and Schuster, 1979.

Sterry, Peter. *The Spirit Convincing of Sinne*. London, 1645.

Van Schurman, Anna Maria. *The Learned Maid*. London, 1659.

Thickstun, Margaret Olofson. "'This was a Woman that taught': Feminist Scriptural Exegesis in the Seventeenth Century". *Studies in Eighteenth-Century Culture* 21 (1991): 149–58.

Thomas, Elizabeth. *Poems on Several Occasions*. London, 1718.

Von Nettesheim, Heinrich Cornelius Agrippa. *The Glory of Women*. Translated by "H. C. Gent". London, 1652.

Walker, D. P. *The Decline of Hell: Seventeenth-Century Discussions of Eternal Torment.* London: Routledge & Kegan Paul, 1964.
Whiston, William. *A New Theory of the Earth.* London, 1696.

"MOTHER OF LOVE": SPIRITUAL MATERNITY IN THE WORKS OF JANE LEAD (1624–1704)[1]

JULIE HIRST

"No one perfect in piety seeks to have children except spiritually".[2]

In the seventeenth century, Protestant theologians taught that women were created for motherhood and that their maternal role was an appropriate way to serve God.[3] Such religious beliefs provided a context and meaning for motherhood, and clergy highlighted biblical texts which promised salvation through maternity. For example, 1 Timothy 2:15 promised women salvation in motherhood, for they "shall be saved in child-bearing, if they continue in faith and charity and holiness with sobriety". Thus, motherhood took on a spiritual significance. This chapter will examine the significance and nature of maternity and maternal imagery in the life and writings of the seventeenth-century visionary and mystic, Jane Lead. First, it will consider how she was perceived as a mother among her followers in the London Philadelphian Society. It will then go on to examine her relationship with her own spiritual mother, Wisdom or Sophia, to show how in Lead's visionary world Sophia's procreative abilities provided hope for a future spiritual generation represented by the second coming of an androgynous Adam. Also, Lead's experiences as a mother will be considered in terms of

---

[1] I am grateful to the following people for their help with this article: Sylvia Brown, Mark Jenner, Chris Maunder, Pamela Ellis, Sheila Wright, John and Helen Ruth Wilson, Cliff and Marcus Hirst. All shortcomings are, of course, mine.

[2] Augustine, *On the Good of Marriage*, 17:19, quoted in Dyan Elliott, *Spiritual Marriage, Sexual Abstinence in Medieval Wedlock* (Princeton: Princeton University Press, 1993), vii. For a feminist critique of Augustine, see Kim Power, *Veiled Desire: Augustine on Women* (New York: Continuum, 1996).

[3] Patricia Crawford, "The Construction and Experience of Maternity in Seventeenth-Century England", in *Women as Mothers in Pre-Industrial England*, ed. Valerie Fildes (New York: Routledge, 1990), 23. See also Sara Mendelson and Patricia Crawford, *Women in Early Modern England 1550–1720* (Oxford: Oxford University Press, 1998), 148–64; Patricia Crawford, *Women and Religion 1500–1720* (London: Routledge, 1996); and Erica Longfellow, *Women and Religious Writing in Early Modern England* (Cambridge: Cambridge University Press, 2004).

how they were translated into religious ideas. Finally, by examining the
Behmenist influence on her use of gendered imagery, this chapter will
conclude by showing how Lead moved beyond these ideas to produce
her own individual version of a maternal Christianity.

Jane Lead: A Brief Biography

Jane Lead was a seventeenth-century prophetess: a mystic and visionary
who became the religious leader of the Philadelphian Society in London
at the end of the seventeenth century.[4] She wrote at least fifteen books
and treatises, including a spiritual diary entitled *A Fountain of Gardens*
which spans sixteen years and is nearly 2,500 pages long. Nearly all
her works were translated into German and Dutch and published in
these languages during her lifetime. Phyllis Mack recognized that as
a "blind, elderly middle-class widow" Jane Lead was to become "the
most eminent female visionary of the 1690s".[5] She was born into an
influential Norfolk family. She had seven brothers and one sister, and
her father, Hamond Warde, served as a justice of the peace. Very little
of her early life is recorded, although she wrote in her autobiography that her father brought her up "with dignity and good manners,
according to his standing".[6] Significantly, during the family's Christmas
celebrations in 1640, her sixteenth year, and without any warning, she
heard a voice saying, "CEASE FROM THIS, I HAVE ANOTHER
DANCE TO LEAD THEE IN; FOR THIS IS VANITY".[7] This sudden experience plunged her into a spiritual turmoil from which she
sought an escape: "nothing was able to give her any satisfaction or
rest, or to ease her wounded spirit...which continued for the space
of three years with very great anguish and trouble".[8] It was then that

---

[4] See Julie Hirst, *Jane Leade: A Biography of a Seventeenth-Century Mystic* (Aldershot,
Hants.: Ashgate, 2005).

[5] Phyllis Mack, *Visionary Women: Ecstatic Prophecy in Seventeenth-Century England* (Berkeley
and London: University of California Press, 1989), 409.

[6] "Lebenslauff der Autorin", in *Sechs Mystische Tractätlein* (Amsterdam, 1697), 3. The
only extant copy of Jane Lead's autobiography is in German. My thanks to Marianne
Jahn for her translations.

[7] Jane Lead, *Wars of David* (London, 1700), 21.

[8] Edward Bysshe, *The Visitation of Norfolk...1664*, ed. A. W. Hughes Clarke and
A. Campling, Norfolk Record Society, vol. 5 (London, 1934), 233–34.

she was determined to become a 'Bride of Christ'.[9] However, she did marry a cousin, William Lead, because, as she tells us, he was "pious and godfearing".[10] They lived in London for twenty-five years and had four daughters, two of whom died in infancy.

The death of her husband in 1670 brought financial distress to the family due to failed business interests abroad. It was two months after her husband's death that Jane Lead started to receive a series of visions of the Virgin Wisdom, Sophia, whom she witnessed as "an overshadowing bright Cloud and in the midst of it a Woman". Three days later it gently commanded, "Behold me as thy Mother", and six days after came the promise:

> I shall now cease to appear in a Visible Figure unto thee, but I will not fail to transfigure my self in thy mind; and there open the Spring of Wisdom and Understanding.[11]

The vision signalled the beginning of a spiritual relationship with Sophia which lasted for the rest of Jane Lead's life, and 1670 was the year she began to write her spiritual diary.

A significant turning point in her life was when she met Dr John Pordage (1607–1681), who introduced her to the writings of the German theosopher Jacob Boehme (1575–1624). Lead moved into Pordage's household as his spiritual partner and 'mate' in 1674. They shared a set of ideas and language to express their mystical experiences.[12] In the year of Pordage's death, 1681, she published her first treatise, entitled *A Heavenly Cloud Now Breaking*, and she also took over his group of followers.

Her first publication aroused the curiosity of Dr Francis Lee, a physician, who travelled from Leiden to meet her. He eventually married her widowed daughter, Barbara Walton. He regarded Lead as his "spiritual mother" and she looked upon Lee as her "spiritual son given

---

[9] "Lebenslauff", 34. 'Bride of Christ' is a common motif in women's religious history. The twelfth-century mystic Hildegard of Bingen described herself as a 'Bride of Christ'. See C. W. Bynum, *Jesus as Mother: Studies in the Spirituality of the High Middle Ages* (Berkeley: University of California Press, 1982), 141–42.

[10] "Lebenslauff", 417–18.

[11] Jane Lead, A *Fountain of Gardens Watered by the Rivers of Divine Pleasure* (London, 1696), 18–21. Hereafter cited as *Fountain*, vol. 1.

[12] Lead, *Fountain*, vol. 1, 328. See also Manfred Brod, "A Radical Network in the English Revolution: John Pordage and His Circle, 1646–54", 119 *English Historical Review* (2004): 1230–53.

to her in old age".[13] When Lead started to go blind, Lee acted as her amanuensis and editor. Even though her outer vision had failed, aged about seventy, her inner vision intensified. As she began to be known by her published writings, a small group of followers gathered at home and in Europe. Known as the Philadelphian Society, named after the sixth of the seven churches in Asia mentioned in Revelation 1:4 and 3:7, they believed in the imminence of the millennium and the concept of universal salvation.

In 1704, however, the death of Jane Lead heralded the death-knell of the Philadelphian Society. Her epitaph in Bunhill Fields reads, "Exuvias Carnis hic deposuit Venerabilis Ancilla Domini JANE LEAD, anno Peregrinationis suae lxxx"—"Here the Venerable Handmaid of the Lord, Jane Lead, has shed the outward garment of the flesh, in the year of her departure, 80".[14]

Spiritual Motherhood

The title 'spiritual mother', a popular term of devotion, was used to describe Lead. She was recognized as a spiritual mother-figure and called the "Mother of Love" by her followers in the Philadelphian Society. A correspondent of the Philadelphians, Richard Roach, referred to Lead as "our Mother" when he wrote, "the Spirit of Wisdom in our Mother appropriated to you that Mystical Name, by which you subscribe yourself". The writer was referring to his pseudonym 'Onesimus', which Lead gave Roach.[15] In a letter of 1695 to Roach, Lead wrote, "your most effectinet Mother to Love and Serve you. Jane Lead".[16] Lead, however, says very little about her own mother or, indeed, her experiences of motherhood, yet she did express spiritual concern for her offspring. In 1696, we know that she was living with her son-in-law Francis

---

[13] Christopher Walton, *Notes & Materials for an Adequate Biography of the Celebrated & Divine Theosopher William Law* (1854), 509.

[14] Francis Lee, "Der Seelig" (1705), 41, quoted in Joanna Magnani Sperle, "God's Healing Angel: A Biography of Jane Ward Lead" (Ph.D. diss., Kent State University, 1985), 17.

[15] Papers of Richard Roach, MS Rawlinson D832, fol. 58r, Bodleian Library, Oxford. Onesimus was a runaway slave who was converted by Paul (Philem. 10) and became a trustworthy disciple (Col. 4:9).

[16] MS Rawl. D832, fols. 57r, 58r.

Lee and her daughter, Barbara.[17] It was during this period that Lead wrote the introduction to *The Fountain of Gardens*, which stated: "there may be some I bear the memorial of a Mother to, natural as well as supernatural, that may possibly succeed in the same spirit".[18] This dual idea of motherhood as both 'natural' and 'supernatural' was a pivotal motif in Lead's writing and will be discussed later. Lead prophesied that a spiritual generation would be born of Sophia, though here she may be referring to her own 'natural' children as well as members of her Philadelphian Society.

Other female religious figures in early modern society were also known as spiritual mothers. The eighteenth-century Shaker leader, 'Mother Ann' Lee, was considered by her followers to be the "spiritual mother in Christ".[19] The Southcottians considered Joanna Southcott and John Ward as "the divine woman and Ward her spiritual son".[20] The Buchanites also believed in the "divinity of Friend Mother Mrs Buchan".[21] As Phyllis Mack has noted, many Quakers were "admirers of the spiritual motherhood of Margaret Fell".[22] Fell was seen as a caring and attentive mother. Quaker Thomas Holme regarded Fell as "A nursing mother...who feeds the hungry with good things, but the fat with judgement".[23] The Quakers' application of spiritual motherhood, however, was grounded in their theology. As Jeanette Gadt has argued, the Quakers believed God was imbued with maternal and compassionate qualities. As such, He was more powerful than a condemnatory God. Gadt suggests that,

---

[17] 24 September 1703, Acts of Court 1687–1707 (Lady Mico's College), fol. 101r, Mercers' Company Archives, London. I am grateful to Dr Mark Jenner who provided the transcript.

[18] *Fountain*, vol. 1, 16.

[19] Edward Whitson Robley, *The Shakers: Two Centuries of Spiritual Reflection* (London: SPCK, 1983), 10.

[20] W. H. Oliver, *Prophets and Millennialists: The Uses of Biblical Prophecy from the 1790s to the 1840s* (Auckland: Auckland University Press, 1978), 153.

[21] J. F. C. Harrison, *The Second Coming: Popular Millenarianism 1780–1850* (London: Routledge, 1979), 34.

[22] Phyllis Mack, "Teaching About Gender and Spirituality in Early English Quakerism", *Women's Studies* 19, no. 2 (1991): 229.

[23] Thomas Holme to Margaret Fell, Chester Castle, 28 August 1655, Swarthmore MSS 1/197 (II, 355), Library of the Religious Society of Friends, London, quoted in Mack, *Visionary Women*, 40.

> To Quakers, God was essentially a non-anthropomorphic being, a force
> of divine love from which radiated mercy and justice, and these attributes
> were often expressed in a feminine, nurturing way.[24]

Unlike the Quakers, however, Lead did not apply maternal attributes to
a male God. Indeed, many of Lead's ideas about God were dualistic.
God represented the Father, and Sophia was often portrayed as a mother
figure. Maternity was important for Lead's visionary life, and Sophia
was a mother figure to Lead. The maternal aspect of Sophia will be
discussed below in addition to other religious figures who were imbued
with maternal qualities and who particularly influenced Lead.

Lead's spiritual ideas and knowledge came primarily from biblical
sources. The Book of Wisdom describes Sophia as the gift of God (8:21),
and Wisdom 7:25–26 states, "She is God's power which is breathed
out, and the image of God's goodness". Sophia is thus described as
an emanation, an outflowing and an effervescence of God. She is
"the breath of the power of God, and a pure influence flowing from
the glory of the Almightie". She is "the brightness of the everlasting
light, the unspotted mirror of the power of God, and the image of
his goodness". Yet Lead also described how she was fed knowledge by
a nurturing Father:

> I was ministered to, by the Nurturing Father of my Spirit, that fed me
> with a white streaming Breath from his own Mouth. Whereby I had
> open'd in me an understanding deep in Knowledge.[25]

Divine sustenance was also obtained from Sophia; as Lead wrote, "my
Spirit still attended eagerly longing to lay my Mouth to Wisdom's Breast,
from which the Word of Life so sweetly did flow".[26] The imagery suggests acts of feeding in which God and Wisdom were united in creating
and disseminating the Word.

Lead emphasized that it was Wisdom's milk and God's white breath,
rather than the sacrificial blood of Christ, which transmitted divine
knowledge directly to her. Lead also did not use the image of 'Mother
Jesus', one of the primary ways of speaking about union with the divine

---

[24] Jeanette Gadt, "Women and Protestant Culture: The Quaker Dissent from Puritanism" (Ph.D. diss., University of California, Los Angeles, 1999), x.

[25] Jane Lead, *A Fountain of Gardens, or, A Spiritual Diary of the Wonderful Experiences of
a Christian Soul, under the Conduct of Heavenly Wisdom* (London, 1700–1), part 2, 211.
Hereafter cited as *Fountain*, vol. 3.

[26] *Fountain*, vol. 1, 34.

used in the Middle Ages.[27] Instead, Lead was concerned to depict *Sophia* as a mother. Milk was a common spiritual metaphor that was usually applied to nurturing by God or Christ, but, unusually, Lead applied this maternal imagery to Sophia.

Interestingly, some of Lead's ideas of spiritual maternity figured Sophia as the biblical Rebecca. "The First Vision" of April 1670 in her spiritual diary, *A Fountain of Gardens*, is worth quoting at length on this point.[28] It invoked two role models central to Lead's ideas about spiritual maternity, namely Rebecca and Sophia. Lead wrote:

> ...this Voice came, saying, Behold I am God's Eternal Virgin-Wisdom, whom thou hast been enquiring after; I am to unseal the Treasures of God's deep Wisdom unto thee, and will be as Rebecca was unto Jacob, a true Natural Mother; for out of my Womb thou shalt be brought forth after the manner of a Spirit, Conceived and Born again: this thou shalt know by a New Motion of Life, stirring and giving a restlessness, till Wisdom be born within the inward parts of thy Soul.[29]

The only reference to non-mystical maternity (besides Mary and Jesus) was the remark about Rebecca and Jacob: "[I] will be as Rebecca was unto Jacob, a true Natural Mother".[30] Rebecca's preferential love for her younger son was emphasized, making her "a true Natural Mother". In the quote above, Sophia assumed the role of Rebecca, while Lead was Jacob. Yet, in order to fully understand Lead's idea of spiritual motherhood, it is necessary to examine representations of Rebecca in a wider context and also to be aware of Jacob Boehme's interpretation of Rebecca.

Lead was clearly influenced by Boehme's ideas. He had also drawn upon the figure of Rebecca, suggesting that she had received God's blessing and was thus covenanted by God. He described Rebecca as "a figure of the Virgin Mary, who brought forth Christ, viz. The blessed of God, who should bless Esau, and all the Adamicall children".[31] Rebecca's sons, Jacob and Esau, however, had different natures representing two unequal nations: "The corrupt Adamicall nature in its Type was represented in the womb in Esau, with the type of Christ in

---

[27] Bynum, *Jesus as Mother*, 162.
[28] *Fountain*, vol. 1, 17.
[29] *Fountain*, vol. 1, 17–21.
[30] See Genesis 27:13.
[31] Jacob Boehme, *Mysterium Magnum, or, An Exposition of the First Book of Moses called GENESIS* (London, 1656), 393.

Jacob". Esau thus represented the "Adamicall sinfull nature" in contrast
with God being manifest in Jacob.[32] When the law of primogeniture
was overturned by Rebecca deceiving Isaac to deny Esau his birthright
blessing, Boehme wrote that the "filial inheritance resteth only upon
[Jacob] the Second New Adam".[33] Moreover, Rebecca's "woman-like,
motherly, natural love" for Jacob was given special significance through
the conjoining of God's love. The bonds of Rebecca's motherly love
were thus a scaled-down version of God's greater love.

Recent feminist scholarship has highlighted the ambiguous nature
of Rebecca, and she is now often depicted as a scheming, deceitful
wife forced to play out her role as a victim of circumstance. Catherine
Smith has noted that,

> Radically interpreting Biblical accounts, Lead 'raises' Eve, and points to
> Ruth, Naomi, Rebecca and Mary as types of the goddess. Their disobedi-
> ence and dependency are recognized as the strategies of victims, disguising
> their original power and keeping it alive in misleading circumstances.[34]

Karen Armstrong has also observed that "Rebekah was forced to resort
to a desperate subterfuge" in disguising Jacob as Esau.[35] Susan Niditch,
however, describes Rebecca as "a trickster heroine" who "formulates
the plan and succeeds, moving the men around her like chess pieces".[36]
Thus, the ambiguous figure of Rebecca, who was noted not only for
being an enterprising and generous mother to her younger son Jacob,
but also for tricking her elder son Esau out of his inheritance and duping
her husband in doing so, would appear to be a curious representative
of Sophia—one which emphasized the resourcefulness of a woman's
cunning and concern for her offspring over more unworldly virtues such
as chastity and self-sacrifice. Rebecca was portrayed by Lead as being
neither disobedient nor dependent, nor did she consider Rebecca a
victim. Yet, Lead clearly accepted the idea of the transference of God's

---

[32] Boehme, *Mysterium Magnum*, 374.
[33] Boehme, *Mysterium Magnum*, 393.
[34] Catherine Smith, "Mysticism and Feminism: Jacob Boehme and Jane Lead", in
Women and Men: The Consequences of Power, ed. Dana V. Hiller and Robin Sheets (Cincinnati: University of Cincinnati Press, 1977), 403.
[35] Karen Armstrong, *In the Beginning: A New Reading of the Book of Genesis* (London:
Harper Collins, 1998), 77.
[36] Susan Niditch, "Genesis", in *The Women's Bible Commentary*, ed. Carol A. Newsom
and Sharon H. Ringe (London: SPCK and Louisville, Ky.: Westminster/John Knox
Press, 1992), 19.

covenant from Rebecca to her equally spiritually receptive son Jacob, thus offering spiritual continuity from mother to son.

Lead elevated Rebecca, as Boehme had, to the role of a spiritual mother comparable to Sophia. Lead, however, adapted the story so that it was applicable to herself. Lead wrote herself into the picture of familial relationships, stating that Sophia

> would be my Mother, and so I should own her and call her, who would now be to me as Rebecca was to Jacob, to contrive and put me in a way how I should obtain the Birth-right-Blessing.[37]

Again, Lead is positioning herself as the child not only of Sophia but also of Rebecca. Positioning herself, in this case, as Jacob, she was worthy of the birthright blessing. On 10 November 1673, Lead wrote that Sophia told her that she could obtain the "Birth-right-Blessing":

> thy Father will come down with his dear Son thy Elder Brother, and I thy Mother, and will hereof take and feed [of a banquet feast], so that the Fountain of Jacob may be thy blessing, which the Eternal Father accordingly pronounced, saying From the Upper and Supercelestial Planets let thy Eternal Nativity again renew, as from its own Originality.[38]

Thus, by adopting the role of Jacob, Lead obtained the blessings of both God and Sophia, which can be seen as an allegorical way of returning to "one's own Native Country and original Virginity".[39]

Lead's phrase "one's own Native country and original Virginity" has been interpreted similarly by Catherine Smith and Brian Gibbons.[40] Smith has considered Lead's visionary feminism as illumining "the human condition by treating the female, not the male, as universal", thus downplaying the "patriarchal limitations of mystical thought" and instead emphasizing mystical women's ability to voice "their reduced condition and their native powers". As such, Smith has interpreted Lead's "native Country and original Virginity" to mean that "Sophia guides her daughters, the souls of humanity, to herself. They find her only by looking inward to the Inner Light of their own individual reflections".[41] Gibbons has also suggested that the aim of Lead's spiritual

---

[37] *Fountain*, vol. 1, 25.
[38] *Fountain*, vol. 1, 34.
[39] Jane Lead, *Revelation of Revelations* (London, 1683), 47.
[40] Smith, "Mysticism and Feminism", 403. Gibbons, *Gender in Mystical and Occult Thought*, 145.
[41] Smith, "Mysticism and Feminism", 403, 408.

project was "to seek existential identity" with Sophia and that unlike
her male Behmenist followers who strove for nuptial union with Sophia,
"Lead's sophiology permitted a positive construction of femininity in
which womanhood itself achieves subjectivity".[42]

Lead's relationship with Sophia was indeed complementary, Sophia
being both mother and daughter to Lead's regenerate soul. Lead
anticipated a new angelical generation of multiple births in which she,
as a mother both 'natural' and 'supernatural', would be involved. In
Lead's vision, Wisdom was Lead's 'true Mother' out of whose womb she
would be spiritually or 'supernaturally' reborn. Wisdom, however, was
born within the "inward parts" of Lead's soul by a "New Motion of
Life, stirring and giving a restlessness"; hence she was both infant and
mother, simultaneously being born and giving birth. Out of Sophia's
womb, she would be "conceived and born again" because "Wisdom
would be born in the inward parts" of her soul.[43] Lead's metaphor of
spiritual motherhood was unique; she broke away from the tradition
where Christ was represented as a Mother whose milk—or blood—was
the salvation of humanity.[44]

Before we can consider Lead's phrase "one's own Native country and
original Virginity" in its proper context, it is helpful to outline briefly
how Boehme represented 'mother nature'. Boehme was interested in the
beginnings of creation, and indeed *Mysterium Magnum* was his exposition
of Genesis. His translator stated that Boehme believed "the beginning
all arose out of one Mother" and he described the "Abyss" as the "one
and only Mother".[45] Boehme also suggested that seven qualities were
generated from the will of the godhead which represented "seven Mothers, out of which the substance of all Substances originally ariseth".[46]
Boehme's writings also used the term "Pregnatress"[47] to represent the

---

[42] Gibbons, *Gender in Mystical and Occult Thought*, 145–46.

[43] Jane Lead, *A Fountain of Gardens, Being a Continuation of the Process of a Life according to Faith, of the Divinely Magical Knowledge* (London, 1697), 19. Hereafter cited as *Fountain*, vol. 2.

[44] For a study of maternal imagery to describe God and Christ in the medieval period see Bynum, *Jesus as Mother*, 110–69. Bynum states that "explicit and elaborate maternal imagery to describe God and Christ, who are usually described as male, is so popular with twelfth-century Cistercian monks" (111); yet, "the theme of God's motherhood is a minor one in all writers of the high Middle Ages except Julian of Norwich" (168).

[45] Jacob Boehme, *Signatura Rerum: The Signature of All Things* (1651), 11, 19, 15.

[46] Boehme, *The Fifth Book of the Author, in Three Parts [Incarnation]* (1659), 138.

[47] Boehme, *Signatura Rerum*, 19.

gestative seventh quality which encompassed the other six, as "they receive their nourishment power, strength alwayes, in their mothers Body or Womb".[48]

Ann Bathurst, also a member of the Philadelphian circle, wrote about spiritual rebirth and suggested the possibility of being born again spiritually many times, yet being born 'naturally' only once. She stated that

> The new birth is the mother of nations: for all must be born again; and we have but one natural mother, but it may be many spiritual mothers and new births, we must pass through before we are born again.[49]

In effect, spiritual rebirth was considered to be a repetitive process in which the soul could be united with the godhead.

Lead's phrase "one's own Native country and original Virginity" was taken from an exposition of Wisdom's Gates "where the hidden track of the Virgins way may be found" leading to the New Jerusalem.[50] The Gates represented the way to heaven as part of the process of a spiritual journey. The opening of all the seven heavenly gates would result, Lead suggested, in "Unity in our selves, and with one another".[51] Lead was trying to explain that the process of spiritual rebirth and unity with the godhead meant a return to a prelapsarian state of "Unity, Harmony and pure Liberty".[52] In Behmenist terms, then, the eternal 'abyss' from which all life comes and to which it is returned to be reunited with the divine was, in Lead's terms, one's "own Native Country and original Virginity". This does not necessarily lead to "the universal feminine" suggested by Smith or Gibbons' interpretation of "womanhood achieving its subjectivity". For Lead, the 'native country' was not gendered as all had equal access to the prelapsarian harmonious state which accorded with her idea of universal salvation; in this way, all souls would eventually be saved and return to the godhead. In Lead's understanding of redemption, Sophia's relationship with humanity was

---

[48] Jacob Boehme, *Aurora, That is, Day-Spring Or Dawning of the Day in the Orient* (1656), 359.

[49] Entry dated 3 July 1693, Diaries of Ann Bathurst, MS Rawlinson D1263, Bodleian Library, Oxford.

[50] Lead, *Revelation of Revelations*, 46. The inscriptions on the seven Gates are: (1) Abnegation or Renunciation of this Outward Principle, (2) Probation, (3) Translation, (4) Bountiful, (5) Wisdom's Factory, (6) Transferring Gate, and (7) Projection.

[51] Lead, *Revelation of Revelations*, sig. B1v.

[52] Lead, *Revelation of Revelations*, sig. B1r.

part of the eschatological scheme, and there existed a complex relationship between Sophia and Mary. As we shall see, many of the feminine attributes of Sophia had parallels with the figure of Mary.

The Virgin Mary and the Virgin Sophia

The most significant mother figure in the Christian faith is Mary.[53] Although Lead was clearly Protestant, some of her thoughts were informed by ideas developed in the first centuries after Christ around the figure of Mary.[54] This section will elucidate some of Lead's religious beliefs surrounding the figures of the Virgin Mary and the Virgin Wisdom to show that they were inextricably linked. Not only was the figure of Sophia imbued with qualities associated with Mary, but in Lead's theology, Mary was a 'type' of goddess who had lesser powers than Sophia. As Barbara Newman has observed

> In the Protestant world, where the divine Father and Son were no longer counterbalanced by the figure of Mary the Mother and Ecclesia the Bride, sapiential theology took on more esoteric and heterodox forms.[55]

Lead produced an unusual account of a female presence in the godhead, recapturing in a different way something that the advent of Protestantism rejected—the figure and power of Mary—although piety associated with Mary clearly survived the Reformation.[56] For example, Thomas Traherne's devotions to Mary are notable for their extravagant language of praise.[57] For Jane Lead, as Gibbons has observed, "Wis-

---

[53] J. Pelican, *Mary Through the Centuries: Her Place in the History of Culture* (New Haven and London: Yale University Press, 1996). See also *Maria: A Journal of Marian Studies*.

[54] Ideas about Mary were subsequently incorporated into the doctrine of the Roman Catholic Church. Of the four declared dogmas about the Virgin Mary—her divine motherhood, her virginity, her immaculate conception, and her assumption into heaven—only the first can be traced to biblical sources (Isaiah 7:14, Matt. 1:23).

[55] Barbara Newman, *Sister of Wisdom: St. Hildegard's Theology of the Feminine* (Aldershot: Scholar Press, 1987), 261.

[56] See Louis Martz, *The Poetry of Meditation: A Study in English Religious Literature of the Seventeenth Century* (New Haven and London: Yale University Press, 1962), 96–107. See also A. M. Allchin, *The Joy of All Creation: An Anglican Meditation on the Place of Mary* (London: Darton, Longman and Todd, 1984), 17–89.

[57] Allchin, *The Joy of All Creation*, 78–89. See also A. Bradford, ed., *Thomas Traherne: Selected Poems and Prose* (London: Penguin, 1991); Thomas Traherne, *A Serious and Pathetical Contemplation of the Mercies of God* (London, 1699). Allchin has noted that the poetry of Traherne "has an exuberance, a freedom, a directness, which is not often found in Anglican writing about Mary" (89).

dom is clearly as personal a figure as the Virgin Mary in traditional
Christian belief, and much of her thought on Sophia has a strong
mariological flavour".[58]

Little is known about Mary if only the sources from the Bible are
used. However, there were four notable views which developed about
Mary in the early church which Lead applied to Sophia: the tradition
of the 'Ever Virgin'; the role of mediator between humankind and
God; the second Eve; and Mary as the image of the Church.[59] Lead,
however, claimed Sophia was "the eternal Goddess".[60] So, according
to Lead, Mary was one of the emissaries of the greatest heavenly virgin of them all—Sophia. Lead described Mary as "the Virgin Mary,
who was the Representative of the Eternal Virgin" and "the Virgin
that brought forth Jesus in a Fleshly Figure".[61] Mary was "a Type of
the Eternal Virgin Mother" who had a role to play at a certain time.
Hence Lead's statement:

> JESUS CHRIST being the Head, and the First-born of this Royal and
> Princely Generation, who was after the way and manner of Human
> Nature conceived in the Womb of that Virgin Mary, that was but a
> Type of the Eternal Virgin, who brought forth the Son of God before
> all Time: But Mary's Womb was sanctified to bring forth in Time, that
> CHRIST who was the Son of God before all Time.[62]

Mary was a representative of Sophia who took on a human form and
made possible the incarnation of Christ. The Cistercian monk and
French theologian, St Bernard of Clairvaux (1090–1153), suggested the
need for another mediator in addition to Christ, and suggested Mary. He
first recognized Mary as a necessary intermediary between humankind
and Christ and compared her to "an aqueduct coursing down through
the city of the faithful".[63] Lead similarly depicted Sophia as a female

---

[58] Gibbons, *Gender in Mystical and Occult Thought*, 145. Gibbons recognised "the association between the Virgin Wisdom and the Virgin Mary, always latent in Behmenist
thought, is made much more explicitly by Lead" (145).

[59] The Council at Ephesus in AD 431 proclaimed Mary 'Theotokos' (mother of
God), and at the Council of Chalcedon in AD 451 Mary was given the official title
'Aeiparthenos' (ever-Virgin), affirming her virginity at the conception. In AD 649, Mary's
perpetual virginity became dogma of the Church. See Marina Warner, *Alone of All Her
Sex: The Myth and Cult of the Virgin Mary* (London: Picador, 1976), 65–66.

[60] Lead, *Revelation of Revelations*, 39.

[61] Lead, *Revelation of Revelations*, 39, 46.

[62] Lead, *Revelation of Revelations*, 32.

[63] Warner, *Alone of All Her Sex*, 286.

intercessor between herself and God, a bridge between the divine and human which she may have drawn from this earlier tradition.

The relationship between Mary and Sophia was a subject that interested other Philadelphians. Francis Lee wrote of the relationship between Mary and Sophia, saying that

> Christ, according to the flesh, was conceived of the Holy Ghost by the Virgin Mary (blessed for all generations), not as she was an earthly virgin only, but as the heavenly Virgin of God's Wisdom had chosen her to represent herself outwardly.[64]

Interestingly, Lee converted to Roman Catholicism after the death of Lead. Lead herself rejected Catholic theology and was selective in what she chose to adopt or reject when considering the figure of Mary. Interpreting the passage where Jesus pointed out his mother Mary to John saying, "Behold thy Mother" (John 19:27), Lead glossed "Mother" as "the Virgin Mary, who was the Representative of the Eternal Virgin".[65] When Lead herself heard the words from Sophia saying, "Behold me as thy Mother", it consolidated her own position as divinely chosen. More generally, the words indicated "a privilege of Adoption, whereby we may entitle this Virgin for our true Mother".[66] The way in which the figure of Sophia was tied in with maternal imagery also included an important account of spiritual rebirth. To complicate things further, spiritual rebirth was not only closely allied to Sophia, but also to the configuration of Adam.

Androgynous Adam and Supernatural Sophia

This section will consider the importance of Sophia's procreative abilities and examine Lead's ideas concerning Sophia as the mother of the androgynous Adam in the 'End Days'. Lead described how, through a spiritual rebirth, souls could recapture the prelapsarian paradise lost at the Fall as well as how the current and future state of humanity rested on the story of Adam and Eve. Interestingly, Lead conflated elements from both Genesis 1:27 and Genesis 2:23 by writing,

---

[64] Walton, *Notes and Materials*, 511–12.
[65] Lead, *The Wonders of God's Creation Manifested in the Variety of Eight Worlds* (1695), 26.
[66] Lead, *Wonders of God's Creation*, 26.

This Virgin Adam had in himself, before ever Eve was taken out of him, but she with-drew as soon as Adam looked outward, as if he were not sufficient of himself to encrease and multiply for the replenishing of Paradise, God having created Male and Female in himself.[67]

The Behmenist view was that the first Adam was an androgynous being, at first "a Man, and also a woman"—his fall from an androgynous state being thus a fall into matter and gender.[68] Lead made the distinction between the physicality of the first Adam after the Fall, and the spirituality of the expected second Adam, as

the First Adam and his Posterity were made living Souls, to move Natural Bodies: But the Second Adam, with his Virgin-Spirit, turns Souls into Spirits, and cloaths them with Glorified Bodies.[69]

Because Adam looked outward towards the world, the Fall caused a separation between Adam and Eve, and between humankind and God. Thus, Adam and Eve no longer enjoyed a harmonious relationship with God after the Fall.

Lead suggested, however, that Sophia's procreative abilities could offer a solution. While the descendants of Eve were subject to sinful natures, the children born of the Virgin Wisdom, or Sophia, could escape this curse through the regaining of original androgyny.[70] Lead wrote that "the first earthly Eve" is "the Mother of all Living in Earthly Property. Her Womb is fruitful, still to bring forth Viperous Thoughts."[71] Eve was, however, to be replaced by a spiritual generation conceived and delivered by the Virgin Wisdom. It was through Sophia, then, that the children of Eve could be reborn and return to an original state through an inward spiritual transformation. In Behmenist terms, it meant a return to a prelapsarian paradise where purity of the soul would triumph over flesh. Lead describes the process here, using Adam as an example:

---

[67] Lead, *Wonders of God's Creation*, 38.
[68] Boehme, *Mysterium Magnum*, 78. For an interesting study of Boehme's ideas of Adam's prelapsarian life, see Gibbons, *Gender in Mystical and Occult Thought*, 95ff.
[69] *Fountain*, vol. 1, 377.
[70] A Behmenist interpretation of Eve's reduced condition is that "Eve unlike Sophia, can no longer be 'a Mother without Generating', that is 'manifesting' images rather than 'generating' fleshy children". James Grantham Turner, *One Flesh: Paradisal Marriage and Sexual Relations in the Age of Milton* (Oxford: Clarendon Press, 1987), 144.
[71] *Fountain*, vol. 2, 76.

> God Created Adam at first to bear his own Image and Figure, who was to represent God himself, the High and Divine Masculine, Male and Female; so that Adam had his Virgin in himself in imitation of his Creator, which in Time was brought forth in a distinct Figure.[72]

This prelapsarian Adam was a symbol of purity and union with the godhead. After the Fall, however, the first Adam had "lost his Virgin Body, wherein his strength did lye".[73] As a symbol of purity and union with the godhead, the prelapsarian Adam was thus a personification of the divine, unlike Christ who was a combination of humanity (from Mary) and the divine. After the Fall, the broken relationship between God and mankind could be healed by Sophia's assistance, allowing the soul to reunite with the godhead.

Lead emphasized how the female population was included in this restoration. She wrote of the Word telling her that "though the holy Scriptures make mention chiefly of the first Adamical Man's Restoration; I say the Woman's Restoration, as well as the Man's".[74] This was entirely in accordance with Lead's ideas concerning the doctrine of universal salvation, where all souls would be saved. As the leader of the Philadelphian Society, however, she would have been aware that she could not have been employed in any official position within the established church. However, she did not trouble herself with the thorny issue of women's full incorporation into the church of man; she was more concerned with the full incorporation of everyone into the church of God. She emphasized the internal, homogenous nature of the soul as being the important connection with God. She wrote, "And as to the outward sex, there shall be no distinction, though the Typical Priesthood admitted none but Males in its day: All that is done away".[75] Lead thus posited an egalitarian model which did not distinguish between the outward physicalities of the flesh, which she perceived as a hindrance.[76]

Moreover, by drawing on Galatians 3:28, "there is neither male nor female: for ye are all one in Christ Jesus", Lead declared,

---

[72] Lead, *Wonders of God's Creation*, 31–33.
[73] Lead, *Wonders of God's Creation*, 36.
[74] *Fountains*, vol. 2, 118. This entry is dated 9 March 1676.
[75] Lead, *Revelation of Revelations*, 106.
[76] The denial of women's full incorporation into the leadership of the Christian Church remains a contentious issue today and will not be elaborated upon here. See, for example, Karen Armstrong, *The End of Silence: Women and Priesthood* (London: Fourth Estate, 1993).

Male and Female are alike here...Where there is neither Male nor
Female, but Christ is all, and in all...Wisdom's Purity and Power in the
Spirit is all that God respecteth.[77]

At the point of the restoration there would be no distinction between
the sexes. For Lead, then, those souls who came after the second Adam
would not have a gender; her idea of a universal restoration meant
there was a place where every soul would be genderless. Lead did not,
however, apply the same criteria to the 'gender' of those who comprised the godhead. God and Christ were clearly male and Wisdom
female, while the Holy Spirit was ambiguous, or at times linked with
Wisdom.

For Lead, however, the gendered Sophia was central to this role of
genderless restoration because she would be responsible for the procreation of the second Adam. Lead wrote, "Wisdom hath recreated
and formed another Adam, being Male and Female, a Production of
her own Virgin-Nature".[78] Lead may have been influenced by Behmenist ideas which had resonances with the Cabbala and Gnosticism
when she suggested that "Adam was androgynous [and] could give
birth parthenogenically".[79] Yet Lead did not state this idea explicitly
in her own writings. She wrote of the spiritual procreation and the
reproductive capability of both males and females who could retain
their identities:

> The male has the Virgin in himself, and so from these may multiply a
> Spiritual Offspring, as was proposed in the first Adam. And on the other
> Hand, the female Virgin shall have like manner, according to the excellent
> might of God-Man so incorporating with the Virgin-mind...to procreate
> these Angelical Births from themselves.[80]

The implication here was that Sophia was in God, as Eve existed in
Adam, and vice versa. Lead's writing, however, suggested a paradox:
the chaste "Virgin" could also "procreate...angelical births". Reproduction occurred through a chaste androgyne, "not limited to Male

---

[77] Lead, *Revelation of Revelations*, 106.

[78] *Fountain*, vol. 1, 79.

[79] Alexander Roob, *The Hermetic Museum: Alchemy and Mysticism* (Cologne: Taschen,
1997), 165. See also Robin Waterfield, ed., *Jacob Boehme* (Berkeley: North Atlantic
Books, 2001), 120.

[80] Jane Lead, *The Signs of the Times: Forerunning the Kingdom of Christ, and Evidencing
When It Is To Come* (London, 1699), 15.

or Female for Angelical Generation".[81] Lead was also concerned to
point out that "the Reign of Christ must be terminated in the Virgin's
seed. Eve's lost chastity will produce a new Generation, to whom this
Kingdom shall be committed in trust". In this way the offspring of the
heavenly Sophia would replace those of the earthly Eve as the "pure
Virgin Spirits, who travel to bring forth Christ spiritually".[82] If Eve's
fall resulted in a separation of the genders, then redemption by the
Virgin Wisdom could be seen as a way of regaining a state of spiritual
androgyny.

Lead's visions highlighted the need for the human soul to be
acquainted with the Virgin Wisdom and regain qualities associated
with Her, such as purity. According to Lead, "The New Paradise will
begin, as it was in the first Paradise, in Male and Female, through the
restoration of the lost Virgin-Nature";[83] i.e. the purity lost at the Fall
and the resulting separation from God. To become a virgin, however,
allowed a move beyond the sphere of sexual polarity because the soul
was created after the image of God and was constituted of male and
female properties which were virginal. When God begins to consort with
the soul, He turns what was human into a virgin again by removing
the degenerate and emasculated passions. External identity is erased in
favour of the pure soul returning to the essence of God. Lead asked,
"How can Sophia introduce herself into that nature, where her pure
chastity hath been violated?"[84] Lead stressed the need for an internal
transformation of the self that pointed to the true nature of the soul,
rooted from the beginning in Wisdom.

Catherine Smith has suggested that Lead was a kind of seventeenth-
century feminist. She argues that mysticism has given women such as
Lead "an indirect language for protesting sexual politics".[85] Yet, as Gibbons has suggested, in Lead's works "sexuality is generally contrasted
with the regenerate life". Lead considered the fallen condition in terms
of lost virginity, and regeneration as a freedom from the constraints of
sexual procreation.[86] For Lead, "Virgin nature, and Godlike Simplicity...

---

[81] Lead, *Signs of the Times*, sig. A8v.
[82] Lead, *Revelation of Revelations*, 38.
[83] Lead, *Signs of the Times*, 13.
[84] Lead, *Revelation of Revelations*, 39.
[85] Catherine Smith, "The Mind and Art of a Seventeenth-Century Protestant Mystic", in *Women of Spirit: Female Leadership in the Jewish and Christian Traditions*, ed. R. R.
Ruether and E. McLaughlin (New York: Simon and Schuster, 1979), 195.
[86] Gibbons, *Gender in Mystical and Occult Thought*, 148.

[have] been deflowered through the subtlety of Reason".[87] The Fall meant turning away from God, resulting in a fall into gender and matter, whereas the offspring born "From God the Father, in conjunction with the Eternal Virgin Wisdom who brought them forth" would be purified, angelical souls.[88] It was as a self-professed child of Wisdom that Lead wished to escape from the Fall and from gender and matter. However, as we shall see, she produced her own version of a maternal Christianity.

Wisdom's Children

Arise, arise, ye virgin daughters, and draw near,
having this name inscribed upon you with the finger of your God.[89]

This section will examine how Lead constructed a sense of self by translating her experiences as a mother into spiritual beliefs. Bodily experiences related to maternity were a common way of describing nurturing functions of the divine. Elaine Hobby has argued that there was a difference in the way that the concept of God as a 'nursing mother' was used by men and women: "God has qualities that are specifically feminine, and women therefore have a privileged access to understanding those aspects of divinity".[90] In her imagery of lactation, for example, the Philadelphian Anne Bathurst, also a mother, applied the experience she had of the capability of sustenance. Expressing her desire of union with Christ, Bathurst transformed her own milk metaphorically, thereby creating a maternal bond where Christ was the child:

I am as pent milk in the breast, ready to be poured forth and diluted into Thee, from whom my fullness flows with such fullness and plenitude, and pleased when eased. O flow and overflow! O thou milk of the world! To the well of life that springeth up in me as a fountain, to reach all the branches...But the word Divine is still too big for me to speak. It fills me with that which is unutterable, sweet and pleasant, yea satisfactory to an

---

[87] Jane Lead, *The Heavenly Cloud Now Breaking* (1681), 22.
[88] Lead, *Wonders of God's Creation*, 32.
[89] Lead, *Wonders of God's Creation*, 78.
[90] Elaine Hobby, *Virtue of Necessity: English Women's Writing 1649–88* (London: Virago, 1988), 42.

excess! O Lord thy fullness is fullness I fill as from a sea, and well I may, when the sea has broke in upon me, upon my understanding.[91]

The metaphorical qualities of bodily milk were easier for Bathurst to articulate than "The word Divine". The milk was an active force which sprang up, spread, and filled, representing a mystical connectedness in a symbiotic relationship between herself and divinity.[92]

Lead, however, reversed the role of 'child' which Bathurst had used, and, in contrast, she used lactation as a metaphor for the way Wisdom's Children would gain spiritual sustenance. For Boehme, such hunger for milk could symbolize the striving for a closer relationship with God: "As a child continually longeth after the breasts of the Mother, so must its hunger continually enter into the love of God".[93] Thus, in accordance with Behmenism, Lead wrote:

> as soon as they [Wisdom's Children] are Spiritually Born, care is to be taken that this holy birth draw the sustenance of Life from no other than its own Virgin Mother, whose Breast must at all times satisfie and nourish it. For according to what it sucks in of such a Kind, Nature and Quality the Birth is, for it draws in the Spirit and Life of its Mother. Therefore watch to it, and hang not upon any strange Breast.[94]

Lead's description of the birth of her own imaginary child, recorded in a night vision on 20 September 1682, shows again how she used the language of androgyny to transcend sex:

> it was the Sight of an Infant, new born, that was brought to me; and it was said to be Mine. But I wondered at it: for I knew it not When, or How, I brought it forth. Then I Questioned, whether it was Male, or Female? And it being examined, there was no Mark of Distinction upon it. Which was Marvelous, to consider what Manner of Child this would be. And when I call'd it over in the Divine Sense, it was said, This Figures Out of the Mysterious High Birth, that will be Mighty in Power, and Wonderful in Wisdom and Majesty.[95]

The unsexed baby transcended gender in a platonic way by embodying an androgyne. The absence of the baby's sex represented part of

---

[91] Entry dated 1693, MS Rawl D1263. For an examination of the subject of milk, see Wendy Wall, *Staging Domesticity: Household Work and English Identity in Early Modern Drama* (Cambridge: Cambridge University Press, 2002), 127–42.

[92] Crawford, *Women and Religion*, 111–15.

[93] Jacob Boehme, *The Way to Christ Discovered* (1648), 86.

[94] Lead, *Wonders of God's Creation*, 35.

[95] *Fountain*, vol. 3, pt. 2, 311–12.

the process of purification, as the new-born infant had "no mark of Distinction".[96] The vision was also prophetic as it indicated Lead's anticipation of spiritual offspring. Like the Virgin-birth, Lead's visionary birth was miraculous as well; as she wrote: "I knew it not When, or How, I brought it forth". The vision showed how Lead anticipated an angelical generation as a way of restoring humanity to God in a

> Resurrection-Birth Which converts all of the dead Body of Sin in those, who have been baptized with Christ in his Death, into a Life of Child-like Innocency, that derives its new Creaturely Being from the contracted matter of the deity in Humanity, which is its risen Body of Birth.[97]

In the "Resurrection-Birth", the soul was imbued with "child-like innocency" instead of a state of sinfulness.

In another night vision dated 12 January 1677, Lead saw monstrous, sinful creatures from which burst beautiful children:

> In the night there was presented unto me, two Forms very displeasing to my Eye, being Cloathed with Hairy Goats-Skin, where spots and blotches did appear so unlovely, as I was disgusted at the sight of them ... And I beheld two sweet amiable children came forth from within this deformed Figure.[98]

There was a similarity between this vision and the story of Esau and Jacob. The "innocent and all-beautiful Babes" who appeared from the "Hairy Goats-Skin" had cast off "that thick and cloudy smothering Body of Sin" which had disguised them.[99] Lead illustrated the point that matter, like sin, could be transformed, or, like the body, could be refigured. The delivery of the infant and the transformation of the "two sweet children" thus both represented a process of spiritual change—spiritual rebirth as part of the purification that could lead to redemption.

In order to return to the godhead, the souls of Wisdom's children had to be transformed. Lead believed that Wisdom would bear such souls as her own offspring. Of divine parenthood, they were "to know themselves as to their original Pre-existence in God the Father, and

---

[96] For interesting accounts of attitudes to the body, see David Tripp, "The image of the body in the formative phases of the Protestant Reformation", in *Religion and the Body*, ed. Sarah Coakley (Cambridge: Cambridge University Press, 1997), 131–51; also Lyndal Roper, *Oedipus and the Devil: Witchcraft, Sexuality and Religion in Early Modern Europe* (London: Routledge, 1994).

[97] *Fountain*, vol. 3, pt. 2, 212.

[98] *Fountain*, vol. 2, 9.

[99] *Fountain*, vol. 2, 10.

brought forth through the Womb of the Eternal Virgin, a pure Simplified Spirit"[100]—the "Simplified Spirit" being androgynous. Lead
considered herself to be one of Wisdom's Children whose soul had
undergone a regeneration. She wrote that

> Wisdom did conceive us in her Womb, and did bring us forth, and so
> passed us over in our Minority to our Jesus; we by him having attained
> to a more grown State, he doth transmit us over to the care and charge
> of the Holy Ghost.[101]

The idea of Wisdom's children was a familiar one. "But Wisdom is
justified of all her children" (Luke 7:35) appears on the title page of
Lead's spiritual diary, in which she kept a record of her spiritual progress
as one of Wisdom's offspring. Of the relationship between Sophia and
her offspring, Lead wrote, "this our eternal Virgin Mother... cannot be
more naturally sympathising with her Children".[102] She considered that
"we are to reckon our selves born anew into the unity tending to all
Purity of Perfection with Christ our First Born from the Dead, and so to
appropriate this Eternal Virgin for our supernatural Mother".[103] Lead's
construction of a theology of motherhood was therefore informed by
Sophia's spiritual maternity as well as her understanding of her own
experiences as a mother.

Lead's images of maternity have caused Diane Purkiss to question
whether she was producing a gynocentric understanding of religion or
whether Lead transcended gender.[104] Purkiss is one of the few scholars
who has written about Lead in terms of the maternal body. Purkiss
is clearly influenced by French feminist writers who interrogate the
meaning and subversion of linguistic signifiers. Using psychoanalyti-
cal theory, they question language and femaleness and their relation
to the patriarchal order.[105] Purkiss suggests that Lead, like many other
early modern women including Elizabeth Poole and Anna Trapnel,
wrote texts which show "women's desire to situate themselves outside

---

[100] Jane Lead, *The Enochian Walks With God, Found out by a Spiritual-Traveler Whose Face Towards Mount-Sion Above was Set* (1694), 28.

[101] *Fountain*, vol. 1, 137.

[102] *Fountain*, vol. 1, 28.

[103] *Fountain*, vol. 1, 26.

[104] Diane Purkiss, "Producing the Voice, Consuming the Body: Women Prophets of the Seventeenth Century", in *Women, Writing, History 1640–1740*, ed. Isobel Grundy and Susan Wiseman (London: Batsford, 1992).

[105] Annette Kuhn, "Introduction to Hélène Cixous's 'Castration or Decapitation?'", *Signs* 7, no. 1 (Autumn 1981): 36–40.

or beyond the body".[106] Purkiss quotes Lead's description of the passage through Wisdom's seventh gate which "causes an unalterable Transmutation of all gross matter, and the vile Body's shape into heavenly consistency: such a celestial body wisdom's Virgin shall have power to put on".[107] Purkiss has interpreted this as a disavowal of the subject body which is "encoded in tropes of physical dissolution and disembodiment".[108]

The transmutation of matter clearly signified a desire for purification, a theme Lead also expressed in alchemical terms.[109] But Purkiss also suggested that "[w]riting out of the body ultimately reproduced the ideology of women's bodily inferiority, even as it allowed women to construct a more stable sense of self.[110] Yet, as Thomas McCray-Worrall has suggested, Lead's gendered figurations "systematically incorporate the bodily associations they ostensibly disavow".[111] This is apparent when Lead writes that "Christ's Glorified Body becomes our Covering; He is in us, and we in Him" causing "the very Outward Body to shine".[112] Such passages suggest a refiguration, not a reduction of the body. This interpretation disrupts the widely accepted understanding in recent scholarship that women prophetic writers simply treat their bodies as empty vessels or passive conduits to receive the Word of God. Lead did deploy this common literary trope, describing herself as "wholly Passive, and the Spirit altogether Active" and writing that God "was to arise, and speak forth himself, through this Earthen and empty Vessel".[113] As a vessel, she was not empty but filled with the Spirit of God. Furthermore, the rhetoric she used showed that her prophetic utterances became a form of delivery, "as a Bodily Birth, going forth

---

[106] Purkiss, "Producing the Voice", 151.

[107] Lead, *Revelation of Revelations*, 53.

[108] Purkiss, "Producing the Voice", 151.

[109] See Hirst, *Jane Leade: A Biography*.

[110] Purkiss, "Producing the Voice", 151–52. Purkiss also writes, "women prophets sought to rewrite the specificity of the female body in metaphysical terms. Jane Lead thus represented the transmission of mystical knowledge in terms of female reproduction (152).

[111] Thomas M. McCray-Worrall, "Wisdom's Body: The Prophetic Writings of Jane Lead" (M.Phil. diss., Cambridge University, 1999), 6.

[112] *Fountain*, vol. 3, pt. 2, 307–8. Entry dated 3 September 1682.

[113] *Fountain*, vol. 2, sig. A2. For scholarship on women's self-deprecation and self-effacement, see Mack, *Visionary Women*, 15–44; Hilary Hinds, *God's Englishwomen: Seventeenth-Century Radical Sectarian Writing and Feminist Criticism* (Manchester: Manchester University Press, 1996); and Hobby, *Virtue of Necessity*.

from me in Outflowing Acts of Power".[114] Lead thus articulated her inner space as an act of communication with the divine, complicating conceptions of herself as a passive, empty vessel.

Conclusion

Lead's texts can thus be read as a dialogue between herself and God and as a record of an embodiment of God's truth, a truth that was produced through a sequence of mystical and revelatory events involving Sophia as Lead's spiritual mother. As we have seen, Lead was not only a 'natural' mother to her offspring, but she was also regarded as a 'mother' by her followers. In addition, Sophia was esteemed by Lead as her 'supernatural' and adopted mother. Lead's representation of spiritual maternity was thus complicated by the fact that these roles were interchangeable. Wisdom was born within Lead's soul, and yet Lead also gave birth to wisdom in the form of revelations of God's truth. Lead also assumed the role of 'supernatural' mother by anticipating Sophia's maternal capabilities in her vision of an imaginary birth. Sophia and Lead were thus both mother and daughter at the same time. As a vessel of the spirit/word, Lead refigured her body and self-identity as a mother, incorporating her maternal experiences into her spiritual beliefs.

Although Lead's understanding of religion is explicitly gynocentric, with Sophia as a pivotal spiritual mother figure, the importance of androgyny cannot be overlooked. In her images of motherhood and the vision of the unsexed baby, Lead transcended gender boundaries. The absence of signs of sexual difference and desire signified part of the process of purification which could lead to redemption. Lead thus prophesied that Sophia would give birth to a purified and androgynous generation, and men and women would be restored to the state that existed before the Fall, a prelapsarian paradise, and be known as Wisdom's children.

What was unusual in the religious and socio-cultural scene of the late seventeenth century is that Lead believed in a spiritual mother figure at all. Her beliefs include aspects of Marian theology transposed by a Protestant. Many of Lead's ideas have parallels with the early

---

[114] *Fountain*, vol. 2, 324.

development of Marian devotion and theology; spirituality can be seen as 'mystical' when repressed. Lead's transposing of Marian theology and spirituality into sophiology was, however, unique. It resulted in a depiction of her female soul in mystical union with Sophia, which in turn gave birth to wisdom from her soul. From this cyclical process, Lead was simultaneously both mother and daughter, naturally and supernaturally.

Bibliography

Manuscripts

Acts of Court 1687–1707 (Lady Mico's College). Mercers' Company Archives, London.
MS Rawlinson D832. Papers of Richard Roach. Bodleian Library, Oxford.
MS Rawlinson D1263. Diaries of Ann Bathurst. Bodleian Library, Oxford.
Walton MS C.5.30. Dr Williams' Library, London.

Printed Sources

Allchin, A. M. *The Joy of All Creation: An Anglican Meditation on the Place of Mary.* London: Darton, Longman and Todd, 1984.
Armstrong, Karen. *In the Beginning: A New Reading of the Book of Genesis.* London: Harper Collins, 1998.
———. *The End of Silence: Women and Priesthood.* London: Fourth Estate, 1993.
Boehme, Jacob. *Signatura Rerum: The Signature of All Things.* London, 1651.
———. *The Fifth Book of the Author, in Three Parts The First, of the Incarnation of Jesus Christ.* London, 1659.
———. *Aurora, That is, Day-Spring Or Dawning of the Day in the Orient Or Morning Rednesse Sun That is The Root or Mother of Philosophie, Astrologie and Theologie from the true Ground Or A Description of Nature by Jacob Behme Teutonick Philosopher Being his First Book.* London, 1656.
———. *Mysterium Magnum or, An Exposition of the First Book of Moses called GENESIS.* London, 1656.
———. *The Way to Christ Discovered.* London, 1648.
Bradford, A., ed. *Thomas Traherne: Selected Poems and Prose.* London and New York: Penguin, 1991.
Brod, Manfred. "A Radical Network in the English Revolution: John Pordage and His Circle, 1646–54". *English Historical Review* 119 (2004): 1230–53.
Bynum, C. W. *Jesus as Mother: Studies in the Spirituality of the High Middle Ages.* Berkeley: University of California Press, 1982.
Bysshe, Edward. *The Visitation of Norfolk... 1664.* Edited by A. W. Hughes Clarke and A. Campling. Norfolk Record Society, vol. 5. London, 1934.
Coakley, Sarah, ed. *Religion and the Body.* Cambridge: Cambridge University Press, 1997.
Crawford, Patricia. *Women and Religion 1500–1720.* London: Routledge, 1996.
Elliott, Dyan. *Spiritual Marriage, Sexual Abstinence in Medieval Wedlock.* Princeton: Princeton University Press, 1993.
Fildes, Valerie, ed. *Women as Mothers in Pre-Industrial England.* London: Routledge, 1990.

Gadt, Jeanette. "Women and Protestant Culture: The Quaker Dissent from Puritanism". Ph.D. diss., University of California, Los Angeles, 1999.

Gibbons, B. J. *Gender in Mystical and Occult Thought: Behmenism and its Development in England.* New York: Cambridge University Press, 1996.

Grundy, Isobel and Susan Wiseman, eds. *Women, Writing, History 1640–1740.* London: Batsford, 1992.

Harrison, J. F. C. *The Second Coming: Popular Millenarianism 1780–1850.* London: Routledge, 1979.

Hiller, Dana and Robin Sheets, eds. *Women and Men: The Consequences of Power.* Cincinnati: University of Cincinnati Press, 1977.

Hinds, Hilary. *God's Englishwomen: Seventeenth-Century Radical Sectarian Writing and Feminist Criticism.* Manchester: Manchester University Press, 1996.

Hirst, Julie. *Jane Leade: A Biography of a Seventeenth-Century Mystic.* Hampshire: Ashgate, 2006.

Hobby, Elaine. *Virtue of Necessity: English Women's Writing 1649–88.* London: Virago, 1988.

Kuhn, Annette. "Introduction to Hélène Cixous's 'Castration or Decapitation?'". *Signs* 7, no. 1 (Autumn 1981): 36–40.

Lead, Jane. *The Enochian Walks With God, Found out by a Spiritual-Traveler Whose Face Towards Mount-Sion Above was Set.* London, 1694.

———. *A Fountain of Gardens.* Vol. 1, . . . *Watered by the Rivers of Divine Pleasure, and Springing up in the variety of Spiritual Plants Blown up by the pure Breath into A Paradise, Sending forth their Sweet Savours, and Strong Odours, for Soul Refreshing.* London, 1696.

———. *A Fountain of Gardens.* Vol. 2, . . . *Being a Continuation of the Process of a Life according to Faith, of the Divinely Magical Knowledge, and of the New Creation in Mutual Entertainments, Betwixt The Essential Wisdom, and the Soul in her Progress through Paradise to Mount Sion, and to the New Jerusalem.* London, 1697.

———. *A Fountain of Gardens.* Vol. 3, . . . *Or, A Spiritual Diary of the Wonderful Experiences of a Christian Soul, under the Conduct of Heavenly Wisdom.* London, 1700–1.

———. "Lebenslauff der Autorin". In *Sechs Unschatzbare Mystiche Tractätlein.* Amsterdam, 1696.

———. *The Revelation of Revelations, Particularly as an Essay Towards the Unsealing, Opening and Discovering of the Seven Seals, the Seven Thunders and the New Jerusalem State.* London, 1683.

———. *The Signs of the Times: Forerunning the Kingdom of Christ, and Evidencing When It Is To Come.* London, 1699.

———. *The Wars of David, and the Peaceable Reign of Solomon Symbolizing the Times of Warfare and Refreshment of the Saints of the Most High God To Whom a Priestly Kingdom is shortly to be given after the order of Melchisedeck.* London, 1700.

———. *The Wonders of God's Creation Manifested in the Variety of Eight Worlds As they were made known to Experimentally to the Author.* London, 1695.

———. *The Heavenly Cloud now Breaking. The Lord Christ's Ascension-Ladder Sent down; To shew the way to Reach the Ascension, and Glorification, through Death and Resurrection.* London, 1681.

Longfellow, Erica. *Women and Religious Writing in Early Modern England.* Cambridge: Cambridge University Press, 2004.

McCray-Worrall, Thomas. "Wisdom's Body: The Prophetic Writings of Jane Lead". M. Phil. diss., Cambridge University, 1999.

Mack, Phyllis. "Teaching About Gender and Spirituality in Early English Quakerism". *Women's Studies* 19, no. 2 (1991): 223–37.

———. *Visionary Women: Ecstatic Prophecy in Seventeenth-Century England.* Berkeley: University of California Press, 1992.

Martz, Louis L. *The Poetry of Meditation: A Study in English Religious Literature of the Seventeenth Century.* New Haven and London: Yale University Press, 1962.

Mendelson, Sara and Patricia Crawford. *Women in Early Modern England 1550–1720*. Oxford: Oxford University Press, 1998.

Newman, Barbara. *Sister of Wisdom: St. Hildegard's Theology of the Feminine*. Aldershot: Scholar Press, 1987.

Newsom, Carol A. and Sharon H. Ringe, eds. *The Women's Bible Commentary*. London: SPCK and Louisville, Ky.: Westminster/John Knox Press, 1992.

Oliver, W. H. *Prophets and Millennialists: The Uses of Biblical Prophecy from the 1790s to the 1840s*. Auckland: Auckland University Press, 1978.

Pelican, J. *Mary Through the Centuries: Her Place in the History of Culture*. New Haven and London: Yale University Press, 1996.

Power, Kim. *Veiled Desire: Augustine on Women*. New York: Continuum, 1996.

Robley, Edward Whitson. *The Shakers: Two Centuries of Spiritual Reflection*. London: SPCK, 1983.

Roob, Alexander. *The Hermetic Museum: Alchemy and Mysticism*. Cologne: Taschen, 1997.

Roper, Lyndal. *Oedipus and the Devil: Witchcraft, Sexuality and Religion in Early Modern Europe*. London: Routledge, 1994.

Ruether Rosemary R. and Eleanor McLaughlin, eds. *Women of Spirit: Female Leadership in the Jewish and Christian Traditions*. New York: Simon and Schuster, 1979.

Sperle, Joanna Magnani. "God's Healing Angel: A Biography of Jane Ward Lead". Ph.D. diss., Kent State University, 1985.

Traherne, Thomas. *A Serious and Pathetical Contemplation of the Mercies of God*. London: Samuel Keble, 1699.

Turner, James Grantham. *One Flesh: Paradisal Marriage and Sexual Relations in the Age of Milton*. Oxford: Clarendon Press, 1987.

Wall, Wendy. *Staging Domesticity: Household Work and English Identity in Early Modern Drama*. Cambridge: Cambridge University Press, 2002.

Walton, Christopher. *Notes & Materials for an Adequate Biography of the Celebrated & Divine Theosopher William Law*. London, 1854.

Warner, Marina. *Alone of All Her Sex: The Myth and Cult of the Virgin Mary*. London: Picador, 1976.

Waterfield, Robin, ed. *Jacob Boehme*. Berkeley: North Atlantic Books, 2001.

"I WISH TO BE NOTHING":
THE ROLE OF SELF-DENIAL IN THE MYSTICAL
THEOLOGY OF ANNA MARIA VAN SCHURMAN

Bo Karen Lee

> Then he said to them all: "If anyone would come after me, he must deny
> himself and take up his cross and follow me".
> Matthew 16:24

The call of Christ to his disciples, as relayed in the Synoptic Gospels,
has wielded enormous power throughout the history of Christianity.
From martyrdoms to rigorous forms of asceticism, the injunction to deny
the self has generated a host of interpretations, both theoretical and
practical. The power of this appeal to self-denial is especially evident
in the writings of Anna Maria van Schurman, the "star of Utrecht" in
seventeenth-century Europe. She went so far as to identify self-denial
as the lifespring of Christianity, without which true Christianity cannot exist, "except one that is counterfeit [*fucatus*]".[1] According to van
Schurman, self-denial was not a *goal* or destination; that is, for mature
believers alone as others were wont to claim. Self-denial was rather a
prerequisite for all who desire even to begin the Christian journey. While
self-denial was not by any means a novel concept, the priority that she
attached to it was surprising to her contemporaries.

For van Schurman, the final purpose of self-denial was union with
Christ. This goal would be utterly unattainable without self-denial,
through which one is fully emptied of the self and thus made ready for
union with Christ. Even before the goal was to be reached, however,
van Schurman yearned for a kind of knowledge that she would label
"the one thing necessary". This *unum necessarium* was an "intimate" or
"inmost" knowledge of God, and this too was inaccessible, apart from a
radical denial of the self. Self-denial, then, would be the engine behind

---

[1] Anna Maria van Schurman to Johannes Jacob Schutz, 12/22 August 1674, MS
G2.II.33, fol. 2v, Basel University Library. Thanks to Joyce Irwin for providing information on these unpublished letters.

an intimate knowledge of God that would, in turn, lead ultimately to union with Christ.

While self-denial was supremely desirable, it eventually proved impossible for van Schurman. A greater, more pleasurable gain would provide the impetus to motivate—and ultimately enable—her to deny herself, as if by sheer coincidence or even accident. Self-denial would not be achieved by sheer effort but would be the by-product of another process. Faithful to the creeds of the Reformed church, Anna Maria held that "the chief end of [humanity] is to...enjoy [God] forever".[2] This desire to "enjoy God" would become the secret to self-denial; it would also lead the seeker, ultimately, towards union with Christ. When the enjoyment of God became the individual's supreme desire, self-denial would inevitably occur. Likewise, a greater self-denial resulted in a sweeter enjoyment of God. Rather than debilitate the soul, self-denial granted deep pleasure and delight to the soul that had learned to deny itself *for the sake of* a greater good. It found both its source and its fruit, its impetus and its reward, in the greater enjoyment of God.

Other theologians of van Schurman's time took issue with her emphasis on self-denial. They argued that it was a "mark of perfection" for mature Christians and feared that its primacy in her writings might oppress or discourage the "everyday" Christian. Against their doubts, van Schurman contended that self-denial need not be a restrictive force or daunting imperative. Rather, it had the power to enlarge and enrich the individual. Indeed, this was the case in van Schurman's own experience. Though the established elite of the day would "deny" her for her decisions, van Schurman found her theological voice. A stronger sense of the self emerged, by the very *means* of her self-denial. She became a key spokesperson for the Labadists, a newly emerging pietistic movement of her day led by Jean de Labadie, and was also a forerunner of German Pietism. Her writings, in fact, arguably shaped this important movement from its outset.[3] At the end of the day, she emerged as poised and confident; her emphasis on self-denial served not to weaken, but to liberate and strengthen her.

---

[2] See the Westminster Shorter Catechism of 1647, as well as the Heidelberg Catechism.

[3] Wallmann argues persuasively that van Schurman influenced the genesis and development of Lutheran Pietism in nearby Germany. Her correspondence with leading figures like Johannes Jacobus Schutz, for example, serves as another link to this important movement. See Johannes Wallmann, *Philipp Jakob Spener und die Anfänge des Pietismus* (Tübingen: J. C. B. Mohr, 1986) for van Schurman's influence upon Frankfurt pietism, and in particular, upon Schutz and Jacob Spener.

In order to understand van Schurman's argument, one needs to uncover the development in her thought. A dramatic shift marks her theological pursuits and indicates the contours of, and the reasoning behind, her spiritual trajectory. This turn in her thought, furthermore, is coupled precisely with her decision to join the Labadist movement— a decision that led to the overthrow of her fame throughout Europe. In 1669, van Schurman made the difficult decision to leave the life of intellectual pursuits in order to devote herself to a life of piety within the sectarian group formed by Jean de Labadie. Labadie was a former Jesuit who had converted to Calvinism—a rare jump given the strident polemic of the era—only to change again to form his own movement. This renunciation of her elite past created upheaval among those who had been van Schurman's most loyal supporters. It also marks an upheaval in her own thinking about what theology and the reading of Scripture were ultimately to attain. This contrast with her past, as she herself presents it in her mature work, *Eukleria*, and as her earlier writings reveal, is almost as stark as her conclusion about the centrality of self-denial. Understanding this radical change will enable us to analyse better van Schurman's rhetoric of self-denial, to which we now turn.

From "Star of Utrecht" to Defamed Arachnephile

Anna Maria van Schurman was widely regarded as the "brightest star" of seventeenth-century Europe, having demonstrated powers of intellect unequalled among women and men alike. While recognized for her intricate artwork, sensitive musical gift, and philosophical acumen, it was van Schurman's linguistic genius that gained her highest praise, and even access to the university (albeit hidden behind a screen in the corner of the lecture hall).

Born in 1607 in Cologne, Anna Maria was the third of four children of Frederik van Schurman and Eva von Harff, devout Calvinists. Instructed by a home tutor in matters of the faith, van Schurman recounts that she was able to "read German accurately" and "recite part of the catechism from memory" by the age of three.[4] Her father took great pains to ensure the education of his children. While testing

---

[4] *Eukleria*, chapter II.2, in Joyce Irwin, ed. and trans., *Anna Maria van Schurman: Whether a Christian Woman Should Be Educated and Other Writings from her Intellectual Circle* (Chicago:

his sons in Latin, he discovered that their younger sister's proficiency far surpassed theirs. From that time on, Frederik initiated Anna Maria in the study of classics and she readily mastered the philosophy of Seneca, as well as the poetry of Homer and Virgil, among others.

In 1622, when van Schurman was only fifteen, this young woman's erudition caught the attention of the renowned Dutch poet Jacob Cats. Her composition of a poem in his honour gained his admiration, and she, in turn, became the object of his praise. A few years later, others also would write elaborate eulogies for her.[5] Not only did Anna Maria van Schurman outshine her older brothers in linguistic prowess, she outshone all of Utrecht (where she had moved with her widowed mother at the age of nineteen) even when it meant defying customary norms. Hailed as Utrecht's finest Latinist, she was invited to compose a poem for the University of Utrecht's opening in 1636, and she was the only female admitted into classes at the university, learning Semitic languages directly from the illustrious theologian, Gisbertus Voetius.

A sophisticated biblical exegete, van Schurman mastered at least twelve languages and compiled the first Ethiopic grammar. She exercised an uncanny command of Hebrew, Greek, Arabic, Aramaic, and Syriac, and wrote treatises in Latin and French; she also composed poems in her native Dutch tongue. Her appetite for knowledge was unbounded and her reputation crossed geographic lines: her fame was sealed. It would be further confirmed with the publication of her *Dissertatio, de Ingenio Muliebris ad Doctrinam, et meliores Litteras aptitudine* ("A Treatise regarding the fitness of the female mind for the study of the arts and sciences") in 1641.

Van Schurman thus travelled in the finest of circles, exchanging letters and gifts with key philosophers, theologians, artists, and poets. Eulogies repeatedly described van Schurman as a *miraculum* or *monstrum naturae*, a "marvel of nature".[6] Indeed, to "have been in Utrecht without

---

University of Chicago Press, 1998), 81. Given the context of Van Schurman's time, the catechism was most likely the Heidelberg Catechism.

[5] Joyce Irwin, "Anna Maria van Schurman: Learned Woman of Utrecht", in Katharina M. Wilson and Frank J. Warnke, eds., *Women Writers of the Seventeenth Century* (Athens: University of Georgia Press, 1989), 166.

[6] See M. de Baar and B. Rang, "Anna Maria van Schurman: A Historical Survey of her Reception since the Seventeenth Century", in *Choosing the Better Part: Anna Maria van Schurman (1607–1678)*, ed. Mirjam de Baar et al. (Dordrecht: Kluwer Academic Publishers, 1996), 5.

having seen Mademoiselle de Schurman was like having been to Paris without having seen the king".[7]

Not only was van Schurman's towering intellect the object of enthusiastic praise, her virtue and modesty were of particular appeal, especially to theologians. André Rivet, for example, when remarking on Van Schurman's intellectual brilliance, characteristically supplemented his words of elaborate praise with salutations declaring his "admiration for your virtues and above all for your exceptional piety and modesty".[8] Had her intellect stood alone, without virtue and piety to match, van Schurman might have seemed a 'monstrous' sort of marvel, indeed. Her humility, however, made her all the more palatable and less intimidating to her male counterparts. Their approval of her work, and in particular of her *Dissertatio*, gained her a wide readership, and her writings were quickly received throughout Holland as well as Europe. This unusual integration of genius and humility was worthy of intense admiration, and van Schurman became the toast of Europe.

Nevertheless, after enjoying nearly five decades of international fame, in the 1660s van Schurman was decried by many as having "gone mad". Her unparalleled splendour was now reduced to a "dimmed, invisible star",[9] and this "*aster éclipsé*" allegedly resorted to the "eating of spiders" ("*on dit qu'elle aimait beaucoup à manger des araignées*")—the equivalent of saying in our day that she had 'lost her marbles' or 'gone batty'.[10] As Eberti explained in 1706, "this crown of the female sex would undoubtedly have been seen by posterity as a shining example of all learned women had she not somewhat tarnished her own luster and her fame by her reprehensible doctrines".[11] Van Schurman herself

---

[7] Joyce Irwin, "Anna Maria van Schurman: The Star of Utrecht", in *Female Scholars: A Tradition of Learned Women before 1800*, ed. J. R. Brink (Montreal: Eden Press, 1980), 84 n. 3. Irwin quotes and translates from Pierre Yvon, van Schurman's earliest biographer, from his work, "Abregé sincere de la vie et de la Conduite et des vrais sentimens de feu Mr. De Labadie", in Gottfried Arnold, *Unparteyische Kirchen- und Ketzerhistorie* (Frankfurt am Main, 1715), II, 1264 ff.

[8] Rivet to van Schurman, 1 March 1632, in *Whether a Christian Woman Should Be Educated*, ed. Irwin, 41.

[9] Quoted in de Baar and Rang, "Anna Maria van Schurman: A Historical Survey of her Reception", 7.

[10] Jacob Thomasiu and Johannes Sauerbrei, *Diatribe academica de foeminarum eruditione* (1671). For the specific charge of spider-eating and what that implied, see de Baar and Rang, "Anna Maria van Schurman: A Historical Survey of her Reception", 7; see also Jean-Pierre Nicéron, *Mémoires*, vol. XXXIII (1736), 18.

[11] Quoted in de Baar and Rang, "Anna Maria van Schurman: A Historical Survey of her Reception", 6–7.

admits in her *Eukleria*, "it is now evident to all from the public writings of a number of celebrated men, who used to be extraordinarily
well-disposed towards me, that my new manner of life displeases them
greatly".[12] What was this "new manner of life"? Which of her doctrines
earned the title "reprehensible", and for what reasons did this star
lose its gleam? Did these detractors object to specific aspects of Van
Schurman's theology, or was mere co-habitation under Labadie's roof
sufficient to raise eyebrows?

As we have seen, Van Schurman's intellect had been celebrated by
her contemporaries for several decades. In the *Eukleria*, however, she
paints a picture of growing dissatisfaction with this life. Her mother
had passed away in 1637, and as early as 1638, van Schurman had
assumed some of her deceased mother's responsibilities—in particular,
works of charity. Nonetheless, she discovered to her chagrin that all
of her learning had imparted not a jot of genuine love in her heart
for the tasks—and people—at hand. It may be reasonable to surmise
that, from these early years, van Schurman had grown somewhat disil-
lusioned with the theological systems that had hitherto buttressed her
life.[13] Finally, in 1653, van Schurman had to leave altogether the life of
focussed intellectual pursuits in order to tend to her ailing aunts.[14]

As one scans the *Eukleria*, it appears that a series of disenchantments
had set her up for her introduction to Jean de Labadie. Though the
treatise does not detail the specific ways in which she gradually departed
from her academic training, hints are scattered throughout. She reports,
in retrospect, that she had become increasingly aware of the spiritual
impotence of her "former ways" of doing theology. In addition to
the lack of change within her own heart, she began noticing the ineffectiveness of the theology that surrounded her. As a result, she "fled"
from the company of those whom she calls "worldly theologians... not
only because they contained not a whit of solid learning or genuine
eloquence, but primarily because they did not savor or give off the

---

[12] Translation of van Schurman, *Eukleria*, chap. 5, quoted in Mirjam de Baar, "The
Eukleria as Autobiography", in *Choosing the Better Part*, ed. M. de Baar et al., 92.

[13] Although van Schurman's responsibilities shifted in part in 1638, she still remained
in the world of the academic elite. Her *Dissertatio* was published in 1641, and her
trajectory continued its course until several years later.

[14] See Anna Maria van Schurman, *Eukleria seu melioris partis electio*, Part 1 (Altona,
1673), 92.

scent of even a drop of that oil that the Spirit of Christ pours into the hearts of his own".[15]

In 1662, her brother Johan wrote to her of the Calvinist minister, Jean de Labadie, reporting that his heart was "set aflame" by his encounter with this "clear and living image of Christ". With these words, van Schurman began to turn in a new direction. She now yearned for a theology that effected change of heart "inwardly". Upon meeting Jean de Labadie in 1669, she concurred with her brother that this man was different from the other "representatives" of Christ she had heretofore known. Her intellectual trajectory had already taken a turn because of the demands of serving others, and now her spiritual journey was to be redirected. In August of 1669, van Schurman became one of the core members of the Labadist community. This was the year that Labadie broke away from (or was expelled from) the official Calvinist church of Wallonia, in order to establish his own sectarian community in Amsterdam.[16] Van Schurman gladly became one of the first to join this new movement.

We know from van Schurman's exchanges with the theological authorities of her day that her decision to join the Labadist movement sparked great controversy. Jean de Labadie had been expelled from both the Reformed Church of Montauban and the Walloon Reformed Church in Middelburg for his sectarian, chiliastic, and mystical tendencies, and her association with the "fanatical Labadie" cast a dark shadow upon her life. Not only did the unconventional living arrangements of the Labadist community appall the authorities, they also had difficulty understanding Labadie's preaching, as well as his passionate, even volatile, approach to religious issues.[17] Why would Anna Maria van Schurman leave her past behind to join *this* man's community? Those who had been van Schurman's strongest supporters now questioned her, and praise was silenced.

From van Schurman's perspective, joining the Labadists was the culmination of a process. She had been dissatisfied by what she perceived to be the ineffectiveness and aridity of airtight Calvinist orthodoxy. As a

---

[15] Translation of *Eukleria*, chap. II.11, in *Whether a Christian Woman Should be Educated*, ed. Irwin, 88.

[16] For an in-depth analysis of Labadie's own theological trajectory, see Trevor J. Saxby, *The Quest for the New Jerusalem: Jean de Labadie and the Labadists, 1610–1744* (Dordrecht: Martinus Nijhoff, 1987).

[17] For a fuller analysis of the problematic nature of Labadie's ministry, both practical and theological, see Saxby, *Quest for the New Jerusalem*.

result, she began to remove herself from the confines of narrow doctrine
and strict theological argumentation. That which she had mastered with
previous delight, the art of "making distinctions", no longer appealed to
her. Theological polemic, rampant in the seventeenth century as Protestantism sought to define and distinguish itself, even proved a hindrance
to the new-found goal of her theological enterprise. Though the core
of her thought would remain Calvinistic,[18] van Schurman expanded
her categories, embracing the thought and spirituality of both nascent
Pietism and Catholic mysticism.

With van Schurman's desertion of the institutional church for the
community of the isolated and controversial Jean de Labadie, mainstream theologians seemed to have had no choice but to disown her.
Her decision to leave her prior way of life led some to believe that
"common sense deserted her at last" as she "fell prey to such weakness" of mind and will.[19] From first to last, however, van Schurman
defended her decision to join the Labadist movement as "the better
choice" (eukleria).

Van Schurman's Theological Shift: From 'scientia' to 'intima notitia'

To understand van Schurman's change of heart, we turn to the pages
of her autobiography, the Eukleria, where her self-portrait emerges.
This masterpiece, noted for its erudition as well as its eloquent Latin
prose, is not only a spiritual autobiography but also a defense of the
Labadist movement, a theological treatise, and a chronicling of Labadist
history. Most importantly for our current purposes, she describes the
break with her past and offers a clear rationale for why this shift of
allegiances was necessary.

How did van Schurman understand her "choice"? In what ways
had she chosen "the better part"? The title itself, Eukleria, can be translated in various ways, as "the better choice", or "good fortune". More
specifically, van Schurman refers to Luke 10:41–42, signalling Mary's

---

[18] See Joyce Irwin, "Anna Maria van Schurman and Antoinette Bourignon: Contrasting Examples of Seventeenth-Century Pietism", *Church History* 60 (September
1991): 301–315.
[19] See de Baar and Rang, "Anna Maria van Schurman: A Historical Survey of her
Reception", 13. This portrait was finally dispelled (though with remaining ambigui-
ties) by the newly authoritative biography of G. D. J. Schotel in 1853 (de Baar and
Rang, 14).

"choice" to sit at the Master's feet as the "better thing". Inscribed on the cover page of her treatise, one finds: "Luc. 10:41,42: *Unum Necessarium. Maria meliorem partem elegit*" ("One thing is necessary: Mary has chosen the better part"). She also provides for her reader the Latin equivalent on that same page: "*Eukleria: Seu Melioris Partis Electio*". Hence, one can render her usage of *Eukleria* as "choosing the better part".

Throughout the *Eukleria*, van Schurman attributes the break with her past to her new-found pursuit of the "one thing" that was "necessary" (Luke 10:41–42). This scriptural passage becomes central to van Schurman's thinking and dominates the whole of her argument. What was this "one thing", however? The reader is invited to discern from the whole of her writing, as well as from the scriptural context itself, that this "one thing" involves an intimate knowledge of God (*intima notitia dei*); that is, an experience of "being taught by the Master directly".[20]

Our task, then, will be to elucidate the contours of this "one thing" as she expands on the notion of direct and intimate, or inmost, knowledge of God. Her thought will come into sharper focus as she contrasts inmost knowledge with that which it is *not*: merely formal or external knowledge (*scientia*). Van Schurman's understanding of this "one thing" becomes the primary lens through which she reconstructs the story of her "change". She defends her choice to join the Labadists as her decision to sit with Mary at the Master's feet in order to learn directly, rather than indirectly, from him.

As van Schurman explains her change, she refers to her *Dissertatio de Ingenio Muliebris ad Doctrinam, et meliores Litteras aptitudine*, published in 1641 (thirty-two years earlier). This treatise was a vigorous defense of the education of women and had contributed to her rise as the "star of Utrecht". Yet now, she could only "blush" to think of its contents. Indeed, one senses regret and remorse over her former way of life. She explains:

> Recently I was truly astonished at the lack of moderation in my studies from which I formerly suffered: when, on the occasion of looking through my dissertation on the studies of a Christian Woman, which I wrote to Andreas Rivet, I could not but blush…At that time I believed that I should learn everything that is knowable and indeed, as I argued there in the words of the philosopher, in order to escape from ignorance. But

---

[20] Translation of *Eukleria*, chap. II.15, in *Whether a Christian Woman Should be Educated*, ed. Irwin, 91.

how far all my thoughts were from the admonition of our Saviour, 'only
one thing is necessary', is clear to everyone from the words alone.[21]

Van Schurman goes on to describe her former writings as "redolent of
such superficiality of mind, or an empty and worldly spirit".[22] Upon
closer examination of her *Dissertatio*, however, it becomes almost impossible to detect anything objectionable or potentially embarrassing to a
religiously sensitive conscience. Indeed, it had won the praise of eminent
theologians including André Rivet and Gisbertus Voetius, precisely
because she had declared in the *Dissertatio* that it is "fitting for women
to study sciences instrumental to theology, since these lead to greater
love of God".[23] In this treatise, she regarded theology as the supreme
"science". Furthermore, the goal of study was to include the glory of
God, salvation, virtue, and magnanimity of spirit. What could be more
noble or lofty? In what lay its "superficiality" or "empty, worldly spirit"?
Van Schurman's previous call for the education of women had been
precisely theological, not secular, in nature. Her turn, or "conversion",
was not from a secular to a religious worldview; rather, she experienced
a dramatic shift within her theological worldview. She now regarded
her former ways of doing theology as sorely insufficient and devoid of
true or lasting meaning.

Previously, neither the study of languages, nor the "arranging into
charts" of subtle theological "distinctions" could lead van Schurman to
a "true" and "intimate" knowledge of God, that "*Unum Necessarium*".[24]
In fact, one could never arrive at the goal of theology by entering
headlong into discussions of theological subtlety. She explains:

> It is evident from this that I did indeed subordinate everything to theol-
> ogy as preeminent but that this subordination extended almost *ad infinitum*
> before one would reach the *goal* of pure theology, since I considered so
> many and such different aids necessary for understanding Scripture that
> this study would easily overstep the bounds of this mortal life. In truth,

---

[21] *Eukleria*, 30, trans. Desmond Clarke, "Anna Maria van Schurman and the '*Unum
Necessarium*'" (unpublished paper, 18 August 1999), 22; see also de Baar, "The *Eukleria*
as Autobiography", 87.

[22] De Baar, "The *Eukleria* as Autobiography", 87.

[23] Eileen O'Neill, "Schurman, Anna Maria (1607–78)", in *Routledge Encyclopedia of
Philosophy*, Vol. 8 (London: Routledge, 1998), 557.

[24] Irwin, "The Star of Utrecht", 81; also see *Eukleria, seu melioris partis electio* (Altona,
1673 [Part 1], Amsterdam, 1685 [Part 2]), 52.

had not the grace of God ordained otherwise, death would have overtaken me while still in these preparations.[25]

The "goal of pure theology", then, could not be reached by the most sophisticated intellectual and theological means. In fact, an "excessive desire to learn", as she puts it, would hinder the "simple and pure knowledge of the crucified Christ".[26] According to van Schurman, theology's proper aim was "union with the Highest Good", namely, God; and the "one thing" necessary for attaining that goal was an "inmost knowledge" (*intima notitia*) of God, as opposed to complicated theological reflection *about* God. This allowed for a deeply felt *experiential* knowledge of God that would penetrate within, while the latter left the individual detached or distant from God, even after complex considerations about the nature of God, world, and self. In van Schurman's view, erudite theological reflections functioned primarily in the realm of externals; God would remain outside the individual, and the individual outside of God. Aridity of doctrine, marked by systems and artificial syntheses, prevailed within this mode, and the things of God would fail to penetrate at a deeper level. Theological propositions might be placed in their proper order, but they would not be placed within the soul.

Inmost knowledge of God, however, was marked by true change of heart and life. It implied *direct* communication with God, and *intimacy* with the object of one's knowledge. Union with God would be attained, in which God is not only "comprehended" but radically enjoyed as the soul's highest good and truest happiness.[27] Furthermore, this intimate connection with God alone had the power to effect a radical change of inward disposition and consequently deepen one's love of God and neighbour. But how could one arrive at this inmost knowledge? Van Schurman notes her own failure to achieve *intima notitia* when she relays her failure to love her aunts, as well as others she was called to serve,

---

[25] *Eukleria*, 30, translated by J. Irwin in "Learned Woman of Utrecht", 179.

[26] *Eukleria*, 204; translations are mine. What, then, qualifies as "excessive"? Van Schurman makes a significant qualification: intellectual pursuits are not inherently contrary to the "inmost knowledge" of God; the danger towards pride and "external" forms of knowledge, however, are all too readily present, and she found herself unable to contend with the risks of intellectual sophistication.

[27] Van Schurman juxtaposes the "excessive desire to learn" ("*nimii sciendi desiderii, multiplicatarum scientiarum comprehensione*") against "*simplici & pura cognitione Christi crucifixi*" (*Eukleria*, 204). Christ, then, is not to be "comprehended" (a term which in the Latin also connotes a grasping, seizing, or arrest), but rather "known" in the most inward parts, "simply and purely".

upon her mother's death. Even after all of her theological investiga-
tions, she had found herself spiritually bankrupt.

In order to understand van Schurman's view of the deficiency of
her former ways of learning, a key distinction between "superficial",
or external, forms of knowledge, and "inmost" knowledge must be
made. Behind the perceived inadequacy of both theological and linguistic sophistication lay a fundamental opposition in van Schurman's
mind between two kinds of "knowing". In the *Eukleria*, she contrasts
scientia (a "*knowledge* so dry and superficial regarding divine matters")
with *notitia* ("true, innermost, and salutary *knowledge* of God and his
glory").[28] While *scientia* connotes knowledge, skill, and expertise of a
more formal and academic sort, *notitia* (from *nosco*) is consistently qualified by van Schurman as true, health-giving, and *intima* (intimate or
innermost). *Scientia* might leave the knower detached and outside the
object of investigation, but *notitia* had the power to effect something—to
create internal change. Doctrine could no longer remain outside the
individual but would have to be incorporated into the very heart of
one's life. She explains further that the object of *scientia* has nothing
within it that "attracts our spirits to the contemplation and *innermost
knowledge*" of God ("*quod animos nostros ad ejus contemplationem intimamque
cognitionem alliciat*") "unless its every essence be contemplated in a holy
fashion". How, then, ought God, the "end" of "true knowledge", to
be contemplated?

According to van Schurman, an inflow of grace was required to
contemplate God "in a holy fashion". Grace would not be given apart
from the reading of Scripture, however. As one meditated upon the
sacred page, divine love would be imparted—a love that would, in
turn, become the key to unlocking Scripture's inmost meaning. As van
Schurman puts it, one must be "instructed, not with philosophical modes
of reasoning, or with human reason, but with the light of grace and
Scripture" as one is "truly imbued with divine love".[29] This kind of
heartfelt instruction would overcome the superficiality and aridity of
scientia. In fact, even the "slightest sense of God's love would provide a
much more reliable and deeper understanding of the Scriptures than

---

[28] *Eukleria*, 39, translation mine (and henceforth, unless indicated otherwise); emphasis
also mine. Van Schurman contrasts "*tam arida ac superficialis de rebus divines scientia*" with
"*veram, intimam, ac salutarem Dei notitiam*".
[29] *Eukleria*, 46.

the most extensive knowledge of biblical languages".[30] Inmost knowledge of God therefore ran parallel to an inmost understanding of Scripture; theological insights would arise from the sacred page as the Holy Spirit shed light upon its hidden, or inner, meaning.

Van Schurman's previous search for Scripture's most hidden meaning had required many tools of inquiry, finely crafted. Now they were replaced by "one thing"—"sitting" with Mary at the feet of the "Master" and learning directly from him in loving adoration. These essential components thus granted inmost knowledge of God: an inner experience of the love of God while reading the Scriptures. God's love needed to be directly, personally experienced.

Had van Schurman stopped at this point, she would have sounded no different from burgeoning Pietists of her day. She makes a more striking turn, however. While love was the necessary handmaid of a "truer and deeper understanding of the sacred page", *even love*, in the end, would be deemed *insufficient*. In other words, love was a necessary but insufficient condition for arriving at an intimate knowledge of God. Not only would the intellect suffer in her theological treatise, so too would love. *Caritas* was in the end powerless, in the absence of one essential element: namely, a *radical overthrow of the self*. One could never arrive at the "one thing needful" (*intima notitia*) without it.

In explicating this requirement, van Schurman makes a three-fold distinction between different forms of comprehension:

> And yet, as in other things, the substance and the conception often differ greatly; thus also, I am learning daily that there is a great difference between those truths comprehended by the intellect, as if pictured in the mind, and even received by a certain love in the heart, and between a total overthrow, conversion, and emendation of mind and heart.[31]

Three types of knowing or "comprehension" emerge: (1) the knowing of the mind, i.e., "truths comprehended by the intellect" (*illas intellectu comprehensas veritates*); (2) knowledge received even "by a certain love in the heart" (*etiam amore quodam in corde receptas*); and (3) the kind of knowledge that can only come from a life radically changed in both mind *and* heart, i.e., "a total overthrow, conversion, and emendation

---

[30] *Eukleria*, 32; Clarke, "Van Schurman and the '*Unum Necessarium*'", 23.

[31] *Eukleria*, 53: "*Atqui, ut in caeteris rebus, res, et conceptus plurimum saepe differunt; ita que inter illas intellectu comprehensas veritates, in mente quasi deppictas, atque etiam amore quodam in corde receptas; et inter totalem mentis & cordis eversionem, conversionem & emendationem multum interesse quotidie addisco*".

of mind and heart" (*totalem mentis et cordis eversionem, conversionem et emen-*
dationem). In other words, if love were not accompanied by a complete
"overthrow" of the mind and heart, it too would be insufficient in
granting the individual *notitia intima*, "inmost knowledge" of God. This
overthrow involved the entirety of the individual and could not occur
simply in one faculty. Loving devotion and direct illumination from the
Holy Spirit therefore had to be complemented by a radical overthrow,
even "destruction" (*eversio*), of the whole self.

In distinguishing different types of comprehension, van Schurman
thus separates two kinds of love. Love alone proves ineffective. Only
when it is accompanied by a radical "overthrow...of mind and heart"
does it gain power. Van Schurman's past loves were insufficient, and
her earlier advocacy of education failed because it stopped at a partial
love. She now sought a more complete and "pure" love.[32]

Throughout her treatise, van Schurman offers examples of the correc-
tives needed for a stagnant intellect and limited love. She also elucidates
the meaning of the term *eversio*, which can be translated variously as
overthrow, subversion, or destruction. What would this "total overthrow"
or "destruction" of the mind and heart imply? As she proceeds, she sets
forth self-denial as the final curative for a mind and heart that are turned
in upon themselves and hence unable to receive the fullness of *intima
notitia*. In her attempts to describe both the goal of theology—namely,
union with God—and the path towards this inexpressible union, she
provides a fuller description of this radical overthrow.

Self-Denial: The Key to Union with God

Expounding upon the overthrow of one's mind and heart, van Schurman sketches out in the *Eukleria* a sort of itinerary, "the true path"
towards the "blessed life" and "union with the supreme good". She
argues that Christianity "teaches correctly and in orderly fashion" this
"true path"[33] and that this teaching leads to the destruction and rejection of the self. While the path to union with God is *impervestigabilem*

---

[32] For a further discussion of "pure love", see van Schurman to Schutz, 22 December
1674, MS G2.II.33, fols. 10r–v.
[33] *Eukleria*, 48.

(literally, "unable to be investigated"), it has been "revealed" by the Mediator.

> Finally, [Christian truth] shows that the Messiah is that unique Mediator who has revealed this uninvestigatable path to restore the union between the creature with his Creator and supreme Good...infusing a new desire on the part of man for his reconciliation and union with his supreme good; and moreover, the salvific knowledge of his supreme good, and love, and the desire for seeking that, rather than the strength for elevating the self, pursuing and possessing the self.[34]

In describing this path, van Schurman contrasts the desire for union with God with the pursuit and elevation of the self. And the pursuit of God *over* the self will provide the key to a successful journey.

Serving as a spiritual guide for her reader, van Schurman presents specific means by which the believer might be united with God. Clear prerequisites are outlined in order to help the soul that is seeking union with his supreme good. For example:

> Altogether other and more lofty means has the Christian religion for arriving at true union with the supreme good: when the Christian, reject-ing himself and all other created things, and through this abandoning imperfect, partial, dependent, and finite good, adheres to the perfect, independent, infinite, and whole, content in that alone, and desires nothing except [the supreme good]...through the sole desire of pleasing [God] himself. And he seeks all his own good outside himself and rejoices to rest in God alone.[35]

A certain progression can be traced, even in the brief passage above. The path to union with God requires that the self be entirely abandoned in order for the individual to cleave more fully to his supreme good. First, the individual is called to "reject" (*abdico*) himself and all other created things. The individual, in the act of resigning or abdicating, is giving up his own rights and desires, subjecting them to something greater. Through this abdication of the self, one abandons or relin-quishes (*relinquo*) "imperfect, partial, dependent, and finite goods". Once the imperfect and the finite are abandoned, however, one is then freed to "adhere" to that which is perfect and infinite. In other words, the finite self proves to be a barrier to full immersion in the infinite; it is a burden. Leaving behind the world of partial goods thus enables the

---

[34] *Eukleria*, 49–50.
[35] *Eukleria*, 48.

individual to enjoy the realm of infinite, perfect good. Freedom and contentment are therefore impossible without having first renounced finite desires. When the self and its creaturely attachments are relinquished, or "destroyed", the individual is able to achieve union with God.[36]

As seen in the frequent appearance of all-encompassing terms such as "total", "alone", and "nothing", it is evident that singleness of heart is of critical importance to van Schurman. No other attachments are to have the slightest leverage in the heart. According to this understanding, singleness of affection, desire, and attention are prerequisites for attaining the supreme good—and this is the precise purpose of self-denial. One is to deny oneself in order to attach oneself to that which is supremely good and that which truly satisfies. The soul is thereby freed from the distractions and cares that keep the individual away from her one 'good', and she becomes free to enjoy all else *in* that supreme good.

---

[36] See Erica Scheenstra, "On the right choice", in *Choosing the Better Part*, ed. de Baar et al., 125. In her later correspondence with Johannes Jacob Schutz, a leading German pietist, van Schurman further explains the content of her *Eukleria*, published in 1673. From 1674–78, at least ten letters were exchanged in which van Schurman responded to queries from Schutz regarding the nature and necessity of self-denial. She argues that self-denial is required of all Christians and gives the following rationale: "And the reason is clear, since God most justly requires the whole heart for himself ... all impediments most greatly opposed to the pure love of God ought therefore [to] be removed" (van Schurman to Schutz, 22 December 1674, MS G2.II.33, fol. 11r). An *impure love* is precisely that which is stained by the *love of self*, and this impure love of self prevents the individual from fully entering the "narrow gate". She continues: "For, if anyone would wish to follow [Christ], it is necessary that he know what separates him from the very threshold of the narrow gate: surely, the love and possession of oneself" (ibid., fol. 10v).

According to van Schurman, self-love is the "bubbling spring of all evil; that most pernicious 'I', which elevates itself up to the throne of God and divides and separates all of ourselves from the true and highest Good, [and] most wretchedly flows from it". In other words, it is this self, this 'I', that robs the individual of her "true and highest Good". It leaves insufficient room for both the self *and* God to occupy the "throne" of one's heart. Two contraries cannot coexist peacefully (van Schurman to Schutz, 12/22 August 1674, MS G2.II.33, fols. 2r–v). An ultimate choice thus needs to be made at every turn between self and God. They are in greatest opposition, for the self resists God's "holy will" and refuses to submit to the "most just love of God" (van Schurman to Schutz, 22 December 1674, MS G2.II.33, fol. 11v). This "pernicious I" must therefore be defeated and extinguished, precisely for the sake of this greater good. Self-denial, for van Schurman, becomes the only means by which one might successfully resist self-love, squelching it by its very opposite. The unwieldy self has proven to be an obstacle to the attainment and enjoyment of God, one's highest good. Removing this barrier is therefore the key not only to reaching union with God but to enjoying Him, even from the start.

Van Schurman presents in the *Eukleria* a radical either/or situation in which one desire alone is allowed to flourish. No rival is welcome into what she calls the "throneroom" of the "King". Two opposing parties cannot share one's attention: either the self rules, or God does.[37] A multiplicity of desires creates confusion, distraction, and paradoxically leads to incompleteness. Singleness of heart—filled with loving desire directed towards its highest Good—ensures fulfillment and wholeness.

Together with the renunciation of self and all created things, however, one must also "cling to" (*adhaeret*) that which is "perfect, independent, infinite, and whole", contenting oneself in that alone. One must "adhere" tightly to God, with a cleaving that is "full of desire" (*desiderat*). Then, seeking all her good outside herself, the individual rejoices to rest in God alone. In "resting" (*acquiescere*), one can also be said to "become quiet", or even, in this particular construction, to "die".

Significantly, the term *acquiescere* also suggests an element of pleasure and delight. One might therefore say that there is a certain pleasure in dying to the self. The individual finally comes to quiet, rest, and peace, finding delight in the singular object of her desire. According to this schema, self-denial thus issues in a profound peace and enjoyment. The self is abandoned and "destroyed" in order to create space, ultimately, for a greater joy. An alternate form of pleasure-seeking is

---

[37] While this assessment of the pernicious 'I' might seem harsh, it is a fair reflection of the Reformed background that van Schurman inherited. The portrayal of the self at enmity with its Creator was part and parcel of the tradition in which she was immersed. However, van Schurman goes beyond this negative depiction to retrieve the self more fully, albeit through a circuitous route. Like Bernard of Clairvaux, she argues that even while self-love is the fundamental problem, one must, in the end, return to the love of self—yet with a purified love. It is not so much the *objects* of one's love that are problematic as the *manner* in which one loves. When vestiges of self-love are expressed in the love of other things, one's love becomes "impure" (van Schurman to Schutz, 22 December 1674, MS G2.II.33, fol. 10v). The problem, then, is an impure love (i.e., love of self) that fails to love God first and foremost.

On the other hand, when one loves God alone, one is able to *return* to the love of both self and creature—but now with a purified love. As van Schurman reminds Schutz, the "love of God" alone "is able to 'love all things purely'". And it is through the school of self-denial that the disciple of Christ "learns to love purely all things in God". In fact, "all things must be denied by the disciples of Christ, [all things] that are not God himself, *until they will have learned to love purely all things in God*" (ibid.). In this Augustinian and Bernardian vein, she continues, "For these can be purely enjoyed, with joy, and with all the benefits of God; no, rather, they can love justly themselves and all creatures in God, and on account of God, since to the pure all things are pure (Titus 1:15)" (ibid., fol. 11v).

thus spiritually validated; and paradoxically, self-denial is the precise means through which the greatest pleasure is achieved.

In a letter to Johannes Jacob Schutz in December 1674, van Schurman further explains:

> Just as we are able to conquer all things, through him who loved us, and therefore especially our very selves, who were by nature the enemies of God, *that practice does not weary or weaken us, but strengthens [us] in a wonderful manner, in the way of life.* Even more, we believe that no Christian can enjoy perfect and constant inward peace, except after he has snatched away his very self and all his possessions, temporal and eternal, with his own hands and cares, through the denial of self and the transfer of all things into the hand and will of God.[38]

Though self-denial may seem like a difficult teaching to the novice Christian, it is the key to great gain, according to this frame. It unlocks an inner strength and ushers in perfect peace and the enjoyment of God. Once finite attachments are removed, the individual is freed to enjoy her supreme good. The self is abandoned, only that it may fasten itself anew to a greater object. In other passages, however, van Schurman's language takes yet another turn.

Van Schurman argues that one more step is necessary if God is to consume the seeker's desire. In addition to denying herself and adhering to God, the individual must be reduced to nothingness. Her logic proceeds as follows: in order for Christ to be all and for the "infinite ocean of divinity" to fill and penetrate the self entirely, the individual, with her partial and incomplete desires, must become nothing. In other words, one cannot join the realm of the infinite if one is still a finite something. As we have seen, the finite becomes an obstruction to being lost in the infinite; it is a weight. Van Schurman explains that union with God, which she describes in various places as "immersion" into the "infinite ocean of divinity", is inextricably linked with an awareness of one's own nothingness. She says:

> Altogether other is the mind of the Christian man and the limit of his felicity, who considers his very self and all his own as nothing, or as if, gazing upon a tiny drop of the ocean, only then judges himself blessed,

---

[38] Van Schurman to Schutz, 22 December 1674, MS G2.II.33, fol. 12r. Emphasis added.

when immersed in the measureless ocean of divinity, enveloped, penetrated, and filled, by that goodness and happiness.[39]

When the Christian has renounced "his very self and all his own as
nothing", it is "only then" that he considers himself truly happy, for now
he has become a tiny drop, "immersed" and "enveloped, penetrated,
and filled" within an infinite and measureless sea.

Although van Schurman employs the language of *becoming* nothing,
she does not go so far as to say that the self is utterly annihilated.[40] The
context of her words is essential. "I wish to be nothing, to own nothing or to do nothing other than that which He always shows through
His workings to be His will".[41] She desires to be nothing "other than"
that which God shows to be his will. In the above passage, similarly,
the individual is to "consider" his very self as nothing—not to become
nothing per se. The key here is one of perspective. When one regards
the self as something, then God becomes a little less than everything to
the individual. Once God becomes all, and the self regarded as nothing, the individual finds himself "enveloped, penetrated, and filled" by
that infinite "goodness and happiness". Again, van Schurman thinks in
spatial terms, arguing implicitly that competing loyalties cannot occupy
the same 'space' in the heart, or in one's purview.

Union with God, then, involves an immersion into something that is
infinite—a measureless ocean of divinity—and a recognition of one's
own 'nothingness'. The way beyond finitude is to embrace one's nothingness. This recognition—that is, the "overthrow" (*eversio*) of self—is
the necessary condition for immersion, as seen above. One is either to
renounce oneself *entirely*, or be left in the world of partial goods. One
cannot have it both ways. This repudiation of the self therefore fits
perfectly with a vision of God as infinite and measureless: because God
is infinite and all-encompassing, the soul can enter that completeness
only when it has become nothing. God becomes all-consuming, leaving

---

[39] *Eukleria*, 46. For more on the image of the "ocean of divinity" prevalent within
mystical literature, see Bernard McGinn, "The Abyss of Love: The Language of
Mystical Union among Medieval Woman", in *The Joy of Learning and the Love of God:
Studies in Honor of Jean LeClerq*, ed. E. Rozanne Elder (Michigan: Cistercian Publications, 1995), 95–120.

[40] See, for example, van Schurman to Schutz, 22 December 1674, MS G2.II.33,
fol. 10v: "finally God himself becomes all things, [and] they themselves truly become
nothing".

[41] See de Baar and Rang, "The *Eukleria* as Autobiography", 94.

room for nothing else. As the soul is lost in God's fullness, it can finally become immersed, surrounded, penetrated, and filled by divinity.

The Impossibility of Self-Denial

Although van Schurman has argued that self-denial is the key to intimate, pleasurable, and life-giving knowledge of God, she concludes ironically that it is an impossible task even for the most determined. The individual is so attached to the 'I' that a greater force is needed to perform the extrication of the unwieldy self. As a faithful Calvinist, she acknowledges that the grace of God alone carries an individual along, empowering her to deny herself and enter into a fuller knowledge of the divine: "this grace of denying all things is poured out into all the elect, in its own time through the Spirit of Christ, who inspires, impels, and leads them there".[42] This grace is given to the "weak", to those who are in fact unable to deny self and the world: "It must not at all be supposed the work of our strength".[43]

Interestingly, van Schurman's own experience confirms her theology of grace. Her theology finds striking parallel in her autobiography, in which she says that she was utterly unable to "deny herself". Convinced that self-denial was the secret to a more vibrant experience of the "infinite ocean of divinity", she strove with all her might to achieve this state. In a key text of the *Eukleria*, however, we find that while she was acutely aware of the need to deny herself, she was ultimately incapable of doing so. Her dilemma is clear in the following passage:

> I was in high expectation of a renewal of grace, such as seemed promised to us from heaven. On the occasion of examining our paths, I was discovering traces of spiritual avarice, of an excessive love for the gifts and good things of God, and a certain impatience with my imperfection, and especially the deficiencies in my own self-denial and my overall love of creation. I was oppressed beyond measure by the burden of this,

---

[42] Van Schurman to Schutz, 22 December 1674, MS G2.II.33, fol. 10r: "...*hanc gratiam abnegandi omnia omnibus electis suo tempore per Spiritum Christi infundi, qui illos eo incitat, impellit, ac ducit*".

[43] Ibid., fol. 11v: "*Talis enim Christianorum imbecillitas non rejiceret hoc jugum Christi, quod revera leve ac lene est. Fit namque amabile per eius Spiritum, quem in suis abnegationis virtutem partier atque amorem producere dixi; adeo ut opus nostrarum virium minime censendum nec iisdem metiendum sit. Indeque natum illud paradoxum Apostoli, cum infirmus sum, tum potens sum* (2 Corinthians 12:10)".

because I seemed to myself rather to be going backwards than advancing in strength and resolution in the ways of the Lord.[44]

Van Schurman's struggle did not end in defeat, however. Something other than herself delivered her from this predicament. She describes a breakthrough in her efforts at self-denial, made possible by the "embrace" of the "vastness of God's own infinite Majesty". In other words, she was simply *unable* to "refuse" (*abnego*) or "forget" herself until she had the experience of being enfolded in God's presence. Self-denial in effect happened to her, rather than van Schurman being the agent of her own self-forgetfulness. In the final analysis, self-denial became contingent upon the divine "embrace". This embrace enabled her to "surrender [herself] entire, all [her] desires, all [her] good and evil circumstances" and to become "profoundly forgetful of [her]self" as a secondary consequence. This profound lack of concern with herself became the source of freedom, and this self-forgetfulness would not be a goal towards which to strive but an inevitable by-product of being consumed in the presence of God.[45] This clearly appears in the text where she confesses,

> but then, instead of my consternation, which deserved divine abandon-ment, divine Mercy gazed at me with such kindness, that, after first quieting my soul a little, it surrounded me with so great a vastness of its own infinite Majesty, and impressed upon me the sense of its own divine presence and goodness, to such an extent that I surrendered myself entirely, and all my desire, and all my good and evil circumstances, both present and still to come, to him, with greater perfection, as if afresh, more completely, and with a purer faith and love than ever before. And I became profoundly forgetful of myself and looked upon myself as though I were the possession of another, that is of God and Christ the Heir of all, and then was stirred up more by shaping myself to his divine will than by anything else.

The "gaze" of "divine Mercy" and the enfolding of God's presence were critical for van Schurman. Her unrest and impatience were first *quieted* by kindness, and she was then *surrounded* "with so great a vast-ness of its own infinite *Majesty*". God's divine presence and goodness were impressed upon her with the result that she was finally able to

---

[44] *Eukleria*, 207.
[45] Notably, self-forgetfulness is tantamount here to the abandonment and denial of the self, as indicated earlier. It is not that she necessarily *becomes* nothing, but that she regards herself as nothing.

surrender herself completely, with a "greater perfection" and "purer faith and love" than before. Only afterwards would she become "profoundly forgetful" of herself and "disregard" herself, now that she was captivated by something much larger than herself. She did not need to focus on the act of denying herself. Rather, a new impulse, a new affection would consume her and consequently expunge her self-loves. In the words of Thomas Chalmers, we witness here "the expulsive power of a new affection". Surrounded and filled with the presence and "infinite Majesty" of God, she realized that she belonged entirely to another. There would be no more room for self, where God reigned supreme.

Van Schurman's theology comes full circle with this pivotal passage. If we carefully heed the sequence described in this keynote passage, however, an inconsistency seems to emerge in van Schurman's thought. Previously, we had looked at the conditions she prescribed for an individual who sought "immersion" into the "infinite ocean of divinity". She had indicated that one must become "nothing" if one is to experience the vastness of God's "infinity". Reversing the sequence here, the imperative to "become nothing" is made possible only by an overwhelming experience of the magnitude and majesty of God. The individual *first* experiences the greatness of God and is *then* made aware of her nothingness. In the end, self-denial becomes impossible without this fuller revelation of God. That which leads to a deeper knowledge of God (i.e., self-denial) is rendered ineffective on its own merit, but it is granted, in fuller measure, by an intimate encounter with the object of one's desire. The goal becomes the impetus that again leads to a deeper appreciation of the goal—namely, the direct experience and enjoyment of the presence of God.

Rather than looking at self-denial as the prerequisite to union with God, one can conclude that deeper levels of *intima notitia* are made possible by deeper levels of self-denial. This, finally, leads to union with God. The goal and the means become interchanged in circular fashion, each leading to a more profound understanding of God. In other words, once an individual experiences the vastness of God, he perceives that he is, by comparison, nothing. Similarly, once he sees how small he is and denies himself, as a "tiny drop in the ocean", he is able more fully to appreciate and enter the vastness of God's infinity.[46] Instead of asking

---

[46] *Eukleria*, 46.

which action comes first, one might rather see them as simultaneous activities, each leading to the other at progressive levels. Indeed, van Schurman had written that "the grace of Jesus Christ" unfolds in a "continuous series" and "stretches out through all steps and intervals of life".[47] While the *Eukleria* argues that union with God is the "end" of Christian theology, the very awareness of God's intimate presence continues to propel the individual toward that goal.[48]

Conclusion

Self-denial, for van Schurman, was not simply a theoretical construct. Her own life involved difficult decisions and the denial of loves she had once cherished. In the *Eukleria*, she portrays her "choice" as one between the theological world of partial goods and knowledge, and a world that provides an intimate, all-consuming knowledge of God. Her choice was costly, however: her fame, intellectual pride, and social prestige were extinguished, together with her former loves and desires. In her own words, she willingly gave up her "good name", as well as the value she had formerly attached to "bourgeois proprieties".[49]

---

[47] Van Schurman to Schutz, 22 December 1674, MS G2.II.33, fol. 10v.

[48] In fact, even union with God (when experienced here on earth as "divine nuptials") serves another purpose. As van Schurman writes to Schutz: "You speak so prudently and spiritually concerning the union of the soul with her Bridegroom, both in the present and in the future life, that it is entirely evident that he not rarely brings you into his wine-cellar and there intoxicates you with his delight. *But to what end, I ask?* Only that you may be delighted with the taste of celestial wine and overflow in joy? I think not: but *in order that*, forgetful of yourself and the world, and strengthened by celestial ambrosia, you may fight bravely and, *above all, conquer love of yourself*, which, as in the first man it was the origin of his accursed falling: so in us now, too, it is the bubbling spring of all evil" (van Schurman to Schutz, 12/22 August 1674, MS G2.II.33, fols. 2r–v, emphasis added).

Again, the circular nature of van Schurman's theology emerges in this passage. An experience of union with God does not serve its own end, however "intoxicating" it may be. Rather, it serves to enable the individual more vigorously to deny herself and the sinfulness that readily attaches itself to the 'I'. Self-denial, in turn, enables the individual to know God more deeply, and to experience the vastness of God more fully. This pattern continues, stretching out "through all steps and intervals of life" until the marriage is consummated in celestial bliss. Toward that goal, the individual is called to wage battle against the insidious 'I' and to follow more wholeheartedly in the steps of Christ. The self must be vigilantly denied until the very end, even as the enjoyment of God marks every interval of the Christian journey.

[49] Irwin, in *Women Writers of the Seventeenth Century*, 181.

However, she regarded this "sacrifice" as nothing—"for the sake of knowing" in a most intimate manner "Christ Jesus [her] Lord". She would gladly give up "dry, superficial knowledge" (*scientia*) for that which she considered "true, intimate, and salutary" (*intima notitia*). On the final page of her *Eukleria*, she identifies her "sacrifice" together with the Apostle Paul's, and describes it as follows:

> As far as the fame of my name is concerned, I have already previously indicated that in countless ways I value above it not only the glory but also the shame of Christ, along with his faithful servant Moses and his chosen vessel St. Paul, who 'considered all things loss on account of the towering importance of the knowledge of Christ Jesus his Lord', and indeed gave up all things, and considered them 'as dung, in order to gain Christ'.[50]

While defamed for her decisions and even derided as a madwoman, van Schurman indefatigably holds that she has made the "better choice". Certainly, van Schurman's new life involved concrete sacrifices. In abandoning her former ways of knowing, she also lost its accompanying fame. Speaking of her past life, van Schurman writes that she "considered it [her] duty to preserve carefully the little honor of [her] fame as a common good of the republic of letters and, as much as modesty would permit, to increase it, so that among the other great lights [she] too, as a star of the sixth magnitude, might contribute some brightness to that sphere of vast knowledge or Encyclopedia".[51] However, her reputation was now tarnished, as she laid down that which she called her "excessive desire to learn". She regarded these prior pursuits as "dung", a loss that she would gladly relinquish for the sake of knowing Christ (*propter eminentiam notitia Christi*).

In fact, she writes that an "unspeakable joy" rose in the place of loves she had previously nurtured but now turned her back upon. She says of her fellow members within the Labadist community:

> We have seen clearly in all of them a complete denial of the world and scorn of all earthly things as well, on the other hand, as a true love of heavenly things and of Christ, a mortification of the old man and a vivification of the new, so much so that there has occurred in our house

---

[50] *Eukleria*, 207.
[51] Translation of *Eukleria*, chap. II.11 in *Whether a Christian Woman Should be Educated*, ed. Irwin, 87.

community a general resurrection; this has brought forth among us all an unspeakable joy which the world does not know.[52]

A striking irony emerges in van Schurman's later years: although disowned by the intellectual elite for her turn towards Labadism, she became more truly "voiced" within her new community. Despite her new-found emphasis on self-denial—or, more properly stated, because of it—a stronger voice made itself known. The feminine humility topos, so prevalent in her earlier writings, vanishes.[53] The shift in rhetoric is astonishing: she ceases to be apologetic both in the *Eukleria* and her letters, and she no longer bows to male authorities to validate her work. Instead, she is open and forthright; the style, tone, and content of her writings reveal a new authority and confidence, rather than a truncated or weakened self. Even as she rails against excessive erudition, she shows no qualms about utilizing her own learnedness in the service of her newly found beliefs. The pages of the *Eukleria* unfold with remarkable precision and erudition. As we have seen, she becomes a theological spokesperson for her superiors within the Labadist movement. In fact, she becomes an 'authority', handing out advice to important leaders throughout Europe and influencing the development of early German Pietism in Frankfurt and beyond.[54]

Having grasped the necessity of self-denial for an intimate knowledge of God, van Schurman seems to have gained a strange and quiet strength. As depicted in the *Eukleria*, she is convinced that she has come to a deeper, more personal knowledge of her "supreme good". Furthermore, the final pages of her treatise describe the powerful effects of being "immersed in the infinite ocean of divinity": she is no longer consumed with herself or her personal fears and strivings, whether spiritual or earthly. Consequently, she is no longer defined or limited by the standards of her time. Confined neither by the demands of Calvinist orthodoxy nor the "proper place" of women in society, van Schurman

---

[52] See de Baar and Rang, "The *Eukleria* as Autobiography", 98.

[53] This topos—e.g., "I, a mere woman..."—riddles her earlier letters. See, for example, her letters to Rivet, in *Whether a Christian Woman Should be Educated*, ed. Irwin, 39–56. In these earlier writings, van Schurman's words drip with the kind of modesty that was expected of women; see p. 193 and n8 of this chapter for Rivet's response. See also de Baar and Rang, "The *Eukleria* as Autobiography", 100, and Mirjam de Baar, "Transgressing Gender Codes: Anna Maria van Schurman and Antoinette Bourignon as contrasting examples", in *Women of the Golden Age: An International Debate on Women in Seventeenth-Century Holland, England and Italy*, ed. Els Kloek et al. (Hilversum: Verloren, 1994), 150.

[54] See note 3.

gained new muscle. Perhaps she experienced that quiet, rest, and delight of which she spoke in her treatise—the enjoyment that comes from denying the self, only to embrace more fully her highest good.

Bibliography

Manuscript Sources

Clarke, Desmond. "Anna Maria van Schurman and the 'Unum Necessarium'". Unpublished paper, 18 August 1999.
Van Schurman, Anna Maria. Unpublished Letters to Johannes Jacob Schutz, July 1674–February 1678. MS G2.II.33 . Basel University Library.

Printed Sources

Andersen, Jenny. "Anna Maria van Schurman". In *Reading Early Women: An Anthology of Texts in Manuscript and Print, 1550–1700*. Edited by Helen Ostovich and Elizabeth Sauer. New York: Routledge, 2004.
Arnold, Gottfried. *Kirchen- und Ketzerhistorie*. Vol. IV. Frankfort, 1729.
Becker-Cantarino, Barbara. "Erwählung des bessern Teils: zur Problematik von Selbstbild und Fremdbild in Anna Maria van Schurmans 'Eukleria'". In *Autobiographien von Frauen: Beiträge zu ihrer Geschichte*. Edited by Magdalene Heuser. Tübingen: Niemeyer, 1996.
Birch, Una. *Anna van Schurman: Artist, Scholar, Saint*. London: Longmans, Green and Company, 1909.
Brandes, Ute. "Anna Maria van Schurman". In *Women Writers in German-Speaking Countries*. Edited by Elke P. Frederiksen and Elizabeth G. Ametsbichler. Connecticut: Greenwood Press, 1998.
Bulckaert, B. "L'éducation de la femme dans la correspondence d'Anna Maria van Schurman et André Rivet". In *La femme lettré*. Leuven: Peeters, 1997.
De Baar, Mirjam, et al., eds. *Choosing the Better Part: Anna Maria van Schurman (1607–1678)*. Translated by Lynne Richards. Dordrecht: Kluwer Academic Publishers, 1996. Originally published as *Anna Maria van Schurman (1607–1678): een uitzonderlijk geleerde vrouw* (Zutphen: Walburg Pers, 1992).
De Baar, Mirjam. "Transgressing Gender Codes: Anna Maria van Schurman and Antoinette Bourignon as Contrasting Examples". In *Women of the Golden Age: An International Debate on Women in Seventeenth-Century Holland, England and Italy*. Edited by Els Kloek et al. Hilversum: Verloren, 1994.
——. "Verleid of verkozen? Anna Maria van Schurman en het huiszezin van Jean de Labadie". In *Op zoek naar vrouwen in ketterij en sekte*. Edited by D. van Paassen and A. Passenier. Kampen: Kok, 1993.
Deyon, Solange. "'S'il est nécessaire que les filles soint sçavantes', un manifeste féministe au XVIIᵉ siècle". In *De l'Humanisme aux Lumières, Bayle et le protestantisme*. Edited by Michelle Magdelaine, Maria-Cristina Pitassi, et al. Oxford: Voltaire Foundation, 1996.
Douma, A. M. H. *Anna Maria van Schurman en de studie der vrouw*. Amsterdam: H. J. Paris, 1924.
Ghijsen, H. C. M. "Anna Maria van Schurman 1607–1678." *De Gids* 90 (1926): I.380–402, II.105–128.
Göbel, M. *Geschichte des Christlichen Lebens in der Rheinisch-Westphälischen Evangelischen Kirche*. Vol. II. Koblenz: Karl Bädeter, 1852.

Holloway, Mark. *Heavens on Earth: Utopian Communities in America, 1680–1880*. New York: Dover, 1966.

Irwin, Joyce. "Anna Maria van Schurman: eine Gelehrte zwischen Humanismus und Pietismus". In *Geschichte der Mädchen- und Frauenbildung*. Edited by Elke Kleinau and Claudia Opitz. Frankfurt am Main: Campus Verlag, 1996.

——, ed. and trans. *Anna Maria van Schurman: Whether a Christian Woman Should Be Educated and Other Writings from her Intellectual Circle*. Chicago: University of Chicago Press, 1998.

——. "Anna Maria van Schurman and Antoinette Bourignon: Contrasting Examples of Seventeenth-Century Pietism". *Church History* 60 (Sept. 1991): 301–315.

——. "Anna Maria van Schurman: From Feminism to Pietism". *Church History* 46 (March 1977): 48–62.

——. "Anna Maria van Schurman: The Star of Utrecht". In *Female Scholars: A Tradition of Learned Women before 1800*. Edited by J. R. Brink. Montreal: Eden Press, 1980.

——. "From Orthodoxy to Pietism: The Self-Reflections of Anna Maria van Schurman". *Covenant Quarterly* 38 (Feb. 1980): 3–12.

——. "Anna Maria van Schurman: Learned Woman of Utrecht". In *Women Writers of the Seventeenth Century*. Edited by Katharina M. Wilson and Frank J. Warnke. Athens: University of Georgia Press, 1989.

Johnson, William Stacy and John Leith, eds. *Reformed Reader: A Sourcebook in Christian Theology*. Vol. I. *Classical Beginnings 1519–1799*. Louisville, Kentucky: Westminster/John Knox Press, 1993.

Kolakowski, Leszek. "Dutch Seventeenth-Century Neo-Denominationalism and *Religio Rationalis*". In *The Two Eyes of Spinoza and Other Essays on Philosophers*. Translated by Agnieszka Kolakowska et al. Edited by Zbigniew Janowski. South Bend, Ind.: St. Augustine's Press, 2004.

——. "The Mystical Heresy and the Rationalist Heresy in Dutch Calvinism at the End of the Seventeenth Century." In *The Two Eyes of Spinoza and Other Essays on Philosophers*. Translated by Agnieszka Kolakowska et al. Edited by Zbigniew Janowski. South Bend, Ind.: St. Augustine's Press, 2004.

McGinn, Bernard. "The Abyss of Love: The Language of Mystical Union among Medieval Woman". In *The Joy of Learning and the Love of God: Studies in Honor of Jean LeClerq*. Edited by E. Rozanne Elder. Michigan: Cistercian Publications, 1995.

Miller, Julie B. "Eroticized Violence in Medieval Women's Mystical Literature: A Call for a Feminist Critique." *Journal of Feminist Studies in Religion* 15:2 (1999): 25–49.

Moore, Cornelia Niekus. "Anna Maria van Schurman (1607–1678)". *Canadian Journal of Netherlandic Studies* 11:2 (1990): 138–161.

——. "Anna Maria van Schurman". In *Women Writing in Dutch*. Edited by K. Aercke. New York: Garland, 1994.

Mülhaupt, Erwin. "Anna Maria von Schürmann, eine Rheinländerin zwischen zwei Frauenleitbildern". *Monatshefte für evangelische Kirchengeschichte des Rheinlandes* 19 (1970): 149–161.

Muller, Richard A. *Post-Reformation Reformed Dogmatics*. Grand Rapids, Mich.: Baker Book House, 1987.

O'Neill, Eileen. "Schurman, Anna Maria (1607–78)". *Routledge Encyclopedia of Philosophy*. Vol. 8. London: Routledge, 1998.

Prozesky, Martin H. "The Emergence of Dutch Pietism". *Journal of Ecclesiastical History* 28, no. 1 (Jan. 1977): 29–37.

Saxby, Trevor J. *The Quest for the New Jerusalem: Jean de Labadie and the Labadists, 1610–1744*. Dordrecht: Martinus Nijhoff, 1987.

Schama, Simon. *The Embarrassment of Riches: An Interpretation of Dutch Culture in the Golden Age*. New York: Knopf, 1987.

Schotel, G. D. J. *Anna Maria van Schurman*. 's Hertogenbosch: Gebroeders Muller, 1853.

Smet, Ingrid A. R. "In the Name of the Father: Feminist Voices in the Republic of Letters (A. Tarabotti, A. M. van Schurman, M. de Gournay)". In *La Femme Lettrée à la Renaissance: Actes du Colloque international Bruxelles, 27–29 mars 1996*. Edited by Michel Bastiaensen. Louvain: Peeters, 1997.

Tschackert, Paul. *Anna Maria van Schürmann*. Gotha, 1876.

Van Beek, P. "De geleerdste van allen: Anna Maria van Schurman". In *Met en zonder lauwerkrans: schrijvende vrouwen uit de vroegmoderne tijd 1550–1850*. Amsterdam: Amsterdam University Press, 1997.

———. "One Tongue is Enough for a Woman: The Correspondence in Greek between Anna Maria van Schurman and Bathsua Makin". *Dutch Crossing* 19 (1995): 22–48.

Van der Linde, S. "Anna Maria van Schurman en haar Eucleria". *Theologia Reformata* 21 (1978): 117–145.

Van Schurman, Anna Maria. *Amica Dissertatio inter Annam Mariam Schurmanniam et Andr. Rivetum de capacitate ingenii muliebris ad scientias*. Paris, 1638. Translated into English as *The Learned Maid, Or, Whether a Maid May Be a Scholar?* London, 1659.

———. *Eukleria, seu melioris partis electio*. Altona, 1673 [Part 1], Amsterdam, 1685 [Part 2].

———. *Opuscula hebraea, graeca, latina, gallica, prosaica et metrica*. Leiden, 1648.

Wallmann, Johannes. "Labadismus und Pietismus: Die Einflüsse des niederländischen Pietismus auf die Entstehung des Pietismus in Deutschland". In *Pietismus und Reveil*. Edited by J. van den Berg and J. P. van Dooren. Leiden: E. J. Brill, 1978.

———. *Philipp Jakob Spener und die Anfänge des Pietismus*. Tübingen: J. C. B. Mohr, 1986.

Weber, N. A. "Labadists". *The Catholic Encyclopedia*. Vol. VIII. 1910.

PART THREE

WOMEN AND RADICALISM
ACROSS EUROPE, ACROSS CONFESSIONS

MOULDERED AWAY IN THE TOWER WITH THE FRUIT OF THE WOMB? ON THE TREATMENT OF PREGNANT ANABAPTIST WOMEN UNDER CRIMINAL LAW

Marion Kobelt-Groch
Translated by Dennis L. Slabaugh

The German Anabaptists wanted to lift the world off its religious-social hinges and, for this, they were persecuted and punished. Heart-rending scenes occurred everywhere the Anabaptists gained a foothold. The records are full of hunting parties, judges, and their victims, who, in the best case, could receive mercy only if they recanted or came across an indulgent government authority. In the worst case, they could expect death. How the leading figures of individual Anabaptist movements met their end is, in many cases, well known.[1] Michael Sattler was burned in Rottenburg and Balthasar Hubmaier in Vienna; Felix Mantz was drowned in Zürich, while Leonhard Schiemer and Hans Schlaffer died in flames in the Tyrol. While these prominent individuals, who made decisive contributions in establishing the Anabaptist movements and in giving them their theological accents, may have been intellectually superior to their many followers, they could hardly claim superiority in their readiness to take on martyrdom and to die for their faith. Lesser-known men and women died no less determinedly for their convictions. Martyrdom was not only the strongest argument in the desperate struggle for the 'true faith', but it was also a levelling act that overcame all social and gender-specific barriers. It confirmed again, and conclusively, what kind of collective consciousness—what sort of 'we'—had been created through believers' baptism. In the final analysis, male and female Anabaptist martyrs did not die as worldly individuals but rather as the

---

[1] A survey (without the Anabaptist kingdom of Münster) is offered by Claus-Peter Clasen, *Anabaptism: A Social History, 1525–1618. Switzerland, Austria, Moravia, South and Central Germany* (Ithaca and London: Cornell University Press, 1972); Hans-Jürgen Goertz, *The Anabaptists*, trans. Trevor Johnson (London and New York: Routledge, 1996); C. Arnold Snyder, *Anabaptist History and Theology: An Introduction* (Kitchener, Ontario: Pandora, 1995); on the Anabaptist kingdom in Münster, see especially Ralf Klötzer, *Die Täuferherrschaft von Münster: Stadtreformation und Welterneuerung* (Münster: Aschendorff, 1992).

spiritual brothers and sisters that the faith had made of them. They were to be pious, renounce their sins, help one another, and "call each other brother and sister"[2]—so ran the message, formulated repeatedly in this or a similar way. Thieleman van Braght's *Martyrs' Mirror* offers graphic insights into this anti-hierarchically conceived world of communal life, suffering, and dying. Regardless of how poor or rich they were, all those men and women who let themselves be sentenced for their beliefs found a place in it. So, for example, hardly more attention was paid to Hans Langmantel, who descended from a noble family, than to his servant and his maid, both of whom were likewise baptized. After all three had suffered much "temptation and torment", they were put to death in 1529: "they killed Hans Langmantel and his servant with the sword, but drowned the maid in water".[3]

Mouldering in the Tower: The Conditions of Imprisonment

It is not violent death alone that made Anabaptist dying so moving. There was more to it than this. Up to the present day, the prayers of those condemned to death, their admonitions, confessions, letters, hymns, and words of farewell, as witnesses of an unbroken resolution, contribute towards preserving that heroic aura that always has surrounded Anabaptist life and death. The fascination with Anabaptist martyrdom can be measured not least by considering all those publications that have been devoted especially to this topic in the recent past.[4]

---

[2] ["Einander bruder und swester haissen".] *Quellen zur Geschichte der Wiedertäufer*, Bd. II: *Markgraftum Brandenburg (Bayern I. Abteilung)*, ed. Karl Schornbaum (Leipzig: Heinsius, 1934), 91.

[3] ["Den Hans Langmantel und seinen Knecht haben sie mit dem Schwerte getötet, die Magd aber im Wasser ertränkt".] Thieleman J. van Braght, ed., *Der Blutige Schauplatz, oder Märtyrer-Spiegel der Taufgesinnten oder wehrlosen Christen*, translated from the Dutch (Aylmer, Ontario and LaGrange, Indiana: Pathway Publishing, 1973), Part II, 14.

[4] See Brad S. Gregory, *Salvation at Stake: Christian Martyrdom in Early Modern Europe* (Cambridge, Mass. and London: Harvard University Press, 1999); B. S. Gregory, ed., *The Forgotten Writings of the Mennonite Martyrs* (Leiden: Brill, 2002); Peter Burschel, "'Marterlieder': Eine erfahrungsgeschichtliche Annäherung an die Martyrienkultur der Täufer im 16. Jahrhundert", *Mennonitische Geschichtsblätter* 58 (2001): 7–36; Peter Burschel, *Sterben und Unsterblichkeit: Zur Kultur des Martyriums in der frühen Neuzeit* (München: R. Oldenbourg, 2004); Nicole Grochowina, "Von Opfern zu Heiligen: Martyrien von Täuferinnen und Täufern im 16. Jahrhundert" in *Vorbild-Inbild-Abbild: Religiöse Lebensmodelle in Geschlechtergeschichtlicher Perspektive*, ed. Peter Burschel and Anne Conrad (Freiburg im Breisgau: Rombach, 2003), 121–50; "Zes onbekende martelaarsbrieven van Jeroniumus Segers (+ 1551)", ed. with an introduction by Piet Vissser, in *Doopsgezinde Bijdragen, nieuwe*

But not all men and women who let themselves be baptized followed the path that led them to the place of judgment—the stake or the bank of a river. Some broke off their journey and, by recanting, turned back as quickly as possible. Still others did not die on a fixed day but suffered an agonizing, long-drawn-out death, such as Melchior Hoffman. Hoffman had been arrested on 20 May 1533, in Strassburg.[5] Ten years later, the man who had once as the "second Elias" filled the hearts of the people with the "darkest fears and the most ardent hopes", died in a Strassburg dungeon, reduced to helplessness, in complete isolation.[6]

Melchior Hoffman does not appear to have been the only Anabaptist to have ended his life in prison under miserable circumstances; others at different times hardly fared better. It is reported that Martin Probst starved to death and rotted away in the tower in 1526,[7] and that two Anabaptists, who had been deported and yet had returned, died respectively in 1573 and 1574 as prisoners in the Alsatian town of Osthofen.[8] A similar fate also awaited the just nineteen- or twenty-year-old Simprecht Kerschbaumer who, in 1529, because of his age, was to be given a reprieve consisting of "eternal imprisonment"[9]—but this only at others' expense. If his relatives did not pay for his maintenance, then the young man was to be executed.[10] Two things draw our attention in these few examples. First of all, death in prison does not appear to have that spectacular quality that generally is expected of a martyr who meets his fate in following Christ. The end comes slowly, unpredictably, and rather quietly—an assessment that may have led to the fact that imprisonment, with or without fatal consequences, has been given little attention in Anabaptist research up to the present.[11] In

---

reeks 29 (2003): 195–249; "Elisabeth's Manly Courage": Testimonials and Songs of Martyred Anabaptist Women in the Low Countries, ed. and trans. by Hermina Joldersma and Louis Grijp (Milwaukee, Wis.: Marquette University Press, 2001).

[5] Klaus Deppermann, Melchior Hoffman: Soziale Unruhen und apokalyptische Visionen im Zeitalter der Reformation (Göttingen: Vandenhoeck and Ruprecht, 1979), 255.

[6] Deppermann, Melchior Hoffman, 335.

[7] Josef Beck, ed., Die Geschichts-Bücher der Wiedertäufer in Österreich-Ungarn von 1526–1787 (1883; repr., Nieuwkoop: De Graaf, 1967), 53–54.

[8] Quellen zur Geschichte der Täufer, Bd. IV: Baden und Pfalz, ed. Manfred Krebs (Gütersloh: Mohn, 1951), 371.

[9] Quellen zur Geschichte der Täufer, Bd. XIII: Österreich, II. Teil, ed. Grete Mecenseffy (Gütersloh: Mohn, 1972), 214–15.

[10] Quellen zur Geschichte der Täufer, Bd. XIII: Österreich, II. Teil, 217. He was to have been executed on 15 February 1531, but he was pardoned by Ferdinand I (ibid., 466n1).

[11] Although prosecution and punitive measures are dealt with in all the relevant portrayals of the Anabaptists, only a few works especially dedicated to this theme

addition, it is conspicuous that the victims mentioned are exclusively
men and not women, which at first glance could suggest a gender-specific, unequal treatment. Were women Anabaptists (as least as far as the
commonly prescribed prison sentences are concerned) on principle given
milder punishment or treated in a more accommodating manner than
men? Rash conclusions of this kind could allow us to miss what really
happened, as seems to be indicated by a case from Zürich. Balthasar
Hubmaier corrects our perception.

In the preface to his "Gespräch auf Zwinglis Taufbüchlein" (Dialogue
on Zwingli's "Little Treatise on Baptism"), published in 1526, Hubmaier
describes the horrors of denunciation, persecution, and imprisonment
that many pious people of both sexes had to endure. Things finally
had gone so far

> that about twenty men, widows, pregnant women, and virgins were
> thrown miserably all at once into dark towers, and judgment was passed
> upon them that from now on they were to see neither sun nor moon all
> their life long and to end their lives on bread and water, and thus remain
> together in the dark towers, the dead and the living, and all die, stink,
> and rot until none of them remained.[12]

This thoroughly plausible and, above all, movingly depicted scene of
horror did not fail to have an effect. Hubmaier's descriptions were taken
over by the *Älteste Chronik der Hutterischen Brüder*,[13] as well as by Josef
Beck's collection[14] and the *Martyrs' Mirror*[15]—in the last, however, with
a minor deviation. While Hubmaier's description of the catastrophic

---

exist. See Horst W. Schraepler, *Die rechtliche Behandlung der Täufer in der deutschen Schweiz,
Südwestdeutschland und Hessen, 1525–1618* (Tübingen: [Fabian-Verlag], 1957) and Hans
H. Th. Stiasny, *Die strafrechtliche Verfolgung der Täufer in der freien Reichsstadt Köln, 1529 bis
1618* (Münster: Aschendorff, 1962).

[12] ["...das man auff ain mal ob zwainntzig Menner, Witfrawen, Schwanger frawen
vnd Junckfrawen in finster thürn ellendigklich geworffen vnd über sy das vrtail gefellet,
das sy füran weder Sunn noch Mon sehen sollen jr leben lang, mit wasser vnnd brott
jhr end beschliessen, vnd also in den finstern thurnen all todt vnd lebendig, biß jr kainer mer vbrig sey, bey ainander bleyben, sterben, erstincken vnd erfaulen"]. Balthasar
Hubmaier, "Ein Gespräch auf Zwinglis Taufbüchlein, 1525–1526", in *Schriften*, ed.
Gunnar Westin and Torsten Bergsten (Gütersloh: Mohn, 1962), 169–70.

[13] *Die älteste Chronik der Hutterischen Brüder: ein Sprachdenkmal aus frühneuhochdeutscher
Zeit*, ed. A. J. F. Zieglschmid (Ithaca, New York: The Cayuga Press, 1943). Here I
would like to thank Gary Waltner, the director of the Mennonitische Forschungsstelle
(Weierhof, Pfalz), who, on the occasion of a visit, made a gift to me of his copy (Nr.
116) of this work.

[14] Beck, ed., *Die Geschichts-Bücher der Wiedertäufer*, 21.

[15] Van Braght, ed., *Der Blutige Schauplatz*, 47.

conditions still appears to indicate that women and men—or leaders and followers—were accommodated in separate quarters, since he speaks of "towers" or of "the dark towers", every form of separation is removed in the *Martyrs' Mirror*. In an account made just a shade more terrible than Hubmaier's description, all of the mentioned twenty men, pregnant women, widows, and young girls are thrown together into a tower and left to their fate. Later, Hubmaier's drastic description was taken up by Heinold Fast in his source collection *Der linke Flügel der Reformation*. Hubmaier, according to Fast's commentary, himself experienced this event in the spring of 1525 in Zürich.[16]

Is this account correct? Certain doubts are appropriate here. Some elements seem to indicate that Hubmaier exaggerated and possibly drafted his account in a form that was meant to arouse understanding and sympathy. It could just as well have been the case that he had only limited information available to him and had no knowledge about the further or final development of matters. However, his account could also have fulfilled the task of strengthening the Anabaptist 'we feeling'. This should not be interpreted as an attempt to deny or to radically moderate the terrors of Anabaptist persecution. It is much more a case of recognizing that Anabaptists, by all means, could tend to surround themselves, as the persecuted, with a certain mystique. Such accounts furthered their own reputation and can be read as an Anabaptist reply to the attacks and demonizations with which they had to struggle. Hubmaier's account in no way strikes one as unrealistic—at least not at first glance. Many details, from the prison sentence encompassing both sexes to the "eternal" imprisonment ending in death, can be substantiated in the sources. What he describes corresponds thoroughly in many points to daily Anabaptist prison life and to that process of suffering that could lead, more or less slowly, from life to death.

Men and women who fell under suspicion of being inclined towards Anabaptism, and who were imprisoned for this reason, had to reckon with the worst. They could expect not only torture, exile, and the threat of execution, but also extreme prison conditions. "Prisons", writes Richard van Dülmen, "were a symbol of terror no different from the

---

[16] Heinold Fast, ed., *Der linke Flügel der Reformation: Glaubenszeugnisse der Täufer, Spiritualisten, Schwärmer und Antitrinitarier* (Bremen: C. Schünemann, 1962), 9n7.

public places of execution".[17] Prisoners were accommodated preferably
in city towers, in the cellars of city hall, or in a castle. Worms, vermin,
and bats lived within the dark, dank, cold, and stinking walls—and mice
pounced upon the food.[18] The straw was seldom changed. A further
torment was to be chained, or to be physically or mentally worn out
by the effects of torture. We learn that the feet of one imprisoned
Anabaptist were frozen in the stocks,[19] and another compares his own
miserable condition in the hole of the Kunibert Tower in Cologne with
that of "Daniel in the lion's den".[20] The fear of another term in the
tower could even lead the father of a family, like Veit Espenlaub in
1587, to leave everything behind and move to Austria because the *Vogt*
of Schorndorf had held him in prison under such harsh conditions.[21]
The generally meagre diet likewise contributed to the further weakening of prisoners, especially if they were not well provided for by their
own families or were not in a position to pay for better conditions.
What Hubmaier suggests with his ominous formulation—that is, that
the incarcerated men and women henceforth would see neither sun nor
moon—strikes one in a thoroughly realistic way as a vivid description
of extreme medieval and early modern prison conditions.[22] Moreover,
the repulsive thought of rotting away in such a dreadful place does
not even appear exaggerated. Whether that could occur depended
first of all upon the length of the respective prison stay. Men as well
as women could spend days, weeks, and months in prison. The length
of the stay was dependent, on the one hand, upon legal factors; that
is, whether, in the modern sense, it was a case of pre-trial, coercive, or

---

[17] Richard van Dülmen, *Theater des Schreckens: Gerichtspraxis und Strafrituale in der frühen Neuzeit* (Munich: Beck, 1985), 21.

[18] Beck, ed., *Die Geschichts-Bücher der Wiedertäufer*, 222, especially n1. The horrors of imprisonment varied. While the Anabaptist Hans Schmidt complained of "ratzen und meise" [rats and mice] in a dirty tower during a stay in prison and feared being eaten alive by vermin, it was penetrating vapours that gave him a difficult time in another case. It smelled like a limekiln: the vapours not only killed all the vermin, but also weakened Schmidt's limbs and drove him quite mad in the head. See *Quellen zur Geschichte der Wiedertäufer*, Bd. 1: *Herzogtum Württemberg*, ed. Gustav Bossert (Leipzig: Heinsius, 1930), 661.

[19] *Quellen zur Geschichte der Täufer*, Bd. IV: *Baden und Pfalz*, 483–84.

[20] Stiasny, *Die strafrechtliche Verfolgung der Täufer*, 136.

[21] *Quellen zur Geschichte der Wiedertäufer*, Bd. I: *Herzogtum Württemberg*, 626.

[22] See here the examples cited by Rudolf Quanter in *Deutsches Zuchthaus- und Gefäng-niswesen: Von den ältesten Zeiten bis in die Gegenwart* (1905; repr., Aalen: Scientia-Verlag, 1970), especially Teil I, and Gotthold Bohne, "Das Aufkommen der Freiheitsstrafe" (Teil I), in *Die Freiheitsstrafe in den italienischen Stadtrechten des 12.–16. Jahrhunderts* (Leipzig: Weicher, 1922), 87–88.

penal detention.[23] In addition, regional differences played a role in the determination of the penalty, not to mention the individual judicial decisions appropriate to each case. Taken in their entirety, these differences underline Claus-Peter Clasen's general assessment that "the hardship of imprisonment varied".[24] Extreme prison conditions with fatal consequences for men and women, like those experienced in 1538 by male and female Anabaptists in Heiligenstadt and at Burg Gleichenstein,[25] are encountered just as often as are mitigated circumstances where the prisoner was very young, sick, or old.

Gender-specific considerations could play a role in the treatment of prisoners. In February 1530, the *Obervogt* Joss Rosa of Blaubeuren reported that Oswald Leber's wife had become so ill in the tower that she had to be removed from it. This was obviously not an isolated case, for "truly, the ladies are not able to stand the tower. For, when we at times put a strong peasant man in there, then it often happens that none of them will either eat or drink".[26] It is not clear what is meant here. Was the stay in the tower so terrible that it took away everyone's appetite, or was it the possible presence of male fellow prisoners that frightened women and made the stay in prison intolerable for them? The obvious problem of sexual molestation arising from mixed-sex accommodation had had consequences as early as the Roman Empire. In the year 340, it was legally prescribed for the first time, against the practice usual up to that time, that men and women held in custody were to be guarded in separate rooms.[27]

It was not only Oswald Leber's wife who suffered. The situation of another prisoner, the wife of the miller Castel, appeared to be hardly any better. The *Vogt* even feared that both women might go mad and put an end to their lives in the tower. His misgivings were made even more serious by the fact that both women were presumed to be pregnant,

---

[23] Schraepler, *Die rechtliche Behandlung der Täufer*, 50.

[24] Clasen, *Anabaptism*, 387.

[25] Günther Franz, ed., *Urkundliche Quellen zur hessischen Reformationsgeschichte*, Vierter Bd.: *Wiedertäuferakten, 1527–1626* (Marburg: Elwert, 1951), 195–96.

[26] ["...firwar, so migen die wiber den durn nit liden. Dann so wir zu ziten ain starken burn darin legen, so mag oft kainer weder essen noch drinken"]. *Quellen zur Geschichte der Wiedertäufer*, Bd. 1: *Herzogtum Württemberg*, 949.

[27] Jens-Uwe Krause, *Gefängnisse im Römischen Reich* (Stuttgart: Steiner, 1996), 178. On the accommodation of men and women together in a single prison, see also Hans von Hentig, *Die Strafe*, vol. II, *Die modernen Erscheinungsformen* (Berlin: Springer, 1955), 187, 192.

and their stay in prison could harm their unborn children.[28] In Württemberg, there was a prison sentence especially for the Anabaptist wives of orthodox-believing men, which meant that the terrors of the tower or the dungeon need not be endured. The women concerned were chained within the four walls of their own homes and placed under the supervision of their husbands.[29] Still, it would be wrong to consider the penal treatment of male and female Anabaptists reductively according to gender, since there was not a rigid separation of this kind. Severity as well as leniency could prevail in regard to both sexes; much depended on the individual case, on the age of the prisoners, on their physical constitution, and on how uncompromisingly or how indulgently the legal provisions were applied. In criminal prosecution, there were, to be sure, some special gender-specific features; for example, when men were sent to the galleys or beheaded and women were drowned. In the final analysis, however, it was not the sex of the perpetrator, but rather the gravity of the crime that was decisive in fixing the penalty. This becomes clear in the relevant levelling formula encountered repeatedly in the fixing of the penalty: whether it be "Manns- oder Weibspersonen" (whether male or female persons).

Mouldering With the Fruit of the Womb? Penal Treatment of
Women and Pregnancy

Hubmaier's account thus appears thoroughly plausible, and he is completely consistent with this idea of equal legal treatment when he describes men and women languishing together in dark towers. Nonetheless, in the case described, there does appear to have been a separation of the prisoners that could have been dependent on gender. In the sources, there are repeated indications that men and women were housed separately. While Hubmaier speaks merely of towers, which suggests separate accommodation, in other cases there appear to have been clear differences in the manner of custody. Thus, Hans Staudach was locked up together with six other persons in the tower, while his wife was put in a barn together with their children and some other

---

[28] *Quellen zur Geschichte der Wiedertäufer*, Bd. 1: *Herzogtum Württemberg*, 949–50.
[29] Marion Kobelt-Groch, "Frauen in Ketten: 'Von widertauferischen weibern wie gegen selbigen zu handlen'", *Mennonitische Geschichtsblätter* 47/48 (1990/91): 49–70.

persons.[30] In a warrant from Württemberg from 14 June 1554, the order was given to arrest those "contentious" people who did not want to be admonished, and to hold them in prison, first of all, for a few days: "the male persons in the attic of the tower and the female persons in a women's prison…".[31] It did not necessarily have to be the feared towers. There were women who found themselves in the *Narrenhäuslein*, a cage in which they were exposed to public humiliation, or in the women's prison of a cloister.[32] If prisoners of both sexes were initially housed together and separated only later, then this definitely could have been of advantage. In this way, they gained the opportunity to comfort each other and to strengthen each other in their faith. This was a trouble spot in the treatment of prisoners, definitely recognized and criticized by the government authorities.[33] While it may be that men and women were locked up together, for such an imprisonment to extend over more than a few days appears to have been the exception.

As moving and plausible as Hubmaier's account may seem, it is only partly convincing. Why, for example, are none of the prisoners mentioned by name? Moreover, a look into the Zürich Anabaptist records confirms that the Anabaptist leader not only further embroidered the judgment in council from 7 March 1526,[34] to which he appears to refer, but also portrayed the threatened shared end of the prisoners as an actual event. They must die together, without the chance of escape. However, it is this precise point that is not correct. Hubmaier relates merely a portion of the decree in a very condensed form. He does not mention the persons by name or their further fate in his scene of

---

[30] *Quellen zur Geschichte der Täufer*, Bd. V: *Bayern, II. Abteilung*, ed. Karl Schornbaum (Gütersloh: Bertelsmann, 1951), 141–42.

[31] ["…die manspersonen inn turm an boden und die frauenpersonen in ein frauengefenknus legen…"] *Quellen zur Geschichte der Wiedertäufer*, Bd. I: *Herzogtum Württemberg*, 129. Another description from 1558 is similar. The men and women, it is said, were first housed together; a short time later, however, they were separated: "Die schwestern auf ein Thor, vnd vns Brueder auf ein Thor" [the sisters in one gatehouse and we brothers in another gatehouse]. *Geschichts-Bücher der Wiedertäufer*, 230n2.

[32] *Quellen zur Geschichte der Wiedertäufer*, Bd. I: *Herzogtum Württemberg*, 480–81, 616.

[33] Franz, ed., *Urkundliche Quellen zur hessischen Reformationsgeschichte*, 191. See also the scene described by Josef Beck: twelve brothers and sisters were left together in prison from 4 a.m. until 10 p.m., "where they then cheerfully and confidently began to praise God together" ["da sie den frölich, getrost miteinander anfingen Gott zu loben"]. Brother Hans prayed so loudly that the people gathered together in a crowd. Later, when they were led through the city, they were said to have sung together. *Die Geschichts-Bücher der Wiedertäufer*, 231.

[34] *Quellen zur Geschichte der Täufer in der Schweiz*, Bd. I: *Zürich*, ed. Leonhard von Muralt and Walter Schmid, 2. Aufl. (Zürich: Theologischer Verlag, 1974), 178.

horror, but rather contents himself with a generalizing reference to
men and women who stink and rot away together in prison, although
the word "fulen" [rot] was struck out in the council's decree. He leaves
out details and adds his own. That the prisoners should henceforth see
neither sun nor moon is a formulation not contained in the council's
decree. It serves merely to embroider the situation of imprisonment,
which is described graphically with all its terrors. In addition, the further fate of the eighteen named male and female Anabaptists shows
that they were not necessarily to moulder away and die together. The
conciliar decree leaves open what should become of each individual.
So much is certain: whoever recants will not end his or her life in the
tower, but will either be punished in another way or even pardoned.
A mandate envisioned for the future is intended, to be sure, to make
clear what is involved in the heavy prison sentence; beyond this, all
those who continue to baptize are also to be threatened with the death
penalty. Felix Mantz, who was one of the most prominent of the, in
all, twenty imprisoned Anabaptists, was drowned in 1527 in the Lim-
mat; his fellow imprisoned Anabaptist brother Georg Blaurock was
executed two years later. What became of Konrad Grebel cannot be
known with final certainty. He probably died of the plague in August
1526.[35] It is known that Anna Widerkehr recanted.[36] This is true also
of Dorothea Kürsin and Hans Hottinger who, after swearing an oath,
were released. Margret Hottinger, Elssbet Hottinger, and Regula Gletzle
likewise confessed that they had erred.[37] The sources are silent about
whether they once again wandered on Anabaptist paths later in life.
However, even these few examples can be used to show that prisoners
of both sexes did not end their lives as part of a suffering Anabaptist
community in the tower.

While discrepancies in Hubmaier's account become visible only
through comparison with the corresponding government records, there
is one particular point that prompts increased doubt about the truth
of his account of the horrible scene. Hubmaier claims that there were
also pregnant women among the doomed prisoners who awaited their
dreadful end in the towers. This is, in view of contemporary principles
and practices concerning the treatment of pregnant women, improbable,

---

[35] Hans-Jürgen Goertz, *Konrad Grebel, Kritiker des frommen Scheins, 1498–1526: Eine biographische Skizze* (Hamburg: Kümpers, 1998), 126.
[36] *Quellen zur Geschichte der Täufer in der Schweiz*, Bd. I: *Zürich*, 179.
[37] *Quellen zur Geschichte der Täufer in der Schweiz*, Bd. I: *Zürich*, 182–83.

if not impossible. Detached from the Anabaptist context of the above-mentioned case, special legal provisions applied to pregnant women mean that an end in the tower, of the kind suggested by Hubmaier, would appear to have been impossible. Pregnant women were commonly treated not only with more consideration and special protection, but also enjoyed special rights. Among these, for example, was the right to satisfy specific desires without incurring legal consequences. Thus, they were allowed to pick fruit, to cut off clusters of grapes, or to fish in forbidden waters. Similar provisions also applied to hunting as well as a variety of comforts that pregnant women could take advantage of.[38] Above and beyond these privileges, a pregnancy could lead to a delay in executing an imposed penalty. As Helga Schnabel-Schüle correctly emphasizes, neither in the *Carolina* nor in the territorial legal codes is there a general mitigation of sentences for women: "In practice, the sentence for women was merely suspended during a pregnancy, but not rescinded".[39] It remains to be considered whether this applies for every imposed sentence, or only for hard corporal punishments. In this connection, one is reminded of the earlier provisions of the *Sachsenspiegel*, in which it was prescribed that pregnant women were not to be punished to an extent greater than that reaching "to skin and hair" ("zu Haut und Haar"). It was permitted to shear their hair and to beat their skin until bloody.[40] As Stiasny emphasizes in his study of the criminal prosecution of the Anabaptists in Cologne, the treatment of pregnant Anabaptists appears to have been oriented on this legal principle of a limited application of violence.[41] In comparison with torture or other corporal punishments, this kind of treatment may strike one as harmless, but, in the last analysis, it too represents a painful personal infringement. At least, it appears in no way to have been the case that pregnant women always remained untouched. On the one hand, there were encroachments in the private sphere, in

---

[38] Hans Fehr, *Die Rechtsstellung der Frau und der Kinder in den Weistümern* (Jena: G. Fischer, 1912), 4–5; Jacob Grimm, *Deutsche Rechtsaltertümer*, Bd. I (1899; repr., Darmstadt: Wiss. Buchges., 1965), 564. A good survey is provided by Eva Labouvie, *Andere Umstände: Eine Kulturgeschichte der Geburt* (Köln, Weimar, and Wien: Böhlau, 1998), especially 77–80.

[39] Helga Schnabel-Schüle, "Frauen im Strafrecht vom 16. bis 18. Jahrhundert", in *Frauen in der Geschichte des Rechts: Von der Frühen Neuzeit bis zur Gegenwart*, ed. Ute Gerhard (Munich: Beck, 1997), 193.

[40] Julius Weiske, ed., *Der Sachsenspiegel (Landrecht), nach der ältesten Leipziger Handschrift*, 8th ed. (Leipzig: Reisland, 1905), 88.

[41] Stiasny, *Die strafrechtliche Verfolgung der Täufer*, 145.

which context one should think first of all of violent husbands who took no consideration of the condition of their wives.[42] On the other hand, the oft-invoked legal protection could also be violated. Thus, in Nuremberg, pregnant women, children, and old men were mercilessly forced to work in the glass-cutting industry, and "four hundred pieces of glass a week were demanded of a woman standing shortly before the delivery of her child, so that she died of exhaustion within a short time".[43] Even executions of pregnant women appear not to have been completely taboo in exceptional cases. In his collection of news items, J. J. Wick (1560–1587) reports on a woman who was hanged and who, after four hours on the gallows, gave birth to a pair of living twins.[44] Interestingly, the children do not die. Completely in accordance with generally accepted expectations and demands, the fruit of the womb remains unhurt, although this is a case of execution. A similar case is reported in the legend told about an Irish saint. The mother of St Fursey had married without the knowledge of her father and had thereupon been condemned to death. Her unborn child is said to have saved her life by rebuking its grandfather for his cruelty, whereupon the latter broke out in tears that extinguished the flames burning at the stake.[45] In this context, we can easily make a connection with the horrible scene in Zürich too.

Determining and Pleading Pregnancy

Hubmaier's account likewise appears to indicate that the usual practice of suspending the sentence during pregnancy was violated or overruled in Zürich, even though this would have amounted to the murder of unborn life. In his account, Hubmaier even chose to use the plural form, which suggests that there were several pregnant women among the condemned. However, a look into the Zürich records does not confirm this picture. Among the prisoners, there was only one pregnant woman, named Aggtli Ockenfuss. Quite conscious of her pregnancy (in about its

---

[42] Labouvie, *Andere Umstände*, 82–85.

[43] Bohne, *Die Freiheitsstrafe*, 89.

[44] Wolfgang Schild, *Die Geschichte der Gerichtsbarkeit: Vom Gottesurteil bis zum Beginn der modernen Rechtsprechung* (1980; Reprint Hamburg: Nikol Ver.-Ges., 2003), 197, with illustration.

[45] Jacques Gélis, *Die Geburt: Volksglaube, Rituale und Praktiken von 1500–1900*, trans. from the French by Clemens Wilhelm (Munich: Diederichs, 1989), 94.

tenth week) and of her rights resulting from it, she not only informed the Zürich council about her condition but also pointed out that the foetus could possibly be harmed. Aggtli Ockenfuss thus requested that she be treated or housed differently from the other prisoners in order to protect her unborn child. This in no way indicates new forms of treatment of pregnant women but rather stands squarely in the line of tradition, the more so since the expectant mother explicitly emphasized her desire only for an "extension" until after her delivery. Apart from this, she gave the council to understand that she wished to maintain her previous religious commitment.

While Aggtli Ockenfuss at first persisted in her opinion, a few days later she appears to have thought the better of it after all and to have recanted, whereupon she was released, on the condition that she pay her costs. As far as pregnancy and birth, as well as her child's future, are concerned, this is likely to have been the best decision. Pregnant Anabaptist women had a difficult time of it. In the worst case, they had to live with the certainty of being permitted to bear their children, of course, but not being able to care for or rear them, since the death penalty was to be carried out after delivery or after the childbed period. In such cases, it can be said that, at best, a pregnancy protected women from execution for only a short period: the execution of the sentence after delivery or after the period of childbed amounted to a death suffered in installments. The *Martyrs' Mirror* and the volumes of Anabaptist records contain a number of cases of this kind. For example, two pregnant women in Ghent were secretly beheaded in 1559 only after birth and childbed.[46] A sister in the faith living in Flanders who, after her period of childbed was ended, died for her beliefs in 1561 also fared no better—although, as was noted sympathetically, she was very devoted to her husband and children.[47] Of course, there could have been exceptions, but, fundamentally, procedures were determined according to the principle of refusing to apply the death penalty to pregnant women.

In order to be able to proceed along these lines, it had to be determined whether the Anabaptist woman was in fact in a family way. When the pregnancy was well advanced, when women were possessed of a "heavy body" ("schweren Leibes"), this was hardly likely to have

---

[46] *Der blutige Schauplatz*, 186.
[47] *Der blutige Schauplatz*, 213.

been a problem. Matters were different when prisoners like Aggtli Ockenfuss, who presumably did not yet look pregnant, first had to draw
attention to their current condition. In doubtful cases of this type, the
authorities attached great importance to obtaining a confirmation of
the alleged pregnancy. This task was incumbent especially upon the
midwives, or "understanding" women ("verständigen Frauen") in the
broadest sense of the term, who knew about such matters. A woman
by the name of Galtzer, a midwife in Berne, received fifteen shil-
lings in 1538 for such expert activity. She was sent to an Anabaptist
woman to see "whether she [the Anabaptist woman] was with child".[48]
Considerable doubt appears to have arisen in another case. An order
from the Innsbruck government was issued on 10 June 1528, to track
down and arrest Anna Rinnerin along with a married couple named
Velcklehner.[49] An additional order was issued six weeks later to release
the aforesaid Anabaptist woman on bail or oath, but on the condition
that she return to prison after delivery of her child. Although clear
opinions about the case existed, the state of affairs still appeared to have
been anything but certain, since the judge was required to submit a
report on whether Anna Rinnerin was in fact pregnant.[50] It is doubtful
whether a pregnancy could always be determined clearly. This is true
not only for the midwives consulted for their advice, but also for the
supposedly expectant mothers themselves, who could not always be
certain about their condition. In this context, one should call to mind
Eva Labouvie's remark that physical 'indispositions' were not unusual
in this hard-working agrarian society with its lack of hygiene and
questionable diet: "Thus, it is not astonishing that young women with
mounting discomfort, nausea, and even abdominal pains did not—or
rather not yet—conclude that they were pregnant".[51] This uncertainty
factor could have been the reason that some pregnancies remained
hidden, which in turn suggests the theoretical possibility that pregnant
Anabaptist women also were executed.

Quite different motives may have been at the root of the authorities' efforts to obtain certainty. The protection of unborn life was one
motive; the suspicion that feminine cunning possibly might be in play

---

[48] ["ob sy mit dem kind gange"] *Quellen zur Geschichte der Täufer in der Schweiz*, Bd.
III, ed. Martin Haas, Quelle Nr. 655 [unpublished manuscript].
[49] *Quellen zur Geschichte der Täufer*, Bd. XIII: *Österreich*, II. Teil, 145.
[50] *Quellen zur Geschichte der Täufer*, Bd. XIII: *Österreich*, II. Teil, 154.
[51] Labouvie, *Andere Umstände*, 19.

was another. The fact that an expected child protected a woman from harsh punishment, at least temporarily, could tempt women to feign a pregnancy or to instrumentalize it to their own advantage. It was definitely possible and usual to exploit the legal shelter of pregnancy,[52] and this is also likely to have played a role in Anabaptist circles. Was Aggtli Ockenfuss really pregnant, or was she feigning pregnancy in an attempt to free herself from her awkward situation? To be sure, such behaviour appears at first glance to contradict the idea of martyrdom, which, however, was not so present in Anabaptist thought that it forbade survival strategies. Anabaptists who escaped from prison could argue, for example, that it was God who had 'helped them out'. It does not always appear to have been absolutely necessary to die for the faith. In addition, not all male and female Anabaptists were necessarily potential martyrs who would go cheerfully to their deaths. There were uncertain candidates, inconstant confessors, and those for whom earthly relationships were more important in the final analysis than Christian discipleship.

It is an open question whether Anabaptist women like Aggtli Ockenfuss were really and exclusively worried about the fruit of their wombs when they indicated their pregnancy and pointed out the possible consequences for the child. Sometimes, the situation developed in such a way that harsh corporal punishments were not only suspended for the duration of the pregnancy, but were not even pronounced, as in the case of Wetzelmeier's daughter, who was expelled from the territory in 1531: "And at the same time she should know that if she was not pregnant with a child, then she would be drowned".[53] The earlier case of Ursula Spanner was dealt with in a similar way. She too, on the basis of her pregnancy, was not executed but rather expelled from the territory[54]—a measure that was not only terrible in the cold month of December but which amounted to social death. Other suspect women or female Anabaptists were dealt with in a milder manner; they did not even have to go to prison or were released and sent home to give birth to their children there. Hans Peissker's wife was treated in such a way in 1535. Since she was not only "burdened with a large pregnant

---

[52] Labouvie, *Andere Umstände*, 80.
[53] ["Und ist ir dabi gsagt, so sy nit schwanger gieng ains kindlins, so würde man sie ertrencken"] *Quellen zur Geschichte der Täufer in der Schweiz*, Bd. II: *Ostschweiz*, ed. Heinold Fast (Zürich: Theologischer Verlag, 1973), 59.
[54] *Quellen zur Geschichte der Täufer in der Schweiz*, Bd. II: *Ostschweiz*, 26–27.

body" ("mit grossem schwangern leib beladen"), but also had other children, she was not put into prison but rather was spared punishment pending further orders.[55] On the condition that she had to remain at home until the end of her childbed, Christine Merk, too, was released from the Rothenburg prison and sent home "after she became pregnant with child".[56] Whether her Anabaptist faith was perhaps not really so firm, or whether her opinion possibly changed under the influence of birth and the newborn child, is difficult to assess. In any case, Christine Merk recanted.

In the end, it could be advantageous from the authorities' perspective to release pregnant women and to send them home. They were then in a position to care for their family and already existing children. In addition, all those precautionary measures that needed to be taken in view of an expected birth were dropped. The special protection that pregnant women generally enjoyed could be completely ignored only with difficulty or in an exceptional case. Anabaptist women who were pregnant were inconvenient since, as prisoners, they required heightened attention and caused additional expense. On the basis of such considerations, those two women "who were great with child"[57] may have been released in February 1543. While their husbands remained in the tower, they were permitted to leave this place of horror. If they had been kept as prisoners, then precautionary measures certainly would have been necessary. Thus, the Innsbruck government on 23 August 1530 authorized the *Hauptmann* of Kufstein to construct a heated room for the pregnant women, in order to protect them from the coming winter cold.[58] When three suspicious persons were arrested in November 1535, the two men among them were sent immediately to the tower, while the very pregnant wife of one of the Anabaptists was accommodated in the house of the bailiff.[59] Hans Velckheimer's wife, on the other hand, appears to have been convinced that she wanted to bear her child in government custody. After she had broken out of Castle Hertenberg in June 1528, together with her husband, she returned to

---

[55] Paul Wappler, ed., *Die Täuferbewegung in Thüringen von 1526 bis 1584* (Jena: Fischer, 1913), 396.

[56] ["...nachdem sie eines kindes schwanger ging"] *Quellen zur Geschichte der Täufer*, Bd. V: *Bayern, II. Abteilung*, 168.

[57] ["...die groß kinds gangen"] *Quellen zur Geschichte der Täufer*, Bd. XVI: *Elsaß*, IV. Teil (Gütersloh: Mohn, 1988), 19.

[58] *Quellen zur Geschichte der Täufer*, Bd. XIII: *Österreich*, II. Teil, 397–98.

[59] *Quellen zur Geschichte der Wiedertäufer*, Bd. I: *Herzogtum Württemberg*, 46.

prison in February 1529 of her own free will, whereupon a directive to keep her securely in custody was issued.[60] This formulation suggested not only a heightened vigilance, but also a certain measure of comfort to be granted to her. Anabaptist women who delivered their children under adverse conditions while in flight, perhaps with no assistance, were hardly in a better position than any of their sisters in prison. Births in the open, in the fields, or in the stable occurred not only in Anabaptist circles, but were usual in a time when women often worked up until their delivery.[61] Thus, it is not surprising to encounter an Anabaptist with two pregnant women in "the high mountains near Ellmau", where they were arrested together.[62]

Of course, it would be an illusion to believe that all pregnant women enjoyed advantages. On the contrary, many a prison warden appears not to have cared at all about a situation of this kind. Indicative of this is, for example, the inquiry into the matter of Anna Gasser: "Why has the Gasser woman lain so long in prison after her miscarriage?"[63] A human tragedy is likely to have taken place here within some dark walls. The sources do not reveal how many occurrences of this kind took place; whether they were, in fact, the exception is an open question. Two and a half months before, the penalty for several male and female Anabaptists was determined, among them Anna Gasser and her husband Hans, who was to be executed. Allowance was made for the "pregnant wives" ("schwangeren Weiber") to the extent that, even in spite of the lack of penance, they were not to be taken before the court. It is uncertain whether whipping at the pillory, to be carried out before imprisonment, also included pregnant women. It was determined merely "to maintain a measure of restraint in regard to them, the wives".[64]

Even more obscure are the circumstances under which Anna Schmid of Uttenreut could have lost her child. She testifies having "carried [it]

---

[60] *Quellen zur Geschichte der Täufer*, Bd. XIII: *Österreich*, II. Teil, 196.

[61] Gélis, *Die Geburt*, 156–57.

[62] *Quellen zur Geschichte der Täufer*, Bd. XIII: *Österreich*, II. Teil, 375.

[63] ["Warum die Gasserin nach ihrer Fehlgeburt so lange im Gefängnis gelegen?"] *Quellen zur Geschichte der Täufer*, Bd. XIII: *Österreich*, II. Teil, 221. On Anna Gasser and other pregnant women, see also Lynda Huebert Hecht, "Anabaptist Women in Tyrol Who Recanted", in *Profiles of Anabaptist Women: Sixteenth Century Reforming Pioneers*, ed. C. Arnold Snyder and Linda A. Huebert Hecht (Waterloo, Ontario: Wilfrid Laurier University Press, 1998), 158–59.

[64] ["…gegen inen, den weibern, etwas beschaidenhait zu halten"] *Quellen zur Geschichte der Täufer*, Bd. XIII: *Österreich*, II. Teil, 189.

alive for nearly four weeks". The flow of information is no less sparse when the subject is the delivery itself, which in most cases undoubtedly took place outside the prison. There is a lack of records that clearly document births in prison. It is possible that they occurred, but the risk and expense were generally too great. Here, one might recall the pregnant Anna Weltzenberger who, differently from the case of many other Anabaptist women, was not to be released on bail but rather held in prison up to the time of her delivery, as was fitting for a pregnant woman—so the source says.[65] The formulation appears to indicate that the prisoner was not to bring her child into the world in the prison, but rather outside it. In the case of Anna Joris also, who, as the *Martyrs' Mirror* reports, died in 1557 while giving birth, it is not clearly evident where this occurred.[66] On the other hand, one learns that a certain Lyntgen not only sat in the Amsterdam jail in 1549 together with other male and female Anabaptists, but also that she bore "a child in her fetters" ("in ihren Banden ein Kind"). However, the birth pains were so great that she lost her mind because of them and then lay confined ("in einem Häuslein") until the end of her life.[67]

The arm of authority was long. Even if Anabaptist women brought their children into the world outside the gloomy walls of the tower and lay in their childbed at home, they still were not always safe from restrictions and infringements. Georg Metzmann's wife, "a rebaptized Anabaptist", was summoned in vain to appear before the church council. Since, at this point, she lay upon her childbed, her husband appeared in her place.[68] Obviously, the official side could hardly wait to end the 'grace period' as quickly as possible. Georg Metzmann was finally released after being ordered to force his wife to go to church. He was not however able to accomplish much in his function as mouthpiece for the authorities. His wife in no way ended her resistance and continued to stay away from the worship service. What took place here strikes one as rather harmless in comparison with the ruthless attempt at conversion carried out in Zürich in 1530. While she was in labour, Anneli von Wattwil was pressed hard by the two birth assistants present to renounce her Anabaptist faith, which amounted to a "highly

---

[65] *Quellen zur Geschichte der Täufer*, Bd. XIII: *Österreich*, II. Teil, 212.
[66] *Der blutige Schauplatz*, 134.
[67] *Der blutige Schauplatz*, 63.
[68] *Quellen zur Geschichte der Wiedertäufer*, Bd. I: *Herzogtum Württemberg*, 456.

effective 'natural torture'".[69] The tormented woman acknowledged her error and was later received again into the good graces of the church. The case is interesting, first of all, because it provides insights into the usual birth practices of the time. In most cases, women from the circle of relatives, friends, and neighbours appeared along with the midwife for the purpose of providing support for a woman in the extremity of pregnancy.[70] This is the case here too, since mention is made of "both wives and neighbours".[71] But contrary to what was expected of midwives and their helpers, they did not stand selflessly and in solidarity by the side of the expectant mother.[72] On the contrary, the women present at the birth brought their power and their supposed religious superiority to bear and, in this way, made themselves into accomplices of an intolerant authority. Such cases of female partisanship belong to the broad spectrum of religious confrontation in the Reformation era, just as earlier radical feminine representatives of the new faith took to the field against their sexual compatriots from the old faith—for example, the former abbess Marie Dentière who attempted to lead confirmed nuns along supposedly better paths of faith.[73] The fronts varied: the case taken from the Zürich records documents that an Anabaptist woman too could be the target of feminized attack.

The difficult birth in Zürich with its ideological side effects is not likely to have been the normal case. There were, conversely, midwives who had Anabaptist sympathies and for this reason fell into disrepute. Among them was a certain Margareta from Miedelsbach, who was entered on the files as an "evil Anabaptist woman". It was said that she delivered the children, but did not appear at their baptisms.[74] And there were likely others who simply fulfilled their function as birth assistants. Midwives had close access to the newborn. What came of this? Former women Anabaptists who had fallen away from their faith

---

[69] Alice Zimmerli-Witschi, "Frauen in der Reformationszeit" (Diss. University of Zürich, 1981), 139.

[70] See Eva Labouvie, *Beistand in Kindsnöten: Hebammen und weibliche Kultur auf dem Land (1550–1910)* (Frankfurt am Main and New York: Campus-Verlag, 1999); also Labouvie, *Andere Umstände*.

[71] ["...biderwen wibern unnd nachpuren"] *Quellen zur Geschichte der Täufer in der Schweiz*, Bd. I: *Zürich*, 336.

[72] See Sibylla Flügge, *Hebammen und heilkundige Frauen: Recht und Rechtswirklichkeit im 15. und 16. Jahrhundert* (Basel and Frankfurt am Main: Stroemfeld, 1998).

[73] Jeanne de Jussie, *Kleine Chronik: Bericht einer Nonne über die Anfänge der Reformation in Genf*, trans. and ed. Helmut Feld (Mainz: von Zabern, 1996), 144–45.

[74] *Quellen zur Geschichte der Wiedertäufer*, Bd. I: *Herzogtum Württemberg*, 505, 516.

in the course of their pregnancy and had recanted are likely to have had few if any problems with infant baptism. Persistent Anabaptist women, on the other hand, would have used every means to protect their children from this much-maligned act or from a threatened forced baptism. Again, mothers who were executed after their childbed had problems of quite another kind.[75]

If there was a death that an expectant mother awaited after her delivery, it was execution. Hubmaier's account of the brothers and sisters in the faith, including pregnant women, ending their lives in agony in the tower contradicts the usual penal practice and does not withstand scrutiny. However, it is exactly this dubious passage in Hubmaier that draws attention to the fact that a martyr's death could also come to pass in prison in an unspectacular way and with little public appeal.

Completely in accord with the tradition of the protection of the life of the unborn and of the expectant mother, pregnant Anabaptist women benefitted from a series of privileges ranging from more comfortable accommodation to the temporary or permanent suspension of the sentence. Since the treatment of pregnant Anabaptist women depended on the facts of each individual case, general judgments are difficult to make. Much depended on the attitude of the pregnant woman herself, her family situation, and the persons looking after her.

Since pregnant women presented an economic and social problem with regard to the privileges granted to them, it was definitely in the interest of the authorities to have the women concerned kept and supervised at a place outside the feared towers and dark prison holes. Births in prison are likely to have been the great exception. Although mandates and decrees against the Anabaptists often formulated the equal legal treatment of men and women, graduated according to the severity of the crime, a pregnancy created gender-specific differences in penal practice and prompted allowances.

On the other hand, it is quite possible that Anabaptist women employed a feigned or actual pregnancy for the purpose of evading a criminal prosecution or for securing mitigated circumstances. Over against this possible instrumentalization of a pregnancy on the part of the woman concerned stands the attempt to use the painful birth process in the authorities' interest for conversion attempts and to persuade the

---

[75] See Marion Kobelt-Groch, "'Hear my son the instruction of your mother'": Children and Anabaptism", *Journal of Mennonite Studies* 17 (1999): 22–33.

expectant mother to fall away from her Anabaptist faith—a case that actually occurred, and yet is hardly likely to suggest the existence of a general practice.

Bibliography

Beck, Josef, ed. *Die Geschichts-Bücher der Wiedertäufer in Österreich-Ungarn von 1526–1787*. 1883. Reprint, Nieuwkoop: De Graaf, 1967.

Bohne, Gotthold. *Die Freiheitsstrafe in den italienischen Stadtrechten des 12.–16. Jahrhunderts*. Leipzig: Weicher, 1922.

Burschel, Peter. "'Marterlieder': Eine erfahrungsgeschichtliche Annäherung an die Martyrienkultur der Täufer im 16. Jahrhundert". *Mennonitische Geschichtsblätter* 58 (2001): 7–36.

——. *Sterben und Unsterblichkeit: Zur Kultur des Martyriums in der frühen Neuzeit*. München: R. Oldenbourg, 2004.

Clasen, Claus-Peter. *Anabaptism: A Social History, 1525–1618. Switzerland, Austria, Moravia, South and Central Germany*. Ithaca and London: Cornell University Press, 1972.

de Jussie, Jeanne. *Kleine Chronik: Bericht einer Nonne über die Anfänge der Reformation in Genf*. Translated and edited by Helmut Feld. Mainz: von Zabern, 1996.

Deppermann, Klaus. *Melchior Hoffman: Soziale Unruhen und apokalyptische Visionen im Zeitalter der Reformation*. Göttingen: Vandenhoeck and Ruprecht, 1979.

Fast, Heinold, ed. *Der linke Flügel der Reformation: Glaubenszeugnisse der Täufer, Spiritualisten, Schwärmer und Antitrinitarier*. Bremen: C. Schünemann, 1962.

Fehr, Hans. *Die Rechtsstellung der Frau und der Kinder in den Weistümern*. Jena: G. Fischer, 1912.

Flügge, Sibylla. *Hebammen und heilkundige Frauen: Recht und Rechtswirklichkeit im 15. und 16. Jahrhundert*. Basel and Frankfurt am Main: Stroemfeld, 1998.

Franz, Günther, ed. *Urkundliche Quellen zur hessischen Reformationsgeschichte*. Vierter Bd.: *Wiedertäuferakten, 1527–1626*. Marburg: Elwert, 1951.

Gélis, Jacques. *Die Geburt: Volksglaube, Rituale und Praktiken von 1500–1900*. Translated from the French by Clemens Wilhelm. Munich: Diederichs, 1989.

Goertz, Hans-Jürgen. *The Anabaptists*. Translated by Trevor Johnson. London and New York: Routledge, 1996.

——. *Konrad Grebel, Kritiker des frommen Scheins, 1498–1526: Eine biographische Skizze*. Hamburg: Kümpers, 1998.

Gregory, Brad S. *The Forgotten Writings of the Mennonite Martyrs*. Leiden: Brill, 2002.

——. *Salvation at Stake: Christian Martyrdom in Early Modern Europe*. Cambridge, Mass. and London: Harvard University Press, 1999.

Grimm, Jacob. *Deutsche Rechtsaltertümer*. Bd. I. 1899. Reprint, Darmstadt: Wiss. Buchges., 1965.

Grochowina, Nicole. "Von Opfern zu Heiligen: Martyrien von Täuferinnen und Täufern im 16. Jahrhundert". In *Vorbild-Inbild-Abbild: Religiöse Lebensmodelle in Geschlechtergeschichtlicher Perspektive*. Edited by Peter Burschel and Anne Conrad. Freiburg im Breisgau: Rombach, 2003.

Hecht, Lynda Huebert. "Anabaptist Women in Tyrol Who Recanted". In *Profiles of Anabaptist Women: Sixteenth Century Reforming Pioneers*. Edited by C. Arnold Snyder and L. A. Huebert Hecht. Waterloo, Ontario: Wilfrid Laurier University Press, 1998.

Joldersma, Hermina and Louis Grijp, eds. and trans. *"Elisabeth's Manly Courage": Testimonials and Songs of Martyred Anabaptist Women in the Low Countries*. Milwaukee, Wis.: Marquette University Press, 2001.

Klötzer, Ralf. *Die Täuferherrschaft von Münster: Stadtreformation und Welterneuerung*. Münster: Aschendorff, 1992.

Kobelt-Groch, Marion. "Frauen in Ketten: 'Von widertauferischen weibern wie gegen selbigen zu handeln'". *Mennonitische Geschichtsblätter* 47/48 (1990/91): 49–70.

———. "'Hear my son the instruction of your mother': Children and Anabaptism". *Journal of Mennonite Studies* 17 (1999): 22–33.

Labouvie, Eva. *Andere Umstände: Eine Kulturgeschichte der Geburt*. Köln, Weimar, and Wien: Böhlau, 1998.

———. *Beistand in Kindsnöten: Hebammen und weibliche Kultur auf dem Land (1550–1910)*. Frankfurt am Main and New York: Campus-Verlag, 1999.

Schild, Wolfgang. *Die Geschichte der Gerichtsbarkeit: Vom Gottesurteil bis zum Beginn der modernen Rechtsprechung*. 1980. Reprint Hamburg: Nikol Ver.-Ges., 2003.

Schnabel-Schüle, Helga. "Frauen im Strafrecht vom 16. bis 18. Jahrhundert". In *Frauen in der Geschichte des Rechts: Von der Frühen Neuzeit bis zur Gegenwart*, edited by Ute Gerhard. Munich: Beck, 1997.

Schraepler, Horst W. *Die rechtliche Behandlung der Täufer in der deutschen Schweiz, Südwestdeutschland und Hessen, 1525–1618*. Tübingen: [Fabian-Verlag], 1957.

Snyder, C. Arnold. *Anabaptist History and Theology: An Introduction*. Kitchener, Ontario: Pandora, 1995.

Stiasny, Hans H. Th. *Die strafrechtliche Verfolgung der Täufer in der freien Reichsstadt Köln, 1529 bis 1618*. Münster: Aschendorff, 1962.

Quanter, Rudolf. *Deutsches Zuchthaus- und Gefängniswesen: Von den ältesten Zeiten bis in die Gegenwart*. 1905. Reprint Aalen: Scientia-Verlag, 1970.

Quellen zur Geschichte der Wiedertäufer. Bd. 1: *Herzogtum Württemberg*. Edited by Gustav Bossert. Leipzig: Heinsius, 1930.

Quellen zur Geschichte der Wiedertäufer. Bd. II: *Markgraftum Brandenburg (Bayern I. Abteilung)*. Edited by Karl Schornbaum. Leipzig: Heinsius, 1934.

Quellen zur Geschichte der Täufer. Bd. IV: *Baden und Pfalz*. Edited by Manfred Krebs. Gütersloh: Mohn, 1951.

Quellen zur Geschichte der Täufer. Bd. V: *Bayern, II. Abteilung*. Edited by Karl Schornbaum. Gütersloh: Bertelsmann, 1951.

Quellen zur Geschichte der Täufer. Bd. XIII: *Österreich, II. Teil*. Edited by Grete Mecenseffy. Gütersloh: Mohn, 1972.

Quellen zur Geschichte der Täufer. Bd. XVI: *Elsaß*. Edited by Marc Lienhard et al. Gütersloh: Mohn, 1988.

Quellen zur Geschichte der Täufer in der Schweiz. Bd. I: *Zürich*. Edited by Leonhard von Muralt und Walter Schmid. 2. Aufl. Zürich: Theologischer Verlag, 1974.

Quellen zur Geschichte der Täufer in der Schweiz. Bd. II: *Ostschweiz*. Edited by Heinold Fast. Zürich: Theologischer Verlag, 1973.

Quellen zur Geschichte der Täufer in der Schweiz. Bd. III. Edited by Martin Haas. Unpublished manuscript.

Van Braght, Thieleman J., ed. *Der Blutige Schauplatz, oder Märtyrer-Spiegel der Taufgesinnten oder wehrlosen Christen*. Translated from the Dutch. Aylmer, Ontario and LaGrange, Indiana: Pathway Publishing, 1973.

Van Dülmen, Richard. *Theater des Schreckens: Gerichtspraxis und Strafrituale in der frühen Neuzeit*. Munich: Beck, 1985.

Von Hentig, Hans. *Die Strafe*. Vol. II. *Die modernen Erscheinungsformen*. Berlin: Springer, 1955.

Visser, Piet, ed. "Zes onbekende martelaarsbrieven van Jeroniumus Segers (+ 1551)". *Doopsgezinde Bijdragen, nieuwe reeks* 29 (2003): 195–249.

Wappler, Paul, ed. *Die Täuferbewegung in Thüringen von 1526 bis 1584*. Jena: Fischer, 1913.

Weiske, Julius, ed. *Der Sachsenspiegel (Landrecht), nach der ältesten Leipziger Handschrift*. 8th ed. Leipzig: Reisland, 1905.

Zieglschmid, A. J. F., ed. *Die älteste Chronik der Hutterischen Brüder: ein Sprachdenkmal aus frühneuhochdeutscher Zeit*. Ithaca, New York: The Cayuga Press, 1943.
Zimmerli-Witschi, Alice. "Frauen in der Reformationszeit". Diss. University of Zürich, 1981.

"THEY ARE BUT WOMEN": MARY WARD, 1585–1645

Pamela Ellis

There is a certain irony in regarding Mary Ward as a religious radical. The main motivation for her activity was the desire to restore the *status quo ante* for the Catholic Church in England, but the means by which she chose to pursue what might almost be called a reactionary aim were seen by that Church as dangerously innovative and subversive. Her apparent conservatism led her into proposing radical ways of preserving or restoring the past, and thus into conflict with the Church she was seeking to champion. As a result of her efforts, her orthodoxy and obedience were called into question by a Church seemingly trapped in conventional thinking and unable to see that obedience might require a creative response to the challenges of the Reformation, and that to cling uncritically to the ways of the past might be to lose an opportunity to shape a Catholic future for England. This paradox lies at the heart of Mary Ward's story.

In 1951 Pius XII described Mary Ward as "that incomparable woman given by Catholic England to the Church in the darkest and most blood-stained of periods". During his visit to Britain in 1982, John Paul II called her "an extraordinary Englishwoman" and commended her for inspiring women today to take their place in the life of the Church. But three hundred years earlier their predecessor Urban VIII had described her life's work as "poisonous growths", which must be "suppressed, extinct, rooted out, destroyed and abolished".[1] Such violent language suggests a deep-seated anxiety on the part of the Catholic Church of the time. In this chapter, I will suggest that this anxiety arose from a perceived threat to traditional views of gender roles, posed by Mary's attempt to establish a religious congregation of women who could engage in educational and other charitable work without being confined by convent and habit. I will trace the journey she made from a conventional understanding of religious life for

---

[1] *Pastoralis Romani Pontificis* (1631), quoted in Mary Wright IBVM, *Mary Ward's Institute: the Struggle for Identity* (Sydney: Crossing Press, 1997), 191.

women to a radical reassessment of that life in light of the particular circumstances of Catholics in seventeenth-century England. I will then look at the hostility that her ideas aroused in certain circles and suggest that this was rooted in a negative estimation of women's abilities and an unquestioned assumption of male superiority. I will also examine Mary's most detailed discussion of what we might today call the gender question. This discussion is found in a series of 'Instructions' to her companions and is forthright in its rebuttal of any suggestion of women's inferiority. Finally, I will look at the consequences, for her personally and for the Institute she founded, of her radical new formulation of women's religious life.

Her early experiences instilled in her a great love for the Catholic Church. Born in 1585 into a family of Catholic landowners in Yorkshire, Mary Ward was the eldest child of Marmaduke Ward of Mulwith, near Ripon, and the widowed Ursula Constable, née Wright.[2] She would have been aware, growing up, of a background of persecution and heroism. Resistance to the imposition of Protestantism was strongest in the north of England, where in 1569 Catholics had risen in revolt, led by the earls of Westmorland and Northumberland.[3] Members of Mary's family were involved in various ways in keeping Catholicism alive; like other Catholic families of their class, the Wards moved house frequently to avoid fines, and Mary spent much of her childhood in other households, including that of her maternal grandmother, Ursula Wright of Ploughland, in East Yorkshire, who had spent a total of fourteen years in prison for her faith.[4] (Two of Mary's uncles, John and Christopher Wright, were involved in the Gunpowder Plot of 1605 and were killed resisting arrest by government troops at Holbeach Hall in Staffordshire. Her father Marmaduke was arrested on suspicion of complicity but released after a few days.[5]) Such an upbringing at first inspired in her a desire for martyrdom that by her mid-teens was transmuted into a longing for religious life.[6] At the time, following the

---

[2] Margaret Mary Littlehales IBVM, *Mary Ward: Pilgrim and Mystic* (Tunbridge Wells: Burns & Oates, 1998), 16–17.

[3] Michael A. Mullet, *The Catholic Reformation* (London and New York: Routledge, 1999), 175; Owen Chadwick, *The Reformation* (Harmondsworth: Penguin, 1990), 287.

[4] Littlehales, *Pilgrim and Mystic*, 18.

[5] Littlehales, *Pilgrim and Mystic*, 33.

[6] Gillian Orchard IBVM, *Till God Will: Mary Ward Through her Writings* (London: Darton, Longman & Tod, 1985), 9.

suppression of monastic life in England in the 1530s, this was possible only on the Continent.

This did not at all accord with the plans and wishes of her family.[7] It was considered that eligible young women such as Mary could best serve the Catholic cause by marrying into the Catholic gentry and aristocracy and raising a family, thus increasing the number of influential Catholics in the land. Mary Ward's father had sought alliances with various northern Catholic families since Mary was ten years old and she is known to have refused at least four such suitors.[8] Eventually, having outworn all opposition, she attained her majority and left England for St Omer, then in the Spanish Netherlands (now in northern France), to seek admission to the religious life.[9]

In her fragmentary Autobiography of 1618, Mary Ward describes the genesis of her sense of vocation and her attraction to religious life. As a child she had heard tales of convent life from an elderly retainer and had been particularly impressed by an account of the severe punishment meted out to a nun who broke her vow of chastity. She recorded, "I immediately conceived a singular love and esteem for religious life, as a sanctuary where all might and must be holy".[10] Henriette Peters notes that this love arose not from any judgement as to the offence or the penalty but as a response to the challenge of a way of life that sought perfection.[11] It may be significant that she uses the word 'conceived' in this context of sexual transgression: she may, perhaps unconsciously, be alluding to the conventional idea of the nun as the 'bride of Christ'. The use of the word 'sanctuary' is also revealing. Mary at this stage still envisages religious life as offering a path to holiness only in return for a complete separation from the secular world. Although the wholeheartedness of Mary's response was to characterise all her later endeavours, she considerably modified her views on the need for 'sanctuary'.

Attracted by such rigour, Mary Ward began to practise "much prayer, some few fasts, and some austerities"[12] in preparation for a life that she

---

[7] Henriette Peters IBVM, *Mary Ward: A World in Contemplation* (Leominster: Gracewing, 1994), 31; Littlehales, *Pilgrim and Mystic*, 49.

[8] Littlehales, *Pilgrim and Mystic*, 21.

[9] Orchard, *Till God Will*, 13–14.

[10] Ward, "Autobiography", 1618, in Mary Catherine Chambers IBVM, *The Life of Mary Ward*, vol. 1 (London, 1882), 46.

[11] Peters, *World in Contemplation*, 46.

[12] Ward, "Autobiography", quoted in Orchard, *Till God Will*, 9.

knew she would not be able to follow for some years. Already at this
early stage her capacity for independent thought is in evidence. Finding herself developing scruples about her thoroughness in carrying out
these practices, she reasoned that "God is not pleased with certain acts
made thus by constraint...I will do these things with love and freedom
or leave them alone".[13] At the age of fifteen she was already able to
recognize that an action not freely undertaken was, though possibly
good in itself, spiritually void.

Another early indication of the later development of her thinking
lies in her comments about the type of religious life she was seeking
at this early stage in the evolution of her vocation:

> I had no inclination to any Order in particular, only I was resolved within
> myself to take the most strict and secluded, thinking and often saying
> that, as women did not know how to do good except to themselves, *a
> penuriousness which I resented enough even then* [my emphasis], I would do in
> good earnest what I did.[14]

At this stage Mary Ward accepts the thinking of the time: that women
were incapable of spiritually benefitting others and should therefore
concentrate on seeking their own perfection. But already something in
her rebels against this limited and grudging 'penuriousness'.

Once arrived in St Omer, and not having any clear idea of which
order would be appropriate for her, she presented herself, with letters
of introduction, at the Jesuit seminary in the town. On the advice of
George Keynes SJ she applied to the Poor Clares, the order founded
in 1212 by Clare of Assisi to follow the Franciscan model of radical poverty and asceticism.[15] Given Mary's desire for "the most strict
and secluded" order, this might seem to have been the ideal choice.
Instead, her life as a Poor Clare was problematic from the beginning.
The convent offered her a place, not as an enclosed ('choir') nun but
as an unenclosed lay sister, which role required her to spend the day
begging around the town and its environs on behalf of her enclosed
sisters.[16] Nothing could be further from Mary's hopes of seclusion
and solitude, but, alone and inexperienced, she allowed herself to be
swayed by Keynes's assurance that this was God's will for her: "These

---

[13] Orchard, *Till God Will*, 10.
[14] Orchard, *Till God Will*, 9.
[15] Peters, *World in Contemplation*, 74–75.
[16] Peters, *World in Contemplation*, 79.

words 'the will of God' so pierced my heart that I had no inclination to say or think of anything else".[17] Thus, attributing her reluctance to pride, she began life as a lay sister, an exhausting and humiliating life to which by inclination and constitution she was profoundly unsuited. Upheld solely by the conviction that she was following God's will, she performed her duties "willingly but with such aversion and grief that death by any kind of torment that I could imagine to myself appeared most sweet to me".[18]

While in this unsatisfactory situation she was, as she puts it, "enkindled with a vehement desire to procure a monastery for the English of this Order",[19] and after much prayer and consultation with her spiritual superiors, she left that convent in 1607.[20] In 1609 she entered a convent for English Poor Clares—a convent that she had been instrumental in founding in Gravelines, on the north coast of France. Details of how she set about this achievement are disappointingly sparse,[21] though she is known to have had support from Bishop Jacques Blaes of St Omer, with financial help from the Governor of Gravelines, who also provided a house and land.[22] She is also known to have travelled to Brussels to seek the approval of the Archduke Albrecht and the Infanta Isabella Clara Eugenia.[23] The founding of this convent was an extraordinary feat for a young woman not yet twenty-two years old and not even a professed religious. It is an early indication of the tenacity of purpose she was always to show when she was convinced that she was carrying out God's will.

On her entry into this new convent she recorded: "I put on the habit with the others, continuing in exact observance of that Rule, the austerity and retirement being extremely to my content".[24] But, as was to become clear, this was only the start of her religious journey not, as she expected at the time, the end. Within weeks she had received another revelation:

---

[17] Ward, "Autobiography", in Orchard, *Till God Will*, 15.
[18] Ward, "Autobiography", in Orchard, *Till God Will*, 17.
[19] Ward, "Autobiography", in Orchard, *Till God Will*, 18.
[20] Peters, *World in Contemplation*, 82.
[21] Peters, *World in Contemplation*, 83.
[22] Peters, *World in Contemplation*, 85.
[23] Peters, *World in Contemplation*, 87–8.
[24] Ward, "Autobiography", in Orchard, *Till God Will*, 22–3.

> Here it was shown to me that I was not to be of the Order of St Clare;
> some other thing I was to do. What or of what nature I did not see,
> nor could I guess, only that it was to be a good thing and what God
> willed.[25]

Mary herself was careful to stress that her 'revelations' were not visions
but intellectual insights.[26] Nevertheless, it is possible that they would
have been regarded with suspicion by church authorities, because
women were considered to be constitutionally susceptible to religious
experience but also to diabolic influence.[27] This consideration may lie
behind the cautious response of her confessor, Roger Lee SJ, to whom
she confided her 'revelation'. He advised her to remain where she was
for the present, while she tested and discerned its origin and nature
in the manner prescribed by Ignatius of Loyola, the founder of the
Society of Jesus.[28] Finally, in 1609, she left the Poor Clares and returned
to England. At this point Mary was very isolated. She had given up
all that had supported her up to that point, without any clear idea of
what was to take its place.[29] All she had was the conviction that she was
following God's will: a truly radical—in the primary sense of 'going to
the root'—place to be. In this place she resolved to "do all the little I
could for God and the good of those there [in London], not to be idle
in the meantime, and the better prepared for whatsoever God should
call me to".[30] In pursuit of this aim she occupied herself with works of
charity and evangelization among the Catholics of London.[31]

This period of her life laid the foundations for all that was to follow.
Since 1570 and the promulgation of Pius V's bull *Regnans in excelsis*,
which excommunicated Elizabeth I and released her Catholic subjects
from their allegiance to her, Catholicism had been equated with treason
by the English state.[32] Adherence to the old faith was both difficult and

---

[25] Ward to Mgr Albergati, 1620, quoted in Orchard, *Till God Will*, 24.
[26] Orchard, *Till God Will*, 53.
[27] Anthony Fletcher, "Women's Spiritual Experience", in *Gender and Christian Religion*,
ed. R. N. Swanton (Woodbridge, Suffolk: Boydell Press for the Ecclesiastical History
Society, 1998), 188; Patricia Crawford, *Women and Religion in England, 1500–1700* (London
and New York: Routledge, 1996), 74.
[28] Orchard, *Till God Will*, 25n.
[29] Martin Chase, "When God is Sought Sincerely: Mary Ward and Dorothy Day",
in *Journey into Freedom: Essays in Honour of the Fourth Centenary of Mary Ward's Birth*, Supplement no. 53 of *The Way* (Summer 1985): 120.
[30] Ward to Mgr Albergati, in Orchard, *Till God Will*, 26.
[31] Littlehales, *Pilgrim and Mystic*, 55.
[32] Mullett, *Catholic Reformation*, 175; Chadwick, *Reformation*, 287.

dangerous, and Mary saw that there was much to be done to alleviate the sufferings of her co-religionists and to strengthen their resolve to endure, and that women could usefully participate in this work.[33] It was this insight that set her on a path that would eventually lead to accusations of heresy and schism. Her decision to seek ways in which women religious could actively support the Church's mission in England was undoubtedly influenced by her experience as a child: she had seen for herself that women were crucial to the survival of Catholicism in England. While Catholic men often conformed outwardly to avoid fines, their wives could organize the household in such a way as to enable Catholic practice as well as raising their children in the faith.[34] In this situation of an underground Church, an order of active consecrated women such as Mary eventually planned for could not act openly: anonymity and flexibility would be required. There was no question of habited nuns being able to operate in England, nor was the clandestine and mobile nature of the task compatible with the confinement and fixed routines of a traditional convent.[35] All Mary's ideas about the nature of her Institute and the rule of life she sought to adopt for it flow from this reality, and always, in discussing her later activities, it must be remembered that the situation in England was the reason why she found herself having to think 'outside the box' in a way that was bound to bring her into conflict with the institutional Church, even though the restoration, or at least the survival, of the Catholic Church in England was her main motive.

Before she left St Omer, Roger Lee had extracted from her a reluc-tant promise to join the 'Teresians' (Carmelites) should he so instruct her,[36] but in London she received a second revelation:

> I was abstracted out of my whole being and it was shown to me with clearness and inexpressible certainty that I was not to be of the Order of St Teresa, but some other thing was determined for me, without all comparison more to the glory of God...I did not see what the assured good thing would be, but the glory of God which was to come through it, showed itself inexplicably and so abundantly as to fill my soul in such a

[33] Ward, "First Plan of the Schola Beatae Mariae" (1612), in Orchard, *Till God Will*, 34.

[34] R. Po-Chia Hsia, *The World of Catholic Renewal 1540–1770*, 2nd ed. (Cambridge: Cambridge University Press, 2005), 85; Randall Martin, "Mary Ward", in *Women Writers in Renaissance England* (London and New York: Longman, 1997), 229.

[35] Peters, *World in Contemplation*, 126.

[36] Peters, *World in Contemplation*, 106.

way that I remained for a good space without feeling or hearing anything
but the sound 'Glory, Glory, Glory'.[37]

Later the same year (1609) Mary Ward returned to St Omer with a
little company of women who had been inspired by her activities in
London, and they began to work within the English *émigré* community
there. They supported themselves by setting up schools for the children
of this community,[38] and this work also contributed to the distinctive
nature of Mary's vision of apostolic religious life for women, a life that
had of necessity to be unenclosed. Mary was not the first to realize the
importance of educating girls: starting with Angela Merici in the first
half of the sixteenth century, several women had sought to establish
religious congregations without enclosure in order to provide schooling
for girls.[39] But Mary was attempting to meet a very specific need, that
of the daughters of English Catholic families, who since the 1530s had
been deprived of any possibility of a Catholic education in England.
The sons of such families had long been sent abroad to study: now
their sisters could follow them.[40] Mary saw that this had implications
for the survival of Catholicism in England, which would depend on
the ability of women to pass on the faith within the home.

While engaging in this work, Mary and her companions followed
a lifestyle which resembled that of a monastic order, but they had no
established rule of life.[41] The discernment of such a rule was Mary
Ward's main preoccupation during this period. In 1611 she fell ill and
nearly died, but on her recovery she had the definitive revelation by
which she felt she had finally perceived God's will for her community.
She describes it thus:

> [B]eing alone, in some extraordinary repose of mind, I heard distinctly, not
> by sound of voice but intellectually understood, these words, *Take the same
> of the Society* ... these few words gave so great measure of light ... comfort
> and strength, and so changed the whole soul that it was impossible for
> me to doubt but that they came from him whose words are works.[42]

---

[37] Ward, "Autobiography", in Orchard, *Till God Will*, 27.
[38] Peters, *World in Contemplation*, 110–11.
[39] Mary T. Malone, *Women and Christianity*, vol. 3, *From the Reformation to the 21st Century* (Blackrock, Co. Dublin: Columba Press, 2003), 95–96.
[40] Littlehales, *Pilgrim and Mystic*, 62.
[41] Peters, *World in Contemplation*, 112; Littlehales, *Pilgrim and Mystic*, 63.
[42] Ward to Mgr Albergati, in Orchard, *Till God Will*, 29.

From this point on she saw her way clearly and knew exactly what her fledgling Institute was being called to. The 'Society' was the Society of Jesus, founded the previous century by Ignatius of Loyola, and by her revelation Mary understood that she was to found an order of women religious who were to live by the Jesuit Constitutions. This implied, among other things, the defence of the Catholic faith under the vows of poverty, chastity, and obedience; intellectual confrontation with heresy and immorality; and a pastoral apostolate of catechesis, social care, and education.[43] This was an extraordinarily radical ambition—no less than the taking on of the public apostolate of male religious—and went far beyond the educational aims of earlier active women's orders. Mary described this revelation as having given her "so great measure of light...so much comfort and strength",[44] but in fact the path it set her on was all but impossible. Not only were all the public activities undertaken by the Society of Jesus regarded as unsuitable for women,[45] but the Society was forbidden by its founder, Ignatius of Loyola, to undertake the direction of women's religious orders.[46] This made it difficult for there to be any formal association of Mary's Institute with the Society, and as she herself records, "all the Society opposed".[47] The absence of enclosure and of habits also caused problems, standing as it did for an apparent disregard for gender and social roles[48] as well as ecclesiastical rules. Lastly, Mary's requirement of self-government for her Institute, which was to be answerable (on the Jesuit model) only to the pope, subverted the accepted model by which female religious communities came under the jurisdiction of the local diocesan bishop.

Even if Mary Ward had not received the revelation to "take the same of the Society" it is likely that the formative influences in her life would have led her towards the adoption of some form of Jesuit-influenced rule for her community. It is known that as a young woman she was familiar with some of the Jesuit spiritual writings of the time, including Robert Southwell's *A Short Rule of Good Life* (1596) and Lorenzo Scupoli's

---

[43] Peters, *World in Contemplation*, 117.
[44] Ward to Mgr Albergati, in Orchard, *Till God Will*, 29.
[45] Mary Daniel Turner, "Woman and Power", in *Journey into Freedom*, 107; Peters, *World in Contemplation*, 252.
[46] Littlehales, *Pilgrim and Mystic*, 66.
[47] Ward to Mgr Albergati, in Orchard, *Till God Will*, 33.
[48] Martin, "Mary Ward", in *Women Writers*, 230.

The Spiritual Conflict (1598).[49] Her early confessors, Richard Holtby and Roger Lee, were both Jesuits. Ignatius's desire for his followers to be able to respond to any demands made on them led to his decision to dispense with the monastic requirement to gather several times a day for communal prayer. Mary sought a similar flexibility for her Institute. Education was another area of shared priorities. The Jesuits themselves were highly educated and regarded education as their primary task. Mary Ward saw clearly that in the "very distressed state of England" one of the most urgent tasks was the education of young Catholic women "in piety, in the Christian virtues and liberal arts",[50] and drew an explicit parallel with the Society of Jesus "which...fruitfully labours throughout the world for the education of youth".[51] Given that Mary Ward's spirituality was to a large extent shaped by the Jesuits and the aims of her Institute were so similar to those of the Society, it is not surprising that she perceived the way of life of the Jesuits as the most appropriate for her company of women, including most especially the Jesuits' freedom to operate in society at large rather than being obliged to recite the Office in choir like a monastic community.

Indecision may have come to an end but problems remained and even increased, as will be seen. The Institute hovered constantly on the brink of financial disaster,[52] while there was opposition to Mary Ward's unorthodox vision both externally and from some members of the Institute itself.[53] The need for ecclesiastical approval to put the Institute on an official footing was becoming pressing, and in 1621 Mary went to Rome to petition the then pope, Gregory XV, for recognition of her Institute. In her petition she refers to "the continual persecutions heaped upon us both by bad and good men ever since our beginnings".[54] These persecutions were about to intensify.

Mary Ward was born into an age which did not much value women outside their roles as wives and mothers. Single women had no independent rights: these were subsumed under those of their nearest male 'protector', and a woman had no status that was not derived from her

---

[49] Jeanne Cover IBVM, *Love, the Driving Force: Mary Ward's Spirituality* (Milwaukee: Marquette University Press, 1997), 33.
[50] Ward, "First Plan of the Schola Beatae Mariae" (1612), in Orchard, *Till God Will*, 34–5.
[51] Orchard, *Till God Will*, 37.
[52] Littlehales, *Pilgrim and Mystic*, 94–95.
[53] Wright, *Mary Ward's Institute*, 10.
[54] Ward, "Memorial to the Holy Father" (1622), in Orchard, *Till God Will*, 63.

relationship to men.[55] They were also thought to have inferior spiritual capacities: Mary Ward overheard one priest claiming that "a woman could not apprehend God".[56] Women entering religious life were expected to spend the rest of their lives within the convent, in a life of prayer and penance. All convents fell under the jurisdiction of the bishop in whose diocese they lay, as women were not deemed capable of governing themselves. One of the controversial requests that Mary Ward made in her petition was that the houses of her Institute should not be under the control of the local bishop, but should be answerable directly to herself. This aspect of her project was a direct response to the needs of English Catholics, always a primary concern of Mary's. Autonomy of governance was the only way in which the Institute could operate in England, where there were no Catholic diocesan bishops, and it would also facilitate her work on the Continent. She therefore asked that the Institute, like the Society of Jesus, should be under the direct protection of the pope,

> not suffering bishops in their dioceses to have any ordinary authority or jurisdiction over us; for that kind of government, though holy in itself and helpful to other religious communities, is not only contrary to our Institute, but would moreover much molest and hinder us, both in the way of our own perfection and in the service we are to perform towards our neighbour.[57]

It was in Rome that the paradox of Mary Ward's mission would come to a head. Intelligent, well-educated, aware of the abilities of women and anxious to harness those abilities for the survival of the faith in England, Mary Ward did not doubt the essential orthodoxy of her project. She certainly did not anticipate the vehemence or the orchestrated character of the opposition to her.[58] But by the time she arrived in Rome in person to petition the pope, it was too late. Those who opposed her already had the ear of the pope, and she was neither properly informed of the accusations against her nor given an opportunity to defend herself.

A month before Mary Ward arrived in Rome in 1621, a document written by the Archpriest of England, William Harrison, was received

---

[55] Antonia Fraser, *The Weaker Vessel: Women's Lot in Seventeenth-century England* (London: Weidenfeld & Nicholson, 1984), 5, 147.

[56] Ward, "First Instruction" (1617), in Orchard, *Till God Will*, 58.

[57] Ward, "Memorial" (1622), in Orchard, *Till God Will*, 63–64.

[58] Peters, *World in Contemplation*, 319; Malone, *Women and Christianity*, vol. 3, 106.

in the Vatican.[59] This document, known as the *Informatio*, was a direct attack on Mary Ward's Institute and is very interesting for the light it sheds on the nature of the opposition.

The first thing that strikes a modern reader is that no attempt was made to establish whether what Mary Ward was seeking to do was in any way necessary. She was not attacked on grounds of irrelevance, or incompetence, or ineffectiveness. Seven 'offences' are listed, and they all relate to the fact that Mary Ward and her companions were women. Briefly, the offences are: (1) women have never before undertaken apostolic work and are not capable of it (2) an unenclosed female order is canonically forbidden (3) these women speak in public about religious matters even when priests are present (4) if women are not properly controlled they will fall into error (5) they "gad about" and frequent mixed society (6) these "idle and garrulous women" bring the Church into disrepute and (7) some of them have bad reputations and bring scandal on the Church. The writer produces no concrete instances of misbehaviour and the language used (for example, *muliercola*, 'little woman') betrays the thinking behind the *Informatio*: preconceived ideas about the role of women in Church and society, and a sense of the natural order of things being threatened by this innovation. As Joan Chittister points out, if women were admitted to be spiritually adult and capable of governing themselves, the entire system of male jurisdiction over women religious would be called into question.[60] It was this perceived threat that forced Mary Ward to choose between bowing to the pressure to conform or pursuing the task she believed God to have laid on her. With her, once 'the will of God' was in question, there could be no hesitation: if conformity meant abandoning the task, she would not conform.

In the *Informatio* William Harrison expresses surprise that the Jesuits should be taking an interest in these women (whom he frequently, and contemptuously, refers to as 'Jesuitesses') in contravention of their Constitutions, which forbade the Society to undertake the spiritual direction of nuns. This surprise is somewhat disingenuous, the intention being to discredit both the Institute and the Society by association. In seeking to adopt the Jesuit rule, Mary Ward had inadvertently

---

[59] Littlehales, *Pilgrim and Mystic*, 111.
[60] Joan Chittister OSB, "Mary Ward: Women and Leadership", in *Journey into Freedom*, 60.

embroiled her Institute in the quarrel then raging between the Jesuits and the secular priests (those not belonging to an order) in England. The hostility arose in part because the arrival of the Jesuits from 1580 onwards was perceived by the state as an attempt by a foreign power to infiltrate the country, and was therefore deemed by the politically less controversial secular priests to endanger the fragile accommodation which Catholics hoped to reach with the state. They also resented the fact that until 1598 they had been under the direction of the Society of Jesus.[61] In this climate of animosity, the appearance of a group of women wishing to associate themselves with the Jesuits must have seemed to the seculars to provide them with timely ammunition with which to attack both the Jesuits and the 'Jesuitesses'. This was ironic, because although since her 1611 revelation Mary Ward and her companions had been living according to the *Formula Instituti* of the Society, and though individual Jesuits encouraged and supported her, there was no formal link between the Institute and the Society. Indeed, the 1611 revelation had not concluded with the words "Take the same of the Society" but had continued, "Father General will never permit it. Go to him".[62] This was borne out in practice in 1612 when the then General of the Society, Claudio Aquaviva, forbade the Belgian Jesuits to direct her order; it had in any case been opposed from the start by the English Jesuits in St Omer. So the Institute was attacked for its links with the Jesuits, while the Jesuits themselves refused to countenance any official connection.[63]

In 1617, well before her journey to Rome and the opposition she met there, something had occurred that forced Mary to confront the inherent misogyny of the Church and to articulate her own position on the capacities of women. While she was away in England, the community in St Omer was thrown into confusion by the remark of a Jesuit to the effect that although the members of the Institute were experiencing success at that present time, they were bound to fail in the long term because "fervour will decay and when all is done, they are but women".[64] In response to this, and to encourage those of her companions who felt themselves and their work to be seriously undermined by this comment,

---

[61] Hsia, *World of Catholic Renewal*, 84.
[62] Ward to John Gerard SJ, 1619, in Littlehales, *Pilgrim and Mystic*, 64.
[63] For the attitude of the Jesuits to Mary Ward's Institute, see Peters, *World in Contemplation*, 118–22.
[64] Ward, "First Instruction" (1617), in Orchard, *Till God Will*, 56.

she wrote three "Instructions", which are usually referred to, collectively, as the "But Women conferences".[65] In a robust repudiation of such a negative opinion of women, Mary argued that

> There is no such difference between men and women…it is not *veritas hominum*, the verity of men, nor the verity of women, but *veritas Domini*, and this verity women may have as well as men.

For Mary, the success of her venture depended on the truth (*veritas*) of God, not on that of human beings, and this truth was as accessible to women as to men—an idea by no means widely accepted at the time, as witness the remark (already quoted) of an unnamed priest, overheard by Mary Ward, that "a woman could not apprehend God".[66] She also points out the error of supposing that service to God hinges on feelings; both male and female religious, she contends, can lose their original enthusiasm because, when the initial feelings of "sweetness" and "content" accompanying their entry into religious life inevitably fade,

> God seeming to leave them, they think that they have lost their fervour. This also is a lie, since they may have fervour in aridity, fervour not being placed in the feelings but in a will to do well, which women may have as well as men.

She refuses to accept that women are incapable of achieving great things and indeed pinpoints with devastating accuracy the true obstacle to such achievement: that women will internalize society's low opinion of them, which then becomes a self-fulfilling prophecy. Having accepted that some roles, such as the priesthood, are not open to women, she continues:

> [I]n all other things, wherein are we so inferior to other creatures that they should term us 'but women'? As if we were in all things inferior to some other creation, which I suppose to be men! Which I dare be bold to say is a lie, and, with respect to the good Father, may say it is an error.
>
> I would to God that all men understood this verity, that women, if they will, may be perfect, and if they would not make us believe we can do nothing and that we are 'but women', we might do great matters.

She argues that holiness is as possible for women as for men:

---

[65] The text of the "But Women conferences" can be found in Orchard, *Till God Will*, 56–60.

[66] Ward, "First Instruction" (1617), in Orchard, *Till God Will*, 58.

Therefore I must and ever will stand for this verity: that women may be perfect and that fervour must not necessarily decay because we are women. Women may be perfect as well as men, if they love verity and seek true knowledge.

Aware that some men regard her and her companions as a sort of freak show, an aberrant example of female achievement that is nevertheless doomed to ultimate failure, she contrasts this view with what she imagines is the attitude of God and the angels:

> You [the members of her Institute] are spectacles to God, angels and men. It is certain God has looked on you as he never looked upon any.... The angels, we may believe, look upon you and upon all other creatures according to the will of God. Men, you know, look diversely upon you...Some thinking we are women and aiming at greater matters than was ever thought women capable of, they expect perhaps to see us fail, or fall short, in many things. Others esteem us 'but women' and, with a kind of emulation that we should compass and bring about things beyond the limit of such weak creatures as they have ever esteemed women to be, expect to see our fervour decay, and all come to nothing, ourselves to shame and confusion.

For Mary Ward, gender is not relevant to the spiritual life. This is contrary to the thinking of the Catholic Church, which had long identified women with the sexual temptation of men[67] and advised them to desexualize themselves in order to obtain sanctity.[68] Mary insisted that the success of her venture ultimately depended not on human qualities, gendered or otherwise, but on God, and the failure to trust God is the only obstacle they should fear:

> The other day, disputing with a father who loves you well, I could not make him think otherwise than that women are yet by nature full of fears and affections, more than men, which, with respect to him, is not so. It is true if we will not place our knowledge right, we shall be full of fears and affections. We shall fear that which is not to be feared and, remaining in troubles, love and adhere to that which is not worthy of love. We know that God only is to be feared and he only is worthy of love. Remember then that he be the end of all your actions and therein you will find great satisfaction and think all things easy and possible.

---

[67] Malone, *Women and Christianity*, vol. 3, 22–23.

[68] Marina Warner, *Alone of All her Sex: The Myth and the Cult of the Virgin Mary* (London: Pan Books, 1985), 73.

Even if Mary had thought it appropriate to advance these arguments in the decade after 1621, during which she appealed in person and by letter to curial cardinals and to Urban VIII (the reigning pope during most of this period), they would have carried no weight. The Council of Trent (1545–63) had decreed the enclosure of all female religious, including those hitherto exempt. Behind this lies a deep-seated sexual anxiety: women represented a threat to clerical holiness, which was equated with sexual purity.[69] As Ulrike Strasser points out in her essay on the forced enclosure of a German convent, this attitude was not confined to the Catholic Church. The fear of unsupervised women was also strong in Protestantism, which regarded convents as "camouflaged brothels", and she suggests that this insinuation may in fact have influenced Trent in its decree.[70] The contemporary Italian saying, *o muro o marito* (either a [convent] wall or a husband)[71] well expresses the perceived need for male control of women. With respect to women's religious congregations, this attitude issued in the enforcement of cloister. In the early sixteenth century there had been the beginnings of a move away from strict enclosure. As already noted, in 1535 Angela Merici had founded the Ursulines, an uncloistered, unhabited teaching order. However, after the Council of Trent had reaffirmed the thirteenth-century rules of enclosure, they had to wear habits and live in convents and, eventually, along with other innovating orders, had to accept full enclosure in order to survive. The intransigence of the Vatican in this matter is well demonstrated by a remark made apropos of Mary Ward's Institute by Francesco Ingoli, the Secretary of Propaganda in the Curia, to the effect that regardless of what the times demanded, the law of the Church on enclosure must be observed.[72] Forced on to the defensive by such attitudes, it was inevitable that Mary would be regarded as 'disobedient' when she sought to mobilize women in the cause of the Church in England.

During the decade from 1621 to 1631, Mary Ward did not only expend much energy in promoting the cause of her Institute, she also opened a school in Rome, in order to demonstrate to the cardinals the

---

[69] Hsia, *World of Catholic Renewal*, 34.

[70] Ulrike Strasser, "Bones of Contention: Catholic Nuns Resist Their Enclosure", in *Unspoken Worlds: Women's Religious Lives*, ed. Nancy Auer Falk and Rita M. Gross (Belmont, CA: Wadsworth/Thomson Learning, 2001), 211.

[71] Littlehales, *Pilgrim and Mystic*, 109.

[72] Mary Margarita O'Connor IBVM, *That Incomparable Woman* (Montreal: Palm Publishers, 1962), 106.

importance of her educational work, and travelled extensively in Italy and elsewhere in Europe, founding communities in Cologne and Trier (1620–21), Naples (1623), Perugia (1624), Munich and Vienna (1627), and Pressburg (i.e., Bratislava, 1628).[73] Many of these journeys were made on foot, as indeed was the original one from St Omer to Rome in 1621, by a woman in almost constant, severe pain from gallstones. But in the end all was, or appeared to be, in vain. From 1628 houses of the Institute began to be suppressed, though, bizarrely, Mary was not informed of this; nor did she see a copy of the 1631 Bull of Suppression until after she had been imprisoned for heresy and then released.[74] The Bull is shocking in its language: Mary Ward's Institute is described as "poisonous growths in the Church" and a "pretended Congregation" which is "null and void and of no authority or importance". It continues:

> [W]e totally and completely suppress and extinguish them, subject them to perpetual abolition and remove them entirely from the Holy Church of God; we destroy and annul them, and we wish and command all the Christian faithful to regard and repute them as suppressed, extinct, rooted out, destroyed and abolished.[75]

The violence of expression is perhaps a measure of the threat that these independent women were felt to pose to the Church; certainly, they were seen as challenging the rightful order of things by undertaking "works which are most unsuited to their weak sex and character, to female modesty and particularly to maidenly reserve".[76] The members of the suppressed Institute were exhorted to enter instead "some order of nuns that has been approved by the said Holy See", in which they will be able to "give edification with innocent hands and pure hearts in the assiduous performance of spiritual works".[77]

For a less determined, or less inspired, woman this would have spelled the end of her venture. But Mary Ward's primary motivation was not her own ambition, or love of her own project, but the conviction that the task had been entrusted to her by God and that God would not let it fail. Under house arrest in a convent in Munich, in very insalubrious conditions and in extremely poor health (at one point her death

---

[73] Susan O'Brien, "Mary Ward" in *ODNB*.
[74] Malone, *Women and Christianity*, vol. 3, 108–9.
[75] Bull of Suppression (1631), in Wright, *Mary Ward's Institute*, 191.
[76] Wright, *Mary Ward's Institute*, 191.
[77] Wright, *Mary Ward's Institute*, 193.

was daily expected), she kept in touch with those of her companions who remained faithful by means of letters written in lemon juice on the paper used to wrap supplies that were sent in to her. In one of these she wrote:

> Who knows what God has determined by these accidents? Truly, neither they [her enemies] nor I, nor do I desire to know or have other than his will....be merry and doubt not our dear Master.[78]

Mary was released after nine weeks and exonerated by Urban VIII himself of the charge of heresy, though Peters argues that the extant accounts of this event may be unreliable in their details.[79] Mary in fact (perhaps naively) never really believed that the pope had consented to the harsh measures taken against her;[80] it is certainly true that after her release Urban permitted her and her companions to live in Rome in a private capacity and to continue their educational work there as lay-women engaged in charitable activities, though the Institute remained suppressed.[81]

Mary left Rome for the last time in 1637 and travelled by slow stages to England, arriving in London in 1639. The outbreak of the Civil War forced her to leave the capital in 1642 and she at last returned to her native Yorkshire with, among others, Mary Poyntz, Winefrid Wigmore, and Frances Bedingfield, all of whom had been her companions for many years. There, in Heworth, just outside York, she died in 1645, her life's work apparently in ruins. Her last words to her companions were, "God will assist and help you; it is no matter the who but the what. And when God shall enable me to be in place, I will serve you".[82]

Three small groups of women—in England, Rome, and Bavaria—kept Mary Ward's vision alive. Despite the Bull of Suppression, the Institute survived, in part because its educational undertakings were valued by the authorities in the localities.[83] It experienced many vicissitudes over the succeeding centuries, but one event, the Apostolic Constitution *Quamvis Justo*, issued in 1749 by Benedict XIV, deserves mention. This document draws a distinction between the 'Jesuitesses'

---

[78] Ward, letter from prison, 14 February 1631, in Orchard, *Till God Will*, 107.
[79] Peters, *World in Contemplation*, 587.
[80] Elizabeth Cotton [Mary Ward's secretary], letter to the Institute members, February 1631, in Orchard, *Till God Will*, 103.
[81] Orchard, *Till God Will*, 113, 115.
[82] Letter of Mary Poyntz, 1645, in Orchard, *Till God Will*, 121.
[83] Wright, *Mary Ward's Institute*, 76.

suppressed in 1631 and what it calls the 'English Virgins' and decrees that these 'English Virgins' must not call Mary Ward their foundress nor honour her name in any way.[84] As a consequence of this, the tradition of Mary Ward as foundress was glossed over by the Institute and eventually almost forgotten, while much archival material was destroyed or hidden[85]—though fortunately the *Painted Life*, a series of fifty paintings from the seventeenth and eighteenth centuries depicting events from Mary's life and also charting her spiritual journey, was preserved in Germany and can now be seen at the order's provincial house in Augsburg.[86] Knowledge of *Quamvis Justo* was slow to reach England, and in the nineteenth century even the nuns of the Bar Convent in York (founded in 1686 by one of Mary Ward's companions, Frances Bedingfield) were unaware that Mary Ward had ever been connected with their Institute of the Blessed Virgin Mary (IBVM), as it was by then known.[87] But gradually the climate of opinion within the Church was changing, as society's attitudes towards women changed. The nineteenth century saw an explosion of unenclosed women's orders, founded to carry out active apostolic work, such as teaching and nursing, and the Institute was able to benefit from this. It had continued to grow and flourish both in England and on the Continent, and was eventually confirmed by the Roman Catholic Church in 1877, although Mary was not officially recognized as foundress until 1909. In 1978 the full Jesuit Constitutions, about which Mary had received a revelation in 1611, were granted to the Institute,[88] and what may perhaps be the final chapter in the story was written in 2003, when the Institute of the Blessed Virgin Mary was permitted to change its name to that desired for it by Mary Ward herself. It is now known as the Congregation of Jesus.[89]

Mary Ward did not set out to be a radical. Indeed she never thought of herself as one, insisting rather that she was "a true and obedient servant of Holy Church".[90] Her activities, however, were regarded with deep suspicion by that Church and resulted in her being imprisoned for heresy and in the suppression of the Institute she had founded. The language of the Bull of Suppression leaves no doubt that what Mary

---

[84] *Quamvis Justo* (1749), in Wright, *Mary Ward's Institute*, 203–4.
[85] Wright, *Mary Ward's Institute*, 77.
[86] O'Brien, *ODNB*.
[87] Wright, *Mary Ward's Institute*, 134–35.
[88] Wright, *Mary Ward's Institute*, 166.
[89] Gemma Simmonds CJ, "Recognition at last", *The Tablet* (7 Feb 2004): 11.
[90] Mary Ward to the Holy Office, 1631, in Orchard, *Till God Will*, 111.

was seeking to do was considered highly dangerous and subversive. To present-day minds the founding of a religious Institute for women, to engage in education and other charitable works and with a special ministry to the persecuted Catholics of seventeenth-century England, does not sound particularly heretical, but in the context of the time it posed a serious challenge to many of the assumptions of the Church, specifically those assumptions pertaining to the nature and role of women, and made a 'radical' of a woman whose only desire was to follow what she perceived to be the will of God in ensuring the survival of the Catholic Church in England.

Bibliography

Chadwick, Owen. *The Reformation*. Harmondsworth: Penguin, 1990.

Chambers, Mary Catherine, IBVM. *The Life of Mary Ward*. Volume 1. London, 1882.

Chase, Martin. "When God is Sought Sincerely: Mary Ward and Dorothy Day". In *Journey into Freedom: Essays in Honour of the Fourth Centenary of Mary Ward's Birth*. Supplement 53. *The Way* (Summer 1985): 119–28.

Chittister, Joan, OSB. "Mary Ward: Women and Leadership". In *Journey into Freedom: Essays in Honour of the Fourth Centenary of Mary Ward's Birth*. Supplement 53. *The Way* (Summer 1985): 59–66.

Cover, Jeanne, IBVM. *Love, the Driving Force: Mary Ward's Spirituality*. Milwaukee: Marquette University Press, 1997.

Crawford, Patricia. *Women and Religion in England, 1500–1700*. London and New York: Routledge 1996.

Fletcher, Anthony. "Women's Spiritual Experience". In *Gender and Christian Religion*. Edited by R. N. Swanton. Woodbridge, Suffolk: Boydell Press for the Ecclesiastical History Society, 1998.

Fraser, Antonia. *The Weaker Vessel: Woman's Lot in Seventeenth-Century England*. London: Weidenfeld & Nicholson, 1984.

Hsia, R. Po-Chia. *The World of Catholic Renewal 1540–1770*. 2nd ed. Cambridge: Cambridge University Press, 2005.

Littlehales, Margaret Mary, IBVM. *Mary Ward, Pilgrim and Mystic 1585–1645*. Tunbridge Wells: Burns & Oates, 1998.

Malone, Mary T. *Women and Christianity*. Vol. 3. *From the Reformation to the 21st Century*. Blackrock, Co. Dublin: Columba Press, 2003.

Martin, Randall. *Women Writers in Renaissance England*. London and New York: Longman, 1997.

Mullett, Michael A. *The Catholic Reformation*. London and New York: Routledge, 1999.

O'Brien, Susan. "Mary Ward". *Oxford Dictionary of National Biography*. Oxford: Oxford University Press, 2004.

O'Connor, Mary Margarita, IBVM. *That Incomparable Woman*. Montreal: Palm Publishers, 1962.

Orchard, Gillian, IBVM. *Till God Will: Mary Ward Through Her Writings*. London: Darton, Longman & Tod, 1985.

Peters, Henriette, IBVM. *Mary Ward: A World in Contemplation*. Leominster: Gracewing, 1994.

Simmonds, Gemma, CJ. "Recognition at Last". *The Tablet*. 7 Feb 2004.

Strasser, Ulrike. "Bones of Contention: Catholic Nuns Resist Their Enclosure". In *Unspoken Worlds: Women's Religious Lives*. Edited by Nancy Auer Falk and Rita M. Gross. Belmont, CA: Wadsworth/Thomson Learning, 2001.

Turner, Mary Daniel. "Women and Power". *Journey into Freedom: Essays in Honour of the Fourth Centenary of Mary Ward's Birth*. Supplement 53. *The Way* (Summer 1985): 104–18.

Warner, Marina. *Alone of All Her Sex: The Myth and Cult of the Virgin Mary*. London: Pan Books, 1985.

Wright, Mary, IBVM. *Mary Ward's Institute: The Struggle for Identity*. Sydney: Crossing Press, 1997.

CHERCHEZ LA FEMME: RADICAL RELIGION IN THE LIFE AND POETRY OF LUISA DE CARVAJAL

José Manuel González

> "Try always to take not the easiest path but the hardest".
> John of the Cross, *Ascent of Mount Carmel.*

The Counter-Reformation called for internal renewal as a reaction against the Lutheran emphasis on the role of faith and God's grace and against Protestant teaching on the number and nature of the sacraments. The disciplinary reforms of the Council of Trent attacked the corruption of the clergy and set out new prescriptions about pastoral care and the administration of the sacraments. In this context, new religious orders and groups were founded to effect the renewal. Not only male orders like the Jesuits but also female ones like the reformed Carmelites were established in Spain to follow the doctrine of the new Tridentine spirit. This led to a great increase in the number of female vocations. To become a sister was regarded as a way of achieving self-fulfilment and spiritual perfection. The convent provided young women with everything they needed to accomplish their religious goal. It also played a fundamental role in their intellectual and spiritual training. Communal reading and writing were part of the daily activities which gave them a humanist and literary education. The life of Sor Marcela de San Félix (1605–1688), an illegitimate daughter of Lope de Vega, provides a good example of this. She inherited her father's literary gifts. Her poems, which are a detailed reflection on daily life in the convent, reveal secular interests in the context of spiritual observance.

Life in the convent was regulated by the patriarchal hierarchy of the Church, which was the censor of religion and culture. The Roman Inquisition was established to combat heresy, to defend the Catholic faith from the attacks of the Reformers, and to punish esoteric and occult activities as well as the type of radical mysticism to be seen in Sor Luisa de la Ascensión (1565–1648), who was prosecuted by the Holy Office in 1634 for being one of the foolish illuminati. In "Romance de la Soledad del alma" (Romance of the Solitude of the Soul) she writes of her union with the divine in extreme emotional terms. Her poetry is powerful, visual, and natural, showing a concern with space, since her desire to be possessed by the divine spouse is related to different locations.

The Counter-Reformation spirit had its best expression in the devotional poetry of women throughout the seventeenth century. However, poetry was used not only as an expression of their Christian faith but also as a subversive and transgressive means of female resistance to male control, and as a denial of fixed gender roles. It succeeded in legitimising female self-expression by the construction of female subjectivity in a context where knowledge and literary activity were seen as potentially dangerous commodities carefully controlled by men. This chapter will discuss the radical poetry and life of Luisa de Carvajal who, although not following the career path of an enclosed nun, dedicated her life to propagating the Counter-Reformation in England.

Luisa de Carvajal was born on 2 January 1566 in Jaraicejo. After being orphaned at the age of six, she was under the tutelage of María Chacón, her great-aunt, who was chambermaid to Philip II's two daughters. As a child, Luisa wished to sacrifice her life to Christ and to pursue a missionary vocation. After her aunt's death, she went to Pamplona where she lived with her mother's brother, Francisco Hurtado de Mendoza, and studied literature and theology. As she resolutely refused to marry, she assembled a little community devoted to prayer. It was not until early 1605 that her Jesuit confessor allowed her to fulfil her desire of setting out for England. On arriving in London, she spent her time visiting Catholics in prison, and going to the houses of others in danger of persecution. Her life attracted the attention of the authorities, as it was said that she was doing more to convert Protestants than twenty priests. On two occasions she was arrested; on each occasion she was released at the insistence of the Spanish ambassador. Attempts were then made by the Ambassador to procure her removal from England. These would probably have succeeded in the end, had they not been prevented by her death. This occurred on her forty-sixth birthday, shortly after her imprisonment for creating a public disturbance in defence of her faith.

A major emphasis of the Counter-Reformation was an ongoing missionary endeavour in parts of the world that had been colonized by Spain. However, there were also attempts to reconvert countries that had once been Roman Catholic. Luisa de Carvajal y Mendoza, a writer and missionary moved by the execution of the English Jesuit

Henry Walpole, decided to devote herself to the cause of the Catholic faith in England. For that purpose she made a journey from Valladolid, through France, and across the English Channel to Dover, where she landed on 2 May 1605. In London she established herself under the protection of the Spanish ambassador to facilitate her activities in a hostile country. She confessed that her vocation to re-convert the English had been an obsession since she was a child.[1] She worked in London as a teacher, missionary, and leader of charitable work for the poor. She was also engaged in a wide range of subversive activities that eventually led King James I to order her return to Spain. For her, the Christian faith meant taking sides and engaging in the propagation of Catholic doctrine through charity and the overthrow of the existing order.

Luisa de Carvajal's life and writings cannot be fully understood without some knowledge of her stay in England, where her subversive spirit was fully manifested during the time of the Gunpowder Plot and in subsequent years. Her activity should be viewed as a form of protest in the historical context of the Plot. Her connection with the Jesuits goes back to the time that she spent in Valladolid, where she became acquainted with them. In her letters we find her involvement with and support of the Jesuit cause that led to the Gunpowder Plot, one of the most dramatic assassination attempts in history and one of the most significant acts of early modern terrorism. A conspiracy of English Roman Catholics planned to blow up Parliament, King James I, the Queen, and their oldest son. The leader, Robert Catesby, together with his four fellow conspirators were angered by James's refusal to grant further religious toleration. The conspirators rented a cellar that extended under the palace at Westminster. There Guy Fawkes concealed over 20 barrels of gunpowder to detonate at the opening of the English Parliament on 5 November 1605. They hoped that the confusion that would follow would provide an opportunity for English Catholics to take over the country, leaving England open to foreign invasion, to re-conversion to Roman Catholicism, and to a brutal struggle for its survival as an independent nation.

However, as the Plot failed, the persecution of Catholics increased. After the conspiracy, Luisa de Carvajal was hidden by Catholic families

---

[1] Albert J. Loomie, "Guy Fawkes in Spain: 'The Spanish Treason'", in *Spanish Documents*, ed. A. J. Loomie (London: University of London, Institute of Historical Research, 1971), 4–5.

and in the Spanish embassy, where she spent several months learning English and preparing herself for her missionary enterprise. Her
connection with and support of the Jesuits continued throughout the
years she was in London. The Jesuit part in the Plot had an immediate
influence on her life. Her activities were mainly devoted to denouncing
English heresy and to missionary and charitable work. De Carvajal
herself depicts the atmosphere of tension, insecurity, and even violence
that existed for Catholics in London where there were frequent raids
to find not only priests but any Catholic, and the charge was one of
high treason:

> At any hour of day and night they attack them out of the blue, at dinner.
> Or supper or in bed. If a 'Credo' is slow in coming when the doors are
> opened, they bring up the first officers from the street, who break down
> the door. For the most part they are bailiffs in the service of the false
> bishops, insolent, and villainous, without any other job or other income
> except what they obtain in this way; and the authorities and neighbours
> are with them and give them all the help they can.[2]

Once more de Carvajal expresses her scorn at the Anglican faith and
authority when she refers to "the false bishops". In this context of
confrontation and religious turmoil she visited Catholic prisoners in
every London prison where they were housed, as she had easy access
to them except in the Tower.

De Carvajal's view of England is negative. Her disgust for every
aspect of English life is a repetitive theme that is omnipresent in her
biography and writings. This may hint at the deep pain and sorrow
that she suffered while she was in such a "wretched land, hateful in
every way",[3] a land full of basilisks and beasts. It was a daily struggle
for her to remain in such a permanent state of tension in a place that
she greatly abhorred. Her longing from childhood to be a martyr for
her faith led to suffering that had a triple dimension: physical, psychological, and spiritual. Physical, as she could not stand the English
weather (her death may have been due to a respiratory illness which
followed shortly after her imprisonment in 1613). Psychological, since
living in England with the English, whom she greatly disliked, distressed
her spirits, and yet, paradoxically, she was also worried that she might

---

[2] In Margaret, A. Rees, *The Writings of Doña Luisa de Carvajal y Mendoza, Catholic Missionary to James I's London* (Lewiston: The Edwin Mellen Press, 2002), 22.
[3] Rees, *Writings*, 14.

be expelled—and therefore unable to complete her work and her mission—at any time. To undertake her missionary activity in those circumstances was hard work, requiring great effort and determination, which she found through her religious commitment. Finally, it was a spiritual martyrdom as she could not achieve her goal of re-converting England to the Catholic creed.

Luisa de Carvajal's life was a reflection of women's aspirations. It was a daily struggle to achieve personal promotion and social acceptance within a patriarchal society designed to keep women away from public life and in a state of subordination and inferiority. Luisa de Carvajal showed that women could be as powerful as and intellectually equal to men, more perceptive, and wittier. She did not merely repeat the traditional women's lament but showed awareness of what being a woman meant historically as well as the realisation that something might be done to improve the situation of women in early modern Spain. She does not represent the society and religion of her day, as she rises above most of her generation—a strong woman ready to overcome all difficulties and to suffer all adversities with patience. Her life became meaningful in a patriarchal world where women were not allowed to fulfil their expectations. Within this negative context, Luisa de Carvajal and other female writers, like Sor Juana Inés de la Cruz (1651–1695), made possible a new construct of the feminine beyond the traditional gender barriers. They wrote about new ways of experiencing the feminine "through which resistance to gendered forms of subordination and oppression were articulated",[4] though this female opposition must be understood within a context where women still suffered from social oppression as they were marginalized by a patriarchy that tried to maintain its predominance at any cost.

However, the key question is whether the activities of Luisa de Carvajal can be labelled as subversive or dissident or not, since her female agency was never contested. Moreover, in analysing her attitude and ability we should consider that Spanish women lived in a dual system, as patriarchy coexisted with matriarchy. If patriarchy privileged all men, matriarchy did the same with women who could make decisions for themselves. But Luisa de Carvajal's life and writings are transgressive in a different way, as she constructed a new form of experiencing the

---

[4] Jean E. Howard, "Was There a Renaissance Feminism?", in *A Companion to English Renaissance Literature and Culture*, ed. M. Hattaway (Oxford: Blackwell, 2000), 651.

feminine beyond the limits permitted. In this case, transgression not only meant to oppose male power or criticise patriarchal impositions, but to create and develop a female subjectivity that allowed a new way of being a woman, appropriating male strategies in order to facilitate the construction of a female self. Luisa's missionary activity was also an instrument to fulfil the roles she was expected to play as a woman and to get rid of the inner tension between her personal freedom and social constraint. In her charitable passion for others she discovered herself as a woman in a more rewarding manner than she might have expected.

Her experience exemplified how women could lead a life of their own beyond the different forms of submission to, and dependency on, the patriarchal systems of family, church, and state which excluded women from public life. She was able to fight male authority. She persisted in defying religious and political power in her struggle for subjectivity. In this way, her persistence in overcoming continuous opposition to the expression of her religious and literary vocation is similar to that shown by Teresa de Ávila. Her religious vocation shaped her life and poetry from the beginning. Her only interest and ambition was to help those who suffered persecution because of their Catholic affiliation. She longed to die as a martyr to the Catholic cause in England, a Protestant country where Catholics were persecuted. Life was a crusade for her as she followed the Hapsburg rulers' determination to fight Protestantism. Thus her religious zeal became a political issue.

For her, the personal and religious became public and political matter. Given the prominence and influence of the Mendoza family—Spain's richest, most noble family—Luisa's actions and decisions, like those of the other Mendoza women, had "a public significance far beyond their own circles of social intercourse". Her life, activity, and convent "served as public arenas in which [she] operated".[5] She became an activist in a crusade of her own in a hostile country that she hated (as she showed on several occasions). Her missionary zeal might have been due to her resistance to the dominance of male power for "the question of woman's desire runs parallel to the question of power".[6]

---

[5] Helen Nader, "Introduction: The World of the Mendozas", in *Power and Gender in Renaissance Spain*, ed. H. Nader (Urbana and Chicago: Illinois University Press, 2004), 2.

[6] Jessica Benjamin, "A Desire of One's Own: Psychoanalytic Feminism and Intersubjective Space", in *Feminist Studies: Critical Studies*, ed. Teresa de Lauretis (Bloomington: Indiana University Press, 1986), 87.

Her subversive activity caused a great scandal even for King James I, who could not understand why a woman of her rank had chosen to live in a foreign country that she hated. Her missionary work can be seen as her way of opposing undervalued female subjectivity and conquering a territory reserved for men. Perhaps she used it to transcend the opposition between genders.

Luisa de Carvajal's lifestyle caused confusion, as she undermined the traditional social order where patriarchal ideology prevailed over feminist claims to equality and promotion. She challenged a world picture in need of change as she showed new possibilities for which women were longing. Her life, from beginning to end, was critical of a historical situation which limited the education of women and reduced them to traditional domestic roles. She was determined to reject her family's proposals of marriage in favour of her missionary zeal for re-converting the English. She made clear her resolution to devote her life to it. She decided to cross the line which divided freedom and self-assertion from alienation and subordination as represented by the authoritarian figure of Don Francisco Hurtado de Mendoza, the uncle with whom she was sent to live when she was ten years old. She was successful in her pursuit of being herself and doing it in her own way without relying, as she might have done, on the advantages of class. She chose the emancipation of leading a different life, being herself instead of just doing housework or enjoying happy days at the Madrid court whose grandeur she openly scorns in "Spiritual Ballad":[7]

> Dos millones de fatigas:
> las unas sobredoradas
> y llenas de amargo acíbar,
> y las otras plateadas
> y por dentro vacías...
> trazas, lisonjas, mentiras,
> intereses, pretensiones,
> temores, melancolías
> correspondencias y amigos
> compuestos de mil falsías...
>
> [Two million troubles:
> some gilded and full

---

[7] *Doña Luisa de Carvajal y Mendoza. Epistolario y poesías*, ed. Jesús González Marañón, Biblioteca de Autores Españoles, vol. 179 (Madrid: Atlas, 1965), Poem 6. All poems are taken from this edition. The translations of the poems are by Rees, *Writings*, 104–93.

of bitter aloes,
and others silver plated
and empty inside...
façades, flattery, lies,
self-interest, pretensions,
fears, bouts of melancholy,
dealings and friends
made up of a thousand acts
of disloyalty.]

She was a nonconformist at the Hapsburg court in spite of her closeness
to royal figures such as her great-aunt Doña María Chacón, lady-in-wait-
ing to the Infantas. One of the most fascinating aspects of de Carvajal's
singular life is that she was an outsider in her own world. She did not
follow the social and courtly conventions of her time. She was neither
a wife nor just a nun. She was a missionary abroad and could be seen
as intruding into a social sphere that had traditionally been male.

Luisa de Carvajal's life and poetry are intimately connected with
Ignatian and Carmelite spirituality. Ignatius of Loyola's *The Spiritual
Exercises* shaped her religious vocation. In this manual of vital and
dynamic spirituality she found guidance and inspiration in her path
to self-fulfilment and salvation, which is achieved at the completion of
a journey of tests and "nights". She sought what Ignatius incessantly
sought: to do God's will. From girlhood she was wholly committed to
God's service, in a spirit of humility but with initiative and action. She
was ready to make her contribution to the universal mission of the
Church. She was resolved, with the grace of God, to be completely
free to seek and find His will in the disposition of her life. Thus she
became a contemplative in action. Many echoes of and references to
Ignatius's *Exercises* can be seen throughout her poems which use the
method of meditation. De Carvajal often uses Ignatian memory tech-
nique to facilitate her understanding of biblical events—particularly of
the Passion—imagining herself a part of these events both to facilitate
her familiarity with them and to achieve her decisions for the improvement of her life.

No less significant was the Carmelite influence. Of all the movements
in the Carmelite order, by far the most important was the reform initiated by Teresa of Ávila which became the discalced Carmelite order. In
spite of difficulties, Teresa of Ávila succeeded in establishing not only
new nunneries but also, with the cooperation of John of the Cross, a
number of friaries. The aim of the reform was to restore the austerity and contemplative character of primitive Carmelite life. From the

Jesuits and Carmelites, Luisa de Carvajal received human and spiritual support. Among her Carmelite correspondents we find Ana de Jesús, prioress of the monastery of Brussels, Mariana de San José, prioress of the Recoletas in Medina del Campo, and Inés de la Asunción. We know that the "Discalced Carmelites and the Augustinian Recollects attracted her". She might even have contemplated the possibility of entering into a Carmelite convent following the wishes of Don Francisco Hurtado de Mendoza, her uncle. However, "she fended off her uncle's growing anxiety to see her settled by claiming that she was unworthy to join those contemplative orders".[8] In her poetry there are many resonances with Teresa de Ávila and John of the Cross's *Cántico Espiritual*; for instance, in the military imagery which refers to the condition of the Christian who must be ready to fight sin in its different manifestations and to live in a permanent state of war in order to, finally, experience the joys of heaven. Spiritual warfare seemed to be the natural state of the Christian in his path to heaven. Arrows, wounds, tournaments, and warriors are some of these images and metaphors borrowed by Luisa de Carvajal which reflect the combative dimension of her life.[9]

De Carvajal's poetry is a reflection of her spiritual anxieties taken to their extremes. Her poems cannot be separated from her daily interests and preoccupations, as they express her most intimate aspirations and aims. They not only reveal her mystic commitment but also anticipate her missionary activity, which is the result of her Catholic faith. Her love for and marriage with Christ, the divine spouse, cannot be fully experienced without love and care for those in need. The spiritual and the missionary element fuse in her life and poetry. However, her poems show how the mystical experience is the most important thing for her. Here, her inner and most authentic self is revealed. Her contemplative vocation comes first, becoming the outstanding feature of her poetry

---

[8] Rees, *Writings*, 7.

[9] Examples of martial imagery include: arrows ("For then he laid me low there with a loving arrow, blessed for me since it pierced my heart" ["Silva's Spiritual Quatrains", 107]; "When the bow homes in on the target, the heart is pierced by its arrow" ["A Spiritual Lyric of Silva's", 141]); wounds ("Amid mortal wounds and extreme pains you live for love, and this life soothes and satisfies you" ["Spiritual Ballad", 117]); tournaments ("You know well, my sweet Treasure, that with his powerful hand in a fierce-fought duel Love overcame you, and spiritedly declared his lordship" ["Silva's Spiritual 'Quintillas'", 129]); warriors ("So as to wound the one who wounded him, Love, dying of love, drew an arrow from his quiver with which he would make a magnificent shot" ["Spiritual Ballad of Silva's", 149]). Pages and translations of Luisa de Carvajal's poems are taken from Rees's *Writings*.

and the most absorbing interest in her life. But her mystic state makes
her aware of the need to care for the corporal and spiritual welfare
of others. Everything she does is a direct consequence of her mystic
engagement with Christ. To love Christ implies helping the needy and
re-converting the English.

However, the difficulties of her life do not diminish her mystic aspirations. On the contrary, those troubles and sufferings increase her love
for Christ, her need of coming closer to Him and being comforted by
her Beloved One, as seen in "Spiritual Ballad of Silva's":

> Amor, el pecho animoso
> de Silva consideraba,
> que cien mil dificultades
> rompiendo, al mar se arrojaba.
> las apacibles riberas
> trueca por aguas saladas;...
> no teme las tempestades
> el mar, ni sus olas bravas,
> que van las del corazón...
> no la encantan las sirenas
> con su voz fingida y falsa,
> porque la tiene el amor
> toda absorta y traspasada,
> cuyos cuidados destierran
> todos los demás del alma...
> porque desde allí hasta el puerto
> adonde su Bien lo aguarda,
> casi siempre camina
> viento en popa y mar bonanza.

> [Love was contemplating the spirited Heart
> of Silva, who breaking through
> a hundred thousand obstacles,
> was throwing herself into the sea.
> she exchanges the calm shores
> for salty seas...
> she is not afraid of the tempests
> nor of its wild waves...
> the mermaids do not charm her
> with their false, deceitful voices,
> for she is entirely absorbed
> and engulfed in love,
> whose cares drive all others
> out of her heart...
> For from there to the port
> where her Beloved waits for her,

there is almost always a following wind
and a quiet sea.]

She (Silva) is well aware of the countless enormous difficulties of living her religious vocation. She confesses that she is forced to leave those quiet banks for troubled waters. The destructive and unbeatable power of the tempest at sea is used as a metaphor to express the hostility and adversity that characterized her life. The poem seems to be an anticipation of her journey and troublesome days in England. It also illustrates the three stages where the drama of de Carvajal's spiritual life is played out. From the heavenly landscape, where she experiences the joys of her relation with the glorious companion, she comes to those "salty waters" of trials that keep alive and inflame the fire of her burning passion and mystical love. Those earthly troubles do not take her away from her spiritual devotion as they are a consequence of the intensity of that relation that makes her engage with those in need of spiritual help and care. The danger of being absorbed and obsessed by her worldly mission disappears as she is taken up by divine love. She finally arrives at the harbour where Christ awaits her, without having been distracted by the "mermaids' songs". Fair weather comes after the tempest and rough sea.

Luisa de Carvajal has been considered one of the best women poets of the period,[10] though she has not had the recognition she deserves. Her poetry presents a remarkable portrait of a woman who aspired to experience a mystic union with God, in spite of suffering and the awareness of not being worthy of it. Her poetry is characterised by its mystic tone and endeavour. She is a writer compelled almost by nature to express her love for God. She followed the tradition of Teresa de Ávila and the Spanish mystics, who combined contemplation with practical outreach, as she came out to the streets of London to reconvert people to the Catholic faith. In this way we can say that her life was a constant transgression of the social conventions and rules of seventeenth-century Spain because, in spite of being a nun, she devoted her life and time to work outside the convent. She went beyond the acceptable limits of her religious status as her love for God needed to be expressed through her love for the others in the streets where she fulfilled her religious duty as a missionary.

---

[10] Ana Navarro, *Antología poética de escritoras de los siglos xvi y xvii* (Madrid: Castalia, 1989), 117.

Her oeuvre consists of about 50 poems. In her youthful poetry may be seen the inspiration that led her to follow a missionary life and seek hardship abroad. Most of these poems were in traditional form, though she also wrote sonnets in the Spanish way. To express her intense religious emotions, she often used metaphors and similes together with antitheses and conceits to render the complexity of her mystic experience as well as the contradictions and tension inherent in her poetry, since she tried to be worthy of divine love in spite of what she thought was her sinful condition.

Since the influential contribution of Anne J. Cruz to a more contemporary understanding of Luisa de Carvajal's religious and literary achievement, subjectivity has become a key concept for a fuller interpretation of her poetry. For Cruz, Carvajal's writings "speak eloquently not of martyrdom but of women's desire of another sort":

> On studying her writings from a feminist perspective, however, the question that arises is not whether Luisa de Carvajal ultimately achieved martyrdom for the Catholic faith...Carvajal's writings speak eloquently not of martyrdom, but of women's desire of another sort: for the subjectivity so often denied them and for which they must constantly negotiate with the dominant hierarchies on their numerous sites and crossings.[11]

She was not only a missionary in London whose "self-sacrificing toil had won her the right to enter the glorious company of martyrs".[12] In her biography, Luisa de Carvajal expresses her religious commitment; her letters refine the picture and reveal the complex religious tensions that defined and limited her identity in early modern Spain.

Her life and writings show how she both constitutes herself as female subject and is constituted by the dominant cultural system of Hapsburg Spain. The contradictions inherent in subject formation can be seen in her poetry, where we can see the tension between courtly and pious values. This tension arises from the desire for an autonomous position in a context where such an aim was difficult to achieve. Nonetheless, for the sake of autonomy, she abandoned her home and her country, rejecting the two options traditionally chosen by noblewomen in early modern Spain: marriage or life in a convent.

---

[11] Anne J. Cruz, "Willing Desire: Luisa de Carvajal y Mendoza and Female Subjectivity", in *Power and Gender in Renaissance Spain*, ed. Helen Nader (Urbana and Chicago: Illinois University Press, 2004), 177.

[12] Rees, *Writings*, 83.

The concept of subjectivity is a complex one in the context of early modern culture. The shift in ideas of the self that took place in Europe at the end of the fifteenth century facilitated the construction of a literary self that was both a fascinating adventure and a controversial issue, often contradictory and unstable. New constructions of the self struggled between the inheritance of earlier literary models and emergent forms of individualism. Subjectivity was considered as the expression of the individual conscience. It was constructed and conditioned by aspects that differ from our concept of the individual. By the beginning of the seventeenth century, new forms of individuality were striving to find expression and a more consistent shape, bringing about a lively dispute about the nature of the subject. Contradiction and instability were outstanding features of the subjectivity that shapes Luisa de Carvajal's poetry, whose voice consistently asserts itself against the social pressures of her time.

The influence of Augustine's construction of interiority on mystical poetry has been broadly discussed and confirmed as one of the origins of the strand of the Western spirituality that seeks God within. Augustine's ideas opened new ways of expressing the self. They were far more pervasive in the seventeenth century than one might think[13]—a driving force that compelled the subject-lover to live outside himself and join the beloved. The poems of Teresa de Ávila and John of the Cross have been regarded as the most elevated example of "the denial of the exterior world, and the internalizing of any perception, idea or feeling".[14] This internalization is an essential experience in mystical poetry, where divine love and human feeling merge, as the poetry of Luisa de Carvajal shows.[15]

Her poems follow certain conventions common to both secular and religious lyrics. In them we find variations on the topic of the absent lover. They also develop a sense of intimacy with erotic overtones in the expression of her love and passion for Christ. It is in her poetry that she articulates her private and spiritual self and is compelled to express her love for the divine. In her poems there are hints of her transgressive

---

[13] See Charles Taylor, *Sources of the Self: The Making of the Modern Identity* (Cambridge: Cambridge University Press, 1989), 131–41.

[14] Guillermo Serés, *La transformación de los amantes. Imágenes del amor desde la Antigüedad hasta el Siglo de Oro* (Barcelona: Crítica, 1996), 96.

[15] Pablo Jauralde, "La condición histórica del *Cántico espiritual*", *Edad de Oro* 9 (1992): 87–97.

spirit which will inspire and encourage her missionary work—a direct
consequence of the social and political contradictions within patriarchy
which create a space for "subversive ideas and dissident behaviour".[16]

The transgressive dimension of Luisa de Carvajal's life and writings
can be best seen in the appropriation of male activities. Preaching
was considered a male preserve. However, it was one of the best ways
for her to re-convert Londoners to the Catholic creed. She set out to
preach to anyone who came within hearing. This activity was a direct
challenge to men's professional control, and this challenge may also
be seen in the poem where Silva appears as a shepherdess in "Silva's
Spiritual Quatrains":

> –¿No encubras, Silva, tu Gloria!
> –Más dime: ¿por qué así dejas
> esparcidas las ovejas
> sin tener dellas memoria?

> Las ovejas que solías
> con tanto gusto guardar,
> que por las apacentar
> los peligros no temías,

> ni sabes si a la majada
> van, ni si van al ejido:
> ¿por qué las diste al olvido?
> ¡aun de ti estas olvidada

> [Silva do not hide your glory!
> But tell me: why do you leave your flocks
> scattered like this, without giving them a thought?

> Those sheep which you used
> to tend with such pleasure that
> you feared no dangers to let them feed

> Now you do not know
> whether they are roaming to the sheepfold or the
>   [common.

> Why have you forgotten them completely?
> you have even forgotten yourself!]

The instability of de Carvajal's subject position is echoed in her poetry
when she becomes Silva, a shepherdess in a natural landscape. In her

---

[16] Catherine R. Eskin, review of *Women in Early Modern England 1550–1729*, by Sarah
H. Mendelson and Patricia Crawford, *Sixteenth Century Journal* 30 (1999): 826.

"Spiritual Ballad by Silva", de Carvajal refers to Silva again as a shepherdess who "fled and left [her] cottage". She went out in search of her shepherd. And the cause was "that strange beauty that [she] saw one day in him who stole [her] heart".

It is a commonplace to find a shepherdess in pastoral poetry. But it is not so normal in a mystical or religious context where Christ is the only shepherd and the rest of his followers are his flock. Silva's appropriation of the role of shepherd suggests that women can carry out the same jobs as men. In this way, she introduces a new female role within a religious context where patriarchal ideology has traditionally prevailed over feminist claims of equality and promotion. Silva, de Carvajal's pseudonym in the poem, challenges a traditional picture in need of change. However, she is not a good shepherdess, as she "has forgotten [the sheep] completely". She doesn't know where her flock is. But there is an explanation. She has also forgotten about herself. She has been seduced by her "fair shepherd", becoming "his slave". Her invasion of the masculine sphere, which has led to an appropriation of masculine roles, has proved to be a failure as she realises that there is only one good shepherd who can take the flock to the right place and care for it.

De Carvajal has also been regarded as a conqueress who tried to gain new souls for the Catholic cause. She appropriated the spirit of conquest of those who went abroad to acquire new territories for the Spanish crown. Her life repeated the pattern that we find in those *conquistadores* who tried to colonise the world: she had the mission of re-converting Anglicans to Catholicism. She was impelled by "a desire for martyrdom" as she proclaims in her autobiography when writing of her wish to sacrifice her life to Christ since she was a young girl.[17] But her appropriation of male roles is taken to the extreme in "Silva's Spiritual Sonnet", dedicated to the Holy Eucharist, where "she transgenders the poetic voice, appropriating the figure of Christ":[18]

> De inmenso amor aqueste abrazo estrecho
> recibe, Silva, de tu dulce Amado,
> y por la puerta deste diestro lado
> éntrate, palomilla, acá en mi pecho.

---

[17] Camilo María Abad, *Una misionera española en la Inglaterra del siglo xvii. Doña Luisa de Carvajal y Mendoza 1566–1614* (Santander: Universidad Pontificia de Comillas, 1966), 128.

[18] Cruz, "Willing Desire", 183.

> Reposa en el florido y sacro lecho,
> y abrásate en amor tan abrasado,
> que hasta que el fuerte nudo haya apretado,
> no sea posible quede satisfecho.

> [Receive this close embrace of vast love, Silva,
> from your sweet Beloved,
> and enter into my breast, little dove,
> through the door in this my right side.

> Rest on the flower-strewn, holy bed,
> and burning such blazing love that
> until the strong knot has closed tight around you,
> you can never be satisfied.]

It is now Luisa—in a poetic appropriation of Christ's voice—who loves and cares for Silva who is invited to "Receive this close embrace...from [her] sweet Beloved". A passionate, erotic experience that will not be satisfied until death comes: it will be the beginning of everlasting love.

Many of de Carvajal's poems have idealized settings:

> the poet loses herself in the scents, sounds and sights that make up the secret garden where she walks with Christ...The scene glows with the whiteness of jasmine and lilies, the vivid colours of sunflowers, anemones, carnations, roses and violets...The fountain waters spring up to meet their Creator....[19]

These idealized settings can be read in the light of ecocriticism. In de Carvajal's poetry, the five senses are appealed to, and life is in harmony with its surroundings. The images of natural beauty present an idyllic landscape which facilitates those loving encounters and joys with the Beloved and which invites a retreat from the world to the countryside. The pastoral setting idealises rural life in contrast to the hard labour and hardships of daily life. It "includes within its celebration the consciousness of the very different present from which the restoration will be a release".[20] It expresses a kind of nostalgia for a state of being and feeling very different from her present condition and situation. For de Carvajal "ecological sainthood" becomes a refuge as it is in nature that her love for Christ can be fully experienced.[21]

---

[19] Rees, *Writings*, 78.

[20] J. Williams, *Wordsworth: Contemporary Critical Essays* (London: Macmillan, 1993), 18.

[21] See Greg Garrard, *Ecocriticism* (London: Routledge, 2004), 42.

Her poetry clearly shows the need for a peaceful nature in bloom and in splendour where man's greatest and most rewarding experiences can happen. De Carvajal was well acquainted with nature in her walks in the countryside near Pamplona and Almazán. She evokes them in "Silva's Spiritual Ballad" in which Nise relates a dream to Inés: "…we sometimes gazed at the pleasant meadow stretching out in extraordinary beauty; sometimes at the deep, crystalline waters of the Duero…".[22] To mysticise the natural environment is a direct consequence of her communion with nature. It was the ideal *locus* for her amorous encounters of mystic transcendence. Her evocation of a Paradise-garden becomes an obsession in her poetry: it is the location where those mystic encounters can take place.

The natural topography used by de Carvajal in her poetry has not only an aesthetic or literary dimension but a personal one as it seems to be the best way to express her feelings and state, her intimacy with and erotic attachment to Christ. But, in this case, the harmonious vision of a utopian nature is broken by the tension and pain she experiences in her search for the Holy Shepherd.

De Carvajal's poems not only refer to familiar religious places like the convent but to different open spaces like gardens or orchards where she can feel free from any constraint and enjoy loving encounters with the divine spouse. But she knows the difficulty of obtaining freedom and being herself. She is very much aware of the suffering and difficulty of being free as her repetitive references to imprisonment show in, for example, "A Spiritual Ballad by Silva":

> ¡Ay, si entre los lazos fieros
> que a mi gloria aprisionaron
> por mi libertad, yo viera
> enlazar mi cuello y manos!
> pero si es atrevimiento,
> porque esos son sacrosantos,
> e indigna toda criatura
> de adornos tan soberanos;
> concédeme, Amor, siquiera
> (pues en dar no eres escaso)
> algunas dulces prisiones
> que le parezcan en algo.

---

[22] Rees, *Writings*, 187.

[Oh, if those same cruel bonds
that imprisoned my glory
to gain my freedom, could bind
my own throat and hands!
but if this be effrontery
to those sacrosanct cords,
and all creatures unworthy
of such regal adornment;
then at least, Love, grant me
(since you never stint in giving)
some means of sweet imprisonment
that somehow simulate yours.]

At least she has tried to get rid of those terrestrial chains and bonds that imprisoned her own glory. However, she would not mind being the prisoner of her Love. To be free means for her to be the slave of her master and lover who is the only one who can satisfy her anxiety for freedom and self-fulfilment. The prison becomes not only a commonplace in her poetry but also an image of her transgressive spirit in life as she herself was taken to prison, and prison visiting in London was that which "most often took Luisa out of her nunnery".[23]

Thus her poetry anticipates and explains her missionary activity in England where "another of Luisa's multiple subject positions may be apprehended".[24] However, in her life and poetry it becomes clear that her only aim was to live a mystic union with Christ. All the other events and activities were mere episodes of a person who was essentially contemplative. Luisa de Carvajal's poetic attempt to challenge a patriarchal order through her transgressive writings and subversive life—though it was not as successful as she hoped—has shown and anticipated new ways of making and experiencing the feminine. Her struggle pointed to future success in the construction of the feminine beyond male interference and control.

Bibliography

Abad, Camilo María. *Una misionera española en la Inglaterra del siglo xvii. Doña Luisa de Car-vajal y Mendoza (1566–1614)*. Santander: Universidad Pontificia de Comillas, 1966.

---

[23] Rees, *Writings*, 33.
[24] Cruz, "Willing Desire", 185.

Benjamin, Jessica. "A Desire of One's Own: Psychoanalytic Feminism and Intersubjective Space". In *Feminist Studies: Critical Studies*. Edited by Teresa de Lauretis. Bloomington: Indiana University Press, 1986.

Cruz, Ann J. "Willing Desire: Luisa de Carvajal y Mendoza and Female Subjectivity". In *Power and Gender in Renaissance Spain*. Edited by Helen Nader. Urbana and Chicago: Illinois University Press, 2004.

Eskin, Catherine. Review of *Women in Early Modern England 1550–1729*, by Sarah H. Mendelson and Patricia Crawford. *Sixteenth Century Journal* 30 (1999): 826–27.

Garrard, Greg. *Ecocriticism*. London: Routledge, 2004.

González Marañón, Jesús, ed. *Doña Luisa de Carvajal y Mendoza. Epistolario y poesías*. Biblioteca de Autores Españoles. Vol. 179. Madrid: Atlas, 1965.

Howard, Jean E. "Was There a Renaissance Feminism?" In *A Companion to English Renaissance Literature and Culture*. Edited by M. Hattaway. Oxford: Blackwell, 2000.

Jauralde, Pablo. "La condición histórica del *Cántico espiritual*". *Edad de Oro*, 9 (1992): 87–97.

Loomie, Albert J. "Guy Fawkes in Spain: 'The Spanish Treason'". In *Spanish Documents*. Edited by Albert J. Loomie. London: University of London, Institute of Historical Research, 1971.

Nader, Helen. "Introduction: The World of the Mendozas". In *Power and Gender in Renaissance Spain*. Edited by H. Nader. Urbana and Chicago: Illinois University Press, 2004.

Navarro, Ana. *Antología poética de escritoras de los siglos xvi y xvii*. Madrid: Castalia, 1989.

Rees, Margaret A. *The Writings of Doña Luisa de Carvajal y Mendoza, Catholic Missionary to James I's London*. Lewiston: The Edwin Mellen Press, 2002.

Serés, Guillermo. *La transformación de los amantes. Imágenes del amor desde la Antigüedad hasta el Siglo de Oro*. Barcelona: Crítica, 1996.

Taylor, Charles. *Sources of the Self: The Making of the Modern Identity*. Cambridge: Cambridge University Press, 1989.

"A WISE AND GODLY SYBILLA": VISCOUNTESS RANELAGH AND THE POLITICS OF INTERNATIONAL PROTESTANTISM[1]

Ruth Connolly

Katherine Jones, Viscountess Ranelagh (1614–91) occupied a prominent position in London political and intellectual society from the 1640s to the 1690s. During the 1640s and 50s particularly, she and her friends put forward ideas of scientific advance and social reform, and their endeavours eventually saw the foundation of the Royal Society in the 1660s. Ranelagh occupied a position as patroness and participant in the manifold plans of men like John Dury and Samuel Hartlib for universal knowledge, the development of science, trade, agriculture, and education and, most significantly for the purposes of this essay, the reunification of the Protestant churches. Her circle explored the possibilities of the conversion of the Jews by supporting the mission of Menasseh ben Israel to England, the fall of the Papacy through Dury's missions to the Continent, and the renewal of England as an educated Protestant paradise.[2]

The significance of their work lies not solely in their aspirations, which were shared by many and disparate groups, but by the fact that this group had close links to and influence with many of the individuals with the political will to see their aspirations realized. Ranelagh played a prominent, yet still unexplored role in the Hartlib circle's work, and her personal dedication to their causes derived from her commitment to Protestantism as the true religion. Her unswerving allegiance was to religious toleration for all Protestant sects as part of the essential

---

[1] The funding for this research came from a Government of Ireland scholarship supported by the Irish Research Council for the Humanities and Social Sciences. Versions of this paper were presented at the "Women and the Divine" conference held at the University of Liverpool, 17–19 June 2006 and at the Perdita-sponsored "Still Kissing the Rod?" conference held at St Hilda's, Oxford, 2–4 July 2006. I would like to thank all who offered advice and ideas at both conferences.
[2] See Mark Greengrass, Michael Leslie, and Timothy Raylor, eds., *Samuel Hartlib and Universal Reformation: Studies in Intellectual Communication* (Cambridge: Cambridge University Press, 1994).

foundations for a future blossoming of England and eventually Europe as a bastion of godly Christianity. This religious stance also committed her to political ideals, which highlights another underexamined aspect of her career: the development in tandem of her religious and political goals and their co-existence as necessary bedfellows rather than as separate entities. However, political reform was only the first step in her religious vision. Ranelagh insisted on the complete separation of church and state and debated the introduction of a republican form of government as the forerunner for the abandonment altogether of earthly politics in favour of a complete submission to and reliance upon God.

Katherine Boyle was born in 1614, the daughter of Richard Boyle, the first Earl of Cork and his wife Catherine. Cork was a New English planter who came to Ireland in 1588 as part of an Elizabethan plantation policy which sought to conquer, convert, and civilise the Catholic Irish and install a reliable Protestant governing class as a counterweight to the Catholic Old English, Ireland's traditional rulers. Cork was phenomenally successful in his ventures, his enormous wealth frequently attracting well-grounded innuendo about the legitimacy of his methods.[3] One of his fifteen children, Katherine Boyle was, like her sisters, married in order to further her father's network of allies.[4] The first match her father arranged for her was to a relative of the duke of Buckingham, Viscount Beaumont of Swords, and Katherine left Ireland at the age of ten in order to be brought up at the home of her future husband. She lived there for six years but, after the death of Buckingham and perceived sharp practice, Cork brought his daughter home and married her, in 1630, to Arthur Jones, the son of Roger, Viscount Ranelagh, a minor Irish aristocrat and his close supporter.

Katherine's early life in England is intriguing, although little remains to indicate what she studied there. However, some clues remain in the writings of Stephen Jerome, sent by Viscount Beaumont to work as a chaplain for Cork in the 1620s, and who served to educate some of the Boyle children. His published writings indicate a number of motifs which were to recur again and again in Ranelagh's mature political

---

[3] See Nicholas Canny, *The Upstart Earl* (Cambridge: Cambridge University Press, 1982).

[4] See Patrick Little, "The Geraldine Ambitions of the First Earl of Cork", *Irish Historical Studies* (2002): 151–168. Little argues that Cork's marriage policy was motivated not by the wish for greater social standing but from a desire to help civilise and convert influential Old English dynasties that also held sway over the native Irish.

thought and which may suggest something of the atmosphere in which
Ranelagh was brought up during her youth in both England and Ireland. Jerome's sermons offer sentiments which recur in her own thinking
in later decades. In a sermon of thanksgiving for the return of Prince
Charles in 1624, without a Catholic Spanish bride, Jerome noted how
qualified the New English were to comment on the Catholic menace
and also emphasised their special position within Ireland:

> We neede no other witnesse of this, but our eyes and eares, in this our
> Ireland; in which we that are Protestants, are planted as some handfuls
> amongst such swarms of Papists, as Israelites amongst Egyptians, as Iacobs
> seed in the lightsome Goshen of the Gospell, it being Popish darknesse
> round about us.[5]

Jerome developed such comparisons between the New English and
the encircled but righteous Israelites by offering a positive gloss on the
Church of Ireland's tendency to welcome all Protestant ministers of
whatever ecumenical shade to preach in Ireland, as the shortages of
Protestant ministers in general made scruples over doctrinal shadings
less important.[6] Jerome praised the unity of the Israelites and wished
similar unity for the Protestant churches. Rather than quarrelling over
ceremonies and giving ammunition to Catholic enemies, Protestants
should concern themselves with that which they had in common, which
was the substance of true religion, and so transform Ireland into an
"Irish-English Israel":

> Oh that as we professe, confesse one God the father of all, one Christ the
> redeemer of all, one Spirit the sanctifier of all the Elect; yea, one Faith,
> one Baptisme, one Hope, one life, one way to this life as one Sunne, but
> one soul in man, one Phoenix in the world, &c so that we would as one,
> in one minde, by one rule, worship this God in Spirit, in truth, in unitie,
> in uniformitie of judgement and affections![7]

The overwhelming theme of Jerome's sermon was of religious uni-
fication as the necessary precursor to ensure the victory of the new
Israelites, the New English in Ireland and the English in general, over

---

[5] Stephen Jerome, *Irelands Jubilee or Joyes Io-Paen for Prince Charles his Welcome Home* (Dublin, 1624), 41.

[6] In another text, Jerome described the enemies of Protestantism as "the Papist, and Pelagian and Arminian". See Alan Ford, "The Church of Ireland, 1558–1634: A Puritan Church?" in *As by Law Established: The Church of Ireland Since the Reformation*, ed. Alan Ford, James McGuire, and Kenneth Milne (Dublin: Lilliput, 1995), 61.

[7] Jerome, *Irelands Jubilee*, 81.

the forces of Papismal darkness and the foundation of a new and renewed nation.

This general theme influences and underpins Ranelagh's own political and religious thought and suggests that it was fashioned initially from the discourses of civility and superiority which accompanied the New English conception of themselves in Ireland. This was then linked in her thought to another discourse which insisted on England's leading role in international Protestantism, a debate fuelled by Charles's misadventures in Spain and by the plight of Elizabeth of Bohemia. Ranelagh also drew further momentum from the rhetoric surrounding Protestant unity, a theme which gathered all European Protestant churches under a single banner and which was predicated on avoiding Protestant schism in the interests of maintaining the strength of the reformed faith and weakening the Catholic one.[8] It was part of Ranelagh's ambition to see this unity come about in practice, and in the scenario envisaged by her and many others in her circle, the problems posed by the varieties of Protestant practice were non-existent in comparison to the threats posed at home and abroad by the forces both of Catholicism and its political counterpart, monarchical absolutism. Therefore any plan that sought the spiritual strengthening of Protestantism must also look to the political structures which might enhance or inhibit it.

Ranelagh spent the 1630s mainly in Ireland and the later years of the decade in London. In 1641, however, she found herself under siege in Athlone Castle for eighteen months, as a consequence of a major rebellion by the Catholic Irish, before finally receiving safe passage from Athlone to Dublin in October 1642. From here she wrote to her father to commiserate on the death of her brother Lewis fighting the rebels, concluding

> since the mortaletie of all my friends makes me certaine they must dye
> once, I confes I think dyeing in the defence of the cause we have now

---

[8] See Anthony Milton, *Catholic and Reformed: The Roman and Protestant Churches in English Protestant Thought 1600–1640* (Cambridge: Cambridge University Press, 1995), 377. This particular ideology was thrown into prominence as the Laudian church, by viewing the Church of England as the only properly reformed Church, refused to endorse Protestant internationalism. This viewpoint is anathema to Ranelagh's perspective. On the challenges this posed to Dury's efforts and the doctrinal views of Dury's supporters and opponents, see Anthony Milton, "'The Unchanged Peacemaker'?: John Dury and the Politics of Irenicism in England, 1628–1643" in *Samuel Hartlib and Universal Reformation*, ed. Greengrass et al., 95–117.

in hand, which is as much god's, as ours, a happyenes both to those that gett their deaths, that way, & to those that are soe deprived of them.[9]

She represents herself in this letter as a militant Protestant English-woman engaged in a holy war: those who die in it take on the role of martyrs. There is not the least doubt in her mind as to the rightness of her cause despite, or perhaps because of, the desolation that has been wreaked by those opposed to it. She also announced in this letter her imminent departure for England, and it was in London, in the ferment of Civil War politics, that Ranelagh was to refine her own perspective on the future of Protestantism and the concomitant destiny of the English nation.

She had already established the broad range of friends who were to make her influence extraordinarily far-reaching for the next six decades. As a member of the Great Tew circle since the 1630s, whose stance on Protestant ecumenism echoed her own, she was closely acquainted with Viscount Falkland and also with Edward Hyde, whose friendship continued into the 1660s.[10] She also met, through Great Tew, Charles I's future chaplain Henry Hammond, Gilbert Sheldon, later the Res-toration Archbishop of Canterbury, and Edmund Waller, with whom she was still corresponding in the 1680s. This group was and remained (with the exception of the wavering Waller) both Royalist and Anglican, though with a concern for religious toleration. In London, Ranelagh was to make further friends whose political allegiances were on the opposite end of the political spectrum but whose interest in Protestant unity and ecumenism made for common ground. She lived with her sister-in-law Margaret Clotworthy and her husband John, a Presbyterian ally of John Pym, but it was through Dorothy Moore, her husband's aunt, that she made the acquaintance of John Dury and of Samuel Hartlib and became involved in the work of the Hartlib circle. The arrival of her brother, Robert Boyle, back to England in the 1640s, her acquaintance with John Milton coupled with the contacts she had from the Great Tew circle, the connections made through her brothers' and sisters' marriages, and the predominantly Parliamentarian circles

---

[9] Katherine Jones to the Earl of Cork, 26 October 1642, uncatalogued Lismore Papers, National Library of Ireland, Dublin. I am indebted to Dr Elizabeth Taylor-Fitzsimon for a copy of this letter.
[10] J. C. Hayward, "The *Mores* of Great Tew: Literary, Philosophical and Political Idealism in Falkland's Circle" (Ph.D. diss., University of Cambridge, 1982).

in which she moved in London, gave her an extraordinary perspective
from which to view the unfolding events of the Civil War.

It was the need to maintain the strength of Protestantism that
ultimately provided the ground from which she interpreted unfolding
political events and which enabled her to actively declare for an English
republic that would act as a beacon for and a bastion of godliness and
Christian virtue. Her religious stance on the necessity for liberty of conscience led her, through natural law and resistance theory, to develop a
political perspective that envisaged a righteous English republic.[11] This
republic required qualities which would enable the people to submit to
God's direction, qualities which were to be instilled by education and
example. Such people could then govern themselves both as individuals and as communities, and eventually the necessity for the state to
interfere with their lives at all would be dispensed with, enabling them
to live for and in God alone.

Her view was that Protestantism comprised a broad church of
believers who held in common three fundamental values. All "owne
that God ought to be worshiped, & both owne that prayer preaching
sacraments, reading the word of God, are parts of the worshipe of
God, & that because they are soe declared to be by God himself in his
owne word",[12] and therefore that the disputes between conformists and
nonconformists of all stripes were quibbles over forms and ceremonies,
none of which breached the fundamentals of Protestantism. Much of
what was disputed among the various denominations of Protestantism
detracted from its real mission:

> I am amazed about the dispute between the authorities and preachers
> in religious matters [and that] they should still argue for so long without
> knowing any end when the indisputable duty consists in the practice
> of their great work, and through which, should they be found faith-
> ful therein, they might obtain greater clarity and revelation, which will

---

[11] Ruth Connolly, "'All our Endeavours Terminate but in This': Self-Government
in the Writings of Mary Rich, Countess of Warwick and Katherine Jones, Viscountess
Ranelagh" (Ph.D. diss., National University of Ireland, Cork, 2005).

[12] "A Discourse Concerning the Plague of 1665", Boyle Papers 14, f. 36r. Royal
Society Library, London. I must once again express my gratitude to Dr Taylor-Fitzsimon
for this reference. In the context of the treatise, "both" refers to Anglicans and to the
Nonconformists who found themselves subject to the penalties of the Clarendon Code
and in particular the Conventicle Act (1664). For the impact of the Code and this
Act on Nonconformists and their increased suffering due to the prevalence of plague,
see Ronald Hutton, *The Restoration: A Political and Religious History of England and Wales
1658–1667* (Oxford: Oxford University Press, 1998), 208–31.

enlighten them as to their disputable rights, which they would not be able to achieve through hotheadedness, when they hurt and wound each other with quarrelling and anger.[13]

Conscience will lead a believer to the form of worship appropriate to the degree of light they receive from God. In this context, it was wholly wrong to impose a form of worship upon any individual. "Otherwise, every action is, for the person who engages in it, not a service to God, but rather a service performed for the person that forces that person to do it".[14] As J. C. Davis argues in relation to the Puritanism and liberty thesis, modern ideas of liberty as personal autonomy do not reflect the intentions of those who, in the seventeenth century, argued for liberty of conscience intended.[15] The opposite term to liberty in this period is not authority but hypocrisy; that is, an insincere profession of religious belief. Breaking down barriers to freedom of conscience meant avoiding the forcible imposition of religious ceremonies on those who genuinely felt them to be unconscionable.

Quite simply, the conscience cannot be commanded by humans, whether kings, bishops, or presbyters, because it is commanded by Christ. Ranelagh argued that "the power over religious matters, which is argued about between the authorities and the preachers, will not be found by either of the two, but in the Lord Christ, who will forever be the living head of the body of his church".[16] In this perspective the Church consists of all the members of Christ's body, undifferentiated by membership of any particular church, sect, or congregation. As a result, Ranelagh advised her circle to act with care and compassion towards all people:

> As soon as it is realised that even the smallest and the lowest among us belong to the Lord Christ, then a lamentation will be pronounced against

---

[13] Ranelagh to unknown correspondent, 14 January 1657, *Hartlib Papers*, CD-ROM, 2 discs, 2nd ed. (Sheffield: University of Sheffield, 2002), 39/2/50B. All the letters cited as to an unknown correspondent are in German. I use my translation in conjunction with that of Kristin Rebien, which was kindly sent to me by Carol Pal.

[14] Ibid. The Biblical passages on which Ranelagh bases her view of proper government may be those contained in the epistles of Paul, particularly Titus 1–3.

[15] J. C. Davis, "Religion and the Struggle for Freedom in the English Revolution", *Historical Journal* 31, no. 3 (1992): 507–530.

[16] Lady Ranelagh, to an unknown correspondent, 14 January 1657, *Hartlib Papers*, 39/2/56A–59B: 39/2/58B.

those that anger them, and it would be best that no-one gives offence, neither to the Jew nor the Gentile, nor the Church of God.[17]

The contract between an individual and God was entirely personal however, a relationship deliberately and specially reserved for Christ. The state had no role to play here. Ranelagh's arguments also echo the calls for toleration made by the Dutch Arminian Simon Episcopius, whose work was cited approvingly in a letter to her from her regular correspondent John Beale.[18] Episcopius argued that stifling the expression of belief could only lead to resentment:

> For no human conscience or intellect is above another, or can judge another. Everybody has equal access to God's word and God's truth. Not only persecution, but ecclesiastical authority, imposed by any form of coercion is wrong, and harms society, not just because it generates resentment, and disrupts political and economic life but still more, because coercion stifles true enquiry into Scripture, reducing the individual to an unthinking cipher or worse, a hypocrite who, in his heart rejects what publicly he professes.[19]

Episcopius' point was that one must submit voluntarily to ecclesiastical disciplinary structures. Forcing an individual to attend a certain form of worship is detrimental both to the individual and to society as a whole. The choice of religious practice must be made by the individual him or herself, according to his or her interpretation and understanding of scripture.

Ranelagh's insistence on the importance of liberty of conscience did not mean that she treated it as a gateway either to personal autonomy or to antinomianism. She realised that there was a challenge posed to this ideal by the ungodly, who refused to be disciplined according to God's light and God's law. But she also understood that secular law must apply to the godly and ungodly alike. Therefore the laws that govern society should be derived from God's laws, laid down in the New Testament. Such laws, governing the interaction between human beings, are under the ministration of the magistrate and are legitimately

---

[17] Lady Ranelagh, to an unknown correspondent, 14 January 1657, *Hartlib Papers*, 39/2/58B.

[18] John Beale to Viscountess Ranelagh, 5 Sept 1660, Boyle Letters, vol. 1, Royal Society, London, ff. 47–50, f. 48r. For Beale, see Mayling Stubbs, "John Beale Philosophical Gardener of Herefordshire; Part I: Prelude to the Royal Society (1608–63)", *Annals of Science* 39 (1982): 463–89 and "Part II: The Improvement of Agriculture and Trade in the Royal Society (1663–83)", *Annals of Science* 46 (1989): 323–63.

[19] Quoted in Jonathan Israel, *The Dutch Republic* (Oxford: Clarendon, 1995), 504.

enforceable by him. The power to punish secular wrongdoing is in the hands of magistrates, and if the laws that these men make and enforce are the right ones, based on the principles of the New Testament, they can and will maintain the order and prosperity of society.[20] All Christians will also be able to obey these laws without fear of contradiction from their conscience, because the laws will be based on the principles of Scripture. Ranelagh believed godly individuals should be guided by their inner light, a stance superficially similar to that of the Quakers, but she set careful boundaries around its expression by also insisting that individuals should also utilise their God-given reason to ensure that their actions were consonant with God's word, thereby heading off the threat of antinomianism.

It is difficult to place Ranelagh herself in any particular church or situate her thought conclusively within any individual branch of Protestantism. Her piety responded to and found resonances in a variety of Protestant religious thought and practice. She appears never to have formally left the Anglican Church, but she also attended the services of Richard Baxter, the celebrated Presbyterian minister, and her house was noted as a visiting place for Presbyterians in 1661.[21] She also had considerable sympathy for nonconformists of all hues, a fact demonstrated by her interventions on behalf of persecuted nonconformists with her friend Clarendon during the Restoration, particularly Baptists and Quakers.[22]

Ranelagh may have believed that God communicated directly with his faithful through dreams and seems to have debated the subject with

---

[20] This is identical to Milton's view in *The Readie and Easie Way to Establish a free Commonwealth and the Excellence thereof* (1660): "And in my judgement civil States would do much better, and remove the cause of much hindrance and disturbance in public affairs, much ambition, much hypocrisie and contention among the people if they would not meddle at all with Ecclesiastical matters, which are both of a quite different nature from their cognisance, and have their proper laws fully and completely with such coercive power as belongs to them ordained by Christ himself and his apostles". In Martin Dzelzainis, ed., *Political Writings*, trans. Claire Gruzelier (Cambridge: Cambridge University Press, 1991), 380.

[21] In 1661, a memorandum to Joseph Williamson, Secretary to Arlington, the Lord Chamberlain, reported Presbyterians meeting at Ranelagh's House (*CSPD* 26 August 1661). She was listed as one of Richard Baxter's 'Lady Auditors' on a list of those attending illegal conventicles in 1676. See Egerton MS 3330, f. 16, British Library, London.

[22] Viscountess Ranelagh to Lord Clarendon, 17 February 1662/3, Clarendon Papers, vol. 79, ff. 73–74; letter to Lord Clarendon, May 1663 (?), Clarendon Papers, vol. 78, ff. 230v–231r, Bodleian Library, Oxford.

John Beale, both of them writing discourses on dreams, although only
Beale's is extant. She also is recorded as a listener to the prophecies
of Sarah Wight.[23] The view of her friend Beale might serve to sum up
her own attitude to the various Protestant groupings she attended or
supported in some way. Writing to her, possibly in 1660, Beale asked:

> shall we exclude holy & humble charitable & reverend brethren from
> our communion for some difference in logicall notions, or about the use
> of water & yet receive them that turn all courts of public justice into a
> craft of oppression, & trade of iniquity? Let us rather tremble to make
> ourselves partakers in the sin and communion of one such transgressor:
> & let us tremble to reject one such brother or sister as God hath allowed
> these titles, though we find him full of weakness & infirmities & very
> much mistaken.[24]

This, in itself, indicates a constant trend in Ranelagh's thought towards
a complete consistency in principle and practice. She placed her stress
on substance rather than form, and a person who conforms in his
churchgoing and sins in the secular sphere should not be preferred
to a nonconformist who strives to live a godly and just life. To do
otherwise would represent a dangerous inversion of the fundamental
truths of Christianity. Her goal is to cause the nation to revert to the
principles and practices of these godly truths, and by developing and
organising schemes to bring this about she was doing the work of God,
for in her eyes

> the best way to be with Him, since while we are still in our bodies we
> are far away from Him, is to be constantly busy in his service, as one of
> his limbs, or the tools in His outstretched hand, which is as far as our
> benevolence can extend, because it cannot reach Him who is the object
> of all our blessings, praise and service.[25]

Her instrumentality to God, offering all she had in his service, was also
her own sincerest means of praising him.

The urgency of praising and honouring God in this way led her to
develop her personal capacities to the utmost, reflected in her extended
involvement with the Hartlib circle. Judging by her letters, she served as

---

[23] Henry Jessey, *The Exceeding Riches of Grace advanced ... in ... Mris Sarah Wight* (1647), 9.
For Wight, see Katherine Gillespie, *Domesticity and Dissent in the Seventeenth Century: English
Women Writers and the Public Sphere* (Cambridge: Cambridge University Press, 2004).

[24] John Beale to Viscountess Ranelagh, n.d., *Hartlib Papers*, 27/16/1A–14B: 12B.

[25] Ranelagh to unknown correspondent, 31 December 1656, *Hartlib Papers*, 39/
2/56B.

one of its leading intellectual lights, encouraging the circle's endeavours in unifying all knowledge and participating in their activities through all the avenues open to her as a woman. Her influence extended into the plans of John Dury to create a unified Protestant church, which would topple the antichristian church of Rome through the freedom of individual interpretation. She reflected optimistically on Dury's work on the Continent to bring the various Protestant churches closer together: "I am of the opinion that our friend, strengthened in his faith and circling among the churches, will perhaps give a more fatal blow to Rome and the whole anti-Christian hierarchy with the guidance and spirit of God's word than any fleet or army could, however strong they could be".[26]

Ranelagh believed that the extension of the reformed faith in Europe would inevitably bring down not only the Catholic church but also the absolutist monarchs who endorsed its faith:

> However, I do not deny that the earthly kings, by the foolish resignation of power to the man of sins /:the Pope:/ have strengthened his reign at the expense of both their and their subjects' consciences. Therefore they are going to be a tool in the hand of God and a means of his dispensation, through which the flesh of the whore will be torn and she will be shown naked, stripped of the decoration and adornment of superficial power, politics and pomp.[27]

Therefore, she is also arguing that it is the very supporters of the Catholic church that will be the ones to destroy it. But although the outer form might be destroyed through a process that is still unclear, the substance would continue. Only when all people abandoned political ambition, resolving to rely on God alone rather than on carnal and mortal means of salvation derived from constant and fickle changes of government, would Ranelagh hope that salvation had finally drawn near. Only then would the spirit of such carnality, which she felt was embodied in the Whore of Rome, finally disintegrate.

She advocated a godly republic then, hoping that this was the first step to establishing a people fit to rule themselves, and promoted schemes of education and legal and agricultural reform in order to encourage

---

[26] Ranelagh to unknown correspondent, 19 February 1657, *Hartlib Papers*, 39/2/60A.
[27] Ibid.

the nation to flourish. Then once liberty of conscience is safeguarded, the need for an intrusive state might be significantly reduced:

> may God grant that Christians subject themselves to the yoke of Christ with a humble and serene spirit, in order to practice those same unquestionable works of piety that are plainly and clearly ordained in His testament. Perhaps then the magistrates, as well as the preachers, might decide to have little to do with such people, except to enliven them, exhort them and to encourage them to wish to become ever better.[28]

Her religious stance places her views close to a group that John Coffey describes as "radical tolerationist", although it is less likely that Ranelagh could accept the toleration of heresy and atheism that was advocated by some of the individuals studied by Coffey.[29] He finds many of the adherents of this view to belong to either Particular or General Baptists, and he also includes Milton as a radical tolerationist. However, Coffey is puzzled by Milton's anti-Catholicism, a characteristic shared by Ranelagh—a seeming contradiction that is resolved through Ranelagh's view of the Roman Catholic church as an antichristian anti-religion, the element which serves to unify all Protestants, whatever their shades of opinion, in a polemical campaign against the church of the Antichrist. To extend toleration to Catholicism as a religion automatically shattered the view of Protestantism as the only Christian religion and even questioned the reason for its very existence.

However, Ranelagh shared the tolerationist insistence that using violence as a means of spreading Christianity was unacceptable. Her faith is based on the individual willingly accepting the yoke of Christ by being convinced of Christ's goodness through reading the Word and seeing the Christian life lived around them. Ranelagh believed that the light of natural reason in every individual would respond to the truths of God in scripture. To force it upon them is the equivalent of the diabolical tyranny practiced by the servants of Antichrist:

> My dear sir, please tell me: with what has God promised to destroy his enemies? Is it not with the sword of his mouth and the whole glory of his future? Is not his word the sword of his mouth, and is this not the

---

[28] Ranelagh to unknown correspondent, 14 January 1657, *Hartlib Papers*, 39/2/57B.

[29] See John Coffey, "Puritanism and Liberty Revisited: The Case for Toleration in the English Revolution", *Historical Journal* 41, no. 4 (1998): 961–85.

armour and weapons which, in the Scriptures, are said to be powerful enough to overthrow everything that rebels against God?[30]

However, errors in the fundamentals of Christianity she could not tolerate, and to combat this she, with her brother Robert, sponsored the publication of the first Bible in Irish.[31] She told the Bishop of Meath that Irish Catholics were ill-served by an English colonial government that failed to effectively banish Catholic priests from Ireland or even to curb their activities:

> And tho its too sad a truth that their Priests have binn to much indulged by the English the liberty of seduceing or hardening them in their Errors & that they have thereby enslaved them to an [implic]ite fayth in their dictates Yet stil the truths of god wilbe found more powerful than the sublelest error. & they wil be in a like way to bee delivered from their miserable bondage when they may heare discourses and reade books that may acquaiant them with those truthes., than while they are left utterly in the darke to be led by them and their great leader the divil Captive at his wil.[32]

Only by building such habits of interpretation for themselves can the individual become open to God's direction of them towards the right path. This ideal formed the basis for Dury and Hartlib's plans to get the Jews readmitted to England, for by exposing them to Christianity and its texts, their conversion might be hastened.[33] Ranelagh too was a philosemite, and extended her sympathy to Jewish suffering at the hands of the Turks in a letter to Henry Oldenburg:

> To London there are send [sic] written sad rela[ti]ons of the heavy oppression, the Jews suffer under the Turke; and the same haveing been seconded with some further informons let me see, that in severall places the Lord is stirring up the hearts of those, that feare his name, to pitty them: which gives me some hopes, that the time of their deliverance may be approaching, in which they shal be taught to see all, & the promises of God to them to be yea and Amen only in that Christ whom they haue crucified, and who even by that act of theirs is made the fulfiller of all

---

[30] Ranelagh, letter to unknown correspondent, 19 February 1657, *Hartlib Papers* 39/2/60A.

[31] T. C. Barnard, "Protestants and the Irish Language, c. 1675–1725", *Journal of Ecclesiastical History* 44, no. 2 (1993): 243–72.

[32] Ranelagh to Bishop Anthony Dopping, 15 April 1682, vol. 1 (21), MS G.11.22., Dopping Correspondence, Armagh Public Library.

[33] See D. S. Katz, *Philosemitism and the Readmission of the Jews to England 1603–1655* (Oxford: Clarendon, 1982).

those profecies, in the fulfilling of which he is proued to be their true
messiah. Oh! That the lives of Christians did hold him forth to them in
his owne glory, and did not rather draw a vayle before their eyes to hide
his beauty from them. It might be only the pourings forth of the Spirit
of the Lord both upon them and us, that can take away that vaile.[34]

The conversion of the Jews formed part of the narrative of Revelation,
but judged on this and other texts, Ranelagh considered the events
depicted in Revelation to be at some remove, for if Christians must
first live the life of service in Christ, they must even prior to that be
reformed through the crippling experiences of pain and loss and finally
realise the futility of violent ambition towards reform. Possibly only free
grace can enable human beings to transcend their carnal weakness:

> But as long as I see that they are pleased by princes and masters and
> their armies, it appears credible that the work on Mount Zion has not
> been completed yet, nor that we should have reasonably waited for the
> lord to punish the proud heart of the king of Assyria. My foolish opin-
> ion about the protesting princes who have united or are about to unite,
> is this: when the most apparent occasion will present itself to destroy
> the Antichrist, but will be thwarted by the unfathomable counsel of the
> Lord, then God will procure deliverance for his people in such a way
> that [the people] will understand that the feebleness of God is stronger
> than the power of humans, and the foolishness of God stronger wiser
> than all human wit.[35]

This passage draws heavily on references to the second Book of Kings
and the destruction of Sennacherib, the King of Assyria who warned
the Israelites not to trust their God for he would not deliver them out of
his hands. An angel destroyed the Assyrians' encampment in the night
after Hezekiah, king of Israel, appealed to God. But Isaiah, God's messenger, also prophesised: "And the remnant that is escaped of the house
of Judah, shall yet again take roote downward and beare fruit vpward.
For out of Jerusalem shall goe forth a remnant, and they that escape
out of mount Zion: the zeal of the lord of Hosts shall doe this".[36]

---

[34] Viscountess Ranelagh to Henry Oldenburg, n.d., "Ex Litt. M. Ra", *Liber Epistolaris*,
MS 1, ff. 190r–194v, Royal Society Library, London.
[35] Ranelagh to unknown correspondent, 19 February 1657, *Hartlib Papers*, 39/2/
61A.
[36] 2 Kings 19:30–31. Biblical quotations are taken from *The Holy Bible: An Exact
Reprint in Roman Type, Page for Page of the Authorised Version Published in the year 1611* (Oxford:
Oxford University Press, 1985).

Ranelagh may not here be explicitly casting the English or Protestants in general as a new chosen people, but she may be proceeding by analogy to imply that the present embattled position of Protestants is similar to the trials of the nation of Israel and that the faith in God which relieved the inhabitants of Jerusalem might and should be called upon to scorn those who, like the Assyrian king, believe that temporal victory also represents a victory over God. Her final quotation is taken from the following passage in Corinthians:

> For the Jewes require a signe, and the Greekes seek after wisdome. But wee preach Christ crucified, unto the Jewes a stumbling block, and unto the Greeks, foolishnesse: But unto them which are called, both Jewes and Greekes, Christ, the power of God, & the wisdom of God. Because the foolishness of God is wiser than men: and the weakness of God is stronger than men (1 Cor 1:23–27).

The crucified Christ matches neither the prophecies of the Jews nor the philosophy of the Greeks, yet residing in it is the truth, and all those who are called, whether Jew or Greek either in religion or mentality, will come to recognise their own weakness and acknowledge God's greatness. What appeared to them to be foolish and humble will be revealed to them in its true aspect once the veil, drawn down by their pride, is stripped away by those called to be instruments of God.

Therefore even the most acute human intellect could not penetrate the inscrutable plans of God: "there is no lesse grosnes in setting up of our reasons against the disposings of his wisdom than there is in setting up in thee motions of our sensual appetites against the dictates of our reason".[37] However much military action might make some inroads against evil, it will be through mysterious and unfathomable ways, and through a means that humans will cast as inadequate and incapable that God will obtain his final victory.

Here too is the corollary of a liberty of conscience which grants priority to the individual's relationship to God: submission to His greater wisdom. Although the individual acts as God directs her, should all her plans appear to be undermined and her hopes dashed, she should nonetheless accept that God's intentions are beyond her capacity to understand, and therefore she should willingly accept incomprehension, disappointment, and loss.

---

[37] Ranelagh to Oldenburg, f. 191r.

However, the failures of the Commonwealth in the 1650s seemed to Ranelagh to be entirely due to human failure, and this led her to express her disillusionment with it in comparison to the heights her hopes for a godly nation had formerly reached:

> if in the beginning of our professions to a reformation in these last 18 years, we had fallen to this practice, and paid as many schoolmasters as we have done military officers, listing regiments of children under them, to be by them train'd up in the nurture and admonition of the lord, instead of so many thousands of poor men sacrificed to the passions and lusts of their rulers, whose ignorance teacheth them to seek an establishment in those things upon which God has decreed an uncertainty, we had by this time reaped better fruits of our labours and expenses, then disappointments, division, poverty, shame and confusion, all of which are in great letters upon the present frames of men's spirits and posture of our affairs.[38]

The fears the Hartlib circle expressed were for the fortunes of international Protestantism, now that its flagship nation had found itself in difficulties. A letter from Peter Figulus, the son-in-law of Jan Comenius, to Hartlib, written after the death of Cromwell commented:

> Wee waite still for the Lords gracious enlightening of his Countenance upon you and the whole state and thus settle all your affaires at home, and your Consultations and Enterprises for Common interests of the whole Protestantcy, that we may see your peace and felicity of the whole Republique daily increased and strengthened.[39]

But Figulus feared that the changes in Britain would presage disaster for Protestants on the continent, and "indeede by this meanes the Prophecies both of that late pious prelate [Ussher] as also of your most wise and godly sybilla Lady Viscountesse Ranalaugh, her pious and truly religious considerations both upon the present and future state of protestant churches & people might well become true of our own fault"—that is, that quarrelling and bitterness amongst Protestants will lead to "the wrath of God" destroying all and that the persecution of Protestants on the Continent will be unbearably intensified.[40]

---

[38] Quoted by Samuel Hartlib to John Worthington, 30 January 1659, in *Diary and Correspondence of John Worthington*, ed. James Crossley, vol. 1 (London, 1847), 166.
[39] Peter Figulus to Samuel Hartlib, 29 November 1658, *Hartlib Papers*, 9/17/51A–52B.
[40] Ibid.

Ranelagh's response to the Restoration is no longer extant, and her correspondence reopens in 1663 with letters to Edward Hyde, now Lord Clarendon, asking for succour for persecuted nonconformists. She reengaged politically with the Whig cause in the 1670s as the Popish plot and the Exclusion Crisis gave rise to fears about the resurgence of Catholicism in England. She never abandoned her religious and political principles, and although it must have seemed as if a prime opportunity had slipped through the fingers of the English nation, she continued to argue resolutely for liberty of conscience and the importance of ruling the self in order to submit to God, and not to a king, pope, or prelate.

It is easy, given the kind of laudatory reception that she received from her male peers, to overlook the problem of her gender when dealing with Ranelagh's work. Her arguments were met with respect for their articulacy and authority and received widespread circulation within the closed public of the intellectual circle.[41] But the question of women's service in the life of Christ was discussed between Ranelagh and Dorothy Moore Dury, although only Dury's letters remain extant.[42] Ranelagh's intellectual and political interventions represent both the extent and the limit to which she, as a woman, could intervene in matters of national and international political and religious importance. The specific issue of gender inequality rarely appears in Ranelagh's writing, and she never resorts to rhetorical gestures in her political and religious arguments which point to her sex as a reason for any shortcomings. The sole reference to it in her extant letters reveals a wry attitude towards the belief in women's shortcomings as a gender, and she was not above poking fun at assumptions about women's weaker

---

[41] Peter Figulus wrote to Hartlib in 1659 that some of Ranelagh's letters had been translated into Dutch and Monsieur de Geer "much delights in them". Peter Figulus to Samuel Hartlib, 29 November 1658, *Hartlib Papers*, 9/17/51A–52B: 51B.

[42] Moore argued somewhat defensively in her letters to Ranelagh that she (Moore) was obligated to use the talents God gave her in the service of others and that she was enabled to act appropriately by drawing on both grace and natural reason. Moore insisted that women, as members of Christ's body on earth, must play their part despite the fact that many thought women incapable of such service. She divided women into the married and unmarried and concluded that the former served God through educating their husbands, children, family, and acquaintances through their good example and edifying conversation. Unmarried women could serve God either through their influence over persons of political or social power or by teaching young girls. See Lynette Hunter, ed., *The Letters of Dorothy Moore, 1612–64: The Friendships, Marriage and Life of a Seventeenth-Century Woman* (Aldershot: Ashgate, 2004).

capacity for self-control. She wrote to her brother Robert asking for permission to open and read a bundle of papers he had composed on religious matters, informing him,

> I would fain open them without your leave, which I hope my being so ingenious a coxcomb as not to do it without asking, will rather bribe you to give, rather than deny me. But if it should not, I know not what I may be tempted to; and you know I am of a sex, that has long been allowed for an excuse of the frailties of those, who are of it.[43]

Like all women in the period, however, she was faced with assumptions about women's role in Protestant religious life: views which veered from considering that women might, through their weakness, have greater access to God, to fears that the expression of such capacities through prophecy, preaching, and publication might in fact represent madness, a desire for power, or an unseemly spiritual whoredom, which breached the social demand for docility and obedience in women.[44]

Ranelagh repeatedly wrote of godly people as instruments of God, a far different metaphor to the description of godly women as vessels which are filled by God. The extent of women's instrumentality was of particular concern to Dorothy Moore Dury. Moore corresponded with Ranelagh on education for girls and engaged in a spirited debate with André Rivet about the role of women as preachers and teachers of God's word.[45] In a letter to Ranelagh, Moore was insistent that natural reason, which was the remains of God's image in postlapsarian humanity, as well as conscience made it clear that all possessed of both had a duty "to render themselves servicable Members to the rest of that body to which they are conjoined with & by Christ the Head".[46] This, Moore insisted, also included women

> who, (because God hath not apointed them, administrators of his word and ordinances in the Church, nor of Justice or Commanding Politick Government of a republicke) many are apt to thinke us alltogeather incapable... of that honour of being Members of that body I must believe that every Member in his owne station may bee proffitable to the rest

---

[43] Ranelagh to Robert Boyle, 14 November 1665, in Michael Hunter et al., eds., *Correspondence of Robert Boyle*, vol. 2 (London: Pickering and Chatto, 2001), 583.

[44] See Hilary Hinds, *God's Englishwomen: Seventeenth-Century Radical Sectarian Writing and Feminist Criticism* (Manchester: University of Manchester Press, 1996) and Gillespie, *Domesticity and Dissent*.

[45] See Hunter, *Letters of Dorothy Moore*, 21–35.

[46] Moore to Ranelagh, 8 July 1643, in Hunter, *Letters of Dorothy Moore*, 18.

(although wee bee judged the weakest & meanest) & therefore bound to intend the imployment of our best strength spirituall & corporall in this service which to mee is very evident may bee attained unto by all sorts in some Measure.[47]

Therefore membership of the Christian body also rendered women members of the body politic, for the requirements of the former insisted that women did all things possible to advance the members of it and this, by necessity in the unified religio-political world of the mid-seventeenth century, meant a concern for and debate about the appropriate political system for a truly Christian body politic.

The use of the imagery of the body is not coincidental. Women were so closely identified with the body that imagining the Christian community as a body which needed ministration and care automatically appealed to the feminine duties of healthcare and housewifery and therefore allowed an effortless segue into spiritual duties. However, this also seemed to posit a married role for such women, a fact Moore reluctantly acknowledged after her own plans to continue her work as a single woman did not come to fruition, telling Ranelagh, in a letter that was later published,

> I conceave that ordinarily a Woman, cannot serue the advance of Christ's kingdome in a single estate, so well as being united to a godly man for the above mencioned Aimes. For surely if she could, God would not have Instituted that, which would prove an impediment to the best way of serving him.[48]

However, Ranelagh's case is one where the extraordinary prevailed. Having left her husband behind in Ireland in 1641, she and he were never reunited, and Ranelagh sued for a separation and maintenance in the late 1650s, her husband reaching neither the level of sobriety or godliness to make a marriage to him tolerable.[49]

This contrast with Moore's struggles highlights Ranelagh's uniqueness. As a society hostess, linked through family, friendship, and intellect to individuals of very disparate political and religious views, she contrived to live the life of a single woman while still married. She also drew on her formidable abilities to win encomia from all sides to join

---

[47] Ibid., 19.
[48] Moore to Ranelagh, 5 May 1645, in *Letters of Dorothy Moore*, 70.
[49] Viscountess Ranelagh to Lord Burlington, 5 July 1659, Lismore Papers, vol. 31(36), Chatsworth. Material from the Lismore Papers is quoted by permission of the Duke of Deronshire.

the international republic of letters and find herself mentioned in her concern and zeal for the future of Protestantism in the same breath as Archbishop Ussher.

The sophistication of her thought and her development of a tolerationist Protestantism based on personal conscience and a republican government intended to eliminate the burden of oppressive tyranny on the godly expresses a bold vision. Ranelagh carefully cultivated the contacts and thinkers who shared and could concretely enact this future. She explored her ideas, however, with a strict eye to the matter of the ungodly and also to the maintenance and religious safety of Protestantism, carefully hedging her ideas against the possibilities of antinomianism and autonomy. Her idea of liberty was the freedom to submit entirely to God's direction and her implementation of it led her to reject the foundations of the state in which she grew up in order to establish a kingdom of Christ on earth. The creation of such a kingdom was a burden to be willingly shouldered by both men and women alike, who did their service not to elevate themselves but to praise the God who made them. Ranelagh succeeded all too well in this aim. It is to be hoped that this and other work by scholars on Ranelagh will cast further light on the career of this extraordinary woman.[50]

Bibliography

Manuscripts

Beale, John. Letter to Viscountess Ranelagh, 5 September 1660. Boyle Letters. Vol. 1. Royal Society Library, London.
Clarendon Papers. Bodleian Library, Oxford.
Jones, Katherine. Letter to the Earl of Cork, 26 October 1642. Uncatalogued Lismore Papers. National Library of Ireland, Dublin.
Leeds, duke of. General Correspondence. Egerton MS 3330. British Library, London.
Oldenburg, Henry. *Liber Epistolaris*. MS 1. Royal Society Library, London.
Ranelagh, Viscountess. Letter to Lord Burlington, 5 July 1659. Lismore Papers. Vol. 31(36). Chatsworth.

---

[50] See Elizabeth Taylor's work, "Writing Women, Honour, and Ireland: 1640–1715" (Ph.D. diss., National University of Ireland, Dublin, 1999). She is now working on an edition of Ranelagh's letters. Carol Pal's work is on Ranelagh's letters in conjunction with those of Dorothy Dury, Elizabeth of Bohemia, Anna-Maria von Schurman, and Bathsua Makin. Dury was a close friend of von Schurman and also served at the court of Elizabeth of Bohemia. See Carol Pal "Republic of Women: Rethinking the Republic of Letters, 1630–1680" (diss., Stanford University, 2007).

——. "A Discourse Concerning the Plague of 1665". Boyle Papers 14. Royal Society Library, London.

——. Letter to Bishop Anthony Dopping, 15 April 1682. Dopping Correspondence. Vol. 1 (21). MS G.11.22. Armagh Public Library.

Published Works

Barnard, T. C. "Protestants and the Irish Language, c. 1675–1725." *Journal of Ecclesiastical History* 44, no. 2 (1993): 243–72.

Canny, Nicholas. *The Upstart Earl.* Cambridge: Cambridge University Press, 1982.

Coffey, John. "Puritanism and Liberty Revisited: The Case for Toleration in the English Revolution". *Historical Journal* 41, no. 4 (1998): 961–85.

Connolly, Ruth. "'All our Endeavours Terminate but in This': Self-Government in the Writings of Mary Rich, Countess of Warwick and Katherine Jones, Viscountess Ranelagh". Ph.D. diss., National University of Ireland, Cork, 2005.

Davis, J. C. "Religion and the Struggle for Freedom in the English Revolution". *Historical Journal* 31, no. 3 (1992): 507–30.

[Dury, John]. *Madam, although my former freedom in writing.* 1645.

Ford, Alan. "The Church of Ireland, 1558–1634: A Puritan Church?" In *As by Law Established: The Church of Ireland Since the Reformation.* Edited by Alan Ford, James McGuire, and Kenneth Milne. Dublin: Lilliput, 1995.

Gillespie, Katharine. *Domesticity and Dissent in the Seventeenth Century: English Women Writers and the Public Sphere.* Cambridge: Cambridge University Press, 2004.

Greengrass, Mark, Michael Leslie, and Timothy Raylor, eds. *Samuel Hartlib and Universal Reformation: Studies in Intellectual Communication.* Cambridge: Cambridge University Press, 1994.

Hartlib, Samuel. *Hartlib Papers.* CD-ROM. 2 discs. 2nd ed. Sheffield: University of Sheffield, 2002.

Hayward, J. C. "The *Mores* of Great Tew: Literary, Philosophical and Political Idealism in Falkland's Circle". Ph.D. diss., University of Cambridge, 1982.

Hinds, Hilary. *God's Englishwomen: Seventeenth-Century Radical Sectarian Writing and Feminist Criticism.* Manchester: University of Manchester Press, 1996.

The Holy Bible: An Exact Reprint in Roman Type, Page for Page of the Authorised Version Published in the year 1611. Introduction by Alfred W. Pollard. Oxford: Oxford University Press, 1985.

Hunter, Lynne, ed. *The Letters of Dorothy Moore, 1612–64: The Friendships, Marriage and Life of a Seventeenth-Century Woman.* Aldershot: Ashgate, 2004.

Hunter, Michael, Anthony Clericuzio, and Lawrence Principe, eds. *Correspondence of Robert Boyle.* Vol. 2. London: Pickering and Chatto, 2001.

Hutton, Ronald. *The Restoration: A Political and Religious History of England and Wales 1658–1667.* Oxford: Oxford University Press, 1998.

Israel, Jonathan. *The Dutch Republic.* Oxford: Clarendon, 1995.

Jerome, Stephen. *Irelands Jubilee or Joyes Io-Paen for Prince Charles his Welcome Home.* Dublin, 1624.

Jessey, Henry. *The Exceeding Riches of Grace advanced . . . in . . . Mris Sarah Wight.* 1647.

Katz, David. *Philosemitism and the Readmission of the Jews to England 1603–1655.* Oxford: Clarendon, 1982.

Little, Patrick. "The Geraldine Ambitions of the first Earl of Cork". *Irish Historical Studies* (2002): 151–68.

Milton, Anthony. "'The Unchanged Peacemaker'?: John Dury and the Politics of Irenicism in England, 1628–1643". In *Samuel Hartlib and Universal Reformation: Studies in Intellectual Communication.* Edited by Mark Greengrass et al. Cambridge: Cambridge University Press, 1994.

———. *Catholic and Reformed: The Roman and Protestant Churches in English Protestant Thought 1600–1640*. Cambridge: Cambridge University Press, 1995.

Milton, John. *The Readie and Easie Way to Establish a free Commonwealth and the Excellence thereof*. In *Political Writings*. Edited by Martin Dzelzainis. Cambridge: Cambridge University Press, 1991.

Stubbs, Mayling. "John Beale Philosophical Gardener of Herefordshire; Part I: Prelude to the Royal Society (1608–63)". *Annals of Science* 39 (1989): 463–89.

———. "Part II: The Improvement of Agriculture and Trade in the Royal Society (1663–83)". *Annals of Science* 46 (1989): 323–63.

Taylor, Elizabeth. "Writing Women, Honour, and Ireland: 1640–1715". Ph.D. diss., National University of Ireland, Dublin, 1999.

Trevor-Roper, Hugh. *The Crisis of the Seventeenth Century: Religion, Reformation and Social Change*. Indianapolis: Liberty Fund, 1967.

Worthington, John. *Diary and Correspondence of John Worthington*. Edited by James Crossley. Vol. 1. London, 1847.

INDEX

STUDIES IN MEDIEVAL AND REFORMATION TRADITIONS

(Formerly Studies in Medieval and Reformation Thought)

Founded by Heiko A. Oberman†
Edited by Andrew Colin Gow

36. MEERHOFF, K. *Rhétorique et poétique au XVIe siècle en France.* 1986
37. GERRITS, G. H. *Inter timorem et spem.* Gerard Zerbolt of Zutphen. 1986
38. POLIZIANO, A. *Lamia.* Ed. by A. Wesseling. 1986
39. BRAW, C. *Bücher im Staube.* Die Theologie Johann Arndts in ihrem Verhältnis zur Mystik. 1986
40. BUCER, M. *Opera Latina.* Vol. II. Enarratio in Evangelion Iohannis (1528, 1530, 1536). Publié par I. Backus. 1988
41. BUCER, M. *Opera Latina.* Vol. III. Martin Bucer and Matthew Parker: Flori-legium Patristicum. Edition critique. Publié par P. Fraenkel. 1988
42. BUCER, M. *Opera Latina.* Vol. IV. Consilium Theologicum Privatim Conscriptum. Publié par P. Fraenkel. 1988
43. BUCER, M. *Correspondance.* Tome II (1524-1526). Publié par J. Rott. 1989
44. RASMUSSEN, T. *Inimici Ecclesiae.* Das ekklesiologische Feindbild in Luthers "Dictata super Psalterium" (1513-1515) im Horizont der theologischen Tradition. 1989
45. POLLET, J. *Julius Pflug et la crise religieuse dans l'Allemagne du XVIe siècle.* Essai de synthèse biographique et théologique. 1990
46. BUBENHEIMER, U. *Thomas Müntzer.* Herkunft und Bildung. 1989
47. BAUMAN, C. *The Spiritual Legacy of Hans Denck.* Interpretation and Translation of Key Texts. 1991
48. OBERMAN, H.A. and JAMES, F.A., III (eds.). in cooperation with SAAK, E.L. *Via Augustini.* Augustine in the Later Middle Ages, Renaissance and Reformation: Essays in Honor of Damasus Trapp. 1991 *out of print*
49. SEIDEL MENCHI, S. *Erasmus als Ketzer.* Reformation und Inquisition im Italien des 16. Jahrhunderts. 1993
50. SCHILLING, H. *Religion, Political Culture, and the Emergence of Early Modern Society.* Essays in German and Dutch History. 1992
51. DYKEMA, P.A. and OBERMAN, H.A. (eds.). *Anticlericalism in Late Medieval and Early Modern Europe.* 2nd ed. 1994
52. 53. KRIEGER, Chr. and LIENHARD, M. (eds.). *Martin Bucer and Sixteenth Century Europe.* Actes du colloque de Strasbourg (28-31 août 1991). 1993
54. SCREECH, M.A. *Clément Marot: A Renaissance Poet discovers the World.* Lutheranism, Fabrism and Calvinism in the Royal Courts of France and of Navarre and in the Ducal Court of Ferrara. 1994
55. GOW, A.C. *The Red Jews: Antisemitism in an Apocalyptic Age, 1200-1600.* 1995
56. BUCER, M. *Correspondance.* Tome III (1527-1529). Publié par Chr. Krieger et J. Rott. 1989
57. SPIJKER, W. VAN 'T. *The Ecclesiastical Offices in the Thought of Martin Bucer.* Translated by J. Vriend (text) and L.D. Bierma (notes). 1996
58. GRAHAM, M.F. *The Uses of Reform.* 'Godly Discipline' and Popular Behavior in Scotland and Beyond, 1560-1610. 1996
59. AUGUSTIJN, C. *Erasmus.* Der Humanist als Theologe und Kirchenreformer. 1996
60. McCOOG S J, T.M. *The Society of Jesus in Ireland, Scotland, and England 1541-1588.* 'Our Way of Proceeding?' 1996
61. FISCHER, N. und KOBELT-GROCH, M. (Hrsg.). *Außenseiter zwischen Mittelalter und Neuzeit.* Festschrift für Hans-Jürgen Goertz zum 60. Geburtstag. 1997
62. NIEDEN, M. *Organum Deitatis.* Die Christologie des Thomas de Vio Cajetan. 1997
63. BAST, R.J. *Honor Your Fathers.* Catechisms and the Emergence of a Patriarchal Ideology in Germany, 1400-1600. 1997
64. ROBBINS, K.C. *City on the Ocean Sea: La Rochelle, 1530-1650.* Urban Society, Religion, and Politics on the French Atlantic Frontier. 1997
65. BLICKLE, P. *From the Communal Reformation to the Revolution of the Common Man.* 1998
66. FELMBERG, B.A.R. *Die Ablaßtheorie Kardinal Cajetans (1469-1534).* 1998

67. CUNEO, P.F. *Art and Politics in Early Modern Germany.* Jörg Breu the Elder and the Fashioning of Political Identity, ca. 1475-1536. 1998

68. BRADY, Jr., Th.A. *Communities, Politics, and Reformation in Early Modern Europe.* 1998

69. McKEE, E.A. *The Writings of Katharina Schütz Zell.* 1. The Life and Thought of a Sixteenth-Century Reformer. 2. A Critical Edition. 1998

70. BOSTICK, C.V. *The Antichrist and the Lollards.* Apocalyticism in Late Medieval and Reformation England. 1998

71. BOYLE, M. O'ROURKE. *Senses of Touch.* Human Dignity and Deformity from Michelangelo to Calvin. 1998

72. TYLER, J.J. *Lord of the Sacred City.* The *Episcopus Exclusus* in Late Medieval and Early Modern Germany. 1999

74. WITT, R.G. *'In the Footsteps of the Ancients'.* The Origins of Humanism from Lovato to Bruni. 2000

77. TAYLOR, L.J. *Heresy and Orthodoxy in Sixteenth-Century Paris.* François le Picart and the Beginnings of the Catholic Reformation. 1999

78. BUCER, M. *Briefwechsel/Correspondance.* Band IV (Januar-September 1530). Herausgegeben und bearbeitet von R. Friedrich, B. Hamm und A. Puchta. 2000

79. MANETSCH, S.M. *Theodore Beza and the Quest for Peace in France, 1572-1598.* 2000

80. GODMAN, P. *The Saint as Censor.* Robert Bellarmine between Inquisition and Index. 2000

81. SCRIBNER, R.W. *Religion and Culture in Germany (1400-1800).* Ed. L. Roper. 2001

82. KOOI, C. *Liberty and Religion.* Church and State in Leiden's Reformation, 1572-1620. 2000

83. BUCER, M. *Opera Latina.* Vol. V. Defensio adversus axioma catholicum id est criminationem R.P. Roberti Episcopi Abrincensis (1534). Ed. W.I.P. Hazlett. 2000

84. BOER, W. DE. *The Conquest of the Soul.* Confession, Discipline, and Public Order in Counter-Reformation Milan. 2001

85. EHRSTINE, G. *Theater, culture, and community in Reformation Bern, 1523-1555.* 2001

86. CATTERALL, D. *Community Without Borders.* Scot Migrants and the Changing Face of Power in the Dutch Republic, c. 1600-1700. 2002

87. BOWD, S.D. *Reform Before the Reformation.* Vincenzo Querini and the Religious Renaissance in Italy. 2002

88. PELC, M. *Illustrium Imagines.* Das Porträtbuch der Renaissance. 2002

89. SAAK, E.L. *High Way to Heaven.* The Augustinian Platform between Reform and Reformation, 1292-1524. 2002

90. WITTNEBEN, E.L. *Bonagratia von Bergamo*, Franziskanerjurist und Wortführer seines Ordens im Streit mit Papst Johannes XXII. 2003

91. ZIKA, C. *Exorcising our Demons,* Magic, Witchcraft and Visual Culture in Early Modern Europe. 2002

92. MATTOX, M.L. *"Defender of the Most Holy Matriarchs"*, Martin Luther's Interpretation of the Women of Genesis in the *Enarrationes in Genesin*, 1535-45. 2003

93. LANGHOLM, O. *The Merchant in the Confessional,* Trade and Price in the Pre-Reformation Penitential Handbooks. 2003

94. BACKUS, I. *Historical Method and Confessional Identity in the Era of the Reformation (1378-1615).* 2003

95. FOGGIE, J.P. *Renaissance Religion in Urban Scotland.* The Dominican Order, 1450-1560. 2003

96. LÖWE, J.A. *Richard Smyth and the Language of Orthodoxy.* Re-imagining Tudor Catholic Polemicism. 2003

97. HERWAARDEN, J. VAN. *Between Saint James and Erasmus.* Studies in Late-Medieval Religious Life: Devotion and Pilgrimage in The Netherlands. 2003

98. PETRY, Y. *Gender, Kabbalah and the Reformation.* The Mystical Theology of Guillaume Postel (1510–1581). 2004

99. EISERMANN, F., SCHLOTHEUBER, E. und HONEMANN, V. *Studien und Texte zur literarischen und materiellen Kultur der Frauenklöster im späten Mittelalter.* Ergebnisse eines Arbeitsgesprächs in der Herzog August Bibliothek Wolfenbüttel, 24.-26. Febr. 1999. 2004

100. WITCOMBE, C.L.C.E. *Copyright in the Renaissance.* Prints and the *Privilegio* in Sixteenth-Century Venice and Rome. 2004

101. BUCER, M. *Briefwechsel/Correspondance.* Band V (September 1530-Mai 1531). Herausgegeben und bearbeitet von R. Friedrich, B. Hamm, A. Puchta und R. Liebenberg. 2004

102. MALONE, C.M. *Façade as Spectacle: Ritual and Ideology at Wells Cathedral.* 2004

103. KAUFHOLD, M. (ed.) *Politische Reflexion in der Welt des späten Mittelalters / Political Thought in the Age of Scholasticism.* Essays in Honour of Jürgen Miethke. 2004

104. BLICK, S. and TEKIPPE, R. (eds.). *Art and Architecture of Late Medieval Pilgrimage in Northern Europe and the British Isles.* 2004

105. PASCOE, L.B., S.J. *Church and Reform.* Bishops, Theologians, and Canon Lawyers in the Thought of Pierre d'Ailly (1351-1420). 2005

106. SCOTT, T. *Town, Country, and Regions in Reformation Germany.* 2005

107. GROSJEAN, A.N.L. and MURDOCH, S. (eds.). *Scottish Communities Abroad in the Early Modern Period.* 2005

108. POSSET, F. *Renaissance Monks.* Monastic Humanism in Six Biographical Sketches. 2005

109. IHALAINEN, P. *Protestant Nations Redefined.* Changing Perceptions of National Identity in the Rhetoric of the English, Dutch and Swedish Public Churches, 1685-1772. 2005

110. FURDELL, E. (ed.) *Textual Healing: Essays on Medieval and Early Modern Medicine.* 2005

111. ESTES, J.M. *Peace, Order and the Glory of God.* Secular Authority and the Church in the Thought of Luther and Melanchthon, 1518-1559. 2005

112. MÄKINEN, V. (ed.) *Lutheran Reformation and the Law.* 2006

113. STILLMAN, R.E. (ed.) *Spectacle and Public Performance in the Late Middle Ages and the Renaissance.* 2006

114. OCKER, C. *Church Robbers and Reformers in Germany, 1525-1547.* Confiscation and Religious Purpose in the Holy Roman Empire. 2006

115. ROECK, B. *Civic Culture and Everyday Life in Early Modern Germany.* 2006

116. BLACK, C. *Pico's* Heptaplus *and Biblical Hermeneutics.* 2006

117. BLAŽEK, P. *Die mittelalterliche Rezeption der aristotelischen Philosophie der Ehe.* Von Robert Grosseteste bis Bartholomäus von Brügge (1246/1247-1309). 2007

118. AUDISIO, G. *Preachers by Night.* The Waldensian Barbes (15th-16th Centuries). 2007

119. SPRUYT, B.J. *Cornelius Henrici Hoen (Honius) and his Epistle on the Eucharist (1525).* 2006

120. BUCER, M. *Briefwechsel/Correspondance.* Band VI (Mai-Oktober 1531). Herausgegeben und bearbeitet von R. Friedrich, B. Hamm, W. Simon und M. Arnold. 2006

121. POLLMANN, J. and SPICER, A. (eds.). *Public Opinion and Changing Identities in the Early Modern Netherlands.* Essays in Honour of Alastair Duke. 2007

122. BECKER, J. *Gemeindeordnung und Kirchenzucht.* Johannes a Lascos Kirchenordnung für London (1555) und die reformierte Konfessionsbildung. 2007

123. NEWHAUSER, R. (ed.) *The Seven Deadly Sins.* From Communities to Individuals. 2007

124. DURRANT, J.B. *Witchcraft, Gender and Society in Early Modern Germany.* 2007

125. ZAMBELLI, P. *White Magic, Black Magic in the European Renaissance.* From Ficino and Della Porta to Trithemius, Agrippa, Bruno. 2007

126. SCHMIDT, A. *Vaterlandsliebe und Religionskonflikt.* Politische Diskurse im Alten Reich (1555-1648). 2007

127. OCKER, C., PRINTY, M., STARENKO, P. and WALLACE, P. (eds.). *Politics and Reformations: Histories and Reformations.* Essays in Honor of Thomas A. Brady, Jr. 2007

128. OCKER, C., PRINTY, M., STARENKO, P. and WALLACE, P. (eds.). *Politics and Reformations: Communities, Polities, Nations, and Empires*. Essays in Honor of Thomas A. Brady, Jr. 2007
129. BROWN, S. *Women, Gender and Radical Religion in Early Modern Europe*. 2007
130. VAINIO, O.-P. *Justification and Participation in Christ*. The Development of the Lutheran Doctrine of Justification from Luther to the Formula of Concord (1580). 2008
131. NEWTON, J. and BATH , J. (eds.). *Witchcraft and the Act of 1604*. 2008